The Invention of Sustainability

The issue of sustainability, and the idea that economic growth and development might destroy its own foundations, is one of the defining political problems of our era. This ground-breaking study traces the emergence of this idea, and demonstrates how sustainability was closely linked to hopes for growth, and the destiny of expanding European states, from the sixteenth century. Weaving together aspirations for power, for economic development and agricultural improvement, and ideas about forestry, climate, the sciences of the soil and of life itself, this book sets out how new knowledge and metrics led people to imagine both new horizons for progress, but also the possibility of collapse. In the nineteenth century anxieties about sustainability, often driven by science, proliferated in debates about contemporary and historical empires and the American frontier. The fear of progress undoing itself confronted society with finding ways to live with and manage nature.

Paul Warde is a Reader in Environmental History at the University of Cambridge. His previous publications include *Ecology, economy and state formation in early modern Germany* (Cambridge, 2006), *Power to the people. Energy in Europe over the last five centuries* (2013) and *The future of nature. Documents of global change* (2013).

The Invention of Sustainability

Nature and Destiny, c. 1500–1870

Paul Warde

University of Cambridge

CAMBRIDGE
UNIVERSITY PRESS

CAMBRIDGE
UNIVERSITY PRESS

University Printing House, Cambridge CB2 8BS, United Kingdom

One Liberty Plaza, 20th Floor, New York, NY 10006, USA

477 Williamstown Road, Port Melbourne, VIC 3207, Australia

314–321, 3rd Floor, Plot 3, Splendor Forum, Jasola District Centre,
New Delhi – 110025, India

79 Anson Road, #06-04/06, Singapore 079906

Cambridge University Press is part of the University of Cambridge.

It furthers the University's mission by disseminating knowledge in the pursuit of
education, learning, and research at the highest international levels of excellence.

www.cambridge.org
Information on this title: www.cambridge.org/9781107151147
DOI: 10.1017/9781316584767

First published 2018
Reprinted 2019

Printed in the United Kingdom by TJ International Ltd. Padstow Cornwall

A catalogue record for this publication is available from the British Library.

Library of Congress Cataloging-in-Publication Data
Names: Warde, Paul, author.
Title: The invention of sustainability : nature and
destiny, c. 1500–1870 / Paul Warde.
Description: New York, NY: Cambridge University Press, 2018. |
Includes bibliographical references.
Identifiers: LCCN 2018003782 | ISBN 9781107151147 (hardback)
Subjects: LCSH: Sustainable development – Europe – History. |
Sustainability – Europe – History. | Human ecology – Europe – History.
Classification: LCC HC240.9.E5 W37 2018 | DDC 338.94/070903–dc23
LC record available at https://lccn.loc.gov/2018003782

ISBN 978-1-107-15114-7 Hardback

For my mother, Brenda Warde,
and in memory of my father, Noel Warde

CONTENTS

ACKNOWLEDGEMENTS

The seeds for this book were sown in a short paper I prepared for a workshop held in Pembroke College in Cambridge in the spring of 2005. Little did I know that the themes of that draft would still be preoccupying me with this book, some 13 years later. The reason for organising the workshop was the fortuitous presence in Cambridge of those distinguished environmental historians, Graeme Wynn and Sverker Sörlin. Neither has contributed directly to this book, but I would like to thank Graeme for the generous assistance he has given me in the years since, along with Chris Smout. Sverker has been a constant intellectual companion, as has, in the intervening years, Libby Robin. Without their support and companionship I would probably not have been in the position to deliver what, from the perspective of 2005, would have seemed a very surprising outcome from me; a work of intellectual history.

The workshop was held at Pembroke College, and supported by the Centre for History and Economics. These two institutions have provided – and still do – intellectual and collegial homes, and many friends to me. I would like to thank them for their faith and investment. Much of the research and writing of the book was undertaken whilst working at the University of East Anglia (UEA) (especially on the commute!), and I would like to thank my colleagues there for their support. It was at UEA that I benefited from research assistance from Hannah Hamilton-Rutter, and collaborative research with Fiona Williamson. That process was assisted by the award of a prize from the Leverhulme Trust.

Some of the ideas in this book have been tested out at research seminars at Harvard University, UEA, the University of Cambridge, University of Warwick and Birkbeck, University of London. Further outings were enjoyed at the Anglo-American conference of the Institute of Historical Research, and the 2016 conference on Malthus organised at Cambridge. A sketch of the argument was published in 2011 in *Modern Intellectual History*. I am grateful for the enthusiasm and interest of the then editor, Anthony la Vopa. I have also benefited from and was privileged to be allowed early glimpses of the writings of Nathaniel Wolloch, Kieko Matteson and Ayesha Mukherjee; advice and tips from Marten Seppel; insight and knowledge from my PhD student, Liz Scott; and from very many of my students, but I would single out in particular those taking the Themes and Sources module 'World Environmental History' at the University of Cambridge.

I am indebted to, and have been delighted by, very many conversations on the themes of this book over the years. Those intellectual debts are covered, I hope, in the footnotes of this volume, but I would like to make space for special mention to Fredrik Albritton Jonsson. For their sins, Emma Rothschild, Felicity Stout and Joanna Warde read parts of the manuscript. I am especially grateful for the reports provided by two anonymous referees to Cambridge University Press, not least their preparedness to navigate early versions of the work.

Finally, I would like to thank my editor at Cambridge University Press, Liz Friend-Smith, for her commitment to and assistance with this book; and those who have smoothed the editorial and production process: Rebecca Taylor, Dawn Preston, Natasha Whelan, Neil Sentance, Rachel Roberts and all those others who work so a book can be.

ABBREVIATIONS

AHEW	Agrarian History of England and Wales
BL	British Library
CSPD	Calendar of State Papers Domestic
EcHR	*Economic History Review*
GUL	Glasgow University Library
JHC	*Journal of the House of Commons*
JHL	*Journal of the House of Lords*
JPQE	*Journals of all the Parliaments during the Reign of Queen Elizabeth*
TNA	The National Archives
WN	*An inquiry into the nature and causes of the Wealth of Nations*

INTRODUCTION

Errors

This book is founded on errors. First of all, mine. When I began to study the agrarian world of early modern Europe over 20 years ago, I made the commonsensical assumption that the peasant cultivators of that era, and by default the rest of the society of which they made up such a large part, were highly preoccupied with issues of what we would now call 'sustainability'. They depended, after all, on the continued fertility of the soil and the availability of resources for not just their livelihood, but their lives. That peasant society endured for so many centuries, or even in certain circumstances millennia, must be testimony to inherited wisdom on that count. It seemed likely to me then, and indeed remains the common wisdom now, that this previous ethic of care (or self-preservation) had been undone only relatively recently, by forces associated with the rise of capitalist economies and modern technologies. If this putative ethos of sustainability was characteristic of the peasants, it seemed likely that it suffused much of the social life of their world. This kind of thinking about the past was also shared by some of the pioneers of modern environmental thought, strident critics of despoliation and the consequences of capitalist development in the middle of the twentieth century. As emblematic of this writing we might take Fairfield Osborn's *Our plundered planet* of 1948, who declared of the European past that, 'people who lived and worked on their land did not think of it so much as a field for exploitation as a sacred trust and means of subsistence... Thus was it protected and cared for.'[1]

But after a while I began to wonder: if the peasants cared so much about sustainability, why did they never talk about it? I believe the reason is that my assumption was wrong.

There is another version of this story of paradise lost that maintains its cachet to this day, although not one with which I ever agreed. This story has the same starting point of a pre-industrial ethic of care, but also argues that ancient and medieval people saw Nature as suffused with a life-force which all shared, and where an interconnection of, and respect for, all things was understood. In a famous essay, first delivered as a lecture to the American Association for the Advancement of Science, the historian of technology Lynn White proposed that modern science was the somewhat delayed offspring of Judeao-Christian thought and the injunction to 'subdue the Earth' that can be read from Genesis 1:28. Thus the story goes that the blighted child of Christian thought and modern science has been a blighted Earth, a mindset that has led to the estrangement of humanity from nature and the technological subjugation of all.[2] Carolyn Merchant has argued that the earlier idea of a vital nature was also seen to have female characteristics, of a mother Earth, that were valued. In her account the 'death of nature' was inflicted by a thousand cuts through the rapiers of the scientific revolution and the reduction of natural processes to the mechanistic interactions of inorganic atoms discovered by experiment. The chief villain in this story is the English statesman, lawyer, and polymathic scholar Francis Bacon (1561–1626). On the other side of that Baconian threshold in scientific thought lies a myopic reductionism. It has led to a fundamental misunderstanding of ecological interaction with hugely destructive consequences, and a valorising of the dominating, male, supposedly dispassionate gaze enshrined in scientific method.[3]

---

[1] Fairfield Osborn, *Our plundered planet* (Boston, MA: Little, Brown, 1948), p. 143.

[2] Lynn Townsend White, 'The historical roots of our ecological crisis', *Science*, New Series, 155 (10 Mar. 1967), p. 1205; Richard C. Hoffmann, *An environmental history of medieval Europe* (Cambridge: Cambridge University Press, 2013), pp. 87–9.

[3] Carolyn Merchant, *The death of nature. Women, ecology, and the scientific revolution* (San Fransisco, CA: Harper & Row, 1980). See also the 'Focus' essays on this work in *Isis* 97 (2006), pp. 485–533; and a restatement of Merchant's belief in the significance of Bacon in Carolyn Merchant, 'Secrets of nature. The Bacon debates revisited',

These stories are not entirely untrue. But they seem to me to be in error in important regards, and this book seeks to explain why, at least for the period and places with which it is concerned, that is, early modern Europe and some of its colonial offshoots. I make no claims at all for anywhere else or previous eras. And Merchant was certainly right that scientific endeavour in the period covered by this book was overwhelmingly dominated by men, its literary output even more than its practice (given that women played many important direct and indirect roles in sustaining scientific practice). Consequently, the pages of this book are also overwhelmingly filled with the voices of men, and by and large rich men, not because they had any intrinsically greater significance than women, but because they were able to participate in debates and leave a record of them in a way that women, and poorer men, were not.[4] The work of remedying this bias is far from complete in our politics today.

Yet much of the thinking attributed to pre-Baconian thought was not widely shared in society but was actually the rather abstruse product of highly educated men drawing their own inferences from classical writers. The scientific revolution did not replace vitalism and a deeper sympathy with the processes of life with an instrumental, de-spiritualised mechanism. This view is wrong – at least in the circles examined in this book. The rather gradual refinement of what we now see as the scientific method did not estrange people from nature. Among the relatively elite groups who conducted botanical, meteorological and silvicultural investigations, the attention to detail and engagement with 'fieldwork' became far greater than ever before. The great mass of the population, about whom we know much less, probably saw very little change in their experience of, and knowledge about the natural world until the later experience of urbanisation and technological revolution that largely came after the early modern period. Far from disappearing, the influence of sixteenth-century 'vitalist' thinkers lauded by Merchant, such as Paracelsus, was long-lasting, including on Francis Bacon. Mechanistic views of nature, far from being all-conquering, had

---

Journal of the History of Ideas 69(1) (2008), pp. 147–62. Merchant's work has been far more warmly received in environmental history than the history of science.

4 The critique of Merchant presented here is of her characterisation of early modern science and understanding of nature, especially the role of experiment and mechanistic thought; not the position of women and the possible influence of science upon that position, or any other issues raised in that book.

a partial few decades of fashion before falling out of favour in the early eighteenth century. Debate about the nature of life and human relationships with their climate and environment intensified from this time. And as a consequence, what we might call sustainability, which previously had not registered in public debate at all, or only in a rather indirect manner, emerged at the *end* of the early modern period, after the 1740s, as an urgent problem that society had to resolve.

I should be very clear at this point. I will argue in this book that the modern framing of 'sustainability', the kind of *problem* it was conceived as in political debate, was a product of the early modern period, and only really appeared in its full-blown form in the latter part of the eighteenth century. This does not mean that I think that the earlier societies of Renaissance, medieval and classical Europe, who did not make sustainability a social and political problem for public debate, were therefore unsustainable. Even less do I wish to argue that modern society, where many people are fully conscious of the problem, is sustainable merely by dint of knowing that it should be. This book does not seek to examine or answer those propositions at all. It is not a study of what people *did*, a search for exemplary sustainable societies. It is largely a history of the ideas that people expressed about whether *whole societies* and economies were dependent on the natural world in some way, and hence how those societies should be governed. One does not have to hold the concept of sustainability in order to engage in practices that might, quite inadvertently, promote that goal. Equally, we are not short of evidence that anxiety and hand-wringing about sustainability does not automatically translate into a collectively sustainable life.

Many studies have shown forces to be in operation in the early modern world that *did* create tendencies towards (what I must always tediously say 'what we now call...') sustainability. These ranged from the very localised wisdom of the peasant planting a field or grazing animals and wanting to know if her or his family will survive this year and the next, and perhaps even the next generation, to shifts in the availability of land or prices that might affect a couple's prospects of marriage, affecting in turn the birth rate and population trends. Ideas that households had a right to the resources (such as wood or grazing) for their subsistence, or that common property should be allotted in a proportional way among communities, were reflected in rules and policies that set limits to the exploitation of the soil and reserved land for particular uses. Such 'homeostatic' forces exerted a balancing force on pre-industrial societies which has been much studied in agrarian and demographic history. But these tendencies usually found their articulation in debates about the justice of allocation or the desire to ensure respectability. These can be powerful forces for sustainability, but they do not need any conscious concern about the fragility of the environment to have force.

Argument

The word 'sustainability' appears only to have emerged in the English language in the early 1970s.[5] It is a remarkably recent coinage, although the German equivalent, *Nachhaltigkeit*, was already established in the mid-eighteenth century and its cognates a century earlier (although this is equally true of the English 'sustain').[6] Like any word, its meaning can be malleable and applied in many different contexts – providing your interlocutors understand what you are trying to say. In this book, I employ a very particular meaning of the term. 'Sustainability' is the idea that to endure, a society must not undermine the ecological underpinnings on which it is dependent. It must not degrade, to use a more archaic term, 'the Earth'. There may of course be many other reasons why a society or a polity does not endure, and indeed there is very rarely only one reason. But here, 'sustainability' is considered as an environmental problem, and I understand it as framing both the problem that people may behave *inappropriately* in regard to the limits of the environment which they inhabit, and that *the environment is changed by the society dependent on it so that society can no longer sustain itself*. Unsustainability, according to this particular definition, is the result of the Earth being modified by human action. I do not want to suggest that sustainability could not be defined otherwise, and usefully so. But that problem of degradation through human action is the issue I am considering here.

This approach begs the obvious question about what should be the social unit to be sustained – whose livelihood is sustainable,

---

[5] 'Sustainability'; *Oxford English Dictionary*.
[6] Paul Warde, 'The invention of sustainability', *Modern Intellectual History* 8 (2011), pp. 153–70.

and is it even desirable that it should continue in its current form? What kind of livelihood should this be? It is frequently pointed out today that discourses about sustainability often do not sufficiently take into account the social distribution of benefits and risks attendant to environmental change. The perils of climate change are not equally distributed, whether geographically or across our very unequal societies. Considering different social or spatial scales of analysis will lead to different answers about what is appropriately 'sustainable' behaviour, and indeed such differences account for the high levels of disagreement in the modern world where nearly everyone, at least notionally, is signed up to sustainability as a good idea. This is not a normative book: it does not seek to make a judgement on what *counts as sustainability*. As the reader shall see, there has never actually been any clear agreement on this question, either what makes for a good and just society, or what resources are required to underpin it. Such debates have been and will remain the stuff of political life. Rather, my interest is how in its emergence the issue of 'sustainability', as what one might call a 'discursive field', a theme to argue about, was bound to particular social and territorial units, and especially the idea of the state as unit of political, economic and environmental management. That is frequently how governments still consider the issue today, although not necessarily the best one. But it is hard to divorce thinking about sustainability from our political organisation, and it always has been.

This is not, then, a book about the basic tenet of farming or gardening, that you cannot endlessly plant certain crops in the same place without the yield declining, whether because of the exhaustion of certain nutrients, or the build-up in ineradicable pests. This fact must have been learned almost immediately during the transition to settled cultivation, and is familiar to anyone who tends a vegetable patch. There is no necessity that repeated cultivation would lead, however, to a *permanent* degradation of soil quality, or that cultivators would have had cause to think so. Of course, other things do lead to such degradation: long-term leaching of nutrients from exposed soils, erosion, and so on. These problems were certainly noticed episodically in classical times, but do not seem to have led to a continuous discourse on the issue stretching into the medieval and modern eras. Neither, importantly, were these general ecological constraints framed as a wider problem for society or the polity at large. It is the emergence of this *wider* social and political discourse that establishes, in my view, 'sustainability' as a general developmental problem. One farmer mismanaging a field is not generally considered worthy of discussion in terms of sustainability. If all farmers are mismanaging their fields, then we begin to worry.

How then did sustainability emerge as a wider issue of debate and focus of anxiety in European thought? Like all profound and troubling ideas, this did not arrive as a revelation to someone one bright morning (even if it sometimes seems that way to individual people, who all share the experience of a private moment of enlightenment), but was the consequence of many things. Thus this book is not about pinpointing some critical juncture, but identifying that array of factors that demarcated a new field for debate. My account begins with the emergence of a more proactive state in the sixteenth century, seeking to transform religious allegiance and practice, regulate markets, increase revenue, regularise military forces, and control indigence. All these activities built on late medieval precursors, alongside the expectation that public authorities should be guarantors of a supply of essential resources to households. This did not mean that the state worried about the general state of 'the environment' as such. This concept simply did not exist, even though authorities were certainly interested in exploiting and managing parts of the natural world. This spirit of reformation, in its broadest sense, began to make the state of that natural world a *political* issue, one by which the polity might be judged. This was most especially in regard to the supply of grain, discussed in Chapter 1, 'Living from the Land', and wood, discussed in Chapter 2, 'Governing the Woods'.

As we move into the seventeenth century, a desire for increased revenue, international competition in commerce, war and religion, and efforts towards post-war reconstruction after the terrible conflagration of the Thirty Years' War posed these questions of public responsibility and resource management in a more dynamic form. Society was expected to *develop*, and wealth to increase over time, and this posed the question of whether the supplies of basic material could be kept in step with growth in population and riches. Should such dependencies be resolved by trade, or, in a world of uncertain geopolitics, be secured domestically? Should certain sectors of the economy receive privileged access? These questions were asked above all in relation to wood. Such issues of balance, population, resources, and an emerging political economy are handled in Chapter 4, 'Paths to Sustained Growth'. Certainly, by this time many European polities, not only the economic trailblazers of the United Provinces and England, expected economic activity and state revenue to expand over time.

However, the intellectual context for those fiscal and political ambitions was only partly fostered by governments. Knowledge about resources was not usually provided by the state. Even when it was debated and developed by men who were public officials, they did so in what we might call a 'personal' capacity that embraced both their own interests *and* the discharge of public office, which was in any case often being done from their own splendid residences. Thus another crucial development for this story, and one that we need to appreciate before examining the rise in thinking about resource use that focused directly on the needs of the state, was the emergence of networks of people (nearly all men) generating, sharing and arguing about nature and its uses: about botany, about agricultural improvement, about trees and forestry, about climate and soil. This knowledge was also generally seen as purposeful, and thus intended to be applied as part of a wider purpose by suitably dedicated and resourced men. This is the subject of Chapter 3, 'Ambition and Experiment'. Much of this literature, which in England from the early seventeenth century can be characterised as the literature of 'improvement', was highly optimistic about the prospects for increasing output. In other words, the concern for 'sustainability' that we are so familiar with today – for limits and their transgression – did not loom large. I argue that this was partly because, despite many opinions offered, the writers of the time had little idea why plants, the essential providers of nearly all basic resources, grew. There were certainly various explanations, but crucially, none of them seemed to imply any fundamental limit, some finitude that might hold development back. Indeed, the problem was rather the opposite: how to unleash the powers that surely lay dormant.

Wider educational currents of the late sixteenth and seventeenth centuries, demands from military activities and navigation, and pressures of estate and fiscal management, gradually spread familiarity and enthusiasm for mathematics and geometrical techniques of surveying. Although their prevalence should not be overstated, in tandem with the drive towards improvement such methodologies provided the basis for a new calculus of resource management that shaped the activities of surveyors, foresters and the 'political arithmetic' that took shape in the seventeenth century. These developments were closely entwined with an interest in extracting more revenue from the land, and hence largely employed by landowning classes. Indeed, throughout the early modern period it was landlords who were much better placed to alter the management of the landscape than central government. States lacked the capacity to do so without a high degree of co-operation from local elites. Hence the techniques for making inventories and surveys, and assessing the future prospects of resource use, tended to be employed in ways to reinforce the dominance of the landed classes. All too often the interests of the ordinary people of Europe (and later the colonies) were considered only as a 'population', a dumb and mute mass. Where resistance to change and policies of 'improvement' was manifest, it was treated as evidence of backwardness and irresponsibility by rulers and their allies.

By the last three decades of the eighteenth century – again, a slow process – such technologies of survey, measurement and control had become widespread, above all in their intellectual esteem and political influence rather than actual practice: a 'new husbandry', a 'scientific forestry', and in the emerging political economy. A quantifiable framework had been provided for thinking about resources – although not yet generally implemented – by which judgements about 'sustained yield' could be made, especially in forestry. This was certainly a new framing and means by which nature was conceptualised, or made 'legible'. These new technologies of power may also have offered the temptation to experts and authorities to treat nature as simpler, more malleable and controllable than the reality, an argument made famously and influentially by James C. Scott.[7] Yet its transformative influence in this period should not be overstated, and an overemphasis on the grand survey seeking to render a territory 'legible' can distract historians from the huge efforts that went into the detailed and nuanced study of natural processes. Hence Chapter 5, examining this history, is more appropriately entitled 'Nature Translated' than implying anything as yet transformed.

The desire for a balanced economy and a sustained yield did not necessarily lead to a concern for the possible *degradation* of the Earth. This required a further step, in what anachronistically but appropriately we can call the 'life sciences' (including chemistry). This is because this step related to ideas about the nature of life itself, a problem that had

---

[7] James C. Scott, *Seeing like a state. How certain schemes to improve the human condition have failed* (New Haven, CT: Yale University Press, 1998).

long puzzled scholars. From the middle of the eighteenth century, the idea rapidly suffused through Northern Europe that the much-debated source of food of plants included some vital element than provided the quickening impulse in living things, and that this substance might be in finite supply. 'Vitalism' was the keystone that bridged the gap between previous ideas about resource management and discourses of sustainability, because mismanagement and loss of this vital element or 'juice' would shrink the life-giving properties available to society. Allied to a new taste for theories of circulation, which emerged across a wide range of thinking including biological debates, hydrology and political economy, the idea emerged of a natural base to society, a recurrent circulation of essential nutrients that must be maintained for survival. Intuitions of these relationships can be found in, for example, the works of Scottish political economists of the mid-eighteenth century, but at that point they were still but a minor theme. They found their true florescence in the writings of agronomists at the turn of the nineteenth century, modelled in a fully-blown quantitative system by writers such as Albrecht Thaer and Johann Gottlieb von Thünen. Modern writers, reading these works, have supposed them to be refined statements of the basic assumptions of the pre-industrial economy. In truth, they were novel. Even if an understanding of the chemical properties of the soil and plants moved on rapidly, above all in the work of Justus Liebig, the basic intuition of finite elements and necessary recycling remained. These crucial developments are set out first in Chapter 6, 'Theories of Circulation', that deals with developments in science and agronomy. Chapter 7 subsequently examines the reception, or indeed indifference to such ideas in 'Political Economies of Nature'.

Chapter 8, 'History and Destiny', examines a new enterprise that then became possible in the light of sustainability thinking; understanding of the past and projections about the future that judged society by the 'sustainability' of its practices. Now environmental concerns were integrated into 'stage theories' of history that could explain the rise and fall of empires, with the expectation that poor husbandry of the Earth would result in similar fates for the profligate in the future. Just as the glittering empires of the Middle East and Rome had crumbled to dust, so would modern societies currently in their pomp. These ideas had particular resonance as a critique of the poor husbandry of the North American 'frontier' (as seen by Europeans or Americans of the eastern seaboard) or in observations of other colonial societies, as well as anxieties about the state of the soil or the forest at home in Europe, which in any case with the emergence of a global trade in raw materials became more than a local question. Hence we perceive the longer history that made possible works now in the canon of modern environmentalism, such as George Perkins Marsh's, *Man and Nature* of 1864. Indeed, in many ways this book itself stands in the tradition established at that time.

The framework was thus laid for modern sensibilities around 'sustainability'. Today, even if not raised in the traditions and thinking of the European West, we hear those conversations still echoing around us. Equally, the writing of the early nineteenth century shaped the way that many people of the twenty-first century think about the pre-industrial world. As memorably expressed by Tony Wrigley, that world was subject to the 'photosynthetic constraint' of an 'organic economy', dependent on plants for the raw materials of life and industry. Wrigley has also noted the irony that at the very moment the classical economists were expressing the notion of an essential limit on growth, Britain was well on the way to its transition to a fossil fuel economy that would, temporarily at least, abolish such concerns.[8] In fact, we might compound 'Wrigley's irony'. For the reasons laid out in this book, the thinkers of previous centuries, with no actual experience of sustained high rates of economic growth even if they sometimes lived in antici-pation of it, did not view 'sustainability' as a problem. They did not even imagine the problem in its modern form. Yet during the Industrial Revolution, it became a major preoccupation and has remained so ever since – albeit in many forms, although always arrayed alongside and in contestation with cornucopian expectations. These currents in the his-tory of economic and environmental thought do not alter the fact that the organic economy *was* subject to a 'photosynthetic constraint' set by the limits of plant growth, and that the Industrial Revolution was, above all else (if not only) founded on an energy revolution as a neces-sary condition.[9] Indeed, long before the encomia to Britain's wealth resting on coal and iron that we hear in the nineteenth century,[10] a

---

[8] E.A. Wrigley, *Energy and the English Industrial Revolution* (Cambridge: Cambridge University Press, 2010).

[9] Astrid Kander, Paolo Malanima and Paul Warde, *Power to the people. Energy in Europe over the last five centuries* (Princeton, NJ: Princeton University Press, 2013).

[10] William Stanley Jevons, *The coal question. An enquiry concerning the progress of the nation, and the probable exhaustion of our coal mines* (London: Macmillan, 1865).

few acute observers had noted how advantageous it was to draw on a subterranean fuel such as coal rather than a space-demanding one like wood.

This is largely a European story, and the narrative focuses on particular parts of Europe: England and Germany, moving later during the eighteenth century to Scotland and France. This choice is not meant to be exclusive; we will also meet the Irish, Swiss, Austrians, Spanish, Italians, Swedes, Danes and Dutch, and towards the end of our story, more Americans. Perhaps equivalent stories could be told in many regions. These choices reflect my own knowledge, ease of access to sources and linguistic capabilities. Yet (perhaps conveniently!), I also believe that the focus of the book reflects the sites of significant transformations in thinking and practice. Those places (which might be London, Paris and Oxford at one moment; Edinburgh and Glasgow in another; courts of German territories for a particular issue, or for another time and issue, transnational and transatlantic debates) attained such significance as part of wider currents that ebbed, flowed and coursed together and apart. So this is a European history, but the reader should not expect a history that handles all of Europe equally. England is particularly prominent in the first half of the book; Germany across the middle chapters; Scotland, France and the United States receive more attention in the final third.

We have already seen some historical hypotheses about human relations with their environment advanced and criticised above. A professional historian will have recognised that the arguments advanced in this book also touch on many other historiographical debates, about the rise of the state, the causes of changes in agriculture and forestry, the underpinnings of the Industrial Revolution, the roles of different kinds of knowledge in social change, the emergence of fields of thought like political economy, to name a few. The approach of this work is to try not to get side-lined into too many such discussions (sometimes they are dealt with in footnotes). They are not the primary concern of this particular volume, important as they might be more generally. I have tried to remain focused on describing the discursive framing of 'sustainability', which is no small topic, and not lose the reader in what might be regarded as parochial, narrowly national and tangential concerns. Thus I beg the indulgence of specialists when arguments about their preoccupations are left implicit, or indeed unjustly neglected.

Lessons

Generally we write books because some life, society or problem has captivated us; as an expression of curiosity and perhaps a will to narrate, if we are fortunate enough to get the opportunity. History needs no further justification. It is interesting.

Sometimes, however, there are also lessons to be learned, not least when people are using, as they habitually do, understandings of historical development to justify political positions in the present. Often it would be desirable if in these circumstances people knew a bit more about the history – which is not to say there is necessarily any consensus about that among historians. It is a cliché, and sometimes a criticism, that to explain historically is to forgive, or to absolve (which is not the same thing at all). But sometimes there is good reason to avoid a blame game. Modern environmentalism is full of blaming for the various very serious problems we face today, and levels of destruction of habitat and varieties of life that make me, at least, sad, indeed at times grief-stricken – an emotion it would be perhaps desirable for politics to take more seriously. Others certainly feel and experience such loss much more keenly than me, and in much more personally devastating ways. Culprits for environmental destruction are legion: 'industrialism', 'capitalism', 'Western thought', 'science', 'ignorance of science', and so on; we have already seen some blaming above. Often these concepts are helpful in framing questions and analyses about our present and past predicaments.

Yet I do not think the problems we feel we face today can be reduced to them. Too much of this blame game assumes that there is a simple relation between some great social force and the thought of the time in which it emerges, whether as a legitimation of it or as a response to the challenges and problems that arise. Such a line supposes that people will eventually wise up and change their minds when confronted with reality (in the second case), or that transformation can somehow be effected by a great collective change of heart (in the first, if our current behaviour no longer seems justifiable). An agrarian society looks after the land; an industrial society is addicted to consumption and squandering resources heedlessly. The wisdom of the former can save the latter (yet – how did we get from one to the other?). I am hardly the first historian to point out that it is a lot more complicated. Certainly, the idea of a correspondence between economic structures ('relations of production') and the prevailing thinking of an age is a powerful idea worth entertaining; thought does not soar unbound from the world which it comprehends, and people like to have an explanation for doing what they feel compelled to do. But that is where the research begins, rather than the conclusion of the story, not least because thought is varied in any age. The proposition that thought (the 'superstructure', in Marxist terms) is linked in some causal way to the socio-economic 'base', however one sees the direction of causation, is no answer in itself, and is possibly neither true nor untrue. It is like asking whether light is a wave or a particle. But unless we choose our tools and set up our observations, we can say nothing about the nature of light at all. This book seeks to set up and draw upon a certain set of observations, as to how and when the discursive field of 'sustainability' emerged, because this work hitherto seems to be lacking, or at best has been fragmented and partial. But such a set of observations makes no claim to completeness. In doing the work of intellectual history, for example, it is undoubtedly the case that much of the socio-economic and political context of early modern thought, and its consequences, is neglected. It would be highly desirable for my arguments to be tested much further both in the crucible of empirical case studies, and in setting this story against other narratives of change over the period, to do with knowledge, class, gender and authority. Whether such work might be stimulated is perhaps the test of the value of what is written here. Indeed, this is what I hope for most of all, because I wish to draw the reader to the conclusion that the way in which sustainability was framed has meant that many *different kinds of argument of what constituted sustainability could emerge within this field*. The lack of consensus was not some kind of imaginative failure, but precisely what would make it political.

In many ways, this work is in a fairly typical exercise in intellectual history – albeit conducted by someone whose background is predominantly in social and economic history, more at ease studying 'cows and ploughs', the 'fuel and the furnace'. It began as a query about findings in court cases brought by peasants, and advice books on agriculture, and ended up veering into the history of political economy, chemistry, theories of life and techniques of quantification and the presentation of knowledge. It takes tried and tested techniques and information and blends them together into a new story.

The reader less familiar with the academic intellectual and cultural history of the past few decades may be surprised that it takes so much work to find the thought of sustainability in history. How can such a simple idea be so elusive! Why didn't we think of that before!? In the universities, the habit of writing the history of an 'idea' – ideas that somehow survived unblemished over time, used 'properly' or 'abused' by different generations – has long since been banished. It even seems a little quaint to write a history book about a concept. But 'de-naturalising' the idea of sustainability, showing that it is not self-evident, and illustrating the web of associations required to make sense of it, is precisely what this book aims to do. Thus while I speak to present concerns, I want to avoid 'Presentism' – judging the past by contemporary standards, looking for 'origins' as if that task may one day be definitively completed, or assuming that when we find similitude of expression or theme in the past, it means that people were thinking the same way as us. (And what, in any case, is 'us'?)

History can guide us away from the idea that particular viewpoints or perspectives (such as the need to act sustainably) should have been obvious to people in the past (or today), and hence behaving in contradiction to them must have come from ignorance, greed or some other strange compulsion. This is not to be exculpatory or to deny that ignorance, greed and compulsions certainly have their place in history (and the present). But evidence that others ignored what we take to be the evidence is not in turn evidence that they acted from the same motivations that would lead us to ignore the evidence. That would be a curious form of empathetic projection. We may think those who disagree with us – or did unwise things in the past, setting in train environmental ruin or other ills – were fools, monstrously self-seeking, or conveniently self-deluded. I certainly do this, as others would doubtless think of me, if they cared what I thought. But leaving it at that is not a route to political persuasion or a civil polity, and if we cannot appreciate that things were complicated for good reason in the past, we are unlikely to be able to resolve political difference in the present, when our opponents are so very alive, annoying and determined. On a more simple level, it can only help our reflections on how to live sustainably on our one planet today if we realise how particular ideas arose, always a little fuzzy and elusive and different, and also appreciate that people may not agree about ideas for precisely the same reasons today. To my mind this behoves us to treat such differences among us not as evidence of betrayal, simple-mindedness or hypocrisy: but instead as a reason to *make our case*, through listening, research and persuasion, for what we regard as desirable and sustainable ways of life in this world. And – this is not a small caveat – to work towards a world where we have *equal chances* to make our case, rather than just the theoretical, legal right to do so. It may help, too, to appreciate that when we argue, self-evidence barely passes muster as evidence at all, that knowledge is a vast, shifting and collective endeavour; that the question of sustainability may not actually have an answer, but that there may be nevertheless good reasons for asking it, over and over.

1 Living from the Land, c. 1500–1620

Bread

'Man doth not live by bread only.'[1] It is true, and repeated twice more in the Bible to underline the point.[2] But when it came to that uttermost necessity of sustaining life, the people of early modern Europe did indeed largely live on bread.[3] This had been true of much of Europe and the Middle East for many, many centuries. Bread might fall in line behind the Word, and arrived on the scene after the expulsion from Eden, but when prophets and scribes sought some metaphor that could convey a notion as being indisputably essential, it was to bread they reached. In the Catholic tradition, God embodied himself in the transformation of bread: the 'bread of life'. The fact that the King James Bible contains 330 uses of the word 'bread' and only 280 of the word

[1] Deuteronomy 8:3, King James version.
[2] 'Man shall not live by bread alone, but by every word that proceedeth out of the mouth of God.' Matthew 4:3; also Luke 4:4.
[3] The literature on bread consumption is enormous and cannot be glossed here. Indeed, as bread or grains (which might also be consumed as beer) constituted the largest share in the diet of the great majority of Europeans, nearly all histories of agriculture and material life must deal with it. There is no doubt too that access to grain and bread was the overwhelming preoccupation of authorities concerned with dearth, even if in some parts of the continent 'its predominance was not nearly so great as many modern assumptions suggest'. Craig Muldrew, *Food, energy and the creation of industriousness. Work and material culture in agrarian England, 1550–1780* (Cambridge: Cambridge University Press, 2011), p. 58. For an authoritative study of the politics of bread in *ancien régime* France, see Stephen L. Kaplan, *Bread, politics and political economy in the reign of Louis XV* (The Hague: Martinus Nijhoff, 1976).

'love' does not perhaps bear witness to the core tenets of Christianity, but might be an indicative of what most graced the tongues of peasants, preachers and politicos, both literally and metaphorically. Bread was everywhere: in dreams, sermons, speeches, banter and bellies; all the places and processes that collectively somehow, mysteriously, made a life.[4]

So when the bread failed it was not just bodies that quailed and suffered, but the whole community, the order of things. Everyone watched the skies and the earth for portents of the harvest and the progress of the crop. There were, no doubt, a thousand different ways how peasants could judge whether God might make a year bounteous. Those hidebound to their books could consult the advice of the ancients who listed the signs to be read in the celestial heavens, in the nether weathery skies, or the behaviour of bird and beast as to how their fortunes might go. Translated by the learned men of the Renaissance, some of these did not perhaps surpass peasant wisdom, if they could make any claim to particular knowledge at all: 'he shall foretell great Abundance of Raine, if the Clouds be darke, deepe and thicke'.[5] At times, it seems that the whole of floral and faunal creation knew more of the coming temper of the airs than did those placed to rule over them:

> Hee shall know before hand that It will be Rain by these and other such like signs… if little birds, haunting the Fens, be continually washing themselves in the water, if the Crow doe wet her head at the brinke of the water, or wade into it, and crie verie much toward evening: if the raven sound out her song from the hollow of her throat, and boast herself of her wings; if the geese crie and flye more than they have been accustomed; if the Bees will not flye farre from their hives; if the Heron wander and and whirle about to and fro in the middest of the Fields all sad and lowring: if Oxen eat more than ordinarie, lye downe upon the right side, looke toward the South, licke their hooves all about: if the Kine looke up into the ayre, and draw in the same: if the Asses bray: if Cockes crow at all hours, and chiefly at evening,

[4] Piero Camporesi, *Bread of dreams. Food and fantasy in early modern Europe* (Cambridge: Polity, 2005).

[5] Charles Estienne, *Maison rustique, or The countrey farme*, trans. Richard Surflet, and further edited by Gervase Markham (London: John Bill, 1616), p. 25.

when they are upon their pearches… if spiders fall downe, not
being blown downe of the wind: if Dogs tumble and wallow
on the earth: if Pigeons come home late to their house: if Flies,
Waspes and Hornets, Fleas and Gnats, bite more keenly than
ordinarily they are wont.[6]

Did any one ever rush to mow their hay to see the beasts through
the long winter ahead at the prompt of a gnat-bite? We cannot know.
But it made perfect sense that the whole of Creation might be aquiver
for what the tenor of the atmosphere might be. When tempests raged,
hail battered ears of corn and soft grapes into oblivion, or deluges
saturated the shallow tilth and rotted crops where they stood, things
appeared awry with the whole order of the world. We know that in certain parts of Europe the clamour might be raised against storm-raising
witches, especially in the exceptional years of 1587–8 and the 1620s
when snows fell in summer across an already war-battered southern
Germany.[7] More often, the message from the pulpit was that more prosaic bad behaviour had incited God's wrath: drunkenness, licentious-
ness, the lack of charity in men's hearts.[8]

People were not resigned to this seasonal wheel of fortune.
Whether bad behaviour triggered the calamities or not, clear-minded
officials knew perfectly well that good governance could ameliorate
the worst. Equally, sharp-eyed merchants saw their main chance. In
the dearth-stricken 1590s, the ships of the Baltic swarmed west and
south laden with grains from the breadbasket of Poland for the bare
warehouses of the Mediterranean and Atlantic coasts. In the popular
imagination the men who stocked up in anticipation of the bad times,

[6] Estienne, *Maison rustique*, p. 25.
[7] Wolfgang Behringer, *Witchcraft persecutions in Bavaria. Popular magic, religious zealotry and reason of state in early modern Europe* (Cambridge: Cambridge University
Press, 1997); also Christian Pfister, 'Climatic extremes, recurrent crises and witch
hunts. Strategies of European societies in coping with exogenous shocks in the late
sixteenth and early seventeenth centuries', *The Medieval History Journal* 10 (2007),
pp. 1–41; Christian Pfister and Rudolf Brázdil, 'Climatic variability in sixteenth
century Europe and its social dimension. A synthesis', *Climatic Change* 43 (1999),
pp. 5–53.
[8] See the essays collected in Wolfgang Behringer, Hartmut Lehmann and Christian
Pfister (eds), *Kulturelle Konsequenzen der "Kleinen Eiszeit" / Cultural consequences
of the "Little Ice Age"* (Göttingen: Vandenhoeck & Ruprecht, 2005); Wolfgang
Behringer, *Kulturgeschichte des Klimas. Von der Eiszeit bis zur globalen Erwärmung*
(Munich: Beck, 2007), chs 3–4.

awaiting the greatest spike in prices and the moment of greatest need for advancing credit, were the cause of the shortages themselves. Oft-times public officials agreed, condemning these 'Caterpillars and Locusts', who 'make a private gaine out of a publike detriment'. Sometimes, those local magistrates and the profiteering middlemen were one and the same.[9] But in many regions statute ordered that grain was to be offered for sale in public places to locals first and foremost. Forestalling and re-grating (stockpiling and speculating through sales to middlemen, not for direct use) were banned. Rioters seized cartloads of grain and redistributed it at what they considered a fair price. Whether the blow was considered providential or from the heartless behaviour of rich individuals, there had to be some culpable, human 'covetousness' involved.[10]

But hunger was endemic, and not just a condition of 'bad years'. The fear of dearth raised basic issues of equity, distribution and responsibility. The misfortunes of vagabonds and beggars, the mob of the *matta-panes* ('bread-crazy') might easily be attributed to their own moral failings; but often the question was not clear-cut. Even small towns in Germany might have a beadle stationed at the town gate to hand out coins to the itinerant poor before barring them entry: a curious combination of beneficence to the stranger with the abdication of responsibility and ejection once this small bounty was extended.[11] In any case the cash dried up when times became hard within the

---

[9] Charles Fitz-Geffrie's sermon, *The curse of corne-holders*, cited in Steve Hindle, 'Dearth and the English revolution. The harvest crisis of 1647–50', *EcHR* 61(S1) (2008), p. 70.

[10] R.B. Outhwaite, *Dearth, public policy and social disturbance in England, 1550–1800* (Basingstoke: Macmillan, 1991); Hindle, 'Harvest crisis', pp. 74–8; Wilhelm Abel, *Massenarmut und Hungerkrisen in vorindustriellen Europea. Versuch einer Synopsis* (Berlin: Parey, 1974), passim; Robert Jütte, 'Klimabedingte Teuerungen und Hungersnöte. Bettelverbote und Armenfürsorge als Krisenmanagement', in Behringer et al., *Kulturelle Konsequenzen*, pp. 225–37; Robert Jütte, *Obrigkeitliche Armenfürsorge in deutschen Reichsstädten der frühen neuzeit. Städtischen Armenwesen in Frankfurt am Main und Köln* (Köln: Böhlau, 1984); Paul Slack, *Poverty and policy in Tudor and Stuart England* (London: Longman, 1988); William John Wright, *Capitalism, the state, and the Lutheran Reformation. Sixteenth-century Hesse* (Athens, OH: Ohio University Press, 1988).

[11] Paul Warde, 'The origins and development of institutional welfare support in early modern Württemberg, c. 1500–1700', *Continuity and Change* 22 (2007), pp. 459–87; on the ambiguities of attitudes to and explanations of dearth, see Ayesha Mukherjee, *Penury into plenty. Dearth and the making of knowledge in early modern England* (London: Routledge, 2015), pp. 21–34.

walls. The Elizabethan government in England exhorted the peers and gentry to 'hospitality', a traditional delivery of alms in hard years at the mansion door (more likely the back door).[12] Poor boxes rattled round the pews and even alehouse benches of an evening to raise funds for the indigent and infirm considered 'deserving', most commonly the old. In towns and increasingly rural parishes in a few parts of the continent overseers and beadles distributed bread, cash and fuel to the poor, sometimes collected through forms of property taxation. Hospitals and religious institutions dominated welfare provision in Catholic countries. More often one fell back on kin, while the cold shoulders of neighbours in very many communities pushed unfortunates on to the road, never to return.[13]

Attitudes to the poor were unquestionably harsh, on many occasion unpityingly so. But welfare was nevertheless understood as a responsibility of government. And this is why this story of sustainability begins here. Long before many people concerned themselves in any detail with the capacity of the land to deliver its benefits over the long run, European rulers were presented with an obligation to ensure the products of the land reached those who needed them. At least officials should do everything in their power to ensure that the honest man could labour to make his own shift. Where people had completely lost the capacity to do so, public officials might step in. Of course, this obligation was rather differently felt, and the experience of welfare was highly varied, in part because of the highly varied polities of Europe and the fact that communities and lordships, even in the greater and more centralised states, retained a high degree of autonomy. But policy (or *police* or *polizei*, that range of measures designed to maintain order, published in *Polizeiordnungen* throughout the period) was not only reactive. Markets sales were regulated, maximum prices sometimes fixed. By the late sixteenth century headmen and magistrates could be found searching through

[12] Steve Hindle, 'Dearth, fasting and alms. The campaign for general hospitality in late Elizabethan England', *Past & Present* 172 (2001), pp. 44–86.

[13] For general surveys, see Jütte, *Obrigkeitliche Armenfürsorge*; Slack, *Poverty and policy*; Steve Hindle, *On the parish? The micro-politics of poor relief in rural England, c. 1550–1750* (Oxford: Oxford University Press, 2004); Bas van Bavel and Auke Rijpma, 'How important were formalized charity and social spending before the rise of the welfare state? A long-run analysis of selected Western European cases, 1400–1850', *EcHR* 69 (2016), pp. 159–87.

the barns of their charges for sacks of grain secreted away, compiling lengthy despatches on the needs and food stocks of their communities so bureaucrats and rulers could assess the balance of supply and demand. Heads of households lined up to swear oaths on how much they generally consumed, what they needed for seed, and what might be spared for distribution. Outside of the major port cities, those places and people whose credit was always good, little enough of this effort had great effect. And rules to obviate scarcity brought confusion in their wake. If grain should be sold to the near locality, how could one get it to great urban centres when the country was hungry? Did the demands of the potentially restive crowds of the capital trump those of the peasantry? Could one trust the reports of public officials who themselves were farmers, grain merchants, shippers? By and large, policy implementation was by necessity local, but it also posed questions about the distribution of resources in the polity as a whole, or at least within the hinterlands of major cities and strategic military regions.[14]

There was another kind of answer to all these quandaries, and to the basic question: how do we get bread? Bread was baked of grains, and since the sin of Adam and Eve grains were coaxed through toil from the tilled earth. Indeed, a preoccupation with earth far outweighs love or bread in the Bible: 960 references in the edition of King James! For bread, for order, one needed tillage, always more tillage. There were other foods to be won of course aside from cultivating the fields and gardens; bounties of hedgerow, lakes, rivers and streams, of wild creatures, although many of these had been declared off-limits and prerogatives of the nobility (who of course had no great need of such things). And *in toto* they were meagre enough measured against the totality of need. In the worst cases people choked down animal feed, adulterated breads that sent them mad, the very grass of the fields. The straw found boiling in small pot over the fire to soften it when neighbours broke into a cottage in the town of Reggio in April 1601, to find three abandoned sons, two dead from hunger, one barely alive

[14] Kaplan, *Bread*, passim; Stephen Hipkin, 'The structure, development and politics of the Kent grain trade, 1552–1647', *EcHR* 61(S1) (2008), pp. 118–25; Abel, *Massenarmut*, passim; Paul Warde, 'Subsistence and sales. The peasant economy of Württemberg in the early seventeenth century', *EcHR* 59 (2006), pp. 289–319; Paul Warde, 'Origins'; Hindle, 'Harvest crisis', pp. 76–7.

and with the halms stuffed between his teeth in a last desperate resort to hold body and soul together.[15] One does not live on bread alone; but even more certainly, one does not live at all from straw. How to get bread? How to increase the supply of crops? It was through asking these questions, and investing them with political urgency, that eventually people would come to turn the question round. Have we over-extended ourselves? Does current plenty store up future penury? It would be a long time before such speculations appeared, but to understand one of the routes by which people got there, we will start with the question of tillage.

Tillage

Sir Thomas More's *Utopia* was a bit of a joke. The perfect place that he described in 1516 was no place that anyone would want to live, but at the same time, it showed that one might live better. So what should one know about this land of *Utopia*, or any polity for that matter? A trusty guide should 'set out in order all things relating to their soil, their rivers, their towns, their people, their manners, constitution, laws'. If the size of individual city populations grew out of balance, the imagined guide to the island, Raphael Hythloday tells us, 'they supply cities that do not increase so fast, from others that breed faster'.[16] He does not tell us why a population could become too much, but clearly there were limits:

> if there is any increase over the whole island, then they draw
> out a number of their citizens out of the several towns, and send
> them over to the neighbouring continent; where, if they find that
> the inhabitants have more soil than they can well cultivate, they
> fix a colony, taking the inhabitants into their society, if they are
> willing to live with them; and where they do that of their own
> accord, they quickly enter into their method of life, and conform
> to their rules, and this proves a happiness to both nations; for
> according to their constitution, such care is taken of the soil that
> it becomes fruitful enough for both, though it might be otherwise
> too narrow and barren for any one of them.[17]

---

[15] Camporesi, *Bread of dreams*, p. 85.

[16] Thomas More, *Utopia, or, the Happy Republic*, trans. G. Burnet (Glasgow: Hamilton and Balfour, 1743), pp. 43, 60.

[17] More, *Utopia*, p. 60.

Self-evidently, then, Utopians managed their soil well. How precisely this was done was not a concern for Thomas More and drew no further comment. In fact, the only real lesson was political. Any society that did not nurture the sod to utopian standards was ripe for justified expropriation.

> But if the natives refuse to conform themselves to their laws,
> they drive them out of those bounds which they mark out for
> themselves, and use force if they resist. For they account it a very
> just cause of war, for a nation to hinder others from possessing a
> part of that soil of which they make no use, but which is suffered
> to lie idle and uncultivated; since every man has by the law of
> nature a right to such a waste portion of the earth as is necessary
> for his subsistence.[18]

Here succinctly expressed was a manifesto for a coming whirlwind of colonisation, forced migrations and subjugation.[19] The voyagers and conquistadors who were launching out from European shores as More wrote this may not have ever considered themselves as spreading an unassailably virtuous order, yet they understood well that any land that did not conform to their ideals of cultivation and civilisation – ideas that could barely be distinguished – was open to claim. By the seventeenth century colonial magistrates would opine from their benches that only 'improved' land – that is, land that had demonstrably received investment in the form of recognised agricultural practices from the Old World – could confer title. The ecology of native farming, and indigenous claims to the land, were rendered invisible.[20]

Yet More's claim related to a more local concern than the practice of great European land grab in the New World. The Utopian

---

[18] More, *Utopia*, p. 60.
[19] A century and a half later Locke made a related argument, implying the native Americans had no store of value and hence no incentive to 'improve' their lands. Nor, by implication, could they justly prevent others from using it. John Locke, *Two treatises of government* (London: Awnsham & John Churchill, 1694), II.V.48–9. Later still, the same argument was employed by Emmerich de Vattel in his *Law of nations* of 1758 to justify claims to colonial sovereignty. Cited in Richard H. Grove, *Green imperialism. Colonial expansion, tropical island Edens and the origins of environmentalism 1600–1860* (Cambridge: Cambridge University Press, 1995), pp. 266, 286.
[20] For example, William Cronon, *Changes in the land. Indians, colonists and the ecology of New England* (New York: Hill & Wang, 1983), ch. 4.

justification rested on an argument that had a widely recognised status in European law: each man [*sic*] had a right to the 'necessary for his subsistence', his *necessitas domestica*, in German his *Notdurft*, all those things that maintained his household. The principle of granting access to necessity, but no more, was frequently applied to common rights, determining the level at which individual households could extract collectively managed resources. Equally, petitioners pressed authorities to ensure that basic necessities were available on the market, and at times, although controversially, it could be claimed as a justification for theft.[21] Subsequently great legists and philosophers would view the labour which fenced a plot of ground and cultivated it to secure enough to eat as the primordial underpinning of private property, and the first justification for extracting a patrimony from the common waste.[22] But in a world distant from treatises and jurists, the rough justice of the squatter also saw a patch of untilled ground as fair game for hungry bellies, and indeed it was conceded in natural law as evoked by Locke 'that men, being once born, have a right to their preservation, and consequently to meat and drink, and such other things as nature affords for their subsistence'.[23] A whole society might be judged by the quality of its environmental management (to use a very anachronistic phrase). And better management, in the view of many, meant more tillage.

Thus across numerous lands in sixteenth-century Europe, people became preoccupied with the balance of tillage and other uses of the soil: pasture, meadow, vineyards, marsh, heath, woodland, although these all played an essential role in the agrarian economy. As populations bounced back from the post-Black Death nadir, cultivated land began to edge out into abandoned territory again, or fill in leys left to grass amid the great open fields. Poorer families without a fortunate inheritance sought 'waste' to colonise, while the better endowed sought to profit as a gap opened up between food prices and relatively lower wages. By default, much of this expansion and assarting was 'enclosure'; in other words, it effectively abolished the possibility of common rights of grazing or fuel-gathering being exercised on the

---

[21] Martina de Moor, Leigh Shaw-Taylor and Paul Warde (eds), *The management of common land in north west Europe 1500–1850* (Turnhout: Brepols, 2002); Hindle, *On the parish*, pp. 89–91.

[22] Locke, *Two treatises*, II.V.27–30.

[23] Locke, *Two treatises*, II.V.25.

newly cultivated land, frequently without any actual legal change in the land's status. When it was a matter of a fraction of an acre here or there, the institutions which governed the common rights frequently turned a blind eye, if they noticed at all. In much of Europe the governing 'institution' over the land was the lord of the manor, or indirectly, the prince of the state who oversaw the local courts. Tillage brought more revenue to landowners and such 'enclosure' was often uncontested.

There was, however, enclosure of another kind to be found in England. This entailed the much larger-scale removal of rights by lords from great expanses of the common waste, or the abolition of collectively agreed regulation over arable fields and pastures. The land was then turned over to more commercially profitable farming, often sheep-raising to supply the textile industry. It might involve large-scale expropriation and drew howls of righteous anger from the affected peasantry. Such enclosure was highly controversial, and a tendency to provoke unrest jangled the nerves of government sufficiently to lead to measures that – at least for the sake of appearances – limited or outlawed the practice, or made it much easier for tenants to defend their rights. Fear of enclosure was a prominent theme in the 1510s and 1520s and a series of commissions investigating the practice had proven a trigger for widespread revolt in southern England in the summer of 1549.[24] Enclosure later in the sixteenth and seventeenth centuries was not usually of this type; it extended tillage into the waste, or undid communal regulation of land already under the plough, although in some parts of the country, notably the East Midlands vales, new commercial incentives saw a shift to pastoral farming and stock-fattening, while other farmers became more flexible in switching land between arable and grass leys ('convertible husbandry') to enhance productivity. But whenever scarcity reared its head, enclosure provided a ready-made scapegoat. It angered those relatively poor commoners who saw the stock of available resources shrunken. In some places it seemed to extend pasture; and it always evoked the bad memories of the sheep ranchers of earlier decades. If England seemed to be bursting at the

[24] R.C. Allen, *Enclosure and the yeoman* (Oxford: Oxford University Press, 1992); Andy Wood, *The 1549 rebellions and the making of early modern England* (Cambridge: Cambridge University Press, 2007).

seams and hungry, then enclosure might be to blame, the devourer of tillage.[25]

The English Parliament thus received many bills on the subject of tillage, often directly introduced by senior government ministers, and some of which became law. Frequently they reacted to dearth and recent or ongoing crisis, as did the great majority of European legislation on welfare, market controls and resources. Bills appeared in 1552, 1555, 1563, 1571, 1589 and 1597. The purpose was sometimes not quite clear: was it 'converting land into tillage', 'the maintenance of tillage', the 'increase of tillage', the 'preservation of tillage'? Sometimes these terms were used for one and the same bill. But the common sentiment was that there should certainly be no less tillage, and preferably more.[26] In the midst of the great European crisis of the 1590s, statesman, lawyer and savant Francis Bacon moved a motion to protect tillage in November 1597, linking it to a simultaneous bill banning forestalling and re-grating, and complaints against depopulating enclosure. At the same time the first bill for the Poor Laws was edging towards the statute book, that over the next three years reshaped English welfare provision into a national, parochial-based system. England was no anomaly. The principalities of Germany published numerous ordinances defending tillage, frequently seeking to arrest a perceived expansion of vineyards (although vineyards often took up land ill-suited to the plough, and in any case provided employment and a ready source of income from exports which grain cultivation could not).[27] But there is little evidence of these efforts by parliaments and privy councils having much effect, certainly in the longer term. In the end, tillage ebbed and flowed with the population, with some regional adjustments in land use as markets became better integrated

[25] J.R. Wordie, 'The chronology of English enclosure, 1500–1914', EcHR 36 (1983), pp. 483–505; Leigh Shaw-Taylor, 'The management of common land in the lowlands of southern England, c. 1500-c.1850', in de Moor et al., Common land, pp. 59–85.

[26] '4 March 1552', JHC 1: 1547–1629 (1802), p. 19; '15 November 1553', JHC 1, p. 30; '12 November 1555', JHC 1, p. 44; '23 March 1563', JHC 1 p. 70; JHL: 'April 1563', The Journals of all the Parliaments during the Reign of Queen Elizabeth (1682), pp. 72–7; 'Journal of the House of Lords: May 1571', JPQE, pp. 145–54. JHL: 'March 1589', JPQE, pp. 424–7; JPQE, pp. 551–66; JPQE, pp. 536–44; JPQE, pp. 660–89; '4 May 1624', JHC 1, pp. 697–8.

[27] Warde, 'Origins'; Walter Achilles, Landwirtschaft in der frühen Neuzeit (Munich: R. Oldenbourg, 1991); Wilhelm Abel, Geschichte der deutschen Landwirtschaft, 2nd edition (Stuttgart: E. Ulmer, 1967).

and specialised. In southern Germany it was a deteriorating climate from the 1560s onwards that would stop the vines in their tracks, especially bitterly cold years around 1600 and again in the 1620s that simply killed the plants and literally froze the peasants' investments.[28] What was more important than the *effect* of such legislation for the story of sustainability was the fact that government attention had been drawn to the problem.

In truth tillage was expanding, but people thought it was not, or that it was not expanding fast enough. How then could it be encouraged? Early modern Europe was not some Utopia where things just got done at a timely moment. Attempts at regulation provoked argument and men were alive to apparent contradiction. Surely the main incentive to till the land was profit, the source of 'gayness' that would inspire more cultivation, argued Sir Thomas Smith? Smith penned a work in the tumultuous, blood-soaked year of 1549 defending enclosure but equally calling for the expansion of tillage through loosening restraints on trade, although it did not see the light of day for three decades. Smith's inspiration to more husbandry was 'To let them have more profit by it then they have, & liberty to sell it at all times & to all places as freely as men may do other things... the ye price would provoke every man to se ye plough in the grounde, to till waste grounds.' According to him higher grain prices would extend tillage, and lower the incentive for depopulating enclosure for pasture. Much of the logic of regulation, that sought to control prices, would militate against the expansion of cultivation.[29]

Similarly, five decades later Sir Walter Raleigh argued at the Parliamentary session of 1601 that bans on forestalling and re-grating, key tools of consumer protection, simply reduced commercial possibilities, and while they squeezed down prices in hard years, they equally

---

[28] Erich Landsteiner, 'The crisis of wine production in late sixteenth-century Central Europe. Climatic causes and economic consequences', *Climatic Change* 43 (1999), pp. 323–34; Paul Warde, *Ecology, economy and state formation in early modern Germany* (Cambridge: Cambridge University Press, 2006), pp. 84–91.

[29] The work was not published until 1580 and for a long time wrongly attributed to Sir John Hale. Smith [published as Gentleman, W.S.], *A compendious or briefe examination of certayne ordinary complaints* (London: Thomas Marshe, 1581), pp. 22–3; Paul Warde, 'The idea of improvement, c. 1520–1700', in Richard Hoyle (ed.), *Custom, improvement and the landscape in early modern Britain* (Farnham: Ashgate, 2011), pp. 127–48.

reduced profit and incentives to investment.[30] In the longer run, it meant less grain to go round – a classic critique of market restrictions and the French and Spanish practice of setting price ceilings that would echo through the seventeenth and eighteenth centuries. Francis Bacon's measure to protect tillage of 1597–8 was thus at best an emergency provision that should be repealed as swiftly as possible (and it should be noted that much of this legislation across Europe was only ever intended for dearth years). Yet the seeds of an idea had been sown, that a goal of government was to promote *expansion* and intensification of the use of the land.

Tudor preoccupation with the extent of tillage seems to have ebbed away in the reign of James I, marked by a single bill on the 'decay of tillage' in 1624. Periodic trade restrictions continued. In response to the dearth of 1622–3, whose manifestation in the Cumbrian uplands is now considered the last famine in English history,[31] the government proposed the setting up of corn magazines to provide both a source of subsidised grain for the poor, and a guaranteed market for farmers. This was a model widely applied in the great cities of the continent, and that with government encouragement had spread into even small settlements in the Duchy of Württemberg. In an England already becoming ill-disposed towards government interference in the grain market, the proclamation does not seem to have been followed up.[32]

If more tillage seemed the solution to Tudor gentlemen, historians have long been schooled by reading Thomas Malthus to view the core problem from the other side of the equation: too many people. The capacity for agricultural expansion would always, necessarily, be limited by technique and land area, and thus the variable that shifted to cause problems was growing numbers of people: 'It

---

[30] Simon d'Ewes (ed.), *Journal of the House of Commons* (Shannon: Irish University Press, 1682), Dec. 1601, pp. 660–89.

[31] Andrew B. Appleby, *Famine in Tudor and Stuart England* (Liverpool: Liverpool University Press, 1978); on the events of 1622–4 in the British Isles, see Richard Hoyle, 'Famine as agricultural catastrophe. The crisis of 1622–4 in east Lancashire', *EcHR* 63 (2010), pp. 974–1002; and a more general discussion can be found in the essays collected in John Walter and Roger Schofield (eds), *Famine, disease and the social order in early modern England* (Cambridge: Cambridge University Press, 1989).

[32] James F. Larkin and Paul L. Hughes (eds), *Stuart royal proclamations. Vol. 1. Royal proclamations of King James I 1603–1625* (Oxford: Clarendon, 1973), no. 248, pp. 585–8; Warde, 'Origins'.

is an obvious truth, which has been taken notice of by many writers, that population must always be kept down to the level of the means of subsistence', wrote Malthus in the first version of his famous *Essay*, published in 1798.[33] Malthus's foray into demography was intended as a private document refuting what he saw as misguided cornucopian optimism among sympathisers of the French Revolution. He would develop an argument in later editions of the book that people could indeed regulate population change by altering the birth rate. But if they did not, they would be repeatedly plunged into periods when the number of people surpasses their means of subsistence, a 'necessary oscillation… constantly subsisting cause of periodical misery' that through higher mortality would bring supply and demand for food back into line.[34]

Two centuries before Malthus people had no notion of restraining population. If pressure became too much, then the indigent were expected to simply head elsewhere, as the Utopians did. Indeed, while the run of opinion in late sixteenth-century Europe was that population had increased, no-one had attempted, or had the capacity, to take the measure of it outside of some limited urban censuses.[35] The great surveyor and mapmaker John Norden delivered a report to the Privy Council on how the Crown might enhance revenue by enclosing parks and chases in 1607; he wrote at a turning point in policy when government no longer shied away from enclosure and began consistently to view it as a tool to enhance productivity and improve the desperate royal finances. The proximate cause of Norden writing was the latter issue, but it did no harm to throw in that: 'It is great providence to adjust of some course to increase not only meadow and pasture but especially tillage in this Kingdom consider the dayly increase of whose wants of corn in years of no extreame necessity.' Shortages sucked coin from the realm to pay for Baltic imports, an issue that had also exercised

---

[33] Thomas R. Malthus, *Essay on the principle of population* (London: J. Johnson, 1798), p. 7. It should be added that Malthus did not imagine agricultural production to be invariant, but that its capacity for growth was always less than 'the power of population', so that even a world turned into a garden would still, eventually, hit a Malthusian crisis; although he also argued that Europe had already reached the crisis point.

[34] Malthus, *Essay*, p. 46.

[35] One Henry Martyn did suggest that the government should keep a register of the entire population, probably in 1612. BL Additional MS 10038.

Sir Thomas Smith. Norden continued, 'if there be no prevension had to increase corn cattle and habitations, there will shortly be (without means of diminishing the multitude of people) neither houses for many destitute families nor food to relieve the mean rank of people if a time of any extra scarceity should come'. Thus both the rescue and promise of the world lay in better husbandry and greater tillage.[36]

There was one celebrated thinker of the age who did raise the issue of population in general, and rates of growth: the Italian theorist Giovanni Botero. He was (and still is) best known for his *Reason of State* of 1589, a counter-blast to Machiavelli that stressed the importance of princely rule through virtue, and that was rapidly translated into German by 1596, and by the end of the century into French. Also bound into the German edition was a treatise of Botero's first published in 1588, and known as the *Greatness of Cities*. Botero was interested in the effects of urban life on population and hypothesised that density of living led to poor sanitary conditions and greater mortality in epidemics, a problem familiar enough to public health officials of the day. But towards the end of the *Greatness of Cities* he wondered why Imperial Rome, and modern metropolises such as Milan and Venice, seemed to settle at certain population ceilings. Indeed, this was not just an urban phenomenon, but one that pertained to 'the whole world': why was the population growth so evident over three millennia since Adam and Eve had left the Garden of Eden no longer (in his perception) taking place?[37] Botero assumed that the 'generative power' of people had changed little or not at all over three thousand years, so the cause of arrested population growth must be the shortage of foodstuffs.

Botero noted that cities could either supply themselves with provisions locally, or by trade. It was however the barriers to trade (hypothesising a merchant travelling to Italy from China or India) that he stressed as limits, in part due to issues economists would today call 'institutional': these ranged across 'the roughness of the places, the height of the mountains, the depth of the valleys, the unstoppable floods, the dangers of the seas, seizure by pirates, the inconstancy of the winds, the great costs, the poor condition of

[36] BL Additional MS 38444 f.5r.
[37] Ioannis Botero, *Von der Stätten / Auffgang / Grösse und Herzligkeit / kurtzer / doch gruntlicher Bericht* (Strassburg, 1596), pp. 432–3.

the roads, the envy of neighbours, the hatred and attack of enemies', and so the list goes on, also covering price rises of goods and religious turmoil. All these combined to set a ceiling to a city's growth, such that dearth and poverty would eventually prompt people to emigrate. Nevertheless, Botero also hypothesised, if rather vaguely, that the world had reached some kind of population limit, that 'the world was so full of people... such that the fruits of the earth, from which people must draw their sustenance, cannot feed a greater number'. As evidence he pressed into service migration to the farthest corners of the world, and strife both current and historical between nations, and the barbarian invasions in Europe which he explained through a lack of domestic resources pushing tribes into the Roman Empire. Further examples of this phenomenon were the selling of oneself and one's family into slavery in contemporary Africa, or cannibalism in the Americas. This rather eclectic mix prompted Botero to make the dismal observation that 'What else can this mean, but that the world is too narrow to satisfy our needs or bring satisfaction to our wants and desires.'[38] Much the same kind of arguments would be made by Matthew Hale in his *The Primitive Origination of Mankind* of 1677, given a providential twist as being part of God's design to limit 'over-plenitude... in the Number of Men'.[39] Yet neither of these dismal prognoses was followed up with further analysis. On the contrary: most thought that there was plenty more that could be got out of the ground yet. We now turn to examine the literature on agriculture to ponder why this might be the case.

Husbandry

If some governments were worried about the production and distribution of food, and their vulnerable subjects all the more so, a few writers focused directly on the means by which farming might improve yields.

[38] Botero, *Von der Stätten*, pp. 434–7. See also Clarence Glacken, *Traces on the Rhodian shore. Nature and culture in Western thought from ancient times to the end of the eighteenth century* (Berkeley, CA: University of California Press, 1967), pp. 368–74; also Giovanni Botero, *On the causes of the greatness and magnificence of cities*, trans. Geoffrey W. Symcox (Toronto: University of Toronto Press, 2012).

[39] Matthew Hale, *The primitive origination of mankind* (London: William Shrowsbery, 1677), p. 215. Also discussed in Glacken, *Traces*, pp. 400–5.

This literature was generally focused on the management of the estates of the well-to-do, and written from the perspective of the lord or the steward concerned to make best use of land, labourers and servants. In developing writing on agricultural practice from its medieval and classical antecedents, authors working in this tradition would eventually have their attention drawn to the very roots of agricultural success. What made plants grow, and what made them yield more profusely? By this means could agricultural 'science' be put at the service of the state. But we are getting ahead of ourselves.

As with so many things, the Renaissance saw a rapid expansion in the provision of books and manuscripts concerned with agriculture. This doubtless reflected both supply, in an expanding literary culture, and demand, in the growing opportunities for profit that a rising population entailed. The classical inheritance of ancient Greece and above all Rome, however, was less to place husbandry at the centre of the polity, than to see the land as an escape from the vice and corruption of the city, an uncorrupted and autonomous place to practise virtue (or, indeed, simply a source of income). Of course, in truth the surviving great classical books of agronomy and household management, penned by men such as Xenophon (Socratic Athens), Cato, Varro, Virgil (in the late Republic), Columella (first century CE) and Palladius (possibly fourth or fifth century CE), were all the products of a moneyed elite who stood close to the heart of either imperial politics, or in the case of Xenophon, had been under the tutelage of Socrates in the busy heart of metropolitan Athens.[40] The assumed seat of residence of the landowner was always the city; he might have a country estate to retire to, or he might ride out to view his fields that lay under the shadow of urban fortifications. So portraying farming as an agrarian idyll could be a stratagem, either an evasion for men who had reason not to antagonise capricious rulers, or itself a form of critique of the dubious morals and priorities of the society in which they were immersed; but in some cases, they were more simply useful sets of notes for farming.[41] Yet if such texts still bore the stamp of politics in the very genre they adopted, that genre ruled out formulating tillage or husbandry as a political cause in itself; in no case do we find the rural estate connected

---

[40] Palladius, *The work of farming (Opus Agriculturae)*, trans. John G. Fitch (Totnes: Prospect, 2013), p. 11.

[41] Of course, these varied purposes were not mutually exclusive.

to the advancement or orderliness of the commonweal through the state of the fields.[42]

The most extensive works of husbandry passed down from antiquity were those of Columella, Varro and Cato, running to many hundreds of pages and providing a rich source of information for those who could read them.[43] Although manuscript copies and some printed works (including translations into Italian) made their way across the Channel into a few libraries, no English translation of the major works would appear until Columella's *On husbandry* was published in London in 1745, although Palladius' *De re rustica*, in many regards a potted Columella, was translated as early as 1442.[44] Thus while the imprint of these classics on contemporary agronomy in continental Western Europe was direct, in England their reception was largely mediated by Renaissance interpreters.

In contrast, many a budding Latin scholar on either side of the Channel was confronted with Virgil's *Georgics*, a poetical homage to animal husbandry and cultivation; while Xenophon's *On the household* was translated into English as early as 1532 and went through numerous subsequent additions. In truth, neither contained much useful agricultural content, especially Xenophon's work which devoted far more space to justifying writing about husbandry at all, and keeping the patriarch's wife in order, than it did to actual farming. While it dignified 'the ordrynge of an house, [with] the name of a science, lyke wyse as phisike is, and masons & carpenters crafte', and thus licensed an interest in these workaday topics by learned men, it nevertheless concluded that husbandry itself was easily learned and differences in agricultural fortunes were to be explained by diligence, not knowledge. The most pressing task for an estate owner was to find a bailiff or steward they could trust.[45] Virgil's stanzas became ever more popular,

---

[42] Nevertheless, some of the authors, such as Cato and Varro, were military commanders, public officials, politicians and commentators of great distinction.

[43] Lucius Junius Moderatus Columella, *Of husbandry*, trans. (London: A. Millar, 1745); Marcus Terentius Varro, *On Agriculture*, trans. William Davis Hooper (Cambridge, MA: Harvard University Press, 1934); Marcus Porcius Cato, *On Agriculture*, trans. William Davis Hooper (Cambridge, MA: Harvard University Press, 1934).

[44] Columella, *Of husbandry*; Palladius, *The work of farming*, p. 23; See also Mauro Ambrosoli, *The wild and the sown. Botany and agriculture in Europe 1350–1850* (Cambridge: Cambridge University Press, 1997).

[45] Xenophon (trans. G. Hervet), *Treatise of housholde* (London: Thomas Berthelet, 1532), esp. pp. ii, 57–8.

reaching an apogee of acclaim in England after Dryden's translation of 1697, but those authors who declaimed that no work of agronomy could surpass him were perhaps better at demonstrating their literary sensibilities than their wide knowledge of agricultural writings. The practical knowledge to be gleaned for farming was relatively scarce and quite possibly entirely drawn from literature.[46]

By the late sixteenth century classical husbandry could be absorbed directly, or through more recent works composed in a range of countries: by many authors in Italy, but prominent among them Agostino Gallo; Olivier de Serres and Charles Estienne in France, and Conrad Heresbach in Germany. These efforts were not themselves entirely novel, having medieval antecedents such as Walter of Henley, and most influentially, the early fourteenth-century *Liber cultis ruris* of Pier de' Crescenzi that drew heavily on Palladius and enjoyed lasting and wide popularity.[47] Such authors drew very widely on the classics, and whilst they were certainly imitative, they were far from slavishly so. The organisation of these books, often written as a kind of manual for managing a country estate for a wealthy landowner as were the works of Antiquity, only loosely resembled their Roman antecedents. In the nineteenth century, the term *Hausväterliteratur* was coined to describe their output: the writings of the patriarchs or 'fathers of the house'.[48] They drew on a variety of authors as seemed appropriate; Cato for constructing a house, Theophastrus or Pliny the Elder on botanical observation. Conrad Heresbach, a senior government official and renowned humanist scholar in the Duchy of Cleve in the lower

---

[46] Varro was obviously a significant source for Virgil, among others. There is no evidence that Virgil was ever directly engaged in farming. It was Virgil in particular who drew a sharp contrast between the city and the 'easy livelihood', of the cultivator. L.P. Wilkinson, 'General introduction', in Virgil, *The Georgics* (London: Penguin, 1982), pp. 35–49; and Virgil, *Georgics*, p. 92. On the reception of Virgil, see Andrew McCrae, *God speed the plough. The representation of agrarian England, 1500–1660* (Cambridge: Cambridge University Press, 1996), passim.

[47] Estienne, *Maison rustique*; Olivier de Serres, *Théâtre d'Agriculture* (Paris: Saugrain, 1600); Conrad Heresbach, *Rei rusticae libri quatuor* (Köln: Johann Birckmann, 1570); Ambrosoli, *Wild and the sown*; Palladius, *The work of farming*, pp. 25–6. See also Martin Grosser, *Kurze und gar einfeltige Anleitung zu der Landwirtschaft, beides im Ackerbau und in der Viehzucht nach Art und Gelegenheit dieser Land und Ort Schlesien*, ed. Gertrud Schröder-Lembke (Stuttgart: Fischer, 1965 [1589]).

[48] Jörn Sieglerschmidt, 'Die virtuelle Landwirtschaft der Hausväterliteratur', in Rolf Peter Sieferle and H. Brueninger (eds), *Natur-Bilder. Wahrnehmungen von Natur und Umwelt in der Geschichte* (Frankfurt: Campus, 1999), pp. 223–54.

Rhineland, cited no fewer than 57 ancient and 18 modern authorities in his work (plus the Bible). He introduced discussion of local agricultural practice too, and where appropriate, drew distinctions between his own observations and those of the illustrious forebears. Columella might argue that dung should be dry when laid on the field, but Heresbach considered him in error, 'as dayly experience teacheth'.[49] In many ways these texts represented an incremental development of agricultural knowledge that had been arrested by the 'Middle Ages'; that enduring historical caricature elaborated since Leonardo Bruni's Renaissance history of Florence in 1442 seems apposite in the history of agrarian literature, at least. As Palladius adapted Columella who had built on Varro who had built on Cato (among over 50 authors he cites), so the sixteenth-century authors introduced local knowledge and new mixes to the genre.[50] Charles Estienne, born of a prominent Parisian family of printers and physicians compiled his *Praedium Rusticum* in 1554. Around 1570 this was translated into French as *La Maison Rustique* by his son-in-law, Jean Liebault, and the sections on arable cultivation were expressly limited as a description of practices in the land lying between the Oise, Marne and Seine.[51]

We may dwell a minute with Heresbach and Estienne because it was their works that would be translated into English and provide a direct route for the classical tradition to reach a wider readership in the Tudor and Stuart polity. Of course, the late sixteenth-century English gentry were well enough lettered in their Latin. But importantly, in translation these works were further embellished with observations derived from local practices known to the translators. The now elderly Heresbach came to England on a diplomatic mission in 1570, having previously dealt with Henry VIII in his courtship of Anne of Cleves in the 1530s. It was probably at this time, just as his *Rei rusticae libri qvatvor* were published in Germany, that he encountered the Lincolnshire squire Barnaby Googe, who was himself clearly familiar with classical authors such as Xenophon, as well as the few native volumes

---

[49] Conrad Heresbach, *Foure books of husbandry*, trans. Barnaby Googe (London: John Wight, 1577), pp. iv–v, 20. On Heresbach, see Joan Thirsk, 'Plough and pen. Agricultural writers in the seventeenth century', in T.H. Aston, P.R. Coss, C. Dyer and J. Thirsk (eds), *Social relations and ideas. Essays in honour of R.H. Hilton* (Cambridge: Cambridge University Press, 1983), pp. 297–9.

[50] See for example, Varro, *On Agriculture*, pp. 165–7.

[51] Estienne, *Maison rustique*, p. 527.

on husbandry. Googe's embellished translation of Heresbach, *Foure bookes of husbandry*, appeared in 1577. Similarly, Liebault's *Maison rustique* was translated into English by Richard Surflet around 1600, and then further recast by that irrepressible scribe Gervase Markham (more of whom later), who added in material from other continental writers as well as asides on English agriculture. Markham was also on Heresbach's case, to ensure it was 'renewed, corrected, enlarged, and adorned with all the experiments and practices of our English nation, which were wanting in the former editions' before his own emerged in 1631.[52] Both Heresbach and Estienne's works ran through several editions, and the genre remained popular until the middle of the eighteenth century.[53] Thus was Renaissance agronomy simultaneously vested with the dignity of classical learning, and acclimatised to the likely experiences of its readership.

It is perhaps not surprising that the politician Heresbach also made husbandry *political*, in that he presented his subject as being of relevance to the fortunes of the polity. The *Rei rusticae* was written in the studied classical style of a dialogue that dramatised what must have been a tension for a man such as himself, privy councillor, leading diplomat and tutor to princes; the antique trope of country living as an easeful retirement, personified by Cono, versus the imperative to take an active role in history, embodied in Rigo. This was an echo of the Socratic dialogue, employed by Xenophon using the person of Socrates himself. Rigo declaimed, 'you know we are not borne to live our selves, nor at our owne pleasures: but for our countrey, our common weale and state whereto we are called'.[54] For this voice the dissemination of agricultural knowledge was neither simply a means to a richer estate, nor a hobby for the leisured gentleman. It was a duty: and as well as a tutor to the princely offspring of Cleves, Heresbach wrote on education

---

[52] Estienne, *Maison rustique*; Conrad Heresbach, *The whole art of husbandrie contained in foure books*, trans. Richard Surflet and enlarged by Gervase Markham (London: Richard More, 1631)

[53] In Germany major works were Iohannis Colerus, *Oeconimicae oder Hausbuch* (Wittenberg: Paul Hefrig, 1598 [1595]); Herr von Hohberg, *Georgica Curiosa Aucta, das ist. Umständlicher Bericht und klarer Unterricht adelichen Land- und Feldleben* (Nürnberg: Martin Endte, 1701 [1682]); Francis Philipp Florinus, *Oeconomus Prudens et Legalis oder allgemeiner kluger und Rechts-verständinger Haus-Vatter* (Nürnberg: Christoph Riegels Wittib, 1750 [1701]); Otto von Münchhausen, *Der Hausvater* (Hannover: Nic. Försters und Sohns, 1765).

[54] Heresbach, *Foure books*, p. 1.

and was friends with Erasmus. Heresbach was still however more in thrall to the classical ideal than that other another scholar-statesman, Francis Bacon. He did not argue that propounding agricultural knowledge should be a mission of government itself.[55]

England produced its own agronomic writings, although very limited in number. The pace of publication picked up from the 1580s, although largely with a horticultural rather than agricultural focus. Before this time, only two works stand out as handling husbandry extensively: the works of Fitzherbert on farming and surveying from the early 1520s, and reprinted ten times up to 1598; and Thomas Tusser's *Fiue hundred pointes of good husbandrie*, which first appeared with a mere one hundred points in 1557, but was expanded and reprinted in nine editions up to 1672. Neither of these men were simple rustics. The books of husbandry and surveying of 1523 were probably written by John Fitzherbert, scion of a family of leading family of gentry, lawyers and justices whose brother published on legal matters.[56] Tusser was a Cambridge-educated court musician who turned to farming.[57]

Yet both of these writers could draw on their own farming experience as the basis of authorial credibility. Tusser delivered his entire *oeuvre* in pithy stanzas of decidedly unVirgilian poesy: 'By practise, and ill speeding/ these lessons had their breeding.'[58] Fitzherbert noted he had been 'an householder this X L yere, and more', and reflected that he had drawn his knowledge 'by experience'.[59] While Tusser's argument suggests wisdom born of trial-and-error, we should remember that the late medieval idea of experience, drawn from Aristotle, saw

[55] That the extant Roman authors made no political points in their husbandry manuals is not to say that the Roman state had no interest in such matters. It seems that the Senate ordered translation of the 28 agronomic volumes of Mago the Carthaginian, who was extensively drawn on by Varro. None of the original Punic or translation survives. Wilkinson, 'General introduction', p. 31.

[56] Indeed, there has been discussion on which Fitzherbert precisely authored the works. E.F. Gay, 'The authorship of the Book of Husbandry and the Book of Surveying', *The Quarterly Journal of Economics* 18(4) (Aug. 1904), pp. 588–93. A brief survey of agricultural writing is also provided in S. Todd Lowry, 'The agricultural foundation of the seventeenth-century English oeconomy', *History of Political Economy* 35(Suppl. 1) (2003), pp. 74–100.

[57] Andrew McRae, 'Tusser, Thomas (c. 1524–1580)', in *Oxford Dictionary of National Biography* (Oxford: Oxford University Press, 2004).

[58] Thomas Tusser, *Fiue hundred pointes of good husbandrie* (London: Henrie Denham, 1580), f.5r.

[59] Gay 'Authorship', p. 589.

it as a category formed from habitual practice and an observation of the usual. It implied neither a theory to explain *why* things were the way they were, nor an attempt to isolate and test the implied relations of cause-and-effect that we would come to name *experiment*.[60] The authority of experience rested on the more commonsensical observation that people who did things for a long time were more likely to know what to do, and for all its place in scholastic thought, had a close kinship with the authority of custom. 'What champion knows/ That custom showes'.[61] Or as Colerus put in Germany a little later, 'one must also, as it cannot be bettered, follow those who have long dwelled on the land and have tilled for a long age before him'.[62]

The learned men did not thus elevate themselves above other farmers. Indeed, their other explicit source of authority was the neighbourly exchange of information. The husbandman was an assayer of fact and feeling who sought an ever more refined intuition from observation and lore. In the end one fell back on an individual faculty of judgement, or as Fitzherbert wrote, 'there is a sede that is called discretion, and yf a husbande have of that sede and myngle it amonge his other cornes, they wyll grow moche the better, for that sede wyll tel hym how many castes of corne every lande ought to have'.[63] This discretion was cultivated in part by observation of neighbour's fields (as recommended when purchasing a farm by Cato and Columella), and in part by conversation; in the words of Barnaby Googe, one drew on, 'the experience and husbandry of our owne hubsandes of England, as farre as eyther myne own observations, or the experience of sundry my freendes would suffer me'. A little later the German writer and

---

[60] Brian Ogilvie, *The science of describing. Natural history in Renaissance Europe* (Chicago, IL: University of Chicago Press, 2005), pp. 18–21; Peter Dear, *Discipline and experience. The mathematical way in the scientific revolution* (Chicago, IL: University of Chicago Press, 1995); Peter Dear, 'Mysteries of state, mysteries of nature. Authority, knowledge and expertise in the seventeenth century', in Sheila Jasanoff (ed.), *States of knowledge. The co-production of science and social order* (Abingdon: Routledge 2004), pp. 205–9; Peter Dear, 'The meanings of experience', in Katherine Park and Lorraine Daston (eds), *The Cambridge history of science. Vol. 3. Early modern science* (Cambridge: Cambridge University Press, 2006), pp. 106–31.

[61] 'Champion' is the name for the open field country of England, with few hedgerows and dominated by arable. The word has the same root as the French *campagne*, and, of course, *champ*. Tusser, *Five hundred* (1580), f.19v.

[62] Colerus, *Oeconomicae*, pp. 2–3. This is also noted by Sieglerschmidt, 'Virtuelle Landwirtschaft', p. 242. See also Grosser, *Anleitung zu der Landwirtschaft*.

[63] John? Fitzherbert, *The boke of husbandrie* (London: Thomas Berthelet, 1533), p. 9.

princely official (with a similar background to Heresbach) Johann Coler (Latinised to Colerus) stated that he would write about managing woods, 'As I have myself seen and experienced. But whoever wishes to learn and experience more in regard to woodlands should seek the counsel of woodcutters, peasants and other wood-worms who deal with such things daily, and there will find much more report. Because they take such matters in hand every day... one can experience and learn much from such people that others do not know or understand.' But as one also comes across divergent opinions, in the end one must also test ideas oneself to find 'who is correct and who is not, because one's own experience teaches everything'.[64]

Despite differences in structure, scope and source, the English works shared with ancient writings a common preoccupation with farming *practice*. They were not concerned to explain *why* things worked, except in the vaguest of attributions to the Gods. Fitzherbert's book launched straight into detailed advice on how thickly to sow seed,[65] ploughing and the appropriate plough for different soils (described as red clay, gravel and sand), sowing time, varieties of oats, barley, paying attention to the weather, and weeding. There is not a hint of theory as an explanatory guide to what bred success. Estienne organised his book around the spatial division of the farm, starting with the farmstead and outbuildings, and moving out through arable and meadows to woodlands, as a landowner might survey his demesne. Others took a roughly calendrical view of sequential tasks, as had Virgil and later Palladius; Tusser's manual took one systematically through the months of the year.[66] Farming success was accomplished by shunning extravagance and performing one's tasks, and ordering one's household diligently, just as Xenophon prescribed. This is why many works of husbandry devoted extensive sections to housewifery and the proper bearing and obedience of a wife (as well as bailiff, overseer, housekeeper, slave or labourer, as appropriate).[67] A key virtue to husband was 'thrift', and to avoid all that was 'unthriftiness,

---

[64] Heresbach, *Foure books*, p. iii; Colerus, *Oeconomicae*, p. 209.
[65] Fitzherbert provided very precise figures but this approach was eschewed by Heresbach who followed the ancients in arguing the variable quality of land undermined such prescription.
[66] Palladius, *The Work of Farming*, p. 14.
[67] Varro wrote his treatise as a compilation of advice for his wife in his eightieth year, so he could dispense with the duties of the patriarch.

slouthfulness, careless and rash'. It was all about modest behaviour, good neighbourliness, sensible use of credit, hard work, honesty and prayer.[68]

In this world, farmers were not expected to understand any of the ecological processes that governed yield. It was enough to read the signs of what was simply 'good' or 'bad'. Here classical authors such as Columella or Varro who organised topographical sections advising on ideal spots for farming with a tripartite division of mountain, hill and plain had little to say of use to the dull, dank flatlands of the north. One merely drew on the observation that different soils were suited to different plants, and you could tell what plants were best suited to each by what grew best there! Cato arranged land into nine categories: suited for vines, a water garden, osier beds, olives, and so on. Varro went a little further in discussing the 'thinness' of soil or whether it was wet or dry.[69] At times this reasoning was entirely circular, as exemplified in Tusser:

> The straw and the eare, to have bignes and length
> Betokeneth land to be good, and in strength.
> If eare be but short, and the straw be but small:
> it signifieth barenes, and barren withall.[70]

But there were other outward signs as to quality: colour; which weeds thrived; taste, how hard it was to work; what birds followed the ploughman. In the end these were signs that led one to apply different varieties of diligence; no-one sought to provide an explanation. The farmer matched his cards to what the ground turned up. 'Each divers soile/ Hat divers toile.'[71]

It was thus possible to get a poor yield by inappropriate use of land: an error in reading the signs. This is why neighbours were of particular use to the novice in any given locality. One could also overtax the land, again as evidenced by the dismal return for one's efforts.

---

[68] Tusser, *Five hundred*, f.8; Columella, *On husbandry*, p. 49.

[69] Columella, *On husbandry*, p. 49; Varro, *On Agriculture*, pp. 191, 197, 203.

[70] Tusser, *Five hundred*, f.21r; Heresbach, *Foure books*, pp. 17–18.

[71] Tusser, *Five hundred*, f.19. See also p. 21. Although Palladius had considered colour an 'unreliable guide to goodness'. Palladius, *The work of farming*, 1.6.1, p. 38; see also Columella, *On husbandry*, pp. 52–3; Sieglerschmidt, 'Die virtuelle Landwirtschaft', pp. 231–2.

Where barlie thee sowe, after rie or else wheat,
if land be unlustie, the crop is not greate.
So lose ye your cost, to your coresie and smart:
and land (overburdened) is cleane out of hart.[72]

Agriculturalists had understood for many centuries, of course, that a piece of land became 'out of heart' if repeatedly cropped.[73] One knew this because the crops got worse. Why did they get worse? Because the land was out of heart. This was one (although not the only) reason for crop rotations; such wisdom was an absolute commonplace: 'you must observe the olde saying of the husbande, Take not too muche of your grounde', just as observers noted native Americans in New England fertilising their maize-grounds with fish when 'bad or worn out'.[74] Vast acreages of fields across Europe were fallowed each year, whether lain in two-, three- or more rarely four-course rotations. Certainly by the latter part of the sixteenth century innovative farmers were beginning to make inroads into this periodically uncropped land with grassed leys, sometimes artificially sown, and new fodder crops. More commonly, fallow persisted on a large scale into the nineteenth century. There were various reasons for this supposed 'conservatism'. Peasants might know of no alternatives; reorganisation of common and open fields to accommodate different cropping patterns was complex and consent difficult to achieve; the quite reasonably risk averse wanted to stick with tried and tested methods, and the use of fallow for flocks of sheep were an important part of the pastoral economy, while the urine and dung collected in the sheepfolds was an almost labourless way of replenishing fertility. But equally, people knew that the land needed 'recreation', and at the very least rotation, a change being in some circumstances as good as a rest. But without having any explanation of why this was so, what could lead one to think that you could reasonably change things? Virgil had already said it

---

[72] Tusser, *Five hundred*, p. 22.
[73] 'herbes and rootes doe so much waste the fertilitie and fatnesse of the ground, that without continuall refreshing it would quickly become so poore and barren, that it would not yeelde the worth of the seede.' John Parkinson, *Paradisi in sole paradisus terrestris or A garden of all sorts of pleasant flowers which are English ayre will permit to be noursed up* (London: Humfrey Lownes & Robert Young, 1629), p. 462.
[74] Heresbach, *Foure books*, f.22v; John Winthorp, 'The description, culture, and use of maiz. Communicated by Mr. Winthorp', *Philosophical Transactions* 12 (1677), p. 1066.

all so many centuries previously in noting the replenishing power of stubble-burning:

> Again, it often pays, when fields are cropless
> To fire the stubble with rapidly crackling flames –
> Whether it is that hence the soil derives
> Mysterious strength and nourishing enrichment;
> Or that the fire burns out all noxiousness
> And sweats our surplus moisture; or that the heat
> Opens new paths and loosens hidden pores
> To let the seedlings drink; or tightens rather
> And closes gaping ducts, less seeping rains
> Or power of parching sun, too fierce, or cold,
> The north wind's penetrating cold, may blast them.[75]

In other words, we have no idea why this works, and the possible proximate reasons are highly contradictory, never mind the occult explanations which actually explain how substances interact. But do it anyway.

And in this pragmatic worldview there was a fundamental optimism about the capacities of farming. One could always make the land productive, more or less. Columella interpreted the obvious fact that newly cleared land gave more abundant crops that declined over time not as evidence of degradation, but simply that the land had been dunged and nurtured to a high degree by leaf fall from trees. 'Stercoration' could imitate this and raise yields to the heights again.[76] If it had become barren, this was the result of permitting it to be cultivated by 'slaves, criminals, and malefactors', in the words of Pliny.[77] Rather, one just had to find the right thing for the right place. Heresbach had Rigo ask if poor grounds may be 'mended by arte'. Cono replied, 'there is no Countrey that the most gratious Lorde hath left without sufficient yeelde, yf labour and travayle not be refused'. We hear an echo of More, perhaps? You will reap what you sow, and those who do not reap are too indolent to sow. All that is required is, 'dounging and diligent labour'.[78]

---

[75] Virgil, *Georgics*, pp. 59–60.

[76] Columella, *On husbandry*, pp. 48–9.

[77] His contemporary Columella made much the same argument. Columella, *Of husbandry*, pp. 1–2.

[78] Heresbach, *Foure books*, p. 19.

Theory

'Dounging'? The adding of manures to the soil was recommended in the earliest husbandry manuals and doubtless was ancient practice then.[79] Manures came in three kinds. Animal dung that had fallen directly on the ground, and that promoted in some circumstances plant growth; observing this was in all likelihood what prompted humans to first 'artificially' manure: 'we might receive a greater product, if the earth was refreshed and cherished with frequent, seasonable, and moderate stercoration'.[80] Second, the use of 'green manures', crops or straw dug back into the soil; and finally, the mixing in of other materials of all kinds, but especially marls, lime and chalk. We know now that the benefit of marling and liming is to alter the acidity of the soil and make it more amenable to cropping. There were perennial debates about which dung was best. Cassius, drawing on a Mediterranean menagerie, commended first pigeon dung (always a popular choice), then human (always a controversial choice), then in sequence the excrement of goats, sheep, asses and finally horses. Varro opined that the very best dung came from aviaries of thrushes and blackbirds. This idea failed to excite the farmers of subsequent centuries.[81]

While the use of manure was ubiquitous, the intensification of agriculture attendant on population growth stimulated a greater interest in anything that might maintain or enhance the productivity of the land. The gradual building up of higher quality fields had long been a characteristic of very marginal communities that lived amid land difficult to till, and who had to carefully maintain 'infields' for their crops.[82] In the sixteenth century, the frontier of intensification

---

[79] Richard Jones, 'Why manure matters', in Richard Jones (ed.), *Manure matters. Historical, archaeological and ethnographic perspectives* (Farnham: Ashgate, 2012), pp. 5–8; Verena Winiwarter, 'Böden in Agrargesellschaften. Wahrnehm ung, Behandlung und Theorie von Cato bis Palladius', in Rolf-Peter Sieferle and H. Breuninger (eds), *Natur-Bilder. Wahrnehmungen von Natur und Umwelt in der Geschichte* (Frankfurt: Campus, 1999), pp. 181–221; Verena Winiwarter, 'Soils in ancient Roman agriculture. Analytical aporoaches to invisible properties', in H. Novotny and M. Weiss (eds), *Shifting boundaries of the real. Making the invisible visible* (Zurich: vdf Hochschulverlag AG an der ETH, 2000), pp. 137–56.

[80] Columella, *On husbandry*, p. 49.

[81] Varro, *On Agriculture*, pp. 263–5.

[82] S. Foster and T.C. Smout, *The history of soils and field systems* (Aberdeen: Scottish Cultural Press, 1994).

arrived on the urban fringe as increased demand made horticulture a commercial proposition and market gardening became established, especially in the Low Countries. The import of vegetables, especially onions, became a major staple of London's trade, largely in the hands of Dutch merchants. With the upheaval of revolt and mass migration in the Low Countries, soon Flemish and Dutch refugees brought their knowledge directly across the sea, settling in Norfolk, Essex and Kent.[83] These trends were mutually reinforcing. The expansion of gardening stimulated greater attention to the qualities of the soil. Equally, urban growth made cities more significant as a store of 'night soil', a resource already exploited in medieval times. It was partly just a straightforward question of cost: cities gave 'great store of Manure... and so consequently [it] is very cheape'.[84]

In keeping with their pragmatism, most of those writing on husbandry cared not a jot why manure worked; or at least they did not discuss it. But the human mind was not so incurious as to never have contemplated mud. Earth was, after all, one of the four elements first isolated by Empedocles in the fourth century BCE.[85] It was fundamental to the order of things, and was part of any schema that sought to explain the physical make-up of the universe, the most influential of which was Aristotle's rendering of the theory. In Renaissance agronomy, it was Charles Estienne who provided a more formal theory of soil that explained its widely noted variation through different combinations of the humours. Soils consisted of two fundamental kinds: clays that were cold and moist, and sands that were hot and dry. All other soils depended on the mix of these two and their humoural qualities. For others, it may have been that this Aristotilean schema was so ingrained it did not require any description.[86]

For Estienne, dunging and meliorating the soil was about providing the correct balance of humours, which had been drawn

[83] This can be found in the customs records, or 'Port Books' of the late sixteenth century. TNA E190, passim. See also Joan Thirsk, 'Agricultural innovations and their diffusion', *AHEW* V, pp. 533–89; Malcolm Thick, 'Garden seeds in England before the late eighteenth century', *Agricultural History Review* 38 (1990), pp. 58–71; Malcolm Thick, *The neat house gardens. Early market gardening around London* (Totnes: Prospect, 1998).

[84] Gervase Markham, *The English husbandman* (London: William Sheares, 1635), p. 82.

[85] Glacken, *Traces on the Rhodian shore*, pp. 9–10.

[86] Sieglerschmidt, 'Virtuelle Landwirtschaft', p. 226.

out unequally by the growth of plants and presented the problem of imbalances for subsequent crops. Animal manures rotted and produced heat, so cold, moist fields were to be dunged more, to heat them and avoid them freezing. But rich and fat clays need little manure. All the different kinds of manure essentially performed the same action of rebalancing. Dung was not an unmitigated panacea; as balance was the key, there could be too much: 'as a field starveth, if it not be dunged at all, so it burneth of it be over-dunged'.[87] This was true of both animal and avian dung, with highly prized bird-droppings especially prone to 'burn' ground if over-applied, and the marls and other earths larded into the fields. Barnaby Googe warned his readers that: 'In some countries they make their land very fruitful with laying on of a Chalke… But long use of it in the end, brings the ground to be starke nought, whereby the common people have a speech, that ground enriched with Chalke makes a rich Father and a beggerly Sonne.'[88] Advice was proffered by authors ancient and modern on what made the best manures, when it should be done, whether it was best wet or dry. There was a theory of sorts here, but the ethos was practical, ever practical, and the explanatory framework based on the humours registered only phenomena straightforwardly present to the senses.[89]

Who was more practical than Hugh Plat? Born in 1552, Plat was a gentleman of extraordinary range and enthusiasm, whose literary career began as a very minor poet in the 1570s, but who dedicated himself to the betterment of the nation through the dissemination of nearly any knowledge that came across his path. He owned a number of properties in the vicinity of London, and a peculiar retail establishment where he collected, made and sold any ingenious device that might promote productivity and health. If he had a profession, it was enthusiasm. Some of Plat's properties nestled in suburban London, including a zone of market gardens, tenements and old estates that bordered the eastern

---

[87] Estienne, *Maison rustique*, p. 536. These kinds of argument endured in the continental *Hausväterliteratur* until the eighteenth century, when arguments shaped by concepts in chemistry won wider influence as discussed in Chapter 6. Sieglerschmidt, 'Virtuelle Landwirtschaft', pp. 236–7.

[88] Heresbach, *Foure books*, p. 100.

[89] See for example the work of the Brunswick father-and-son double-act, Jacob and Johann Colerus whose discussion of dung and manure went no further than to note positive effects and a descending list of preferred manures. The focus on vision, smell and taste can be found throughout the husbandry literature and into the eighteenth century. Colerus, *Oeconomiae. Bd. II*, pp. 29–30.

fringes of the capital around Bethnal Green. Here he could observe, exchange, and banter with horticulturalists working their soils hard to provide the city with fresh vegetable fare.[90] In the 1590s Plat became preoccupied with projects to enhance national welfare through more productive use of its resources, and produced two volumes dedicated to this cause: the *The iewell house of art and nature Conteining diuers rare and profitable inuentions, together with sundry new experimentes in the art of husbandry, distillation, and moulding* (1594) and a more narrowly botanical volume, *Floraes Paradise* (1608). He was, as we have seen, in tune with times that were blighted with dearth and the need to expand tillage. Where he stood out was not, as with the English legislation on tillage, in any *effects* of his ideas on productivity, but his desire to bring *theory* to bear on the problem. Indeed Plat never won the attention of his Italian near contemporary, Camillo Tarello, who in 1566 won the right from the Venetian state to receive payment for every acre of land planted according to his direction.[91]

At first sight Plat's publications are an encyclopaedic and highly idiosyncratic mix of observations and projects, *The iewell house* arranged according to the alphabet – in other words, apparently randomly when measured against the standards of calendrical or spatially orientated works. But we can read this very differently, as has been pointed out by Ayesha Mukherjee: the 'alphabetical index' provided the means by which the actively engaged and thoughtful reader could select topics of particular interest and enjoy the wealth of advice that the polymathic Plat had assembled. He did not write for the owner of the country estate, or the family member coming into their inheritance, or even the simple husbandman. He wrote for anyone who desired the enhancement of the 'weale publicke', and produced a work that was in

[90] For example, Hugh Plat compiled a manuscript for his own use of 'what is to be done euery moneth', apparently compiled from the 'Rules of Gardening by Clement King Gardner to the Lo.Burghley Lo. Threasurer of England'. Mukherjee, *Penury into Plenty*, esp. pp. 65–8, 82; Sidney Lee, 'Plat, Sir Hugh (*bap.* 1552, *d.*1608)', rev. Anita McConnell, in *Oxford Dictionary of National Biography* (Oxford: Oxford University Press, 2004); Plat (1594), p. 2v; Deborah Harkness, *The Jewel House. Elizabethan London and the scientific revolution* (New Haven, CT: Yale University Press, 2007), pp. 211–12; Malcolm Thick, *Sir Hugh Plat. The search for useful knowledge in early modern London* (Totnes: Prospect, 2010).

[91] See *The Complete Farmer; Or a General Dictionary of Husbandry in All Its Branches, Containing the Various Methods of Cultivating and Improving Every Species of Land*, 4th edition (London, 1793), p. 529.

fact user-friendly in that it did not assume the precise context in which the knowledge might be used.[92] *Floraes Paradise* would be organised more conventionally, as a very roughly calendrical list of tasks.

Not long afterwards, Plat might have been called an 'improver'; after a few decades in obscurity his work was taken up with enthusiasm by the projectors of the mid-seventeenth century, who we will meet in Chapter 3, and his works reissued. But it was too early for that: 'improvement' still had the more limited meaning of raising rents, not the glorious imprimatur of a national mission.[93] Perhaps because of his own immense curiosity, perhaps because of his wide social network embracing the rapidly growing metropolis, its suburbs and rural hinterland, for Plat the intensely pragmatic, the *how*, was always linked to the *why*. He was a man of theory – despite his book that appeared to have no system except the alphabet. He was determined to use knowledge that contemporaries would have called 'occult', meaning that he wanted to look behind those easily legible signs that indicated that something was good or bad for a particular purpose, to the hidden relations that actually *caused* phenomena. Thus theory could be combined with 'sundrie observations, drawn from experience herselfe the undoubted mother of all true and certaine knowledge'[94] to create new, innovatory routes to profit. He was trying to create a new kind of agricultural expert.

But before he could make the world better, first Plat needed to address an age-old question: were things just getting worse? More precisely, was the Earth itself ageing and going into decline? So said Virgil, though perhaps with a poet's licence: 'everything by nature's law/ Tends to the worse, slips ever backward, backward.'[95] Arguments about the 'senescence' of the world – whether it aged like all living things – were part and parcel of discussion of nature in Antiquity and would remain a matter of heated controversy across the seventeenth century.[96] The discussion was however pitched at an extremely general level and might seem to have no relevance to any particular farm, or indeed manual of husbandry. But when *regions* seemed to decline

[92] Mukherjee, *Penury into plenty*, pp. 66–7.
[93] Warde, 'Idea of improvement'.
[94] Sir Hugh Plat, *The iewell house of art and nature* (London: Peter Short, 1594), p. 1.
[95] Virgil, *Georgics*, p. 63.
[96] Glacken, *Traces on the Rhodian shore*, pp. 383–90, passim; Columella, *On husbandry*.

in fertility, then the question was posed more forcefully as to whether the advancing decrepitude of the very Earth would eventually preclude efforts to make it more productive. In our twenty-first-century terms, we might understand this not so much as a sustainability problem, as one of managing ageing; raising yields would be akin to extending an active life and seeking to hold decrepitude at bay. Heresbach noted the alleged phenomenon, drawing on Pliny: 'You must remember also, that ground wyll some times change, and of fruitefull become barren, whiche hath been seens, as Plinie reporteth, in the olde time in Thessali, and in our time, in sundry places of our Countrey.' Pliny in fact denied that declining fertility came from ageing, and blamed it on poor husbandry.[97]

But Plat bought it. 'For what eie doth not pitty to see the great weakness and decay of our ancient and common mother the earth, which now is grown so aged & striken in yeares, & so wounded at the hart with the ploughmans goad, that she beginneth to faint under the husbandmans hand, and groneth at the decay of her natural Balsamun.'[98] His explanation is both based on senescence and the impact of human intervention, that farming has somehow bled the Earth. Yet if husbandry could cause infertility, this was not for Plat an issue of diligence but ignorance. The 'Balsamun' was being lost. There was a substance that was ebbing away from the soil, and his mission was to restore it. Decrepitude could be delayed.

The idea of an active agent, a first cause of fertility and the need to conserve it, will be a red thread running through this book. The idea was not Plat's. He tapped into a school of thought that had been gathering force across Europe for decades, a train of speculation and experiment that was strongly shaped by the Swiss physician, mine assayer, and searcher after occult lore, Paracelsus; or as he was baptised, most splendidly, Philippus Aureolus Theophrastus Bombastus von Hohenheim (1493–1541). Paracelsus would play a prominent part in the history of Renaissance medicine and chemistry.[99] But while Plat drew on the Paracelsian tradition through English adherents such as John Hester, the immediate source of his

[97] Heresbach, *Foure books*, p. 18; Columella, *On husbandry*, p. 47, n.1.
[98] Plat, *The iewell house*, p. 3.
[99] Allen G. Debus, *The chemical philosophy. Paracelsian science and medicine in the sixteenth and seventeenth centuries* (Mineola, NY: Science History Publications, 1977).

thinking about the fertility of the soil was Frenchman Bernard Palissy (c. 1510–1589) and his *Discours Admirables* of 1580.[100] Palissy has been disarmingly referred to as a potter, but while this captures much of the everyday activity of the man, it captures his significance and essence in the same way that one might comprehend all that was important about Louis Bourbon (XIV) by calling him an 'actor'.[101] Palissy was a surveyor, a ceramicist who harboured a famous and ultimately futile obsession to reproduce Chinese porcelain; friend to royals; a portraitist; engineer; and lecturer who can fairly be called a Renaissance man, an embodiment of his age. The service that Plat would render to English agronomy was to translate Palissy in his *Diverse sorts of soil*. He set agronomy on the search for *causes*: a theory to explain what could be observed.

Of course, this causal agent was occult; it was hidden, beyond measurement, and it is perhaps not surprising that the Paracelsians were not entirely clear or consistent in explaining what it was. Yet while their theorising about the occult would come to seem fantastical and chimerical to later empiricists, the Paracelsian chemists made important contributions to the development of what we now think of as the experimental method, seeking to isolate the properties of objects and transformations that are not immediately apparent to mere observation. For Bernard Palissy, the key agent in the soil that brought life was a salt: the fifth element (although in his text Plat also suggests that this element was, in fact, a special kind of water that could draw heat from salt, a notion that also had Paracelsian origins).[102] 'Salt' was a term used much more liberally than today, and embraced substances like copper and sugar, although writers correctly tended to stress the alkaline properties of salts. Consequently, the bleaching properties of plant ashes could be taken as clear evidence of a saline presence in vegetable matter.[103]

---

[100] See Allen G. Debus, 'Palissy, Plat and English agricultural chemistry in the 16th and 17th centuries', *Archives internationals d'histoire* 21 (1968), pp. 67–9, 71, reprinted in Allen G. Debus, *Chemistry, alchemy and the new philosophy 1550–1700* (London: Variorum Collected Studies, 1987).

[101] G.E. Fussell, *Farming technique from prehistoric to modern times* (Oxford: Pergamon, 1965), p. 91.

[102] Plat, *iewell house*, p. 23; See also Debus, 'Palissy, Plat and English agricultural chemistry', pp. 73–6.

[103] Plat, *iewell house*, p. 11.

Thus Plat declared:

> And it is a salt that maketh all seedes to flourish, and growe, and although the number of those men is verie small, which can giue anie true reason whie dungue shoulde doe anie good in arable groundes, but are ledde thereto more by custome than anie Philosophicall reason, neuerthlesse it is apparaunt, that no dungue, which is layde vppon barraine groundes, coulde anie way enrich the same, if it were not for the salt which the straw and hay left behinde... it is not the dung itselfe which causeth fruitfulnes: but the salt which the seed hath sucked out of the ground.[104]

As a theory this did not perhaps have anything more to recommend it than the idea of the humours, but it contained a key notion, and one that will have some significance in one of the stories told in this book. There was a finite substance in the soil that could be identified by the experimenter and the master chemist, and it was the circulation of this substance – and mastery of this circulation – that would lead to the growth of plants. Dung contained the residual salts of consumed plants and this had to be restored, else 'the hungry seede in time will drinke vp all the salt of the earth, whereby the earth being robd of her salt, can bring forth no more fruit untill it bee dunged againe, or suffered to lie fallow a certaine time: to the ende that it may gather a newe saltnesse from the cloudes, and raine that falleth vpon it'.[105] Here lay the germ of later theories of plant nutrition, a substance found in the earth, in the air and in rainwater that could explain why plants prospered from contact with all three. It also introduced an essential idea for later thinking: at a particular place, at least, in any given field, this substance could become deficient. It would be a long time before

[104] Plat, *iewell house*, pp. 14–15; on the degree to which this is a direct translation of Palissy, see Debus, 'Palissy, Plat and English agricultural chemistry', p. 72; see also the helpful discussion on salts and Palissy in Mukherjee, *Penury into plenty*, pp. 98–9, 104–13.

[105] Plat, *iewell house*, p. 16. In her book on Plat and 'dearth science', Ayesha Mukherjee makes a case that circulation theory was an important part of Plat's work and not anomalous at the time. I have not found any clear evidence in her text of this type of thinking (that is, as I understand it, circulation as thinking about 'circular processes', as opposed to simply the flowing movement of things), although Plat opened up the possibility of this approach. Mukherjee, *Penury into plenty*, p. 88, and for discussion of circulation, e.g. pp. 106, 109; for the sake of clarity I note that her statement on my work on p. 141 is contradicted in Warde 'Invention of sustainability', p. 156.

this view became widely significant, but at the end of the sixteenth century, drawn from the alchemical tradition, it was being articulated.

The 'Skilfull Clowns'

A giant of English intellectual life in the early seventeenth century, although much more with hindsight than at the time, was the lawyer, statesman and polymathic thinker Francis Bacon: often considered the founder of modern experimental science and the tradition that led to expertise being defined by method and institutional training, subsequently being both praised and blamed for all the results of those 'scientific' habits of mind in the modern world. Gervase Markham, however, cut a rather different figure. Markham is best known now as the writer of a popular book on the duties and callings of housewives. He was from a well-to-do Nottingham gentry family, and probably enjoyed a university education before serving as a soldier in Ireland. From 1593 he was residing in London and began an extraordinary literary career, as a poet of some distinction, and writing books on a vast array of topics, especially matters veterinary and relating to horsemanship (where his capacity for self-plagiarism led to five rather similar volumes being on the market simultaneously, leading to the stationers' company that controlled publishing in London forcing him into an agreement in 1617 to have no more printed on the topic!). Hitching his fortunes to the Earl of Essex, he too crashed with the disastrous failed rebellion, disgrace and execution of his patron in 1601. Markham spent the next decade as a modest tenant farmer, and on taking up the pen again, agricultural works became a major part of his output.[106] It was Markham who dominated publishing on matters agricultural in the 1610s and 1620s. Rather like Plat, much of his oeuvre was derivative of older works, especially the continental *Hausväter* like Estienne and Heresbach whom he edited.[107] But in his recasting of this knowledge,

[106] Matthew Steggle, 'Markham, Gervase (1568?–1637)', in *Oxford Dictionary of National Biography* (Oxford: Oxford University Press, 2004); online edn, Oct. 2006. Somewhat bizarrely, this entry makes no mention of his extensive agricultural writing. On a surprisingly limited survey of Markham's contributions, given her mastery of the contemporary sources, see Thirsk, 'Plough and pen', pp. 302–3.

[107] George Fussell, *The old English farming books from Fitzherbert to Tull 1523–1730* (London: C. Lockwood, 1947), pp. 13, 29.

and combining it with his own experience, he presented the reading world with a novel approach to farming: he made the enrichment of the soil the first and most central issue in his work.

This manoeuvre was most manifest in *Markhams farwell to husbandry or, The inriching of all sorts of barren and sterill grounds in our kingdome, to be as fruitfull in all manner of graine, pulse, and grasse as the best grounds whatsoeuer*, published in 1613 and that went through at least nine further editions from 1620. This was more original than his later *The English husbandman* which still discussed house and climate first, in the manner of the estate-owning *Hausvater*. Markham was clearly well read in sixteenth-century agricultural writing, and the classics. Arguably *Markhams farwell* was the first manifesto for improvement, as it later came to be understood. Good crops could be won out of barren soils! One did not simply have to adapt to what providence, or nature, had bequeathed your land. Rather, the task of the husbandman was to 'nobly and victoriously boast the conquest of the Earth, hauing conquered Nature by altering Nature, and yet made Nature better than shee was before'. Here was Markham's call to action, a sentiment simultaneously so reminiscent of the famous prescription of the still more famous Francis Bacon that nature could be commanded by being obeyed; yet more pragmatic, and yet more immodest, and perhaps truer to the times.[108]

Markham also looked to the future in that he claimed to be not a peculiar genius in his own right, but a reporter of the wisdom of correspondents, filtered through his own experience of farming. These were comments reminiscent of Fitzherbert almost a century before, but the earlier author, and many later, would claim simply to have spoken to wise neighbours, rather than being, 'a publique Notarie, who record[s] the most true and infallible experience of the best knowing Husbands in this Land.' Markham was allegedly a hub, a role later exemplified in actuality in the middle of the century by Samuel Hartlib, and later on men like the John Worlidge and Houghton (see Chapter 3); and a century after them, Arthur Young (see Chapter 6). Markham desired his book to 'belongeth... to the plaine russet honest Husbandman... and the Kingdomes generall profit'.[109] By this, like Thomas Tusser, he meant a substantial farmer with perhaps one or two servants, but someone of

[108] Markham, *English husbandman*, p. 9.
[109] Markham, *English husbandman*, pp. iii, 147.

a lesser social rank than each of those downwardly mobile men was born into.

Markham recognised that, in fact, the combination of soils tended to determine the husbandry applied, and local and regional variations in farming practice were to be explained thus: 'every man in his owne workes knows the alteration of climates'.[110] His theory did not move beyond Estienne, whom he drew on extensively, dividing soils into the clays, sands, gravels, and their mixes and properties. As well as the mix of soils, a fine-grained tilth was important to bring a 'soft libertie' that prevented dense earths from choking plants and allowing the ground to heat. In fact, Markham's intent was not to promote theory at all, and this was not his service. His focus on soil was practical, and for practical men, that they might understand through his provision of 'fixt rules' how different soils affected crops, so the simple farmer could follow his prescriptions 'without the study of his braines'. Yet he proclaimed himself determined that men should not settle for what they found, and that husbandry should not be mere habit. It should be a transferable skill, an applied art, and a process of betterment, and the route to this was to read men such as himself.

> Yet for so much as this labour of Husbandry, consisteth not for the most part in the knowing and understanding breast, but in the rude, simple, and ignorant Clowne, who onely knoweth how to doe his labour, but cannot give a reason why he doth such labour; more than the instruction of his parents, or the custome of the Country, where it comes to passe (and I have many times seene the same to mine admiration) that the skilfullest Clowne which is bred in the Clay soyles, when he hath beene brought to the sandy ground, hee could neither hold the Plough, temper the Plough, not tell which way in good order to drive the Cattell.[111]

Implicit in earlier arguments about ideal husbandry was the idea of farming as a slow, evolutionary process of adaptation that had brought the wisest methods to each particular place and clime. This, as we will see in Chapter 3, would no longer satisfy the improving mood of the seventeenth century. And of course the fact of change was not new either; in practice one could never be sure if 'optimal' methods had been

[110] Markham, *English husbandman*, p. 95.
[111] Markham, *English husbandman*, pp. 95–6.

attained, even if one was schooled to think in such terms (and Tudor cultivators certainly were not). In practice, then, there was always a degree of innovation going on, and probably rather more failure than success. In some regions of the country, however, the Elizabethan era had seen notable changes in technique that were inspiring to authors such as Markham and John Norden, the former describing his inspiration from new meadows around Chatsworth in Derbyshire, on Exmoor and north Devonshire – 'allmade by industry & not nature'.[112] This was the age of the advancing water meadow and convertible husbandry, of greater opportunities for profit as prices rose but real wages were depressed, and to some degree the agricultural writers moved in the wake of pioneers on the ground.[113] Literature could help in the dissemination of best practice, and thus also facilitate change that was not based on anything genuinely new, but just more widely applied, such as the description by surveyor John Norden of how 'In *Shropshire, Denbighshire, Flintshire* and now lately in some parts of Sussex they fetch limestone, erect kilns, and burn it on their own farms... On the south-east coast from Rye to Suffolk they burn pebbles for the same purpose.'[114] In the farm accounts of Robert Loder of Harwell in Berkshire we can trace how one farmer, albeit one who for those times somewhat eccentrically kept meticulous records of all his expenditure, experimented with the use of malt dust and black ashes to meliorate the soils on his open-field farm between 1610 and 1620.[115]

Markham, although a self-styled herald of change, was more unusual than original in his breadth of interests and writings. For the most part, the old and classical ways remained central to his work, and

[112] Gervase Markham, *Markhams farwell to husbandry or, The inriching of all sorts of barren and sterill grounds in our kingdome, to be as fruitfull in all manner of graine, pulse, and grasse as the best grounds whatsoeuer together with the anoyances, and preseruation of all graine and seede, from one yeare to many yeares. As also a husbandly computation of men and cattels dayly labours, their expences, charges, and vttermost profits. Attained by trauell and experience, being a worke neuer before handled by any author: and published for the good of the whole kingdome.* (London: Roger Jackson, 1620), p. 69.
[113] For example, Hadrian F. Cook and Tom Williamson (eds), *Water meadows. History, ecology and conservation* (Oxford: Windgather, 2007); Eric Kerridge, *The agricultural revolution* (London: George Allen & Unwin, 1967).
[114] John Norden, *The surveyors dialogue* (London: Hugh Astley, 1607), p. 228; Fussell, *Old English farming books*, p. 100.
[115] Fussell, *Old English farming books*, p. 101.

much of his writing was derivative. One would not find any author a few decades later attributing mysterious ailments of crops to 'planet strooke... sometimes from the euill aspects of the Starres, sometimes from the rotten corruptions of the ayre, sometimes from the contagion and unfection of the winds, and sometimes from the euill habits of dewes'.[116] Authority on farming remained, as it had been earlier in the Renaissance, a mixture of ancient writings, more contemporary writers and observations from the authors' own experiences or those of their wise neighbours. Little or no consideration was given to the active agents in promoting plant growth, and this had next to no impact on recommendations for husbandry, which remained highly practical. For the most part Markham's writing was heavily orientated towards practice, so even more theoretical passages posited a range of possible causes for phenomena, without deciding on what was the most likely; it was not considered possible or necessary to verify any particular one. Equally, no consideration was given to what made the soil fertile, aside from noting the obvious benefits of externally observable factors, such as heat, moisture, or the colour and texture of soils. Growing crops successfully was thus simply about balance and climate, and good husbandry. Raising output was largely a question of what kind of agriculture was applied to each ground: and the extent of tillage was either a juridical matter, determined by manorial and legal controls over the land, or one shaped by market incentives and opportunities to profit.

But nevertheless Markham's works contain the germs of later developments, and a framework that could absorb the thoughts of men like Plat: an emerging focus on soil management, and concern for the quality of land and labour, rather than the more general descriptions of techniques of ploughing, sowing density or the timing of work found in Tusser and Fitzherbert. In filtering earlier works Markham foregrounded the soil, and the possibility of enhancing its productivity; by no means an entirely new theme, but one given much greater prominence. Equally, men like Palissy and Plat, though apparently of minor influence before the 1640s, presented a theoretical and chemical approach to agriculture that would draw attention to the role of manures and especially dung in promoting soil fertility by suggesting there was some unique, single causal agent at work. They presented their works as a means not only to extend the area of tillage onto

---

[116] Markham, *Markhams farewell*, pp. 100–1.

'barren' soils, but to improve the output of those soils already under the plough, arguments calculated to appeal not just to the profit-maker, but those concerned with the needs of the polity.[117] Agronomic writers would persist in framing their work in a reflex condemnation of custom and conservatism for centuries to come, and we must always take such caricatures of general practice with a pinch of salt. But as the seventeenth century advanced the role of knowledge and the possibility of changing and shaping nature were emerging with greater clarity in the printed text, with the idea of the possibility of enhancing the soil would come, eventually, the concomitant notion of degrading it.

[117] Mukherjee, *Penury into plenty*; see also the complementary development of rhetoric around national needs and profit that would become discredited by favouritism in Elizabethan and Jacobean 'projecting', in Joan Thirsk, *Economic policy and projects. The development of a consumer society in early modern England* (Oxford: Clarendon, 1978).

2 Governing the Woods, c. 1500–1700

Wood

'Who can enumerate all of the uses of wood? Wood is the greatest and most necessary thing in the world, of which man has need and cannot dispense with.' So wrote one Martin Luther in 1532.[1] Perhaps he exaggerated a little; Luther was not a man to temper his rhetoric. It was doubtful whether wood was more necessary than bread, although according to the petitioners of Bourbévelle in the Franche-Comté on 17 March 1789, it was 'a necessity as vital as bread'.[2] Bread, however, was only good for eating. Wood could not be eaten but it could be used for nearly everything else that people put their minds to, from fuel for the bakery, the home and industry, through the equipment used in the production of essentials such as textiles, to things actually manufactured or constructed from it. Trees themselves provided both the key raw material of the early modern world, and played a central role in landscapes, whether economic, ecological or aesthetic; they were for '*Timber, Shelter, Fuel,* and *Ornament*' as John Evelyn put it in 1664.[3]

---

[1] Cited in Joachim Radkau, *Holz – wie ein Naturstoff Geschichte schreibt* (Munich: Oekom verlag, 2007), p. 11.

[2] Cited in Kieko Matteson, *Forests in revolutionary France. Conservation, community, and conflict, 1669–1848* (Cambridge: Cambridge University Press, 2015), p. 69.

[3] Although in some circumstances bark was ground into flour for consumption. I am grateful to Felicity Stout for pointing this out. John Evelyn, *Sylva. Or, a discourse of forest trees* (London: Jo. Martyn & Ja. Allestry, 1664), p. 6.

Tending to trees, a practice only later formalised as forestry, silviculture or arboriculture, presented a rather different case to arable or pastoral farming. From an early date people linked the durability of local wood supplies with the fortunes of the state itself. It was then most markedly and influentially in the case of wood that governments and communities came to imagine their dependency on natural resources, and the possibility that bad management could put them at risk. This led to widespread legislation that *did* have concrete effects, including the development of forestry administrations and conflict over the proper use of both woodland and the material itself. Yet curiously – to modern eyes – such responses remained peculiar to wood. It was not yet taken as a particular instance of a more general phenomenon. The politics of wood also foreshadowed the modern politics of sustainability: sustainability of what? And for whom?

In part, these developments rested simply upon the biological properties of wood. These things do matter. Any concern with wood operates on a different time horizon to crops and animals. Both food and wood are products of the 'organic economy', and are dependent on the flow of solar radiation to grow. The annual round of tasks involved in felling, pollarding (a type of which was also called 'shrouding' as the branches were known as 'shrouds') and seasoning timber, 'shredding' trees for fodder, or setting acorns, were included in the calendrical husbandry manuals, an endlessly repeated part of the cycle that traced the stations of the sun.[4] Yet while food is largely (although not wholly) delivered as an annual flow, and in the long run the annual harvest of wood in any one place cannot exceed the annual input of insolation, any particular harvest reaps from a stock accumulated over years or decades. It took several years' growth before anyone could usefully harvest wood from a sapling. Some European trees took 120 years to reach full maturity, and could live for substantially longer. When you planted a tree you were planning ahead. The consequences of decisions taken in woodland management stretched far into the future. When you choose to use land as tillage or woodland, you are also making a decision as to how long you are prepared to wait for a return: a few months, a few years, or for your unknown heirs? Thus while states legislated in an attempt to control the *distribution* of both food and

---

[4] For an excellent discussion of pollards in England, see Charles Watkins, *Trees, woods and forests. A social and cultural history* (London: Reaktion, 2014), pp. 128–39.

wood, legislators came to think at an early date that wood *supplies* required a different kind of management, exercising a more pervasive princely authority – or attempting to do so.

Equally, from late medieval times wood supplies were seen to have a direct bearing upon the great matters of state in a way that agricultural output was not. Yes, dearth bore with it the risk of disorder and disruption to the best-laid plans of princes. Yet wood supplies, or more accurately timber supplies, shaped the capacity of the state to enforce its will and realise its glory. The Venetian republic was literally built upon the oak and larch piles that hoisted it above its artificial lagoon. The fleet that policed and protected its maritime empire was of course a wooden one; every maritime polity needed wood supplies for shipping, but in Venice's case its galleys were the very sinews of power, and its merchant vessels the wellsprings of its essential trades. Venetian naval construction, both military and civil (insofar as they can be separated) was directly organised by the republic's government and therefore it had a paramount interest in obtaining a plentiful supply of raw materials. This was less usual in other parts of Europe, where naval fleets were often nearly all re-flagged merchant vessels, and the purpose-built warship only came to predominate during the seventeenth century.

Where particular interests such as shipbuilding were prominent they would have a strong role in shaping perceptions and policy around timber, although the actual volume of wood required for shipping relative to other uses was small; even tiny compared to the amount of wood consumed by domestic hearths across Europe. Princely rulers also often claimed direct ownership of large swathes of sparsely populated land, the right of *regal* to uncultivated grounds, which prompted an interest in how such resources could be turned into revenue. These reserves were linked to other strategic industries such as metal-smelting or salt production that focused the interest of rulers of landlocked regions on wood resources in a way that shipping did in the maritime world.

The 'forest' laws of various territories, whether (as in England) they pertained to particular localised jurisdictions within the realm, or the polity as a whole, were initially intended to encourage and protect a population of game for the noble sport of the chase. But they also gave rulers an avenue into, and interest in, regulating the use of trees and woodlands. In these cases we must distinguish between the use of 'forest' as a general term to describe wooded areas, and the much more specific sense of the 'forest' rights of rulers that related to jurisdiction over hunting, and restricted any activity that might limit opportunities to hunt. In England the 'forest laws' pertained only to those areas designated as Royal Forests and that in theory at least were subject to separate juridical systems in matters covered by those laws. These districts, such as Dean, the New Forest, Sherwood or Alice Holt, did have large stands of trees but they were far from being densely wooded. In England legislation that dealt with the state of the woods more generally was about 'timber', and was not part of forest law. In other territories, 'forest' (*Forst, Fôret*) regulation more frequently had wood supplies as a central preoccupation, even if the sport of the chase was also important.

Wood was of course not a single product with undifferentiated qualities, as the reference above to the needs of the navy makes clear. Every species had its particular virtues and habitats, although it would be a mistake to think they were always put to the most 'appropriate' use; people used what was to hand. The diarist, royalist gentleman and general enthusiast John Evelyn provided the most comprehensive listing of uses to that date in his *Sylva, or a Discourse of forest trees* of 1664.[5] Evelyn was another one of those (late) renaissance men whose lust for learning and the exchange of information led him to write one of the more influential texts of his age, running into numerous editions and finding its niche in the bookshelves of gentlemen (or women) inclined to take a care for their landed estates, and consulted by an international readership. It is doubtful that Evelyn personally possessed intimate knowledge of the full range of subject matter covered in *Sylva*, but he

---

[5] It would appear however that the layout of *Sylva* is indebted to the much more limited approach taken in the second book of Conrad Heresbach's *Foure books of Husbandry* (1578), pp. 100–10. Subsequent authors such as Florinus and Carlowitz would also include extensive chapters on individual tree species, although not obviously modelled on the work of Evelyn (a book Carlowitz knew well). Florinus, *Oeconomus Prudens*; Hanns Carl von Carlowitz, *Sylvicultura oeconomica oder haußwirthschaftliche Nachricht und naturmäßige Anweisung zue Wilden Baum-Zucht nebst gründlicher Darstellung wie zu förderst durch göttliches Benedeyen dem attenthalben und unsgemein einreissenden grossen Holz-Mangel...* (Leipzig: Johann Friedrich Braun, 1713). Some English authors, such as John Mortimer, closely followed Evelyn's approach. John Mortimer, *The whole art of husbandry. Or, the way of managing and improving of land*, 2nd edition (London: H. Mortlock & J. Robinson, 1708 [1707]), pp. 311–70.

was a diligent and eager correspondent and observer, and was assisted by the physicians Jonathon Goddard, Christopher Merret (the inventor of sparkling wine) and governor of Connecticut, John Winthrop.[6] *Sylva* would be expanded in numerous subsequent editions, and in turn inspire Carlowitz's *Sylvicultura oeconomica* of 1713, often seen as the first true book of forestry (see Chapter 4).[7]

Oak was the great building timber, strong but pliable, and widely available in its different varieties. Elm was a hard-wearing and water-resistant wood: recommended for all waterworks, mills, pipes, pumps, ship-planks beneath the waterline (although there is not much evidence of this being a major use), for wheelwrights, weatherboards and dressers.[8] Its sprays of leaves could be used as winter cattle fodder, especially when stripped off the female tree and dried in the sun at the end of August. In England beech was used for domestic wooden vessels, buckets, furniture, bellows, shovels and spades, and as a source of fuel, although its charcoal was 'one of the least lasting'. The French preferred walnut for utensils. Beech leaves could be gathered in the autumn and made excellent mattresses, not becoming musty as fast as straw.[9] Ash was beloved of the toolmaker, a fine, workable wood with good tensile properties that Evelyn thought should make up a third of woodlands. 'The best *Ash* delights in the best Land (which it will soon impoverish)', noted Evelyn, 'yet grows in any.' He did not perceive the issue of impoverishment to be important; he was more concerned to encourage the planting of ash. It was used very extensively in tools, weapon-handles, carts, hop-poles, spars and made a durable charcoal, 'the sweetest of our

---

[6] Beryl Hartley, 'Exploring and communicating knowledge of trees in the early Royal Society', *Notes and Records of the Royal Society of London* 64(3) (20 Sep. 2010), pp. 229–31; Blanche Henrey, *British botanical and horticultural literature before 1800. Vol. I. The sixteenth and seventeenth centuries* (Oxford: Oxford University Press, 1975). Certainly, another consulted at that time was John Smith, later author of *England's Improvement reviv'd* in 1673, who may have been an important source for Evelyn. Lindsay Sharp, 'Timber, science, and economic reform in the seventeenth century', *Forestry* 48 (1975), pp. 60–1. Ulbrich Grober, *Die Entdeckung der Nachhaltigkeit. Kulturgeschichte eines Begriffs*, 3rd edition (Frankfurt: Kunstmann, 2010), pp. 87–97.

[7] Carlowitz, *Sylvicultura oeconomica*; Sharp, 'Timber', p. 64.

[8] Evelyn, *Sylva*, p. 20.

[9] Evelyn, *Sylva*, p. 21; a similar listing was provided, probably largely in imitation, in John Worlidge, *Systema agriculturae* (London: Samuel Speed, 1669), pp. E1–2 (f.10v–11r).

Forest-fuelling, and the fittest for *Ladies* chambers'. Leaves could also be used for fodder.[10]

'The use of the *Cheß-nut* is (next the *Oak*) one of the most sought after by the *Carpenter* and *Joyner*: It hath formerly built a good part of our ancient houses in the *City* of *London*, as does yet appear.'[11] In southern France and Italy chestnut was famously cultivated as a bread-crop, the nuts being ground into flour. Latin Europe adored the look of the walnut that also gradually crept into fine English furniture, and was used for interior panelling and gunstocks. Not everybody appreciated its charm, however. When Sully administered France in the early seventeenth century, 'there was a resolution of adorning all the *High-ways* of *France* with *Elms, &c [and walnuts]*. but the rude and mischievous *Paysans* did so hack, steal and destroy what they had begun, that they were forc'd to desist from the through prosecution of the design'. For the peasant, firewood and not adornment was the priority.[12] Evelyn ran through service, maple, sycamore, hornbeam, lime and birch, the latter being 'the worst of *Timber*' but used for ox-yokes, hoops, paniers, brooms, wands, fuel and coals.[13] Birch is a good coloniser of poor ground, at the vanguard of the re-treeing of Northern Europe after the Ice Ages, and found widely in the scrubby pastures of much of Northern and Central Europe. In Scandinavia great birch forests were a key resource, and its bark was used to clad houses.

In much of lowland Europe most deciduous trees could be coppiced, that is not left to grow to maturity but constantly harvested back to a stool and valued for the young shoots and rods that re-grew (hence it was called 'spring' in England). In many coppices, only a few trees were left to grow into mature timber (called 'standils' or 'staddles'). For some species coppice-wood was the only widespread use. Chief among these was hazel, which Evelyn recommended as ready to coppice after 12 years, and subsequently every seven or eight years. It was used for poles, spars, hoops, hurdles, forks, angling rods, faggots (bundles of smaller diameter sticks for the fire or as infill in building and drainage ditches) and charcoals.[14] Charcoal from alder,

[10] Evelyn, *Sylva*, p. 23.
[11] Evelyn, *Sylva*, p. 25.
[12] Evelyn, *Sylva*, p. 27. Evelyn recommended the reading of Columella on the walnut, a text at that time only available in Latin.
[13] Evelyn, *Sylva*, pp. 28–32.
[14] Evelyn, *Sylva*, p. 35.

another lover of damper ground, was excellent for gunpowder. Its resilient properties in its natural habitat made it ideal for pipes, pumps, piles, troughs, sluices and drainage trenches.[15] The coal made from the sally (sallow) was good for pencils and artists.[16] Another specialist tree was the box, a Mediterranean import to the north, prized by turners, engravers, mathematical instrument makers, comb and pipe makers, and for cabinet and inlay work. According to Evelyn, its 'chymical oyl' cured venereal disease.[17]

Fir was native to the north and mountainous regions and as yet rare in the lowlands. In England it was almost entirely imported until the nineteenth century, and used for masts, wainscot, floors, laths, boxes, beams and timber-work, 'being both light, and exceedingly strong, where it may lie dry *everlasting*, and an extraordinary saver of *Oak* where it may be had at a reasonable *price*'.[18] By the 1660s the ancient yews that adorned many an English churchyard were no longer used for the famous bows that had characterised the onslaught of English and Welsh armies in late medieval times, although some of these were actually imported from Eastern Europe, and the trade was hit when Tudor armies switched to firearms.[19] It was good for millworks, axles and for the body of lutes or tankards.[20]

We should not, however, be distracted from the priorities for woodland management by this plethora of qualities and uses. Most craftsmen and women would not pay a large premium for high-quality timber if it was not easily obtained. And compared to total growth, most of the itemised uses of wood took up a vanishingly small proportion of the harvest. Firewood was overwhelmingly the most important product, taking up something like three-quarters to nine-tenths of all wood consumed. This would have been followed by construction and fencing (with which we can bracket the millions of vineyard poles used in Central and Southern Europe). Fencing could also be burned if it had not already become too rotten after a few years in the ground, as the wood was not coated in any preservative. It was the major uses of fuel,

[15] Evelyn, *Sylva*, p. 39.
[16] Evelyn, *Sylva*, p. 41.
[17] Evelyn, *Sylva*, p. 65.
[18] Evelyn, *Sylva*, p. 54.
[19] Detlef Krannhals, *Danzig in der Weichselhandel in seiner Blütezeit vom 16. bis zum 17. Jahrhundert* (Leipzig: Hirzel Verlag, 1942), p. 34.
[20] Evelyn, *Sylva*, p. 65.

shipbuilding and construction that preoccupied men of policy, from village magistrates to princes and doges. Italian cities kept reserves of firewood, just as they did for grain.[21]

Scarcity

Almost everywhere, people complained that the woods were in decline. The fact was proverbial: *'Let them that live longest, fetch their wood farthest.'*[22] This belief arose out of both a longer-term view of how ancient landscapes had once been and how the process of cultivation and civilising inexorably gnawed away at the forest mantle of the Earth; and a short-term view of general laxity in the husbanding of resources, in which every difficulty in getting hold of raw materials was blamed on covetous and neglectful people. It was generally believed that much of Europe had once been swathed in great forests. Thus in 1598 John Manwood's *Treatise and discourse of the laws of the Forrest* began its history of English forests noting 'this realme, at the first being a wilderness ful of great huge woods', where 'at first' appears to be set sometime vaguely before the reign of the eleventh-century Danish King Canute.[23] William Harrison similarly noted in his topographical and social survey of 1577, *A description of England*, 'It shoulde seeme by anncient recordes, and the testimony of sundrie authors, that the whole countries of Lhoegres and Cambria now England and Wales, have sometimes been very well replenished with great woods and groves.' Sometimes evidence was more direct: the agricultural writer Walter Blith based his belief on the early prevalence of great woods on the discoveries of bog oak.[24] England had of course been more wooded in

---

[21] Karl Appuhn, *A forest on the sea. Environmental expertise in Renaissance Venice* (Baltimore, MD: Johns Hopkins University Press, 2009), p. 29.

[22] Norden, *Surveyors dialogue*, p. 213.

[23] John Manwood, *A treatise and discourse of the laws of the Forrest* (London: Thomas Wight & Bonham Norton, 1598), f.11v, 15v; in Michael Drayton's *Poly-olbion* of the 1610s, this stereotypical process of deforestation was presented as an inevitable, rather melancholic transition from a putative Golden Age as the inevitable consequence of time and human activity, in a deliberately Ovidian style. Sara Trevisan, '"The murmuring woods euen shuddred as with feare". Deforestation in Michael Drayton's Poly-Olbion', *The Seventeenth Century* 26(2) (2011), pp. 240–63.

[24] William Harrison, *An historical description of the Island of Britain* (London: John Harrison, 1577), f.90v; Walter Blith, *The English improver improved or the survey*

the distant past, although the nature of that woodland cover remains hotly debated among ecologists. Yet as early as the Domesday survey of 1086 it seems that no more than 15 per cent of the land surface was covered by trees, and the total was probably not very much lower by the end of the fifteenth century.[25] The belief in the truth of this supposition about the history of civilisation as a narrative of deforestation would have global consequences. When imperial foresters took these 'lessons' elsewhere, they would claim that allegedly more backward peoples, at an earlier stage of development, were destroying the forests that only they, newly enlightened with ideas of sustainability, could be trusted to restore.

In Scotland the myth of a once-great swathe of impenetrable trees gained traction during the early modern period, as misreadings and fabrications came to be more widely disseminated by print. Classical texts were a major inspiration. Tacitus had almost defined the nature of Germania by its great gloomy arbours, where the legions of Varus had blundered their way into ambush and annihilation.[26] The Scottish stories of a 'Great Wood of Caledon' drew on a very vague identification in Ptolemy's second-century atlas, reproduced with further liberality in its location by Waldseemüller in 1513 and Blaeu in 1654. Even greater literary licence was displayed by Hector Boece in 1527 and later Camden in the 1570s, allowing the great wood to spill out of the heart of the Highlands and seed itself across all the imagined mountains that lay north of the Forth and Clyde. The notion perhaps won further traction by the fact that the Picts of the north, just like the German tribes under Hermann who defended the Hercynian Forest, remained unsubjugated by the legions of Rome.[27] Massed ranks of trees could provide a satisfactory explanation of how such a historical anomaly could have happened. German writers relied on classical

<hr/>

of husbandry surveyed discovering the improueableness of all lands, 3rd edition (London: John Wright, 1652), p. 37.

[25] Oliver Rackham, *Ancient woodland. Its history, vegetation and uses in England* (London: Edward Arnold, 1980), p. 134.

[26] Nevertheless, Tacitus also noticed that alongside the 'horrid forests' it was 'full of sheep' which does not suggest endless dense woodland. Publius Cornelius Tacitus, *On Germany*, trans. Thomas Gordon (New York: P.F. Collier & son, 2012), ch. V.; see also Simon Schama, *Landscape and memory* (London: Fontana, 1996), pp. 81–120.

[27] T.C. Smout, Alan R. MacDonald and Fiona Watson, *A history of the native woodlands of Scotland, 1500–1920* (Edinburgh: Edinburgh University Press, 2005), pp. 20–4, 45.

sources such as Tacitus to demonstrate the earlier prevalence of trees in Germany, while also seeing their forests as a providential gift to northern nations.[28]

Nevertheless, neither the Scots, nor the English, nor the Germans required lax classical scholarship to discover the scarcity of trees. A 1504 parliamentary act in Scotland was already deemed necessary, 'considering that the wood of Scotland is utterly destroyed'.[29] The problem was not the unfolding of a general historical process, but a keen lack in the here-and-now. An Act passed under Henry VIII in 1543, much like German counterparts that appeared in the first decades of the sixteenth century, spoke of 'the great decaye of Tymber and Woodes' meaning 'a great and manifest likelihood of scarcity'.[30] We must take care in interpreting such passages: was this undoubtedly widespread feeling of scarcity because demand for wood had risen with population growth, or because competing uses for the woodland such as grazing and hunting were reducing yields of wood, or because the wooded area itself was shrinking, being turned into pasture by hungry beasts or grubbed up to go under the plough? Any one, combination, or none of these factors might be at play.[31] Although texts that proclaimed wood scarcity frequently placed it in the near future rather than the present, that future was becoming a less distant prospect. By 1577 William Harrison was concerned about the possibility of general shortage of wood for fuel: 'it is to be feared that brome, turfe... heth, firze, brakes, whinnes, ling... straw, sedge, reede, rush, & seacole will be good marchadze [merchandise] even in the citie of London'.[32] He was already behind the times, as the quantity of coal shipped down the east coast from the Tyne and Tees to the Thames was rapidly expanding.[33] The squeeze was most apparent in big cities without an adjacent source of fuel. Venice experienced crisis during the tough, cold years around 1531: 'our mint cannot function, nor can many artisans such as glassmakers, dyers and metalworkers. And

[28] Carlowitz, *Sylvicultura oeconomica*, pp. 3–7, 61.

[29] Smout et al., *Native woodlands*, p. 38.

[30] Statutes of the Realm 35 Hen. VIII c.17, p. 977.

[31] Paul Warde, 'The fear of wood shortage and the reality of the woodland in Europe, c. 1450–1850', *History Workshop Journal* 62 (2006), pp. 28–57.

[32] Harrison, *Historical description*, f.91r.

[33] John Hatcher, *The history of the British coal industry. Vol I. Before 1700. Towards the age of coal* (Oxford: Clarendon, 1993), p. 41.

unless opportune and proper provisions are made, no one can doubt but that there will be no longer a shortage, but an absolute lack of fuel in our city.'[34] A dearth of firewood and the loss of woodland was not simply a matter of industrial prosperity or comfort, but health and the very survival of a republic founded on mud and wood. Lack of material to burn would prevent 'purifying the air of malignant winter vapours' while deforestation was blamed for the silting of the lagoon.[35]

Writers frequently blamed the vanishing of the woods on neglect or greed. For cities and princes, with their eye on concentrated sources of supply and the ensuing potential for collecting revenue, creating extensive reserves of woodland was desirable and cost-effective. The issue for the farmer and peasants was very different, even though their views became incorporated into the same, universalising discourse. Peasants rarely owned or leased entire woodlands, and thus hedgerows or copses were often a major source of fuel, especially in those regions of *bocage* or 'severalty' where the landscape was characterised by small fields and numerous copses. These concerns were reflected in writing on husbandry. In 1649 Walter Blith blamed the poor condition of hedgerows on the fact that people did not root them in 'good mould' when they were set, protect them from grazing, or weed and fertilise them. For husbandmen who saw hedges primarily as barriers that could also be conveniently lopped for firewood, such efforts doubtless did not seem worthwhile (measures such as protecting a hedgerow from pasturing animals for five years!). Blith was probably incorrect to assert that 'All which were it done upon all Opportunities, No man almost in the Nation would be either at want of Firing, or Timber', but this suggestion indicates the important place of hedges in the English rural economy.[36] If just a little imagination and ingenuity were required to deliver the timber desired, then of course Hugh Plat was on the case: 'When your Trees are young, you may bow them to what compasse you will, by binding them down with packthread to any circular form, or other shape that pleaseth one best. And by this means your Timber will grow fit for Ships, Wheels, &c. whereby the great waste of Timber in time would be avoided.'[37]

---

[34] Appuhn, *Forest on the sea*, p. 137.
[35] Appuhn, *Forest on the sea*, p. 138.
[36] Blith, *The English improver improved*, pp. 113–14.
[37] Sir Hugh Plat, *Floraes paradise* (London: William Leake, 1608), p. 148.

Although no-one expressed it thus at the time, the fear of wood scarcity was frequently a classic case of how the incentives to the individual farmers of the land did not match the wider needs of a growing populace or specialist users such as the navy. The landlord took the mature timber so there was no incentive for the tenant to husband it. Demographic and tenurial uncertainty meant that the likelihood of one's heirs harvesting mature timber was low. Yet few seemed to grasp that this was a quite reasonable clash of interests. Shortages might also come from bottlenecks in labour supply for felling and transport, especially at times of high demand. They did not have to arise from neglect or ill will or covetousness.[38] In the 1650s it came to Samuel Hartlib's observant eye that chestnut wood was commonly to be found in old buildings in the vicinity of Gravesend, 'although there is scarce a chestnut within twenty miles'. He went on to conclude that: 'This shows that in former times those places did abound in such timber; for people were not so foolish surely in former times to runne up and down in the world, to procure huge massey timbers for barnes and such buildings when as there was plenty of *Oakes* and *Elmes*, at their doors.' But the wise habits of former times clearly did not extend to thinking about how subsequent generations might be taken for fools because they had to replace the timber that was never renewed with imports from far afield, increasingly the woods of Norway or the Baltic shore; as a man from the eastern Baltic port of Elbing must have been well aware.[39]

The necessity of trade was also taken as evidence of scarcity. It was not until later in the eighteenth century that this geography of supply could be more widely celebrated as a rational division of labour. The need to import timber and other wood products such as tar, pitch and potash also fed into fears of the negative consequences of the balance of trade, and the draining of specie from the nation. These precious metals were themselves a scarce commodity that could only be obtained from overseas, and it seemed an ill-starred policy to vent them on goods that could as well be produced at home. As Evelyn wrote, 'I will not complain what an incredible mass of ready *Money* is

---

[38] Appuhn, *Forest on the sea*, p. 32, Paul Warde, 'Early modern "resource crisis". The wood shortage debates in Europe', in A.T. Brown, A. Burn and R. Doherty (eds), *Crisis in economic and social history* (Woodbridge: Boydell Press, 2015), pp. 137–59.

[39] Samuel Hartlib, *The compleat husband-man; or, A discourse of the whole art of husbandry; both forraign and domestick* (London: Edward Brewster, 1659), p. 18.

yearly exported into the *Northern Countrys* for this sole commodity, which might all be saved were we *industrious* at *home*. Likewise from *Fir* we have the most of our *Pot-ashes*.' Thus did he complain.[40]

We can find such fears of scarcity expressed throughout the period, but in each place there was a gradual shift from an uneasy anticipation to reporting the experience of a generation past. In England this came in the late sixteenth century. The surveyor and author John Norden had his imagined bailiff declare in 1607: 'within these twenty yeares [woodlands] have bene diminished two parts of three: and if it go mo by proportion, our children will surely want'. His Surveyor interlocutor replied: 'I find, that it hath vniuersally receiued a mortail blow within the time of my memorie: notwithstanding there is a Statute for the preseruation and maintenance of the same.' In his own voice fellow surveyor Rock Church, who in 1612 published *An old thrift newly revived*, also spoke of 'spyles and devastations' since Henry VIII's time. 'For my selfe have knowne certain grounds, upon which within this twentie or thirtie years was growing great store of Underwood and Timber, and did yearely pay to the late Queene a rent, but now the wood is all gone, the soyle turned to a Common, and the rent quite lost, and not any paid.'[41] In 1611 Arthur Standish produced the first edition of his *Commons Complaint*: the first grievance of which was 'the generall destruction and waste of woods in this kingdome', there being 'too many destroyers, but few or none at all doth plant or preserve'. The consequences could be dramatic: 'so it may be conceived, no wood, no kingdome'. In 1614 Standish proposed that in the relatively recent past there was 'ten times so much Timber and Fire-wood in this kingdome, as there is at this instant'.[42]

---

[40] Evelyn, *Sylva*, p. 54.

[41] Norden, *Surveyors dialogue*, p. 212; Rock Church, *An old thrift newly revived* (London: Richard Moore, 1612), p. 3.

[42] Arthur Standish, *The commons complaint* (London: William Stansby, 1611); Arthur Standish, *New directions of experience authorized by the kings most excellent Maiesty, as may appeare, for the planting of Timber and Fire-Wood* (London: Nicholas Okes, 1614), p. 1; re-issued as Arthur Standish, *New directions of experience authorized by the kings most excellent Maiesty, as may appeare, for the increasing of Timber and Fire-Wood* (London: N. Okes, 1616). Joan Thirsk connects Arthur Standish as being the son of the rector of Wigan but this appears to be conjecture with a long chronological gap between his putative father's will of 1552 and first writings in the 1610s. Joan Thirsk, 'Standish, Arthur (*fl.* 1552–1615)', in *Oxford Dictionary of National Biography* (Oxford: Oxford University

Both he and Norden's bailiff were wildly wrong, but the anxiety seemed plausible enough for his publisher to pump out several editions of his work in these years, and he also managed to gain royal sanction.[43]

In many parts of Britain pressure on wood supplies had already been alleviated by the use of mineral coal (often called sea-coal, reflecting that it was delivered to London down the east coast, or the more self-explicable pit-coal, in contrast to the traditional usage of 'coal' to mean charcoal). Both Standish and the surveyor Rock Church pondered the prospects for what we now know to be the fossil fuel economy. They considered its long-term viability to be low; for notwithstanding some chemical theorists who imagined that stones and minerals grew in the ground, animated by the same forces that inspired living creatures, these men saw that coal was a non-renewable resource. 'For if Coale should faile', Church wrote, meaning mineral coal, '(as it is too apparent it beginneth to grow deere and scarce, and in many places there is none to be had) how then should we doe for this materiall of fuell? for doe we thinke that wood alone can beare the brung to satisfies euery mans chimney? Assuredly no, except it were more plentifull.'[44] At this time the price of firewood ran ahead of that of coal, explaining much of the transition to a mineral economy that marked early modern Britain out from the entirety of the rest of the world.[45] But this was not widely perceived as a great boon, a liberation from millennia of constrained energy supplies. In the 1650s Hartlib articulated a general unease with dependency on the unseen and capricious reserves of the east and this 'subterranean forest': 'if

Press, 2004), www.oxforddnb.com/view/article/26229, accessed 19 Sep. 2014. See also Henrey, *British botanical and horticultural literature*, p. 114.

[43] It may have been these works that led Gervase Markham to add a substantial section on woodland management and timber supply to the second book of his *English husbandman* that appeared in 1614 and was republished along with his first book in 1635. I am grateful to Felicity Stout for pointing this out. Markham, *The English husbandman*. See also Sharp, 'Timber, science, and economic reform', pp. 53–5; Henrey, *British botanical and horticultural literature*, p. 114.

[44] Church, *Old thrift*, f.i, v.

[45] See Paul Warde, *Energy consumption in England and Wales 1560–2000* (Naples: Consiglio Nazionale della Ricerche, 2007); Wrigley, *Energy and the English Industrial Revolution*; Hatcher, *British coal industry*, passim; Kander et al., *Power to the people*, pp. 107–12; Robert C. Allen, *The British Industrial Revolution in global perspective* (Cambridge: Cambridge University Press, 2009), pp. 84–96.

we had not *coales* from *Newcastle*, and *Boards* from *Norway*, *Plough-staves* and *Pipe-staves* from *Prussia*, we should be brought to great necessity'.[46]

Scarcity was almost universally proclaimed across Europe, and the problems it could lead to were couched in all-embracing terms by authors such as Norden, Standish and Church. We have already seen however that wood was a highly differentiated product, and even firewood was put to many different uses. Historians must ask, as has increasingly been the case since the 1980s, whether fears of wood shortage (*Holzmangel*) reflected a general crisis, or the problems experienced by particular groups of consumers. In more radical inter-pretations of the literature, it has been argued that there was scarcely a shortage to speak of at all, but rather powerful interest groups used the fear of such to seize control of valuable assets obtain them at subsidised rates. It is certainly striking how quickly the discourse of wood shortage spread across Europe and prompted a legislative response in the sixteenth century, embracing polities with radically different extents of woodland.[47] It is hard to believe that shortages were growing at the same rate.

---

[46] Hartlib, *Compleat husbandman*, p. 45.

[47] Warde, 'Fear of wood shortage'; Joachim Radkau, 'Holzverknappung und Krisenbewußtein im 18. Jahrhundert, *Geschichte und Gesellschaft* 4 (1983), pp. 513–43; Joachim Radkau, 'Zur angeblichen Energiekrise des 18. Jahrhunderts. Revisionistische Betrachtungen über die "Holznot"', *Vierteljahrschrift für Sozials-und Wirtschaftsgeschichte* 73 (1986), pp. 1–37; Joachim Radkau, 'Warum wurde die Gefährdung der Natur durch den Menschen nicht rechtzeitig erkannt? Naturkult und Angst vor I Iolznot um 1800', in Hermann Lübbe and Elisabeth Ströker (eds), *Ökologische Probleme im kulturellen Wandel* (Paderborn: Wilhelm Fink Verlag, 1986), pp. 47–78; Joachim Radkau, 'Das Rätsel der städtischen Brennholzversorgung im "Hölzernen Zeitalter"', in Dieter Schott (ed.), *Energie und Stadt in Europa. Von der vorindustriellen 'Holznot' bis zur Ölkrise der 1970er Jahre*. Beihefte der Vierteljahrschrift für Sozials und Wirtschaftsgeschichte 155 (Stuttgart, 2007), pp. 43–75; Bernd-Stefan Grewe, *Der versperrte Wald. Ressourcenmangel in der bayerischen Pfalz (1814–1870)* (Köln: Böhlau, 2004); Bernd-Stefan Grewe, '"Man sollte sehen und weinen!" Holznotalarm und Waldzerstörung vor der Industrialisierung', in Frank Uekötter und Jens Hohensee (eds), *Wird Kassandra heiser? Die Geschichte falscher Ökoalarme* (Stuttgart: Steiner, 2004), pp. 24–41; Christoph Ernst, *Den Wald entwickeln. Ein Politik- und Konfliktfled in Hunsrück und Eifel im 18. Jahrhundert* (Munich: De Gruyter Oldenbourg, 2000); Margaret Grabas, 'Krisenbwältigung oder Modernisierungsblockade? Die Rolle des Staates bei der Überwindung des "Holzenergiemangels" zu Beginn der Industriellen Revolution in Deutschland', *Jahrbuch für europäische Verwaltungsgeschichte* 7 (1995), pp. 43–75.

There can be no question that scarcity of particular kinds of wood was easily inflated into a problem with the resource as a whole. As economists understand well, 'scarcity' may well mean that something is more expensive than we would like it to be, which may come from any number of reasons, to do with changing relative prices of a host of different goods, or shifts in the cost of delivering a good to market, and changes in demand for the product, as well as the actual prevalence of the resource itself. We can note James, Duke of York (later the unfortunate James II of England and VII of Scotland) writing to the Lord Treasurer on 8 October 1661 that the Crown forests were needed for naval supply because of 'the want of money to buy timber from private men'.[48] Hence a request for afforestation on crown property, which made up only a small share of the national woodland, was the consequence of straitened royal finances, not the availability of timber. Andreé Corvol has argued convincingly that efforts to reform the forests of France at the same time were rather more to do with the hunt for royal revenue, and such efforts soon relented when financial concerns moved on.[49]

The 'perpetual struggle of jarring interests', as an observer of the 1780s put it, over the use to which the woods should be put, was political as well as economic.[50] The republican Samuel Hartlib reckoned that ironworks 'mightily destroy Woods', and that good had been done by shutting down the industry of Dean to preserve wood for shipping. In the 1650s the beginning and rapid growth of iron imports from Sweden combined with an overriding government preoccupation with obtaining timber for naval construction as the English squared off with the Dutch across the North Sea. Hartlib noted the myth (while conceding it was perhaps not actually true) that in Elizabethan times Spain sent an ambassador to get the woods of Dean destroyed and prevent the construction of a navy. What was true, on the other hand, was that it was worries about securing naval timber that prompted the Spanish monarchy into efforts to reserve and itemise timber from the mid-sixteenth century. Hartlib hoped that technological advances would render the competition over timber between iron and ships

[48] Sara Morrison, 'The Stuart forests. From venison pie to wooden walls', PhD thesis, University of Western Ontario, 2004, p. 364.
[49] Andrée Corvol, 'La decadence des forêts. Leimotiv', in Andrée Corvol (ed.), *La Forêt malade. Débats anciens et phénomènes nouveaux XVIIᵉ–XXᵉ siècles* (Paris, 1994).
[50] *HCJ* 43, 18 Jun. 1788, p. 561.

redundant: 'There are some ingenious men, who lately have got a *Patent* for making *Iron* with *Sea-coale*; I hope they will accomplish their desires; for it would wonderfully advance this *Island*, and save *wood*.'[51]

Hartlib's fortunes crashed with the Restoration of 1660, and he died soon after. In his wake it was the royalist Evelyn who presented himself as the saviour of the forests, placing the blame for their allegedly woeful state squarely at the feet of his republican predecessors – as one might expect in a book dedicated to Charles II. He inveighed against those 'sacrilegious *Purchasers*, and disloyal *Invaders*, in this *Iron-age* amongst us, who have lately made so prodigious a *Spoil* of those goodly *Forests*, *Woods*, and *Trees* (to satisfie an impious and unworthy *Avarice*) which being once the Treasure and Ornament of this *Nation*, were doubtless reserv'd by our more prudent *Ancestors* for the repairs of our floating *Castles*.'[52] In reality the merry monarch's father had perhaps not been considered among the most prudent of men. The commonwealth period had however brought depredations in the *Crown* forests, which we must stress again only accounted for a small proportion of the national total. Great debates in Parliament from 1648 to 1659 had raged over whether to disafforest and sell these reserves, especially as for a period they had been earmarked as a means to pay the vast arrears of the army.[53] Certainly, both the political turmoil of the Interregnum, and wars with the Dutch causing shipping losses and generating demand for an expanding navy were proximate causes of the publication of Evelyn's *Sylva*. Naval commissioners had been in discussion with the lessee of rights to the Crown forest of Dean in the summer of 1662, culminating in a plea delivered to the Royal Society and the king in September of that year to respond to 'so great a scarcity of Tymber for the Supply of his Navy' by replanting the royal forests and giving the crown first right to timber even on private land. Society members, including Evelyn, responded with a selection of papers less than a month later, and in the winter of 1664 these were collated by Evelyn and written up into the famous work

[51] Hartlib, *Compleat husbandman*, p. 48; John T. Wing, 'Keeping Spain afloat. State forestry and imperial defense in the sixteenth century', *Environmental History* 17 (Jan. 2012), pp. 126–8.

[52] Evelyn, *Sylva* (1664), f.iv.

[53] Morrison, 'Stuart forests', pp. 232–86.

that has borne his name since.[54] In this Evelyn repeated several of the recommendations of the naval commissioners directly, suggesting draconian powers of purveyance and limits to oak use that were enacted in various European states, but would not be in England.

Yet in truth the jarring interests reflected a basic structural problem with the 'organic economy', the pre-industrial world order in which nearly all raw materials and energy could only be obtained from the products of the land: the 'photosynthetic constraint'.[55] Relative scarcity was the inevitable by-product of rising demand for all kinds of products that had to draw on the produce of the same narrow ground. Thus while Evelyn could place a blanket blame on Parliamentarian regicides for the 'sensible and notorious decay of [the] *Wooden-walls*' of the nation, he was more astute when he noted 'it has not been the late increase of *Shipping* alone, but the multiplication of *Glaß-works*, *Iron-Furnaces*, and the like, from whence this im-politick diminution of our *Timber* has proceeded; but from the disproportionate spreading of *Tillage*'.[56] Yet Chapter 1 has already shown how generations of rulers were devoted to the extension of tillage – as well as subject to fears of diminishing wood supplies. From the perspective of the 1660s, as population pressures on agriculture slackened, a case for the priority of timber might be made, but we should remember that the previous regime had struggled through extremely hard dearth years from 1647 to 1649.[57] The spread of tillage had already been noted as a problem for the woods in Venice in 1531; in southern Germany blame was laid on vineyards whose extent grew proportionately at a faster rate than arable lands in the sixteenth century, often up slopes previously covered by trees.[58] It was easy to make the culprit whatever you happened to desire less at a particular moment, especially if it shifted responsibility onto other shoulders. In the German Palatinate officials of the monastery of Offenach informed their ruler Duke Johann I that they could not provide the wood usually due to his palace at Lauterechen because

---

[54] Hartley, 'Exploring and communicating knowledge of trees', pp. 229–31, 245; E.S. de Beer, 'John Evelyn F.R.S (1620–1706)', *Notes and Records of the Royal Society of London*, vol. 15 (Jul. 1960), p. 234.

[55] E.A. Wrigley, *Continuity, chance and change. The character of the industrial revolution in England* (Cambridge: Cambridge University Press, 1988); Wrigley, *Energy*.

[56] Evelyn, *Sylva*, pp. 1–2.

[57] Hindle, 'Dearth and the English revolution'.

[58] Appuhn, *Forest on the sea*, p. 137; Warde, *Ecology*.

of excessive theft by the peasants. But it is rather more likely that the lack of wood to spare came from the increased demand of the monastery itself. Such examples could be multiplied many times over.[59]

Different consumers competed over woodland space. Undoubtedly many accusations of wastefulness arose from this competition, although this by no means denies the possibility that total wood supplies were simultaneously declining. The two narratives are not mutually exclusive. But it also became recognised that the exploitation resulting from commercial and industrial expansion and exclusions did not *necessarily* reduce the actual yield of wood. John Evelyn conceded that his own father, and Christopher Darell of Surrey, had considered ironworks 'a means of maintaining, and improving his *Woods;* I suppose, by increasing the *Industry* of *planting,* an[d] care'. The requirement of a sustainable supply of coppice-wood to forges was more likely to be an invitation to good husbandry than a temptation to rapacious clearances, as the forge could not relocate once all the wood was gone. Evelyn pointed to how the iron industry near Bilbao was based upon a sustainable pollarding system.[60] In this vein, the projector, improver and surveyor Andrew Yarranton argued in 1677 and 1681 that deficient internal navigation was leaving valuable resources isolated and unexploited. He was particularly excited by the prospects of the River Slaney in Ireland, on whose upper reaches great timbers rotted that could be taken to build ships at Wexford. Yet there were similar stands of unused and rotting timber in Essex or Wiltshire.[61] Wood was not generally scarce; it had simply, and understandably, been logged out in those places closest to consumer demand. Yarranton considered this to be common knowledge. 'For it is now evidently known to all persons, building Ships or dealing in Timber, that all, or the greatest part of the best Timber, near all Navigable Rovers are already destroyed, and most of such Timber, as is growing in all these Countries, which are landlockt and at a good distance from the Sea, and from Navigable Rivers, is as yet growing, and commonly that Timber is the very best, and of the greatest quantities.'[62] Where pit-coal dominated the domestic fuel

---

[59] Joachim Allmann, *Der Wald in der frühen Neuzeit* (Berlin: Duncker & Humbolt, 1989), pp. 105–6.

[60] 'Without at all diminishing the stock of *Timber*'. Evelyn, *Sylva*, p. 110.

[61] Andrew Yarranton, *England's improvement by land and sea*, vol. 1 (London: T. Parkhurst & N. Simmons, 1677), pp. 38–9.

[62] Yarranton, *England's improvement*, p. 61.

supply, Yarranton noted that coppice-woods would have been grubbed up were it not because of the demand from the iron industry.[63] The untapped reserves could equally lie overseas. It was already the case by the 1670s that vast amounts of wood were consumed in Russia and Ukraine making potash for the soapboilers of London, while Finnish tar and pitch caulked the hulls of English vessels; wharfs were stacked with the boards of Norway and oaken wainscot of Germany.[64] By the 1710s shiploads of pitch and tar were crossing the Atlantic from the Carolinas. Why not vent the great reserves of these sparsely populated lands?: ''twere better to purchase all our *Iron* out of *America*', opined Evelyn, 'than thus to exhaust our *Woods* at *home*'. He harked back to the Elizabethan statute protecting timber of one foot square against use for ironworks, so it could be raised for timber.[65] In practice something like this happened, but not in the colonies where shipping rates remained too high for the transoceanic transport of any cargo except valuable mast timbers. English iron output stagnated for a century from the 1630s, and Swedes and then Russians became major suppliers.[66] Such spatial zoning of supply was already stipulated in various Acts of Parliament. Although the Weald of Kent and Sussex was exempted from laws barring larger trees from use in the iron industry, an Elizabethan Act of 1582 protected any wood within 22 miles of London from the ironmasters, and at this time the Crown tried to extract promises of minimal timber use when granting contracts to ironfounders.[67]

Industry and commerce were blamed for depredations in the woodlands throughout the period, and of course continue to face opprobrium today. By the latter part of the seventeenth century however, an alternative discourse was well established that saw commerce

---

[63] Yarranton, *England's improvement*, p. 148.

[64] H.S.K. Kent, *War and trade in northern seas. Anglo-Scandinavian economic relations in the mid-eighteenth century* (Cambridge: Cambridge University Press, 1973); Paul Warde, 'Trees, trade and textiles. Potash imports and ecological dependency in British industry, c.1550–1770', *Past & Present* (2018); Christian van Bochove, *The economic consequences of the Dutch. Economic integration around the North Sea, 1500–1800* (Amsterdam: Aksant, 2008).

[65] Evelyn, *Sylva*, p. 110; TNA Customs 3.

[66] Peter King, 'The production and consumption of bar iron in early modern England and Wales', *EcHR* 58(1) (2005), pp. 1–33. On the early American wood trade, see Charles F. Carroll, *The timber economy of New England* (Providence, RI: Brown, 1973), esp. p. 86.

[67] 23 Eliz C.5; Harkness, *The Jewel House*, p. 152.

as a solution to scarcity, whether in providing for a new geography of supply making best use of the world's endowment of resources, or in itself providing the incentive to conserve and improve. Profit was itself an incentive to good husbandry, and if some leases encouraged the lessees to strip the land of trees, this was because of the incentives built into the leases, not covetousness. It was noted in reports on the woods of James I that poor security of re-entry into the tenancy gave the lessee little incentive to replace the wood that they felled.[68] Such arguments suggested that scarcity could be resolved by the correct configuration of property rights and guarantees of trade, but their application was limited. Trade was only a realistically affordable prospect if conducted over water to regions of low population density; profit to the owner only worked as an incentive to conserve on a substantial scale when the cutting cycles were short. Mostly, government had recourse to law.

Law

In the late medieval centuries, many Central European cities had already taken active steps to secure wood supplies by purchasing woodlands, especially in the muddled and fractured polities of the Holy Roman Empire where the threat of blockade or economic ransom loomed large. From the late fifteenth century the governments of the large territorial states of Europe began to pass legislation on the supply of wood and the condition of the forests, pioneered in Italy and in a particularly developed form in Germany. These ratcheted up to the level of the territory by-laws and regulations on resources that had been applied to particular communities and woodlands since the fourteenth century, or perhaps earlier.[69] Everywhere the word was of impending

---

[68] BL Additional MS 10038, f.8.v. 18 Sep. 1612.

[69] See examples in August Bernhardt, *Geschichte des Waldeigenthums, der Waldwirtschaft und Forstwissenschaft in Deutschland* (Berlin: J. Springer, 1872–5); Helmut Brandl, *Der Stadtwald von Freiburg* (Freiburg: Wagnersche Univ. Buchhandlung K. Zimmer, Kommissionsverlag, 1970); Albert Hauser, *Wald und Feld in der alten Schweiz* (Zurich: Artemis Verlag, 1972), pp. 110–12; Ernst Schubert, 'Der Wald. Wirtschaftliche Grundlage der spätmittelalterlichen Stadt', in Bernd Herrmann (ed.), *Mensch und Umwelt im Mittelalter* (Stuttgart: Deutsche Verlags-Anstalt, 1987), pp. 257–69; Siegfried Epperlein, *Waldnutzung, Waldstreitigkeiten und Waldschutz in Deutschland im hohen Mittelalter. 2. Hälfte 11. Jahrhundert bis ausgehendes 14. Jahrhundert* (Stuttgart: Steiner, 1993).

shortages and scarcity. Legislation relating to Württemberg's forests from 1495 onwards was justified by the 'common complaint' of shortages of fire- and building wood, and of 'marked wastage' of the woodlands; in Bavaria the looming wood shortage in 1568 would imminently lead to men '[leaving] their goods, homes and sustenance including even their wives and children and go from the same because of its lack'.[70] For the most part the new legislation was unenforceable on a national scale. But it was a major signal of intent and was promulgated in the majority of German states between the 1530s and 1580s.[71] The justification for legislation was the common good. 'The kinge... perceiving... the great decaye of Tymber and Woodes universally within this his Realm of Englandde to be such, that unless speedy remedy in that behalf be provided there is great and manifest likelyhod of scarcity.'[72] European rulers had to be seen to be taking responsibility. Indeed, a 'pragmatic' issued by Ferdinand and Isabella for their kingdoms in 1496, largely aimed at reducing disputes, indicated that they were happy to accommodate local solutions; although by 1518 Charles I's legislation on the matter was speaking more typically of 'a great shortage of firewood'.[73] Of course, in some cases there was money to be made too, but for the most part princes received no direct pecuniary benefit from such laws. Indeed, they created the costs of enforcement, although these fell in theory on part-time and often ill-motivated local officials.

---

[70] Warde, 'Fear of wood shortage', p. 42; Dorothea Hauff, *Zur Geschichte der Forstgesetzgebung und Forstorganisation des Herzogtums Württemberg im 16. Jahrhundert* (Stuttgart: Landesforstverwaltung Baden-Württemberg, 1977), pp. 14–15; A.L. Reyscher, *Vollständige, historisch and kritisch bearbeitete Sammlung der württembergischen Gesetze*, vol. XII (1841), p. 9.

[71] K. Krüger, *Finanzstaat Hessen 1500–1567. Staatsbildung im übergang vom Domänstaat zum Steuerstaat* (Marburg: Elwert, 1980), p. 153; Allmann, *Der Wald in der frühen Neuzeit*, pp. 35, 44; Burkhard Dietz, 'Wirtschaftliches Wachstum und Holzmangel im bergisch-märkischen Gewerberaum vor der Industrialisierung', www.lrz-muenchen-de/MW/Hardenstein/Dietz.htm, pp. 5–6; Ernst, *Den Wald entwickeln*, p. 52; Christa Graefe, *Forstleute. Von den Anfängen einer Behörde und ihren Beamten Braunschweig-Wolfenbüttel 1530–1607* (Wiesbaden: Kommission bei Harrassowitz, 1989), p. 74; Friedrich Mager, *Der Wald in Altpreussen als Wirtschaftsraum* (Köln: Böhlau, 1960), pp. 36, 54; Kurt Mantel, *Forstgeschichte des 16. Jahrhunderts unter dem Einfluß der Forstordnungen und Noe Meurers* (Hamburg: Parey, 1980), pp. 158, 273.

[72] Statutes of the Realm 35 Hen. VIII c.17, p. 977.

[73] Wing, 'Keeping Spain afloat', pp. 124–5.

Shortage was usually blamed not on general habits, and certainly not structural problems inherent to the pre-industrial economy, but the profligacy and covetousness of a few. In common with much Renaissance legislation, acts that threatened welfare and order were seen as arising from individual moral failings, a weakness of the will that led to sinfulness.[74] Superfluous wood consumption was bad neighbourliness on a national scale.

> Some burneth a lode, at a time in his hall/
> some never leave burning, til burnt have they all,/
> Some making of havock, without any wit,/
> Make many poore soules, without fire to sit.[75]

Problems also arose out of dimwittedness and laziness. Valuable timbers were cast into the fire. Crooked timbers should be reserved for ship- or millwrights, the sturdy elm for carts and ploughs, hazel for making forks. Of course, what appeared to be profligacy might well make perfect sense to someone with different priorities. The production and management of oak coppice in parts of England was heavily influenced by the demand for bark, and the tannins it contained, for use by tanneries in leather-making, a major industry. This did not necessarily chime well with other potential uses of the tree.[76] Indeed, the timing of oak-felling in England was largely determined by the moment best-suited for the removal of bark which put English practice out of line with the rest of Europe where oaks were felled when the sap was at its lowest ebb to assist seasoning the wood.

The very earliest market controls on wood were similar to those imposed on other essential products like grain. It was to be sold only at central markets where supply could be scrutinised, the best timbers reserved and fraud identified. Of course, these measures inevitably created smuggling and a black market, as Venice found in seeking to control supplies from Belluno on the Italian mainland as early as the 1400s and 1410s.[77] Here the imposition of rules from the new colonial ruler may have exacerbated resentment. The price ceilings widely imposed on wood and grain seemed good for consumer in short run,

---

[74] Warde, *Ecology*, pp. 165–9.
[75] Tusser, *Five hundred*, f.33.
[76] Tusser, *Five hundred*, f.44v
[77] Appuhn, *Forest on the sea*, p. 81.

but they discouraged supply, either because in times of acute need merchants did not want to pay the costs of shipping available goods to market or because they created a disincentive for their production in the first place. The greatest profits in the timber trade were always made by middlemen, and they were acutely sensitive to such policies; if they did not hold an inventory of the goods, there was no reason to acquire one if the price wasn't right. Such policies were however explicitly temporary measures, usually only applied in crisis years: by Venice in 1437–8 and 1441–3.[78]

As well as consumer protection, governments legislated for the wood supply that they directly controlled. The Swedish Crown made all uninhabited land, much of which was forested, Crown property in the 1540s.[79] In the early eighteenth century one-third of the vast Russian forests were state-owned.[80] Here there was an incentive to use it to derive revenue and to try to ensure that the use-rights of peasants over this land did not diminish that revenue. The same was potentially true of all woodland owned by rule-setting institutions, whether village communes, cities or princes. Legislators thus followed three basic strategies aside from the general habit of market controls.

First, they extended powers of jurisdiction and regulation over their own property or where the land was already invested with Crown rights, sometimes deriving from forest rights connected to hunting. Where 'state' or 'public' woodlands were large, these had the potential to resolve any perceived problems of supply. On occasion, this policy also meant making concrete claims to property rights in the first place. Second, they extended powers over others' property as a function of rights or duties of a prince to provide for the welfare of a populace. This could mean regulating the management of woodland and uses to which its products could be put, with legislation enforced either by special forest officers, or the normal judicial machinery of the state and the municipal, communal and lordly jurisdictions within it. In Castile, the Crown re-asserted – as it claimed – rights over common lands granted

---

[78] Appuhn, *Forest on the sea*, p. 83.
[79] Jorma Ahvenainen, 'Man and the forest in northern Europe from the Middle Ages to the 19th century', *Vierteljahrschrift für Sozials- und Wirtschaftsgeschichte* 83 (1996), p. 19.
[80] V.V. Alexejev. Y.V. Alexejeva and V.A. Shkerin, 'Russian forest. Its dimensions and use', in Simonetta Cavaciocchi (ed.), *L'uomo e la foresta secc.XIII-XVIII* (Florence: Le Monnier, 1996), pp. 1087–8.

by earlier monarchs to municipalities, and that it retained the power to enter the commons to extract timber.[81] Finally, they sought to facilitate the development of better supply networks, by for example permitting rafting of timber, removing or arbitrating with competing uses of the rivers (millworks or fish weirs), and negotiating trade agreements. Officials set up warehouses and pounds for timber, and provided commissions to factors to obtain supplies. Much of this activity was ongoing and had been part of late medieval processes of market integration. By 1530 Venice explicitly recognised that some of its scarcity problems related to transportation.[82]

During the second half of the fifteenth centuries monasteries and cities in south-west Germany had begun to limit peasant use-rights in woodlands, a move they sometimes claimed was simply the enforcement of neglected entitlements but that was seen as an unwarranted novelty by rural communities. Thus the already age-old clash of rights between the urban and rural populace was replayed, as later centuries would see equivalent struggles over unevenly distributed resources such as drinking water.[83] The use of these woods was a major source of contention in the years up to and including the great peasant revolt of 1525. Where the state had *no* direct rights, and market controls could not entice the desired supply (at least at the desired price), more draconian measures were employed. In 1471 Venice, having no domestic forests, seized control of rights over some community woodlands in the Montello district,[84] having already made an area in Cadore on the upper Piave a reserve for masts in 1463. By 1476 the Doge issued regulations on the use of oaks throughout community forests on the *terrafirma*, and by mid-sixteenth century the state held 40 reserves, where local use-rights were limited and the timber designated for particular uses, especially for the arsenal.[85]

Such legislation can be found almost everywhere. It would be redundant to list all of it. Timing of course varied according to many

[81] Wing, 'Keeping Spain afloat', p. 122.
[82] Appuhn, *Forest on the sea*, p. 121, see also Katia Occhi, *Boschi e mercanti. Traffici di legname tra la contea di Tirolo e la Repubblica di Venezia (secoli XVI–SVII)* (Bologna: Il Mulino, 2006).
[83] See for example Harriet Ritvo, *The dawn of green. Manchester, Thirlmere and modern environmentalism* (Chicago, IL: University of Chicago Press, 2009).
[84] Appuhn, *Forest on the sea*, p. 94.
[85] Appuhn, *Forest on the sea*, pp. 100–1, 111, 114.

factors – perhaps the sudden concern of a duke or prince out on a hunting trip who found himself dissatisfied with the woodlands he rode through. Bursts of administrative vigour were often found at the beginning of reigns, or where for financial reasons rulers found themselves constrained to call parliaments. We should not necessarily read much about the state of the woodlands in any particular place from the existence of legislation: many contingencies affected its emergence. Sometimes drafts took time. The Swedish diet asked for a new law in 1642, but it was enacted in 1647.[86] Laws might be in sub-sections of more general Acts, such as the 20 paragraphs devoted to the forest in the great Russian *Sobornye ulozheniye* of 1649 that provided a new legal underpinning to the Empire after the Time of Troubles.[87] Laws were not newly invented responses to whatever challenges perceived, but had their own genealogy, lifting measures from neighbouring states, or following the careers of the men who made them. The jurist and bureaucrat Noé Meurer, one of the first to write on forests, specialised in woodland matters in the service of the Duke of Württemberg in southwest Germany and went on to the nearby Palatinate where he worked on the forest ordinance (*Forstordnung*) of 1572. This also referred back to previous laws of the 1540s and 1550s promulgated 'because of the felt shortage and retreat of the woodlands in the Neckar Valley'.[88] The 1572 text was then copied into sections of the forest laws for the Upper Palatinate, a separate principality in the south-east of Germany in 1585, 1596 and 1611.[89] On a more local scale, we can trace the similar translation of by-laws between southern German villages, sometimes even in different lordships.[90] Once laws were made there were many reiterations and emendations. If we include only the major legislation Württemberg's laws were made in 1540, 1552, 1567 and 1614. Scotland saw Acts in 1503, 1535, 1592, 1594, 1607, 1617 and 1661.[91]

---

[86] Ahvenainen, 'Man and the forest', p. 14.
[87] Alexejev et al., 'Russian forest', pp. 1087–8.
[88] 'Die sie wegen gefühlten Mangels und abgangs wegen der hölzer im Nekkarthal'. Allmann, *Der Wald in der frühen Neuzeit*, p. 43.
[89] Allmann, *Der Wald*, pp. 35, 43–4.
[90] Paul Warde, 'Imposition, emulation and adaptation. Regulatory regimes in the commons of early modern Germany', *Environment and History* 19 (2013), pp. 313–37.
[91] Warde, *Ecology*, ch. 3; Smout et al., *Native woodlands*, p. 45.

The content of this legislation was largely concerned with demarcating forest space, preventing waste, and in some cases subjecting felling to the approval of a new forestry administration (or at a village level, local magistrates or forest wardens): a power that was largely negative and juridical in that it sought to limit consumption, and its efforts to enhance supply rested on maintaining best traditional practice rather than large-scale intervention in the woodlands to reconfigure their management and use. Cutting (especially in state woodlands) with authorisation from officials might be limited to certain days, and particular species were reserved for special uses. Grazing animals were to be barred from areas of new growth to assist regeneration, and marked trees, or set numbers protected from coppicing to grow into mature timber. Woodland was also generally explicitly made subject to noble and princely hunting irrespective of ownership.[92] In centres of consumption, officials were re-tasked with often long-established duties of seeking out supplies and regulating stores and public warehouses, and purchases on the part of state.[93]

In some states newly created forest officials were tasked with enforcement of the law, or foresters who had previously only managed Crown or princely domains were granted power over all kinds of property throughout the polity. Communities that held their own woodlands were expected to appoint woodwards. In England, forestry officials and the forest courts (which as we have seen were medieval jurisdictions relating to a bundle of rights initially connected with hunting) remained limited to their ancient, sometimes revived bounds;[94] on the Crown estates woodwards employed by each manor watched over treed land, as was often the case on private estates if they had extensive woods, while the Acts on timber were enforced by magistrates. Often the reach of princely officials was weak in practice, and only the regal or princely properties were closely regulated. More frequently oversight was extremely lax, corruption rife and knowledge

---

[92] Allmann, *Der Wald in der frühen Neuzeit*, p. 70; for an extensive study of the Danish laws, see Bo Fritzbøger, *A windfall for the magnates. The development of woodland ownership in Denmark, c.1150–1850* (Odense: Syddansk Universitetsforlag, 2004).

[93] Appuhn, *Forest on the sea*, pp. 83–5.

[94] The attempt to extend forest bounds under the regime of Charles I of England, essentially for revenue-raising reasons, was one of the many sources of antagonism in the run-up to the Civil War.

of the laws apparently limited. Traditional practice and custom remained the dominant force. Rock Church created an imaginary but representative woodward for his book of 1612, who stated that in his work he was governed 'partly by custome', that he did not set any trees, but he did obediently only fell them when granted special authority by his superior, and he protected coppices from cattle for five to six years.[95] Church had doubtless met plenty of woodwards in his surveying work and the account is plausible. Indeed, many a village warden across Western Europe could have said much the same. This underlines the fact that many statutes 'merely formalized what was already a universal practice', as Karl Appuhn has described the Venetian law of 1476.[96] The men who enforced rules, whether village by-laws or statutes, were the linchpin of the whole system. Were they sufficiently well-paid and incentivised to do their work? If not, did venality and corruption undermine their authority? Were they aided or hindered by their neighbours, and were there sufficient feet on the ground to police the bounds of their wards and the activities within it? Watching the watchers became one of the major preoccupations of legislators, not least in France where venality of office was a significant underpinning of the whole bureaucratic system.[97] Evelyn highlighted the 'Continual duty' of woodward 'to walk about, and survey his young *Plantations* daily; and to see that all *Gaps* be imemdiately stopp'd; trespassing *Cattle* impounded; and (where they are infested) the *Deer* chas'd out'.[98]

From the very beginning of the new systems of forestry administration that appeared form the late fifteenth century, conflicts arose from perceived intrusions into traditional rights, overbearing behaviour, arbitrary rulings, favouritism and venality. The compendious laws of Württemberg quickly became preoccupied with regulating official behaviour, watching the watchers, the provision of receipts and scrutiny of accounts. The aim was not simply to get the duke what was due to him, but to generate trust in the whole system. In the English royal woodlands the accounting paper trail led in theory from local woodwards right up to the Exchequer in London, but it was a trail

---

[95] Church, *Old thrift*, p. 2.
[96] Appuhn, *Forest on the sea*, p. 112.
[97] This was, for example, one of the main goals of the legislation of 1661. Andrée Corvol, *L'homme et l'arbre sous l'Ancien Regime* (Paris: Economica, 1984), pp. 3–4.
[98] Evelyn, *Sylva*, p. 77.

that as often as not found its way into deadends or was a path simply never taken.[99]

For all the making of rules, the debates of parliaments and committees, solemn proclamations of monarchs and employment of liveried men to guard and mind the forest, it remained the fact that in nearly every case the traditional users actually managed the woodland. They might have to – in theory – ask for permission to do so – but the forest was not yet handed over to professional experts in the seventeenth century. Foresters and wardens were policemen, not engineers. In Denmark the guardians of Crown woods were, in fact, simply one of the local tenant farmers who were exempted from other services and received some additional payment in kind.[100]

However, in the long term the creation of this cadre would provide a crucial basis for the development of modern forestry. Another long-term consequence would be the gradual erosion of trust. Wood for what, and for whom? Who was to judge what a regulation or behaviour cost another? Onerous requirements to ask permission for many activities generated evasion and a cat-and-mouse game between locals and officials. If the victim of transgressions was perceived to be the distant and unimaginably wealthy Crown, rather than one's neighbours, petty infractions could become an easy and guilt-free habit. Foresters could become distrusted because they were distant; every peasant, a potential infractor. Where wardens were better embedded in local communities, they could equally be undermined by factionalism and rivalries to which early modern villages were often prone.[101] Yet without being able to swim in a sea of peasant sympathy, foresters' power was very limited. This sympathy was not automatically withheld. Indeed, left to their own devices village authorities frequently introduced rules that were much the same as princely laws. As with much law enforcement, a basic mechanism in Germany was that peasants had to report annually under oath any infractions of which they knew, a practice that raises the suspicion that those caught were those whom their neighbours

[99] Philip A.J. Pettit, *The royal forests of Northamptonshire. A study in their economy 1558–1714* (Gateshead: Northumberland Press/Northamptonshire Record Society, 1968).

[100] Fritzbøger, *Windfall for the magnates*, p. 230.

[101] Warde, *Ecology*, pp. 220–3; Allmann, *Der Wald in der frühen Neuzeit*, p. 109.

generally wanted to be caught.[102] In the Venetian *terrafirma* village heads were personally made liable for damage.[103]

Although not yet widely practised, the deliberate setting (planting) of trees and acorns was well known in antiquity and medieval times. While the requirement to sow trees only rarely appears in the sixteenth century, and usually in regard to specific locations rather than as a general rule,[104] the presence of increasing numbers of forest officials (as well as the stewards of private estates) offered the possibility of the state pursuing a more active managerial style. Eyeing what were considered the neglected and wasted coppices in royal ownership in 1607, James I instructed his woodwards: 'To replant our new coppice where the soyl will naturally breed wood where it may be conveniently done without impediment to our Game or disgrace of our parks forests or Chases.' All coppices were to be surveyed, 'To certify the quantity present age and yearly value of all coppices whatsoever', and leases reviewed.[105] Of course, the caveats remind us that wood production remained only one aim among many. Addressing the House of Lords on 21 March 1610, James had stressed the importance of protecting woods, for the '*esse bene esse*', but specifically listed 'the navy, for fuel, lastly for sports and pleasure, which is for my honor'.[106] Interests became similarly entangled and tense over the use of commons, where according to Fitzherbert in the 1520s, lords could sell wood and other woody plants from the common, although peasant farmers had rights to grazing and sometimes 'estovers', 'ploughbote' or 'housebote' (wood for domestic fuel or repair).[107] The often vaguely specified rights that were exercised over common land would lead to a well-documented history of perennial friction, court disputes and sometimes violence.

---

[102] Allmann, *Der Wald in der frühen Neuzeit*, p. 137.

[103] Appuhn, *Forest on the sea*, p. 161.

[104] Planting quotas were set under Phillip II for the regions of northern Spain most involved in naval supply, but proved difficult to enforce. Johann Coler talks about collecting seed and cones for sowing as quite normal practice in Brunswick in the 1590s, and Heresbach describes the sowing of acorns. Colerus, *Oeconomicae*, pp. 210–11, 217–18; Heresbach, *Foure bookes*, p. 101; Wing, 'Keeping Spain afloat', p. 129.

[105] BL Add 38444. f.19.

[106] Morrison, 'Stuart forests', p. 68.

[107] John Fitzherbert, *Boke of surveyinge and improumentes* (London: Rycharde Pynson, 1523), f.6v, p. 13.

Perceptions of scarcity were shaped by different needs, opinions of the activity of others, and indeed the many varied forms that any woodland might take. Similarly, the motivation for law-making was shot through with overlapping and potentially contradictory impulses. The debate about the woodlands in England between 1604 and 1614 tapped into the time-honoured narratives of woodland decline, and a perception of accelerating problems in recent decades. But the state of the royal finances was also dire, and the Crown forests seemed a vast, under-utilised asset. In the 1630s Charles I would push its potential to the fisc much further, attempting to extend the forest bounds far beyond even their great medieval extent as a means of claiming various fines and perquisites (by this time the actual woodlands had largely been leased out or sold). These venal manoeuvres undermined the legitimacy of the forest jurisdictions and contributed to a resistance that led to civil war. Yet by the end of the war the finances of the new Commonwealth were no better, and there was an army to pay. In July 1649, the royal forests were turned over to the army to pay their arrears, although standard timber for the navy was protected on all Crown land within 15 miles of navigable waterways, all trees to be surveyed, marked and reserved for navy in a few months, and sales completed by summer 1657. In practice, it was beyond the capacity of the state to achieve this and the trees were reprieved.[108]

Such concerns and limits of power were equally evident across the Channel, where the famous forest ordinances produced by Colbert were simply one step in an ongoing process of debate and regulation, whose character was already largely shaped during the reign of Henri IV (1597–1610) just as, contemporaneously, James I's officials attempted to reform the Crown forests of England.[109] The laws of 1661 and then the great Ordinance of 1669 were predicated, among other things, with getting royal forests in shape to be leased and hence the stipulations about preservation of trees and set cutting cycles for coppicing were a means to determine the potential profits; a fiscal rather than ecological concern. Episodic fears about the provision of naval

---

[108] Morrison, 'Stuart forests', p. 201.
[109] Andrée Corvol, 'La belles futaies d'antan', in Andrée Corvol (ed.), *La Forêt malade. Débats anciens et phénomènes nouveaux XVIIe–XXe siècles* (Paris: L'Harmattan, 1994), pp. 22–3; and Andrée Corvol, 'Les communautés d'habitants et l'approvisionement énergetique. Les combustibles ligneux', in Simonetta Cavaciocchi (ed.), *Economia e energia secc. XIII–XVIII* (Florence: Le Monnier, 2003), pp. 737–64.

timber were a repeated stimulus to action for the French and Spanish crown, particularly with cycles of warfare, attrition and budgetry squeezes across the late seventeenth and early eighteenth century that were often motivated by keeping costs down. As with Evelyn's *Sylva*, such concerns could have a spin-off in literature, as a commission to examine procurement of material for the French navy in 1731 eventually lead to Duhamel du Monceau's treatises on rope-making and forestry in the later 1740s and 1750s. The imposition of laws originally drawn up for Crown forests to all kinds of property in 1669 was immediately perceived as draconian and inappropriate by the jurists asked to ratify them.[110]

A seeming paradox of legislation protecting the woodland, or more vigorous restrictions on use-rights, was that trees became useless excrescences for much of the population, limiting the rights that they still did enjoy. Many forest commoners treasured grazing rights and the fodder that could be stripped from trees more than the wood; infinitely more, if that wood was reserved for some distant fleet and the tree cast a shadow over the grass. Where Swedish officials marked oaks for the navy, peasants followed in their wake and opened up the scar, allowing rot to enter the tree, stunting its growth and eventually killing it.[111] Woodwards cutting browse for deer could accidentally produce the same effect.[112] The same was true on private estates where tenant farmers had no rights to the timber: 'if wee pore farmers take paines to plant young trees and sow Acornes, these great landlords will be sure to have the crop thereof: so that we have nothing but our labours for out hire, which indeed doth greatly discourage all honest men in that kind'.[113]

The truth was that there was a vast distance between a law being on the statute book and people obeying it. Hartlib noted it in the

---

[110] However, the offer of compensation to those potentially losing use-rights also made it unforceable from a fiscal point of view. Andrée Corvol, 'La decadence des forêts; Leimotiv', in Corvol, *La Forêt malade*, pp. 7–9, 13; C.C. Gillispie, *Science and polity in France. The end of the Old Regime* (Princeton, NJ: Princeton University Press, 2009), pp. 339–44, 356–60. Tamara L. Whited, *Forests and peasant politics in modern France* (New Haven, CT: Yale University Press, 2000), p. 23.

[111] Per Eliasson and Sven G. Nilsson, 'Rättat efter skogarnes auftagende – en miljöhistorisk undersökning av den svenska eken under 1700- och 1800-talen', *Bybeyggelsehistorisk Tidskrift* 37 (1999), pp. 46–51.

[112] Church, *Old thrift*, p. 18.

[113] Church, *Old thrift*, p. 9.

1650s: 'It is well known, we have good lawe, but it's better knowne, they are not executed.' A virtually identical sentiment was expressed regarding Danish laws in 1758: 'We surely do have the finest forest ordinances, but does one let the cat out of the bag by saying they are just observed in a few places?'[114] Yet this was already apparent as a problem as soon as laws were promulgated, and the laws themselves were full of loopholes. William Harrison noted as early as 1577 the egregious lapse in the Statute of 1543 that ruled when a coppice was cleared, 12 staddles were to be left, but there was nothing to stop these staddles being cut down the next time the coppice was felled so long as 12 new ones were left in turn. The consequence was no prospect of mature timber.[115] If licences to cut timber did not specify precisely where they applied, they could easily be used multiple times.[116] There was no shortage of law, noted Andrew Yarranton, 'as little put in practice as any Laws whatsoever'. But in a thrice he had a remedy: 'and I will make it appear that our fears and jealousies as to want of sufficient Timber, are groundless, provided that a short law were made'. Old habits died hard on all sides.[117]

Posterity

What increasingly marked writing on wood was its concern for, as we might say, intergenerational justice: a new conception of struggles over allocation. Propertied families had long been concerned with the inheritance of their holdings, and in that domain thinking ahead was nothing new. However, concern over wood appears to have presented something unusual in the scale of the *public* and *political* debate about the obligation to leave resources in a proper state for the future.

Trees planted by any individual might only be harvested by their grandchildren, or even more distant generations. In turn, people reaped what their ancestors had sown, and could reap no

---

[114] Hartlib, *Compleat husbandman*, p. 45; Fritzbøger, *Windfall for the magnates*, p. 240; also Corvol, 'La belles futaies d'antan', p. 30.

[115] Harrison, *Historical description*, f.91r; also repeated in Norden, *Surveyor's dialogue*, p. 213.

[116] Appuhn, *Forest on the sea*, p. 188.

[117] Yarranton, *England's improvement*, pp. 69-70.

more. As Noé Meurer put it in 1576 (echoing in fact language I have seen in court cases from the 1550s), forestry officials were to prevent anyone over-cutting wood, so that 'not they alone, but also their descendants, heirs and children, will always have from their woods what they need (*die notdurft*) for building and burning'.[118] By the eighteenth century in Germany it had become proverbial to commend the wisdom of forefathers in planting trees, and a story was told of how Emperor Maximilian II (r. 1562–76), on enquiring of a peasant in Italy why he was planting a tree received the answer that it was 'to honour God, and do the best for those coming after [*Nächste*]'.[119] As Evelyn put it in his famous *Sylva*, each generation was not born for itself, but for 'posterity'. The same word justifying action, '*posterité*', was employed in Colbert's great forest ordinance of 1669. This approach was decidedly original in addressing basic resources.[120]

Evelyn set his argument within a lineage; a wood supply was to be secured by respect for the order of familial authority. 'Posterity' was originally a notion that literally referred to one's progeny, and of course the notion of husbanding a family estate was familiar to the gentry and nobility of Europe, and to those much lesser proportions of the peasantry who could anticipate the possibility of inheriting the same land over generations. The great project of national tree planting demanded by Arthur Standish in the 1610s responded to a time when men were 'desiring to become heyres of their owne time, without respect had to such heyres as shall succeed them'. He thought that recent history contained a salutary lesson: 'forty years ago... the poorer sort scorned to eate a piece of meate roasted with sea-coles, which now the best Magistrates are constrained to do'.[121] In 1637, John Shaw thundered that 'every one ought to know that no man is born only for himself, and that Fathers are to provide for their Children; therefore if we would leave our Countrie to our Children, and have our Childrens

---

[118] Noé Meurer, *Jag und Forstrecht* (Frankfurt: Paul Keffeler, 1576), p. 5; see also Allmann, *Der Wald in der frühen Neuzeit*, pp. 103–4.

[119] This was told by Döbler in his 1680 book on the responsibilities of state officials, and repeated in Florinus, *Oeconomus Prudens*, p. 785 and Carlowitz, *Sylvicultura Oeconomica*, 2nd edition (Leipzig: Johann Friedrich Braun Erben, 1732), p. 70.

[120] Evelyn, *Sylva*, p. 111; Clarence Glacken, *Traces on the Rhodian shore*, p. 492.

[121] Around the same time Michael Drayton's *Poly-olbion* grumbled that no-one planted trees for posterity. Standish, *New directions* (1614), pp. 2, 26; Trevisan, 'The murmuring woods', p. 243.

Children enjoy the same, let us then providently forecast, to provide such materials for our Grand-children'.[122]

Such sentiments suited Evelyn very well: a royalist writer currying favour with a restored monarchy, praising the 'prudent *Ancestors*' of Charles II in contrast with the 'unhappy *Usurpers*' and 'late prodigious *Despoilers*' of the Commonwealth – adding for good measure that if a good number of royalists seemed to have been enthusiastic in grubbing up woodland, this was forced on them by the 'unparallel'd *Tyranny*' of the regime. Indeed, not least because of their use in creating the military hardware that underpinned a maritime power, the states of 'our *Oaks* [are] the truest *Oracles* of the *perpetuity* of our *happineß*'.[123] His arguments combined the idea of woodlands as a sensitive indicator of national well-being with the implicit claim, found frequently in subsequent centuries, that only a certain type of government or institution had the perpetual character and vision to ensure timber supplies. Ensuring that the 'the whole *Nation* were furnish'd for *posterity*' became both a defining mark, duty and legitimation of a royal regime that knew what was best for its subjects: 'his *Majesty* must assert his power, with a firme and high Resolution to *Reduce* these men to their due *Obedience*, and to a necessity of submitting to their *own*, and the *publick* utility'.[124] It also implied that the fortunes of the future were dependent on the present delivering to it at least as much wood as could be secured in the here and now. In a marginal subtitle in his work of 1607 John Norden had declared, 'A commoditie present should not depriue future times of a better.' It is a startling observation in a world raised on the novelty of the Brundtland Commission's definition of 'sustainable development' penned 380 years later. Norden was not referring to wood, but the issue we have elaborated at length in Chapter 1; it was potentially short-sighted to use enclosure to replace tillage with pasture.[125] But whether talking of 'need', 'commoditie' or 'utility' the idea was abroad that it was the responsibility of present society as a whole to bequeath the means to satisfy wants of future

---

[122] He published a number of agronomic tracts in the mid-1630s, but it is unclear who exactly he was. John Shaw, *Certaine easie and profitable points in husbandrie* (London: Barnard Alsop, 1637), p. 5; see also John Shaw, *Certaine helpes and remedies vnder God to prevent dearth and scarcitie* (London: B. Alsop, 1638).

[123] Evelyn, *Sylva*, p. 111.

[124] Evelyn, *Sylva*, p. 112.

[125] Norden, *Surveyor's dialogue*, p. 221.

generations. By the mid-eighteenth century, agricultural writer Thomas Hale could, alongside the public benefits of tree-planting, present it as a means of moral restoration: 'it is of all methods the best in which a man can make atonement to his successors for his own extravagance. He who sets about it with spirit, should consider he is working for himself, his heirs, and posterity.'[126]

How to do this? One solution was deceptively simple. Rock Church suggested that landlords should have three or four young trees set for every one that is cut, a policy already declared in parts of the continent. 'For by this meanes also we should have Wood and Timber perpetually without want... we might in very few yeeres haue the whole Realm sufficiently furnished with Wood, to serve our selves and posteritie for euer.'[127] According to him and others, it was simple dim-wittedness that did not see this done. A few decades later Sir Robert Gordon of Strauloch reckoned forests near Aberdeen had been 'entirely cut down through the carelessness of those concerned'.[128] Elsewhere Church suggested that government should make people plant five times as much as they felled.[129] It was already the case in the 1590s that a proposed lease of Crown woods included a stipulation to plant two trees for every one felled, and in 1577 William Harrison had expressed the hope, which he conceded unlikely to be fulfilled, that every land-holder with more than four acres would plant an acre of trees.[130]

The problem was that these solutions, so elegant and self-evident, were not actually happening. Hale went on, in the 1750s, to note that his call to moral reformation went unheeded: 'The heir cuts his wood without the least thought of providing for his heir.'[131] The ratios of planted to felled trees were not in fact a guarantee of success, because of the high attrition rate of young saplings. In naturally regenerating woodlands hundreds of thousands of plants might germinate in a single hectare, but only a tiny fraction, probably a few dozen, will

---

[126] Thomas Hale Esq., *A compleat body of husbandry. Containing rules for performing, in the most profitable manner, the whole business of the farmer and country gentleman... Compiled from the original papers of the late Thomas Hale... Illustrated with a great number of cuts...* vol. 1, 2nd edition (London: Tho. Osborne, Tho. Trye & G. Crowder, 1758–9), p. 287.
[127] Church, *Old thrift*, p. 23.
[128] Smout et al., *Native woodlands*, p. 46.
[129] Church, *Old thrift*, p. 163.
[130] CSPD 1591–4, pp. 288–9; Harrison, *Historical description*, f. 91r.
[131] Hale, *Compleat body*, p. 287.

ever grow into maturity. In 1652 Blith looked abroad for examples of a policy that might work.

> The sixt Prejudice [against improvement] is the not compelling men to plant woode where they do cut downe, then to set againe a treble proportion or more that they doe destroy, especially now so much of the gallant wood of the nation is exposed to sale: we forget that it is a mighty pillar in the upholding this poore island, and how honourable a custome it is in other nations, that they looke what timber they cut downe, they must plant five or ten times as much in stead thereof.[132]

Compulsion to replace felled trees had a long if sporadic history in Europe. In parts of the German Palatinate it was already found locally in 1344, again in 1478, 1528, and in larger forest ordinances of 1568 and 1608, and was quite widespread in sixteenth-century forest ordinances, especially in regard to oak and beech.[133] It was ordered in Venice in 1531.[134] Compulsion could be justified by the fact that too many people were too selfish; as Shaw put it, 'Surely the reason why this *Husbandrie* is not used, is because the profit thereof would not presently arise to our selves.'[135] Alternatively, the difficulty lay in 'the known untowardness of the major part of the people, who being wonderfully wedded to old customes, are not easily wonne by any new course'.[136] In other words, reverence for the settled practice of the past stymied attempts to be recalled gratefully in the future. So was the core of the problem that people had too great a sense of themselves *as* posterity, or not enough respect for their own posterity?

These contradictory messages illustrate how commentators had not yet got to the root of the problem. Nearly all of their rhetoric was directed at the supposed mismanagement of supply. No-one had much to say about demand. Evelyn praised the chimneys and stoves of the Netherlands and Germany as 'an extraordinary expedient of

---

[132] Blith added this to the 1652 edition of his book, possibly a reflection of debates about the use and fate of the forests at that time. Blith, *The English Improver improv'd*, f.6r.

[133] Allmann, *Der Wald in der frühen Neuzeit*, pp. 46, 110; Florinus, *Oeconomus Prudens*, p. 785.

[134] Appuhn, *Forest on the sea*, p. 138.

[135] Shaw may well have read Church, as some of his language is very similar to the earlier author's. Shaw, *Profitable pointes*, p. 5.

[136] Hartlib, *Compleat husband-man*, f.2v.

husbanding our *Fuel*. Plat and Robert Boyle conducted experiments on alternative fuels.[137] Yet only a very few occasions brought the issue of balance to the fore. One such was the burst of English naval construction after 1649 combined with debates about the selling off or leasing of the royal forests.[138] This prompted the appropriately named Silvanus Taylor to suggest that some 30,000 acres of Dean, New and Windsor Forests should be reserved and sown with oaks for 70–80 years, which would provide 150 acres of mature trees each year for the navy. He acknowledged that as it stood it was actually cheaper to get timber from New England than transport it 10–15 miles in England, but suggested that this supply would soon be logged out and remarked how Dutch blockades had cut off England from the Baltic. At the same time, he argued that the navy should estimate the number of ships needed in next 30–40 years, with projections for each year. Once this figure was known, the timber requirements could be demanded as rents from the lessees or purchasers of Crown land.[139] This would require the enclosure of the forests.

While these authors called on government to act, in the absence of intervention they appealed to a range of more or less estimable motives that might prompt the private landowner to change their ways. Silvanus Taylor appealed both to a supposedly natural inclination to provide for one's posterity, but also the spur to improvement as a godly mission and unfolding of providence: 'What, hath not God made us a Commonwealth... Are not we to bless God for it, by improving those blessings he bestows on us to the best advantage, that the many thousands unborn may bless God for the Change he hath wrought for us, by putting the opportunity of doing good in our hands?'[140] Private estates held the greater share of the nation's woodland. Another motive was, of course, profit. If, argued Evelyn, there were four fruit trees set in each of England's twenty-five million acres, the timber and produce would come to 10*d* per acre annually, earning some £2 million. This would be far better than the practice

---

[137] Evelyn, *Sylva*, p. 98.

[138] Morrison, 'Stuart forests', pp. 220–2.

[139] Silvanus Taylor, *Common-good; or, the improvement of commons, forests and chases, by inclosure, wherein the advantage of the poor, the common plenty of all, and the increase and preservation of timber, with other other things of common concernment* (London: Francis Tyton, 1652), p. 48. See also Morrison, 'Stuart forests', pp. 222–3.

[140] Taylor, *Common-good*, pp. 23–4, 45.

of turnip-planters uprooting hedgerows near London 'to give *Sun* to a few miserable *Roots*', although he failed to estimate the value of turnips that might have explained such behaviour.[141] In providing these kinds of calculations Evelyn and others encouraged the idea that the estate-owner's handling of his plantations was linked to the fate of the nation, a sentiment reinforced by the rise of the language of 'improvement' that will be discussed in Chapter 3. The desire for a perpetual wood supply was thereby closely linked to an ideology of *expansion*, both political and economic.

Husbandry manuals had long handled timber as part of the management of an estate and household, but its effects on the wider social order operated only indirectly by maintaining estates. Fitzherbert suggested in the 1520s that land unsuited for arable could be sown with acorns collected in the autumn, carefully stored and set in February or March, very likely reflecting a general practice. In 1557 Thomas Tusser recommended the same, along with the protection of young saplings to prevent grazing animals biting their tops off. As befits a text aimed at the stolid yeoman, Tusser was concerned above all with wood for fuel.[142] Cato, Theophastrus and Pliny were renowned for writing on these themes. But these tasks were undertaken for the benefit of the husbandman, whose success was not given any wider significance.

In the seventeenth century the ground shifted. Rock Church and John Evelyn wrote works that drew upon the *Hausväterliteratur* and classical tradition. They did so, however, in the context of demands that raised their focus to national concerns, or at least the concerns of a large part of political elites: the state of Crown lands and revenues, and the Naval Board's preoccupation with timber supplies that led to a request to the newly formed Royal Society to examine the issue. It was this context that gave a new resonance to often quite traditional advice. The setting up of a nursery on an estate became, for Evelyn, part of a 'universal plantation'.[143] Another significant change had become established in public debate by the mid-seventeenth century, as will be

---

[141] Evelyn, *Sylva*, pp. 177–8. Actually, it would come to almost £3 million on these figures, which underestimate the size of England, although Evelyn excluded fens and roadways.

[142] Fitzherbert, *Boke*, p. xlvi; Tusser, *Five hundred*, f.19v, 33, 43v; see also Heresbach, *Foure bookes*, pp. 100–9; Esmond Harris, Jeanette Harris and N.D.G. James, *Oak. A British history* (Macclesfield: Windgather, 2003), p. 19.

[143] Evelyn, *Sylva*, p. 2.

elaborated further in Chapter 3: men began to write with a conviction, almost a mania, that the dissemination of knowledge might act as a spur to better practice and general reformation. It was also becoming not only a question of *how many* trees were planted, but again in the mode of Renaissance agronomy, which trees were best suited to particular uses. By the seventeenth century commerce and exchange could lead one to contemplate the plantation of species previously unknown. Church looked to the introduction of firs, already extensively imported and used in shipping: 'and now of late, for want of other Timber, we begin to use them for building of houses: and I see no reason to the contrarie, but that in time we might have as goodly trees and whole Woods of this kind growing in our owne country (if men would endeavour to get them, as easily they may)'. He noted examples of firs already established by innovators in Scotland and Wales, some brought over from Newfoundland.[144] Evelyn argued that sown trees were in fact stronger and less prone to moss. Pruning should be diligently practised too, producing trees 'infinitely preferable to such as are abandon'd to *Nature*, and *Accident*, without this discipline'.[145] He singled out Felbrigg in Norfolk as an example of a leader in the field. In turn, the masters of Felbrigg became avid readers of *Sylva*, establishing a nursery in 1676 and planting large numbers of sweet chestnuts and firs (which died), walnuts, chestnuts, oaks and limes.[146]

Yet this work was not merely for money, or even national defence. It was also an act of beautification. Already in 1612 Church thought that trees should be set so they were 'much pleasing to the eye, especially when they grow & begin to beare leaves'. Coppice wood ('spring') 'greatly delighteth the sight wuth the varietie of his greene and pleasant colours, the harmonie and musicke of the birds is pleasant to the eare'. There was, of course, still plenty of talk of profit.[147] Ideally plantings could, as with Sir Harbotle Grimstone, 'wonderfully improve both the beauty, and the value of [the] *demeasnes*'.[148]

Sixteenth- and seventeenth-century Britain was living through an age of energy transition. Coal was substituting wood, which helps

---

[144] Church, *Old thrift*, pp. 7–8.
[145] Evelyn, *Sylva*, p. 3.
[146] R.W. Ketton-Cremer, *Felbrigg. The story of a house* (London: Rupert Hart-Davis, 1962), pp. 61–2.
[147] Church, *Old thrift*, pp. 10, 29–31.
[148] Evelyn, *Sylva*, p. 9.

explain why fears about scarcity in the island became increasingly focused on shipbuilding timber, or supplies to a few key industries that still used charcoal. In continental Europe the situation was quite different. Transition to a fossil fuel economy, with the exception of the Low Countries, did not occur until the mid-nineteenth century or later. In continental European states the 'wood shortage' debate would be conducted close to the heart of government and the emerging arts of political administration, which in turn would exercise a profound influence upon forestry, as we will see in later chapters. In England, by way of contrast, concern for posterity remained largely the concern of the improving gentleman or -woman who read *Sylva*, strolled down their stately avenues of perhaps exotic trees and contributed to national well-being through running a profitable estate, or at least hiring a good steward to run a profitable estate for them. Despite a flurry of interest among men associated with the early years of the Royal Society with the more efficient use of timber in shipbuilding and construction, public debate was largely framed by reissues of *Sylva* into the second half of the eighteenth century.[149] Posterity was first and foremost a family matter, in a rather traditional mode; the great projecting tracts of Standish or Silvanus Taylor were soon forgotten within the literature of arboriculture and nurserymen, and for the most part woodland management remained an adjunct to husbandry.

A curiously hybrid figure was Timothy Nourse. His *Campania Foelix* penned in the 1690s was in many ways a quite traditional, beefed-up manual for the country estate that was not much different from Columella. We find the commonplace chapters on coppicing, timber trees and fruit trees, as well as the admonition that 'Men are not born only for themselves, but must be mindful also of Posterity

---

[149] The colonies were an interestingly different case, where governors, perhaps viewing their charges as might the lord of an estate, were more prone to intervene. Richard Grove has traced this history in the St Helena Forest Act of 1731, but as we have seen, this was hardly a 'precocious programme of interventionist land management' seen in the context of what was the norm in many regions of Europe. Similarly, measures enacted to preserve timber in the Cape Colony were little different from those to be found in many a Dutch common. Grove, *Green imperialism*, pp. 109–11, 118–20, 123, 135, 141. On Dutch management practice, see the magisterial Jaap Buis, *Historia forestis. Nederlandse bosgeschiedenis* (Utrecht: HES, 1985); On England, Sharp, 'Timber, science, and economic reform'; and Anthony Turner, 'Natural philosophers, mathematical practitioners and timber in later 17th century England', *Nuncius* 9 (1994), pp. 619–31.

whether descending from themselves, or such as shall rise up in succeeding Ages', as a moral injunction to plant coppice-woods that might only mature beyond one's own life.[150] Attached to the end of this work, however, was an *Essay on the fuel of London*, an altogether different matter. By this time, 'sea-coal' had been the primary fuel of the city for many decades, and had given rise to debates over the impact on health of coalsmoke. John Evelyn (who else?) had published a tract on this subject, *Fumifugium*, in 1661, and managed to get an (unsuccessful) bill introduced to Parliament to limit emissions.[151] Nourse, an Oxford-educated Tory clergyman and Catholic convert of Newent in Gloucestershire, pondered the hazards of pollution and whether a return to wood might be advisable. We should not slip into labelling such men as prescient before their time. For all that coalsmoke might seem self-evidently a severe nuisance, to a large degree the debate over its health impact was not based on any direct evidence of a link between mortality and smoke, but rather more scholastic arguments about the nature of matter itself, and whether smoke was in fact composed of sharp particles that could damage the lungs when inhaled.[152]

For Nourse the idea of wood substituting coal raised three 'general points to be resolved'. 'The First is what Quantity of Wood may probably be sufficient, to serve the occasions of so vast a City? Next, whether such a sufficient Quantity may be found for this occasion? And Lastly, Whether the Profit and Benefit arising from this Exchange of Fuel, be greater than the Dammage we may suffer by a

---

[150] Timothy Nourse, *Campania Fœlix. Or, a discourse of the benefits and improvements of husbandry; containing directions for all manner of tillage, pasturage, and plantation*, 2nd edition (London: Tho. Bennet, 1700), p. 110.

[151] John Evelyn, *Fumifugium, or, The inconveniencie of the aer and smoak of London dissipated together with some remedies humbly proposed* (London: G.Bedel & T. Collins, 1661). See also Mark Jenner, 'The politics of London air. John Evelyn's Fumifugium and the Restoration', *The Historical Journal* 38 (1995), pp. 535–51; William Cavert, 'The environmental policy of Charles I. Coal smoke and the English monarchy 1624–40', *Journal of British Studies* 53 (2014), pp. 310–33; William Cavert, *The smoke of London. Energy and environment in the early modern city* (Cambridge: Cambridge University Press, 2016).

[152] Peter Brimblecombe, *The big smoke. A history of air pollution in London since medieval times* (London: Methuen, 1987), pp. 44–6; Evelyn, *Fumifugium*; on Nourse, see David Souden, 'Nourse, Timothy (c.1636–1699)', in *Oxford Dictionary of National Biography* (Oxford: Oxford University Press, 2004), www.oxforddnb.com/view/article/20376, accessed 19 Sep. 2014.

want of Sea-Coal?'[153] To answer these questions Nourse could draw on traditions established during the previous century of estimating yields and projecting future wood supplies by simple processes of multiplication, which we will discuss further in Chapter 5. He also operated in the wake of John Graunt and Gregory King's studies of the demography of London and national estimates of land use, and supply and demand for particular products differentiated by social group. Using these ideas he could become the last of the wood projectors of the seventeenth century.

Nourse estimated that London had 400,000–500,000 inhabitants, a quarter of whom being temporary visitors, by the expedient of reckoning each generation lived around 20 years and knowing that about 23,000 people died every year from the city's bills of mortality. There were 40,000 houses in the city and its suburbs with an average of nine chimneys. Each chimney would consume around a load of cordwood, and so total consumption was about 400,000 loads superficial.[154] He speculated that demand might actually be less because currently the veil of choking smoke over the city made it colder and without this pall the poor would have to burn less fuel.[155]

On the supply side he reckoned an acre of coppice would produce 60 'Cords or Loads of Wood', if felled every dozen years. Thus 'Sixty Thousand Acres of Land well planted with Wood, will afford us the quantity we are now seeking'.[156] To protect woods from theft there should be a ranger for every 1,000 acres, regulated by a court staffed by aldermen of the City of London. Each hundred acres would support four families, and give a return to the owner of 30 shillings per acre. The edges of coppices could be used for timber for 'Naval Magazines'.[157]

---

[153] Timothy Nourse, Of the fuel of London, in Campania Foelix, p. 349.

[154] 'Superficial' means a measure of stacked, not solid timber, so the real volume of timber is much lower. On Nourse's assumption that a load equals a cord, annual consumption would be a million cubic metres (superficial), although actual loads appear to have been smaller, which would lead to an estimated consumption of around 625,000 m³. Of course, Londoners mostly burned coal so these figures are entirely hypothetical. Nourse, On the fuel of London, pp. 350–1.

[155] Nourse, On the fuel of London, p. 361.

[156] This implies a coppice giving about 150 cubic metres superficial, 90 metres solid timber, or 8–9 cubic metres p.a. – extremely high even by modern standards although not impossible.

[157] Nourse, On the fuel of London, p. 355.

Nourse's estimates were probably not very accurate. The yield of coppice-wood was taken as given, and entirely unexplained. His essay was written as a potential solution to a problem that the vast majority of the population probably did not entertain at all, and it had no great impact. Yet the *Essay on the fuel on London* represents a transitory moment that both gathered together traditions of accounting wood resources and projecting potential yields, as so often based on the problem of supplying a particular location; and pointed towards an emerging concern for balance between demand and supply related to a new 'political arithmetic'. This equation, this balancing act that also had to extend across the generations, formalised a spectre that had sent a shiver down the official spine since late medieval times and that was particularly related to wood. As this question of balance came to be elaborated in the 'enlightened' eighteenth century, largely outside of England, the jurisdictional and administrative structures set up in the sixteenth and seventeenth century would play a profound role in how thinking and policy developed.

3 Ambition and Experiment, c. 1590–1740

Improvers

In 1649, Walter Blith, one-time officer in the Parliamentary army and now Midland farmer, continued his mission of national reformation with the publication of *The English improver, or, A new survey of husbandry discovering to the kingdome, that some land, both arable and pasture, may be advanced double or treble other land to a five or tenfold*... He did not rest on his laurels as the book quickly won renown, but demonstrated his commitment to his own message by bringing out *The English Improver Improved* three years later, thus making a virtue of the self-plagiarism beloved of contemporary scribes. The subtitle of these volumes encapsulated the ethic that Blith's publications seem to embody: calculating, pragmatic, attached to concrete and demonstrable methods: '*clearly demonstrated from principles of sound reason, ingenuity, and late but most certaine reall experiences, held forth under six peeces of improvement*'.[1]

---

[1] The 'six pieces' were floating meadows; draining boggy ground; ploughing and sowing exhausted pasture, with enclosure; composting and manuring; planting of woods; and 'moderate Improvement' of other lands 'by more common experiences'. Walter Blith, *The English improver, or, A new survey of husbandry discovering to the kingdome, that some land, both arable and pasture, may be advanced double or treble other land to a five or tenfold, and some to a twenty fold improvement, yea, some now not worth above one, or two shillings, per acree, be made worth thirty, or forty, if not more: clearly demonstrated from principles of sound reason, ingenuity, and late but most certaine reall experiences, held forth under six peeces of improvement* (London: J. Wright, 1649); Blith, *The English improver improv'd*. Joan Thirsk,

The idea or even 'project' of improvement has become a familiar theme in the historiography of environmental change. It has been viewed as the basis of an ideological assault on traditional and customary values, the dream of an engineered return to Eden, a fantasy of control, a merciless and remorseless utilitarian ethic.[2] In short, it encapsulates, for some, all of the hubristic vices that have led to our current condition of unsustainable development, and may well have been a major contributing factor to destroying previous ways of living that were, in fact, sustainable. The English statesman and prolific writer on education, knowledge and development, Francis Bacon, is sometimes presented as the father of this way of thinking.[3] As is so often the case, the detailed history of 'improvement' is both more prosaic and rather more complex. In the first decade of seventeenth century Bacon was in his forties and at last reaching high office after a chequered, if by any reasonable standards, blessed career at law and as a Member of Parliament. He endured fluctuating fame and fortune by a typically Tudor mix of patronage, misalliance and occasional writing. At this moment, when Bacon began to publish his influential works, 'improvement' had a very limited meaning. It referred to the augmentation of rental value, and for a long time yet it would generally be used to refer to practices that raised the rent of land, without any wider implications. However, around this time preachers began to use the term metaphorically, to talk about augmenting the qualities of a person, implying a calculus of virtue as well as landed income. It was this manoeuvre that began to shift the idea of 'improvement' in its more general usage, to shape it into a sensibility that might guide an ambitious maritime power.[4]

By the time Blith was writing, 'improving' was still rooted in its traditional usage, as a very concrete investment in the land. While the word had become unhitched from its more precise reference to a

'Blith, Walter (*bap.* 1605, d. 1654)', in *Oxford Dictionary of National Biography* (Oxford: Oxford University Press, 2004).

[2] For varieties of these arguments, in much more nuanced forms than are presented here, see Carolyn Merchant, *Reinventing Eden. The fate of nature in Western culture* (New York: Routledge, 2003); Richard Drayton, *Nature's government. Science, Imperial Britain, and the 'Improvement' of the world* (New Haven, CT: Yale University Press, 2000); John C. Weaver, *The Great Land Rush and the making of the modern world* (Montreal: McGill-Queen's University Press, 2003).

[3] Merchant, *The death of nature*, pp. 176–90.

[4] Warde, 'The idea of improvement', pp. 127–48.

higher monetary return, it was still a description of the activities that would have that end result. Yet immediately after this moment, usage of the term exploded, the task of improvement becoming an exhortation to betterment of any kind, going far beyond its agrarian roots. What also became a core aspect of this exhortation was the *improver.* Improvement was undertaken by a certain kind of person, displaying virtue and ingenuity. And rather than representing a dismal narrowing of the human capabilities and ambitions to a utilitarian core, the notion of 'improvement' had power because of its appeal to what we might now call 'self-improvement' or 'character-building'. In turn, the multiplication of improvers within the nation would lead to an equivalent process of national regeneration and expansion. Thus could the improvement of trade, arts, navigation, fruit-trees, the military, London and any number of other things be part of a common mission engaged in *England's Improvement*, by the title of Andrew Yarranton's publication of 1677. So too did this thinking apply to colonial endeavours, as we find in Gerard Boate's path-breaking *Ireland's Natural History* of 1657, that discussed the improving properties of lime and ashes in soils. Private virtues, and the resulting profits, became harnessed to a vision of national progress.[5]

Thus the striving for greater rents became intimately connected with an educational ethos that stretched at least as far back as the early sixteenth-century works of Desiderius Erasmus. Sermons played a role in promoting this ethos; so did educational tracts, as well as texts on husbandry, and all the unrecorded allusions and allegories of everyday conversation.[6] But not just anyone could become an improver. His was a special kind of exemplary character, and it may be that the popularity

[5] Yarranton, *England's improvement*; John Smith, *England's improvement reviv'd digested into six books* (London: Tho. Newcomb, 1670); Gerald Boate, *Irelands naturall history being a true and ample description of its situation, greatness, shape, and nature, of its hills, woods, heaths, bogs, of its fruitfull parts, and profitable grounds* (London: John Wright, 1657); Adam Fox, 'Printed questionnaires, research networks, and the discovery of the British Isles, 1650–1800', *The Historical Journal* 53 (2010), pp. 595–6; see discussion in Paul Slack, *The invention of improvement. Information and material progress in seventeenth-century England* (Oxford: Oxford University Press, 2014), pp. 4–5.

[6] Warde, 'Idea of improvement'. Surprisingly, 'improvement' does not even have an index mention in the great work of Charles Webster, although it is very much about this nexus in mid-seventeenth-century English life. Charles Webster, *The great instauration. Science, medicine and reform 1626–1660* (London: Duckworth, 1975).

of the term was also linked to the ill-repute of a precursor, 'projectors' as a result of various ill-starred schemes for economic development that often seemed little more than ways to extract money out of gullible or corrupt government ministers.[7] Writers were keen to evoke exemplary improvers as a club of earthly saints to which one might aspire to join. Herefordshire was 'the Countrey where *Rowland Vaughan* began his Waterworks; and I can name you a great number of admirable contrivers for the publick good', opined one.[8] You could look to the example of:

> The Lord *Scudamore*... a rare example, for the well-ordering
> of all his family, a great preserver of woods against the day
> of *Englands* need, maintaining laudable hospitality regularly
> bounded with due sobriety, and alwayes keeping able servants
> to promote the best expediencies of all kinds of Agriculture. And
> Sr. *H. L.* hath heartily prosecuted the same encouragements.
> Our learned Mr. *B.H.* drives on the same design, as far as the
> glances of a most sedulous imployment will permit. Mr. *R.* of *L.*
> is excellently apt, and constantly diligent in the pursuit as well of
> delicacies, as necessaries. Mr. *S.* of *W.* hath in few yeares raised
> an under-tenement, from 8^l. yearly, & so rented, to be well worth
> 60^l. yearly, and so rented, or thereabouts. He never failes in any
> point of good husbandry.[9]

Indeed, the precise virtues of these men were less clear than the fact they were virtuous. If anything, they were model *Hausväter* in the manner promoted ever since Xenophon (see Chapter 1). The activity of these good husbands, however, was now being more directly linked to the 'publick good'. A stand of trees not grubbed up was a resource for the navy. Wealth was used for the succour of the deserving poor, as had been admonished by Elizabethan and Jacobean governments in hard times.[10] These men were sober, industrious, innovative and getting richer.

    Improvers were a forward-looking and rather comfortably-off version of the honest labourer, and labour itself was a godly virtue that

---

[7] Thirsk, *Economic policy*.
[8] Blith, *The English Improver improv'd*, p. 37.
[9] Blith, *The English Improver improv'd*, pp. 37–8.
[10] Hindle, 'Dearth, fasting and alms'.

would get its just reward. Yet there remained a distinction between the virtues of the 'industrious' labourer and the *innovative* capacities of the improver.[11] Improvement would lead to the expansion of tillage and the greater provision of bread that had so worried sixteenth-century polities, examined in Chapter 1. The Book of Proverbs provided rhetorical underpinning to this endeavour:

> He that tilleth his land shall be satisfied with bread: but he that followeth vain persons is void of understanding. (Proverbs 12:11) Love not sleep, lest thou come to poverty; open thine eyes, and thou shalt be satisfied with bread. (Proverbs 20:13)

In a world saturated with providence, was it possible to imagine that virtuous men would *not* be rewarded for their efforts? Improvement meant the implementation of best practice and openness to the wisdom that agricultural writers could provide. But if all these could be combined, it was reasonable to expect that the soil would respond in kind; 'the people being industrious... there should be found victuals ynoughe at the full in all bounty to suffice them all'.[12] As Blith put it, with what seems in hindsight an extraordinary blind optimism,

> All sorts of lands, of what nature or quality soever they be, under what Climate soever, of what constitution of condition soever, of what face or character soever they be (unless it be such as Naturally participates of so much fatnesse, which Artificially it may be raised unto) will admit of a very large Improvement.[13]

Yet improvers be warned, if godly improvers needed such a warning, that in the final reckoning the divinity and not themselves was the source of fecundity and success. Did the Psalm not state the rules of success and failure clearly? 'He that planteth and watereth are nothing of themselves, but God alone, who by his gracious blessing giueth a

---

[11] On labourers, see Muldrew, *Food, energy and the creation of industriousness*, ch. 7; for a survey of the language of industriousness, see Alexis D. Litvine, 'The industrious revolution, the industriousness discourse, and the development of modern economies', *Historical Journal* 72(2) (2014), pp. 531–70.

[12] Hakluyt, cited in Muldrew, *Food, energy and the creation of industriousness*, p. 303.

[13] Blith, *The English Improver improv'd*, p. 17.

most happy increase' (1 Corinth 3.7), and 'So saith the Prophet: A
fruitfull land God maketh barren, for the sins of them that dwel
therein' (Psal 1.7.34).[14] Samuel Hartlib reminded his readers that
the husbandman must always 'walk as becometh a Christian, in all
Sobriety, Righteuousnesse and Godlinesse; not to trust in confidence
in his own labours, and good Husbandry; but on the Lord that hath
made all things'.[15] It did not much trouble the improving mind that the
Lord was socially selective in distributing those blessings that inspired
confidence and encouraged experimentation. It was the wealthier land-
holder who in practice could proceed with less fear about 'the many
Contingences which lie beyond his Care and Foresight'.[16] Somehow
the patriarch of a solid gentry household was able to scrape together
the capital, confidence and character that counteracted disincentives
to innovate that were listed by the Tory cleric Timothy Nourse at the
end of the century: fear of being laughed at by neighbours, singled
out for mockery at the marketplace, as well as 'The streightness of...
Circumstances [that] will not suffer them to venture a certain Expence
upon an uncertain Return.'[17] That God might assign worldly wealth
and good character in a similar manner was entirely in keeping the
expectations of the age. For rich beneficiaries of such providence, He
did not act in mysterious ways.

Across the seventeenth century a rising tide of 'improvers'
emerged. The godly could hardly envisage failure, never mind actual
environmental degradation as a result of their efforts to improve yields.
Far from a concern for limits, critique was levelled squarely at those
who rejected or were indifferent to improvement. It was a question
of character. We know most, of course, about those who left behind a
paper trail of correspondence or estate records indicating enthusiasm
for experiment, or burgeoning yields and new crops. But we also find
traces of the mood in the endeavours of tenant farmers or yeomen who
gradually adopted new crops, watched and noted the results of innovatory techniques, or indeed might be pushed into some desperate expedient by inclement times. In the end, the improver knew that virtue was

---

[14] Cited in J. Moore, *A target for tillage briefly containing the most necessary, pretious,
and profitable vse thereof both for king and state* (London: William Jones, 1612),
pp. 6, 14.

[15] Hartlib, *The compleat husband-man*, p. 81.

[16] Nourse, *Campania Fœlix*, p. 39.

[17] Nourse, *Campania Fœlix*, p. 39.

not enough: one also needed knowledge. It might be, as Gabriel Plattes averred, that 'Nature is no niggard, but giveth riches to all that are industrious'.[18] Industry, however, had to be wedded with knowledge of what nature demanded. Hence Francis Bacon's unforgettable injunction that 'nature is only to be commanded in obeying her'.[19]

Yet here is the strange twist: one of the legacies of that closer investigation of nature demanded by the improver, as we will see in Chapter 6, was a new understanding of ecological process that also had deep roots in the Paracelsian experiments we met in Chapter 1, and that would give rise to doubts. Perhaps the lack of improvement was not the long-run problem? Could fertility decline as well as be enhanced? But first would come two centuries of haranguing, self-important optimism.

Bacon's precept has frequently been seen as an irreversible step down the road to secularisation, a firm if elegantly executed shove that displaced the theologian in favour of the empiricist. Yet as is now widely recognised in the history of science, it was no such thing. If the idea of the improver as a model Christian made the enhancement of profit and agricultural innovation the badges of heavenly favour, then the acquisition of the knowledge necessary to this process became part and parcel of the mission; and nature itself was imagined as the raw material on which godly faculties could act to demonstrate their virtuous properties. The deity had left enough traces of the Edenic state for the sharp-eyed and well-informed to strive for its 'restauration'.[20] What Bacon did decry was the Aristotelian preoccupation with final causes

---

[18] Gabriel Plattes, *A discovery of infinite treasure, hidden since the worlds beginning* (London: George Hutton, 1639), p. 78. This also reflected Francis Bacon's view that *industry* and *utility* were key characteristics of the virtuous investigator, as a critique of dillentantish and undirected habits of natural history in Elizabeth's reign. See Paula Findlen, 'Francis Bacon and the reform of natural history in the seventeenth century', in Donald R. Kelley (ed.), *History and the disciplines. The reclassification of knowledge in early modern Europe* (Rochester, NY: University of Rochester Press, 1997), pp. 239–60; also Webster, *The great instauration*, pp. 356–7.

[19] Francis Bacon, *Novum Organum*, in *Works of Francis Bacon*, ed. Basil Montagu (London: William Pickering, 1825), p. 157; an earlier version from a speech in 1592 proclaimed, 'if we would be led by [nature] in invention, we should command her in action'. Cited in Stephen Gaukroger, *Francis Bacon and the transformation of early-modern philosophy* (Cambridge: Cambridge University Press, 2001), p. 72.

[20] Nourse, *Campania Fœlix*, p. 2; Keith Thomas, *Man and the natural world* (London: Penguin, 1984), p. 256; Peter Harrison, *The Bible, Protestantism, and the rise of natural science* (Cambridge: Cambridge University Press, 1998), pp. 226–49; Webster, *The great instauration*, pp. 324–9; Gaukroger, *Francis Bacon*, pp. 75–83 and

and teleological reasoning in explaining material phenomena, following
the Greek philosopher Epicurus. The proper activity of the investigator
should be to assign 'the causes of particular things to the necessity of
matter'.[21] This whole enterprise was expressed, posthumously, in the
collected writings of Thomas Hale, echoing the master but with greater
clarity nearly a century and a half after Bacon's *Novum Organum*:

> It has pleased the creator of the earth, to cover it with different
> soils; and in some places to leave it more barren, in others naturally
> improved. We are to use our understanding in observing what is
> the kind of that natural improvement; and our industry in imitating
> nature is obeying God.[22]

Knowledge

We have seen in Chapter 1 the great esteem attached to experience in
agricultural discourse. 'Experience' in the Aristotelian usage meant the
'usual', and hence one could be 'expert' (not yet 'an expert') if a particular activity had been mastered as a commonplace.[23] This meaning,
seeing knowledge as standing on an accumulating bedrock of time, has

on Italian developments, pp. 92–3. Bacon did, however, distinguish clearly between
natural and theological knowledge. See Francis Bacon, *The advancement of learning*,
ed. William Aldis Wright (Oxford: Clarendon [1605], 1868), Book II, pp. 108–14;
another source that valorised labour as the route back to a golden age was Virgil's
Georgics. A. Low, *The Georgic revolution* (Princeton, NJ: Princeton University Press,
1985), pp. 126–42. On similar views in France, Chandra Mukerji, 'The great forest
survey of 1669–1671. The use of archives for political reform', *Social Studies of
Science* 37(2) (2007), p. 229; on generic argument that gardening was a restoration
of Eden, see Harold J. Cook, *Matters of exchange. Commerce, medicine and science
in the Dutch golden age* (New Haven, CT: Yale University Press, 2007), p. 318; and
John Prest, *The garden of Eden. The botanic garden and the re-creation of paradise*
(New Haven, CT: Yale University Press, 1981).

[21] Bacon cited in John Bellamy Foster, *Marx's ecology. Materialism and nature*
(New York: Monthly Review Press, 2000), pp. 40–1. While 'proponents of the new
science', to use the phrase of Harold Cook, may have rejected teleology in explaining
particulars they certainly did not abandon it in the general (contrary to Cook's argument), and indeed revived it in new forms in physico-theological writing. Cook,
Matters of exchange, p. 6.

[22] Hale, *A compleat body of husbandry*, p. 112.

[23] For a discussion in the context of renaissance natural history, see Ogilvie, *The science
of describing*, pp. 17–21; on the word 'expert', see Eric H. Ash, 'Expertise and the

not yet vanished today. For Francis Bacon, experience was no more or no less important than for any other writer of the time. However, in his direct challenge to Aristotle's methods in the *Advancement of Learning* of 1607, and *Novum Organum* of 1620, he sought to fundamentally shift the grounds on which experience stood. Thinking, he argued, was worth nothing if it was rooted in the *habitual*.[24] It was a grave weakness of the human mind that it was so easily overwhelmed by the comforts of the familiar, the desire for order, and the need to avoid contradiction. The experience of such minds was beholden to unreflected and probably erroneous prejudices that Bacon named 'idols':

> idols and false notions which are now in possession of the human understanding, and have taken deep root therein, not only so beset men's minds that truth can hardly find entrance, but even after entrance is obtained, they will again in the very instauration of the sciences meet and trouble us, unless men being forewarned of the danger fortify themselves as far as may be against their assaults.[25]

This kind of experience was the experience of being trapped in Plato's cave. Bacon demanded that these idols must be killed, and only when they were slain could experience proceed on the basis of induction to discover the truth of the world. To revert to explanations simply from their established antiquity or as the arcane property of occult masters was to engage in 'shifts of ignorance'.[26] Bacon made experience

---

early modern state', in Eric H. Ash, 'Expertise. Practical knowledge and the early modern state', *Osiris* 25 (2010), p. 4.

[24] Bacon, *Advancement of Learning*. His aversion to Aristotle may already have been established in his university years during the 1570s. Gaukroger, *Francis Bacon*, p. 43. For a biographical account of Bacon, see Lisa Jardine and Alan Stewart, *Hostage to fortune. The troubled life of Francis Bacon* (London: Gollancz, 1998).

[25] Much of the content of the *Novum Organum* had been developed since at least the 1590s. Bacon, *Novum Organum*, XXXVIII; see Gaukroger, *Francis Bacon*, pp. 106-7, 118-20. In the 1640s, now inveighing against the Descartian critics of Aristotelianism in favour of his own brand of experimental empiricism, a young William Petty declared in a letter to Samuel Hartlib how he 'never knew any man who had once tasted the sweetness of experimental knowledge that ever afterward lusted after the Vaporous garlick & Onions of phantasmaticall seeming philosophy'. Cited in Ted McCormick, *William Petty and the ambitions of political arithmetic* (Oxford: Oxford University Press, 2009), p. 64.

[26] Francis Bacon, *Sylva sylvarum; or A naturall historie In ten centuries* (London: William Rawling, 1627), p. 12. For Restoration critics of theorising without empirical

a sceptical endeavour, which was by no means entirely new given that the knowledge of the ancients, as we have seen in Chapter 1, was already far from uncritically received. In fact, he stood as a particularly successful self-promoter amid a stream of such men, such as the less renowned Hugh Plat whom we have met, or the highly influential Paracelsus, who scathingly declared:

> I do not compile my textbooks from excerpts of Hippocrates or Galen. In ceaseless toil I create them anew, founding them upon experience. If I want to prove anything I do so not by quoting authorities but by experiment and reasoning.[27]

This would become the tediously rehearsed clarion call of every agronomic writer who thought himself worth their salt for the next three centuries. It was a self-vision that displayed extraordinary faith in the wit and character of the observer to transcend the accretions of mere customary knowledge and discover the truth. Of course, Paracelsus is not generally remembered as a founder of empiricism because he left behind the unfortunate hostage of a set of chemical and medical theories that turned out to be wrong.

Bacon and his peers were not sceptical about induction itself, as David Hume would be so strikingly over a century later.[28] And it is a little hard to see how Bacon's sceptic is any different from the peasant farmer described by Jacques Bernouilli in the *Ars conjectandi*, published posthumously in 1721, who was adept at drawing inferences from the effects of weather and circumstances on crops. But the peasant did not know how to express himself, or have the correct deportment. Thus was he no improver. Indeed, it is clear that renaissance naturalists or agronomists were not at all averse to drawing information from the lowly, but they very rarely

foundation, such as Glanvill, see Barbara Shapiro, *A culture of fact. England, 1550–1720* (Ithaca, NY: Cornell University Press, 2000), p. 147.

[27] Cited in Ian Hacking, *The emergence of probability*, 2nd edition (Cambridge: Cambridge University Press, 2006), p. 40. On the wider culture of experimentation in Elizabethan London, see Harkness, *The Jewel House*.

[28] Nevertheless, Hume's scepticism led him to insist upon the importance of personal judgement in a fashion not dissimilar to the attribution of trust among seventeenth-century thinkers. David Hume, *A treatise of human nature. Being an attempt to introduce the experimental method of reasoning in moral subjects* (London: James Noon, 1739).

permitted the lowly to stand forward as exemplars or quoted them directly as bearers of knowledge.[29] Bacon's works both formed and gave licence to men who saw themselves as improvers, and helped place the opposition to improvement into a place of backwardness, an archaic mode of being. Equally, Bacon forcefully promulgated an argument that knowledge of nature and knowledge of good policy were in essence the same thing, 'For there is a great consent between the rules of nature, and the true rules of policy: the one being nothing else but an order of government in the world, and the other an order in the government of an estate.'[30] By the end of his life, Bacon had made the study of natural history 'the foundation of all', in both the development of knowledge and the polity.[31] In truth, neither Bacon himself nor his many followers were so blinkered as to treat every problem as a *tabula rasa*. Yet the repeated thrust of Bacon's aphorisms could instil that idea that the old kind of experience was actually holding improvement back. What would be needed was a new kind of empiricism that rested on the ability of the improver to wrestle free of all those idols (except, perhaps, the genius of Bacon himself); a 'thoughtful prudence' in regard to the learning of the past which described well a certain gentlemanly self-identity.[32]

Some situations demanded new knowledge with greater forcefulness than others. The first attempt to write a general 'natural history' of a region in English came from the pen of a Dutch physician writing about Ireland. Gerard Boate was an adherent of the Parliamentary cause, although previously appointed to the king. He began to write on Ireland in 1644 where his brother was settled, despite never having visited it and relying on second-hand reports from said brother, and the surveyor-general Sir William Parsons. In 1649 he secured a position in Cromwell's army but would die soon after his arrival in Dublin. His notes were edited and published by Samuel Hartlib in 1652 as a *Natural History of Ireland*.[33] What was both original and striking about the work, despite Boate's personal distance, was his addressing

[29] Hacking, *Emergence*, p. xxvi; see for example, Ogilvie, *Science of describing*, p. 56.
[30] Bacon, cited in Gaukroger, *Francis Bacon*, p. 17.
[31] Findlen, 'Francis Bacon', p. 240.
[32] Cited in Gaukroger, *Francis Bacon*, p. 122.
[33] Elizabeth Baigent, 'Boate, Gerard (1604–1650)', in *Oxford Dictionary of National Biography* (Oxford: Oxford University Press, 2004); Webster, *The great instauration*, p. 429.

of a problem of knowledge bound up with the process of colonisation and plantation. How did you improve a place of which you knew little, and that apparently had no traditions of much value? Boate's answer was that you systematically gathered information from scratch, preferably of course through the eyes of the planter community, and thus produced one of the first works of economic geography.

The cleric John Dury, an ardent Protestant and educational reformer who wrote a tract in 1649 on the proper ordering of libraries, wrote the introduction to Hartlib's edit of Boate's notes. 'I can conceive none more profitable in Nature', he declared,

> than that of Husbandry. For whether we reflect upon the first settlement of a Plantation, to prosper it, or upon the wealth of a Nation that is planted to increase it, this is the Head spring of al the native Commerce & Trading... Now to advance Husbandry either in the production and perfection of earthly benefits... I know nothing more usefull, than to have the knowledg of the Natural History of each Nation advanced & perfected: For as it is evident, that except the benefits which God by Nature hath bestowed upon each Country bee known, there can be no Industrie used towards the improvement and Husbandry thereof.[34]

Boate's work provided a template and exemplar for the systematic gathering of useful knowledge that found an echo in the English county studies of Robert Plot in the 1670s and 1680s, and Robert Boyle's outline of 'General Heads for the Natural History of a Country', themselves an echo of earlier endeavours by surveyor and cartographer John Norden and the rather less exact chorographical 'praise' works of men like John Speed and William Camden. In the same period colonial officials were compiling reports as they went about their duties, searching for resources such as timber, medicines and valuable crops in South Asia and the Dutch East Indies. The application of natural history both domestically and in the colonies can both be seen as simultaneous outgrowths of a desire to harness knowledge to power, although some writers in the seventeenth and eighteenth centuries complained that colonial natural history was simply a glamorous and very expensive

---

[34] John Dury, in Boate, *Naturall history*, p. 4.

version of work that could better be done at home.[35] But it was the peculiarly blank canvas of an occupied colony that demanded and justified the greatest effort of manufacturing a new experience of it.

The successor to the *Natural History* was William Petty's *Anatomy of Ireland*, published in 1691. The slippery Petty is still considered the founder of 'political arithmetic', the quantitative framing of a polity through compiling records on land use, demography, economic activity and fiscal returns. He learned to learn, especially the art of mathematics, as a student in the Netherlands and France and mixed with luminaries such as Gassendi, Hobbes and Mersenne. Petty prospered under the Cromwellian regime to become general surveyor of Ireland after brief stints working with the Hartlib circle, as an Oxford academic and a private physician, and in the 1650s both created knowledge and a new land by being the lead official in the surveys that facilitated the massive expropriations and plantations of those years in Ireland. After the Restoration, Petty easily adapted to the monarchical regime.[36] He bequeathed a more refined model of what the creation of new knowledge, of new experience, might be. In truth, Petty was rather inconsistent in the rigour he applied. After the empirical care with which he conducted the 'Down Survey' of Irish land, his 'political arithmetic' generally included a mishmash of both carefully collected datasets and fantastical improving projects, leavening the limited amount of information that was in fact available to him with breathtaking extrapolations and what we might somewhat generously call 'guestimates'. In short, he showed himself in practice

---

[35] Robert Plot, *The natural history of Oxfordshire, being an essay toward the natural history of England* (London: Moses Pits & Millers, 1677); Robert Plot, *The natural history of Staffordshire* (London: Theater, 1686); Robert Boyle, *General heads for the natural history of a country great or small drawn out for the use of travellers and navigators* (London: J. Taylor & S. Hedford, 1692); Alix Cooper, *Inventing the indigenous. Local knowledge and natural history in early modern Europe* (Cambridge: Cambridge University Press, 2007), pp. 119–20; Emma Spary, '"Peaches which the patriarchs lacked". Natural history, natural resources, and the natural economy in France', *History of Political Economy* 35(Suppl. 1) (2003), pp. 14–41; 'Hartley, 'Exploring', pp. 232–3; McCrae, *God speed the plough*, ch. 8; Slack, *The invention of improvement*, pp. 16–31, see also Fox, 'Printed questionnaires'; Cook, *Matters of exchange*, pp. 305–8.

[36] Toby Barnard, 'Petty, Sir William (1623–1687)', in *Oxford Dictionary of National Biography* (Oxford: Oxford University Press, 2004); for a recent biographical study of Petty and political arithmetic, see McCormick, *William Petty*; Webster, *The great instauration*, pp. 435–43.

to be prone to several of the vices of the mind identified by Bacon. But he also pointed the way to a future, by which a land's fortune could be anatomised, turned into numbers, and predicted. The tools to do this would be a powerful spur to imagining a land that might *fail* as much as a route to success. We will return to these themes, and Petty, in Chapters 4 and 5.

Discovering ways to improve on the 'mere Irish' was one matter. How about in long-settled and so-civilised England?: 'our English husbandmen are allowed by all nations to have a genius in Agriculture superior to those in any other country, yet it is rare to find one among them that ever attempts any new discovery; or even can give any other reason for what he does, than that his father did the same before him', lamented Richard Bradley in 1727. The bulk of farmers had not, it seemed, moved beyond Gervase Markham's 'clowns' a century before. This recalcitrance provided Bradley for the justification of his writings 'to enquire into the nature of such lands that are most capable of improvement, and to propose the most proper method for fertilizing them'. The ensuing improvement would be 'like a new acquisition of territories to our nation'.[37] Bradley doubtless exaggerated the ignorance and sloth of farmers, as did nearly every writer with a book to sell. His own expertise perhaps rested mostly on enthusiasm, a knack in acquiring recommendations from influential patrons such as James Petiver and Sir Hans Sloane, and tireless correspondence. Yet he attained (but probably did not often warm) the first chair of botany at Cambridge in 1724.[38] His career and writings, like those of Boate and Petty, exemplify the essential unity of this quest for new knowledge in the early Enlightenment, mapping spaces but also delving into the inner life of plants and soils, as the prerequisite to improving a yield, a rent, a nation. The quest was carried out by experts whose prestige rested above all on a self-identification as improvers, as being of the right turn of mind, combined with the financial means and communicative skills to get their work (or others' work under their own name) printed.[39]

[37] Richard Bradley, *A general treatise of agriculture, both philosophical and practical* (London: W. Johnston etc., 1757 [1727]), pp. 1, 3–4.
[38] Frank N. Egerton, 'Bradley, Richard (1688?–1732)', in *Oxford Dictionary of National Biography* (Oxford: Oxford University Press, 2004).
[39] On this movement in regard to timber, see Sharp, 'Timber, science, and economic reform'.

We have already met in Chapter 2 another of these self-certified savants, who in fact exploited a much wider network of thinkers and experimenters, the royalist gentleman John Evelyn. Best known for his writings on trees and his extensive diaries, these were but a subset of his wide horticultural interests. On 29 April 1675 he presented the Royal Society with *A philosophical discourse on Earth relating to the Culture and Improvement of Vegetation, and the Propagation of Plants*, publishing it the following year. Evelyn suggested there were no fewer than 179 million kinds of earth; mercifully, as John Houghton noted, 'tho' he names but few'.[40] And indeed reading it can feel like wading through a vast sea of mud. In this inquiry Evelyn sought to focus on first principles, isolating the processes that lead, eventually, to the final desired result. Without earth, he declares, 'there could hardly be any such thing [vegetation] in Nature'.[41] With this justification Evelyn the gardener devoted not just a day in the life of the Royal Society, but an entire book to the properties of the soil. His attention was literally microscopic, employing the newly invented instrument to inform us on the form of different kinds of dung.[42]

Improvers such as Blith, his contemporaries Cressy Dymock and Andrew Yarranton, or the many correspondents of John Houghton and Richard Bradley into the eighteenth century were largely concerned with discussing the efficacy of agricultural techniques. Nevertheless, since Gervase Markham had foregrounded knowledge of the soil, and Hugh Plat translated the Paracelsian preoccupation about a putative life-giving element, a strand of thinking had become intertwined with agrarian thought that viewed knowledge of the intimate processes of germination and growth as being crucial to agricultural success. These preoccupations featured prominently in widely read compendia such as John Worlidge's *Systema agriculturae* of 1669, a great synthesis of current knowledge poured into the vessel shaped by the classic writers and their elaboration by Charles Estienne.[43] Hence Evelyn squinted

---

[40] John Evelyn, *A philosophical discourse on Earth relating to the Culture and Improvement of Vegetation, and the Propagation of Plants, etc.* (London: John Martyn, 1676); John Houghton, *A collection for the improvement of husbandry and trade* (London: Woodman & Lyon, 1727–8), p. 12.

[41] Evelyn, *Philosophical discourse*, p. 9.

[42] Evelyn, *Philosophical discourse*, pp. 36–7.

[43] Worlidge, *Systema agriculturae*.

down his microscope at dung. Agriculture came closer to botany. The botanist Nehemiah Grew, born in 1641, was educated at Pembroke College in Cambridge and Leiden and became a physician in Coventry; through word of mouth his investigations came to the attention of leading figures in the Royal Society. By the 1670s he secured funding from the Society to pursue his researches, becoming a secretary to the organisation, alongside teaching at Gresham College in London.[44] Seeing himself an anatomist of plants, Grew was a pioneer in revealing their physiology, but for him this painstaking work was a teasing enterprise and a laborious courtship:

> For what we obtain of *Nature*, we must not do it by commanding, but by courting of Her. Those that woo Her, may possibly have her for their Wife; but She is not so common, as to prostitute her self to the best behaved *Wit*, which only practiseth upon it self, and is not applied to her. I mean, that where ever Men will go beyond Phansie and Imagination, depending upon the Conduct of *Divine Wisdom*, they must Labour, Hope and Persevere.[45]

Nature's jewel house was not easily prised open. Simple observation could not reveal how and why things happened; as long as improvers were mired in mere description of nature and the agriculture that they found, innovation could not emerge. But neither was abstract thought adequate to the task: 'reason', Blith declared, 'hath sometime deceived me, and so many others, but Experience never shall'.[46] '[T]rue *Axiomes* must be drawne form plaine Experience, and not from doubtfull', wrote the editor of Bacon's posthumous collection *Sylva sylvarum* of 1627.[47] But why should one not also doubt one's experience?

There was a test by which the mettle of experience forged in the Baconian crucible could be measured: 'unlesse you can produce me some Experiment, wherein my directions have been observed, and

---

[44] Michael Hunter, 'Grew, Nehemiah (*bap.* 1641, *d.* 1712)', in *Oxford Dictionary of National Biography* (Oxford: Oxford University Press, May 2009).

[45] Nehemiah Grew, *The anatomy of plants with an idea of a philosophical history of plants, and several other lectures, read before the royal society* (London: W. Rawlins, 1682), p. 23.

[46] Blith, *The English Improver improv'd*, p. 140.

[47] This is hardly true of much of the contents of the book, the most popular of Bacon's works in the seventeenth century, which drew heavily on Pliny and other ancients

your Prejudice succeeded, otherwise you say nothing'.[48] Or 25 years later, from Moses Cook, 'I also always was very wary of taking things upon trust... and if any man told me any thing, unless he had sufficient Experience of it, or could give very good Reasons why it was so, I always was incredulous of it, unless my Judgement told me it were possible, or he by Discourse made it plain to see.'[49] Repetition of the deliberately framed experiment, or faith that a trustworthy individual had conducted such a thing, was becoming the touchstone for sure knowledge. Improvers were not to be believed because their ideas fitted some theory, but because they could deliver accounts of men who really had doubled, trebled or further fantastically augmented the rental of a field.[50] Authority rested with those who had tried it out and succeeded, whether from the weight of anecdote, the long reputation the author could draw on in advancing farming, or from the methodical comparison of results on experimental plots as envisaged by Grew:

> To make tryal of the growth of Plants, in all kinds of simple Soils;
> either Earthy or *Mineral*, as Clay, Marl, Oker, Fullers Earth, Bole
> Armeniac, Vitriol, Allum, *&c.* or *Vegetable*, as Rotten Wood,
> Brans, Starch, or Flower, *&c.* or *Animal*, as Dungs, pounded
> Flesh, dried and powdered Blood, and the like; that it may
> appear, how far any of these may contribute to the growth of a
> *Plant;* or to one, above another.[51]

The rise of experimental culture is of course a very familiar story in the history of seventeenth-century 'natural philosophy'. For the most part, it

---

and seem to transgress many principles argued for by Bacon himself. W. Rawling in Bacon, *Sylva sylvarum*, f.5r; Gaukroger, *Francis Bacon*, pp. 32–3.

[48] Blith, *The English Improver improv'd*, p. 112. Gaukroger argues that the Baconian interest in experiment was a model developed out of a familiarity with legal procedure and the process of determining what was reliable testimony from witnesses. Gaukroger, *Francis Bacon*, pp. 60–7.

[49] Moses Cook, *The manner of raising, ordering, and improving forrest-trees. Also, how to plant, make and keep woods, walks, avenues, lawns, hedges etc. With several figures proper for avenues and walks to end in, and convenient figures for lawns* (London: Peter Parker, 1676), f.vii.

[50] This in turn still rested on the authority and trustworthiness of the witnesses, which higher status compounded but did not produce of itself; numerous scholars have noted this borrowing from legal practice in establishing 'fact'. See Shapiro, *A culture of fact*.

[51] Grew, *Anatomy of plants*, p. 22.

remained very distant from the actual practice of farmers. What is peculiar about its role in developing agricultural knowledge is that it was not only place-specific in its styles and capacity to produce results, to which historians of science have recently taught us to be alert, but experimental knowledge of the soil remained absolutely site-specific. It could provide no guide to what to do in one place unless the practitioner *knew the place*. That qualities like colour could be deceptive and mean different things in different places had already been highlighted by Columella.[52] Plant growth might be affected by any number of qualities produced by the mix of earths; and remember, Evelyn argued there were over 179 million kinds of earth! Consequently, Blith was not very worried at the prospect that an experiment might be successfully conducted to disprove him: 'which Experiment you have found, I shall not question but to discover your mistake, either you are mistaken in the nature of the Land, or else in the way of Husbandry and Ploughing'.[53] Agricultural thought could thus not produce knowledge that could be applied independently of the virtuous improver. Facts, we might say, were *social facts*, but also *embodied facts*.

The agriculture of the early Enlightenment required a rooted knowledge, a localised virtuosity. Nature could be enhanced, but also had to be wooed as she was found. Improvement in agriculture was neither a mechanistic nor abstracted method understanding nature. After working as a customs office and brewer, William Ellis settled on a Hertfordshire farm and by the 1730s worked as an agent for agricultural goods and as a kind of consultant, disseminating advice about good practice, and writing.[54] He became famous enough to draw a visit in 1748 from Pehr Kalm, the Linnean pupil and traveller. In the early 1730s Ellis assembled notes on the agricultural practice of the Chilterns and adjacent vales, and he could reflect on over a century of improvement and writing on husbandry. For him, it remained 'certain, that Art helps Nature to a great degree, and the more, according to its better being adapted'.[55] In other words, the farmer had to carefully respond to the demands of the immediate locality. Ellis had strong grounds then for his ritual condemnation of those who were no more

---

[52] Columella, *Of husbandry*, p. 9.
[53] Blith, *The English Improver improv'd*, p. 111.
[54] Anne Pimlott Baker, 'Ellis, William (c.1700–1758)', in *Oxford Dictionary of National Biography* (Oxford: Oxford University Press, 2004).
[55] William Ellis, *Chiltern and vale farming explained, according to the latest improvements* (London: Weaver Bickerton, 1733), p. 257.

than 'theorists'.[56] Yet he had certainly learnt much from his precursors who engaged with theory: understanding different soils was the key to agriculture, and he aimed to disseminate 'experimental Rules of different Cases'.[57]

Agricultural experiment had to grapple with two sources of variation: that of the soil and the weather. Ellis meticulously recorded the disastrous effects of the wet summer of 1732 on his crops, and noted how changing precipitation might make one kind of land best suited for a bumper yield one year, another the next.[58] In such circumstances, Hale would later note that 'Accident... is as often the mother of improvement, as necessity is of invention'.[59] All learning was local; 'a particular instance is not to be advanced into a general rule', echoing Googe's translation of Heresbach almost two centuries before: 'but we shoulde foulie deceaue our selues yf we shoulde obserue the lyke in euery place'.[60] Hale particularly liked the example of Devon men discovering the virtues of sea salt as a fertilising agent when a field was flooded by an unusually high spring tide.[61] There was experiment, and there was experiment by default. Ellis recorded how one of his neighbours, the 'oldest Farmer in our Parish' of thirty years' experience, mistakenly sowed rye for sheep too late on moist, cold soils and little came up. He 'was not sensible of his Mistake, until Experience became his Monitor'.[62] Whether intentional or not, whether learning by doing or not doing, experiment was widespread by the early eighteenth century. We see it in stewards' accounts, in probate inventories recording cropping, in correspondence and description (sometimes with injunctions *against* experiment!). It seems to have gone far down the social scale; Ellis recorded the various responses of his neighbours to the contingencies presented by bad weather in the early 1730s.[63]

Yet if experiment was widespread, the writers of the mid-eighteenth century seem to have been less sanguine than their

[56] Ellis, *Chiltern and vale farming*, p. vi.
[57] Ellis, *Chiltern and vale farming*, pp. 1–2; ii.
[58] Ellis, *Chiltern and vale farming*, pp. 199–200. For all the contempt that some authors expressed of the clowns who tilled the fields, the 'old farmer' remained a useful figure of authority to draw on. See Sieglerschmidt, 'Virtuelle Landwirtschaft', pp. 234–5.
[59] Hale, *Compleat body*, p. 125.
[60] Heresbach, *Foure bookes*, p. 30.
[61] Hale, *Compleat body*, pp. 126; 288.
[62] Ellis, *Chiltern and vale farming*, p. 255.
[63] Ellis, *Chiltern and vale farming*, pp. 201–4.

predecessors about the prospects for a rapid improvement of agriculture. This was because they had seen it happen and knew it took time. Ellis pondered change and its cause:

> It is true that Custom does not authorize a wrong Practice,
> no more than Antiquity should anticipate a better one; for
> undoubtedly, all Improvements has their rise from industrious
> Disquisitions, and experimental Trials, that by time spread their
> Knowledge, and become general Practices.

He observed how the previous six to seven decades had brought the rise of turnips, clover and lucerne. 'So likewise the goodness of Soots, Salts, Ashes, Lime, Rag[e]s, etc. were hidden Secrets about a Century ago, that are now common to the most rustick Swain.'[64] Such an account did not render easily visible how one got the hidden secrets to the mind of the rustic swain. If new knowledge could only reasonably be both discovered and applied in 'local places', how could one move beyond the 'skilfull clowns' of each parish to disseminate, and perhaps more to the point accept as trustworthy, good practice? How could one become an expert in things one did not directly experience? It was thing to be in oneself virtuous and knowledgeable. But who could you trust?

Networks

Many men trusted Samuel Hartlib. Hartlib was a kind of media guru, a networker *extraordinaire* who had made his way deftly through an unfamiliar world. He had migrated to England from the eastern Baltic port of Elbing which by the 1620s was plunging into steep decline as the staple trade of the English Eastlands company, once its mainstay, moved elsewhere. He studied in Cambridge in the year 1625–6, and was domiciled in England permanently from 1628, escaping the chaos of war-battered Northern Europe.[65] He settled in London three years later. His Elbing roots brought him into contact and a deep friendship with John Dury, minister in the city from 1625 until

[64] Ellis, *Chiltern and vale farming*, pp. 253–4.
[65] On Hartlib's life, see Charles Webster, 'Introduction', in C. Webster (ed.), *Samuel Hartlib and the advancement of learning* (Cambridge: Cambridge University Press, 1970), pp. 1–72.

1630. Dury became the linchpin in a great network of correspondents that Hartlib built up during the 1630s, exchanging knowledge and dreams of a reconciled, educated and godly Protestant Europe. Years later Dury wrote the introduction to Gerard Boate's *Natural History*. Hartlib became an 'Intelligencer', a channel and purveyor of ideas and information. Although over 60 publications bore his name, Hartlib generally at best wrote only introductions to them and recounted and compiled the works of others. His was a career devoted to being 'serviceable unto... *Publicke Concernments*'; 'For mine owne part, although I can contribute but little; yet being carried forth to watch for the *Opportunities* of provoking others, who can do more, to improve their Talents, I have found experimentally that my *Endeavours* have not been without *effect*.'[66] He was the English republic's great impresario of knowledge.

Hartlib, Dury and Comenius, a Bohemian educational writer whom the former brought to London in the early 1640s, committed themselves to 'Pansophy', an encyclopaedic project that aimed at nothing less than the restoration of knowledge lost at the Fall (lathered with the irony that, of course, the temptations of knowledge had led to the Fall, although Bacon had been careful to distinguish between knowledge of nature and moral knowledge of good and evil that had led to the expulsion from Eden).[67] The scope of this ambition ran far beyond agricultural concerns, and their attitude to the proper disposition for improvement was exemplified in the book title of 1651, *The reformed husbandman*.[68] In principle, there were no concerns that it did not embrace. However, as the largest sector of the national economy, agriculture inevitably came within the sights of the 'Hartlib Circle'. In 1649 Hartlib secured a well if unreliably remunerated position as head of an 'Office of Address for Communications' in Oxford, tasked to be 'Center and Meeting-place of Advices, of Proposalls, of Treaties and of all Manner of Intellectual Rarities'.[69]

---

[66] Samuel Hartlib, *An essay for advancement of husbandry-learning* (London: Henry Hills, 1651), p. ii.
[67] Webster, 'Introduction'.
[68] Samuel Hartlib, *The reformed husband-man* (London: J.C., 1651).
[69] Mark Greengrass, 'Hartlib, Samuel (c. 1600–1662)', in *Oxford Dictionary of National Biography* (Oxford: Oxford University Press, 2004); Webster, 'Introduction', especially pp. 50–60; Webster, *The great instauration*, pp. 370–6, 422–5.

At the centre of a countrywide web, Hartlib was the resort for men seeking to expound their views on improvement. Earlier agrarian writers such as Surflet, Googe or Markham had relied on access to the London publishers' monopoly, and had as often as not built their reputation on the translation or paraphrasing of more esteemed works. In the English Republic, little platoons of projectors and intelligencers emerged in the counties; in fact, their authority was based on deep knowledge of the practices of the places they lived and worked in. Hartlib published among many others Beale's and Dymock's writings on Herefordshire orchards and farming; the texts of Richard Weston reporting on Flanders, and Gerard Boate on Ireland, in essence both intelligencers themselves but reaching a wider audience through the 'Hartlib Circle'.[70]

Being a 'conduit pipe' for correspondents of highly varying quality was nevertheless not the ideal. These mid-century pedagogues had been inspired, of course, by Francis Bacon, and especially his utopian notion of a college of the advancement of arts and sciences, the 'House of Salomon', an academy of experts who would build the foundations of the new knowledge and use it to govern providentially and progressively.[71] One of Hartlib's earlier publications in 1641 was *Macaria*, a slim volume almost certainly drafted by his friend and largely unheeded projector Gabriel Plattes, who also ventured into agricultural writings. *Macaria*, allegedly a near neighbour of *Utopia*, was presented to Parliament in 1641 and included the thoroughly Baconian institution of a series of six colleges to order learning, including one on agriculture. A decade later Hartlib was still propounding that 'in the *Science* and *Trade* of *Husbandry*, which is the *Mother* of all other

---

[70] Thirsk, 'Agricultural innovations', pp. 546–50; Webster, *The great instauration*, pp. 473–4.

[71] Deborah Harkness has rightly stressed that the model for this approach to science was not a creation *ex nihilio* of the genius of Bacon, but was a formalisation – and one might say narrowing – of a disparate and active scientific community already established in Renaissance Europe. Nevertheless, the savants of the mid-seventeenth century doubtless looked back to Bacon as their inspiration, who had presented the notion of a state-supported central library, garden and workshops in 1594. It was also the case that there were a number of continental precedents for gentlemanly learned societies, in both Italy and Germany. From 1631, there was the exemplar of Renaudot's *Bureau d'Adresse* in Paris in the 1630s. Harkness, *The Jewel House*, p. 7; Webster, 'Introduction', pp. 29–32, 44; Gaukroger, *Francis Bacon*, p. 72; Webster, *The great instauration*, pp. 328–9, 341.

Trades and *Scientificall Industries*, a *Collegiall* way of Teaching the *Art* thereof will be of infinite *Usefulnesse*'.[72] This college was to exemplify the character of improvers and the qualities of the new experience, as he declared (echoing Markham, as well as Bacon):

> That there may be a *Colledge* or *school* of all the sorts and
> parts of *Good-Husbandry* erected; that so the knowledge and
> practise become more universal. and men may... practise it to the
> advancement of a more *general* and *Publique good*: not as now in
> a *sordid clownish way*, for *meer selfe-profit*; nor as now according
> to *unsound* and rather *Customary* then *rational rules* and *grounds*;
> nor as now in a *dishonourable drudging way*; which indeed is the
> *grand cause* that hinders or takes off the most *ingenious spirits*
> (which yet are most fit to be engaged.)[73]

After the Restoration in 1660 the Royal Society would come to perform some of the functions imagined of these colleges, albeit as an information exchange rather than a dedicated house of learning. Its secretary Oldenburg – another immigrant from the east, and son-in-law of John Dury – would play, more modestly, Hartlib's role.[74] The Society's 'Georgical Committee' would briefly aspire to collect and collate reports on the best agricultural practice of the entire nation in the mid-1660s, but floundered after a brief period although the extent reports provide a treasury of information to historians.[75] If they could not yet erect 'Solomon's House', nevertheless a scientific community could be built that would help secure one of the foundations of

---

[72] Hartlib, *Essay for advancement*, p. ii.
[73] Hartlib, *Essay for advancement*, p. 8. Later William Petty would draft a similar proposal, which for all of its insistence on the importance of practicality and the wider good, is hard to distinguish from the projecting proposals from many seeking an income from their monarchs during the reigns of James I and Charles I. McCormick, *William Petty*, pp. 66–74.
[74] Marie Boas Hall, 'Oldenburg, Henry (c.1619–1677)', in *Oxford Dictionary of National Biography* (Oxford: Oxford University Press, 2004); Marie Boas Hall, *Henry Oldenburg. Shaping the Royal Society* (Oxford: Oxford University Press, 2002).
[75] Anon., 'Enquiries concerning Agriculture', *Philosophical Transactions* 1 (1665–6), pp. 91–4; Reginald Lennard, 'English agriculture under Charles II. The evidence of the Royal Society's "Enquiries"', *EcHR* 4 (1932), pp. 23–45; Allen G. Debus, 'Palissy, Plat and English agricultural chemistry', in Allen G. Debus, *Chemistry, alchemy and the new philosophy* (London, 1987), pp. 85–6; Thirsk, 'Agricultural innovations', pp. 563, 566–7.

knowledge. With little in the way of centralised institutions to generate knowledge, the Royal Society's network of correspondents would have to do.[76] Hartlib himself would reap none of these benefits. Widowed, half-blind and cut off by the new regime, he passed away in 1662.

A network of agricultural expertise was not to be institutionalised in England until the Board of Agriculture emerged nearly a century and a half later. Instead, it remained the role of intelligencers to act as nodes in the networks of ideas, whether metropolitan hacks, self-styled model farmers, or the familiar neighbourly parsons. Some of these would imagine themselves able to 'comprehend all the Labour and Wit of our Ancestors, and be thereby able to supply the defects of one Trade with the perfections of another'.[77] Yet others, like Hartlib himself, were more modest. They set their correspondence before the world in the hope that better minds might draw better conclusions, and that more voices would manufacture better knowledge. As Moses Cook, leading arboriculturalist and gardener wrote in 1676, 'For the Gifts of God are improved by communicating, and Knowledge thriveth as Ingenuity is improved and communicated: for Ingenuity hath these Properties of Memory and Charity, the more you use it, the better it is; and the more you give of it, the more you shall have.'[78] This was a work that had already been ongoing through less celebrated networks of correspondents and seed-exchangers in parts of sixteenth-century Europe.[79] When he published an exchange he had incited on the nutrition of plants (he and his circle were admirers of Plat), Hartlib did not yet take the step of later Enlightenment minds in thinking that existence of the *conversation itself* might yield a better answer. But publicity, a wider public, gave better hope of finding the genius who could provide solutions: having 'received from [some Friends] the three severall Answers, which I have here imparted unto thee: but because they are not yet clear and satisfactory to my self, as somewhat varying from each other, I hope to procure for the Publick Good a more full discovery of this Subject'.[80]

---

[76] Shapiro, *A culture of fact*, pp. 118–21.

[77] William Petty, *The advice of W.P. to Mr. Samuel Hartlib for the advancement of some particular parts of learning* (London: na, 1647), p. 10.

[78] Cook, *Manner of raising*, f.vii r.

[79] Ogilvie, *The science of describing*, ch. 2; Harkness, *Jewel-house*; Ambrosoli, *The wild and the sown*.

[80] Samuel Hartlib, *A discoverie for division or setting out of land, as to the best form published by Samuel Hartlib esquire, for direction and more advantage and profit of*

Neither did these networks, yet, trust to the free and spontaneous desire to exchange knowledge; virtue was not so sure that a steadying and promoting hand could not be of service. This was no wisdom of crowds. We have seen how these men remained inspired by the Baconian vision of a college of experts, and how Hartlib briefly won a stipend from the state for his intelligencing. In the case of improving the woods, there was already the example to hand of forestry administrations that had been set up all over Europe, sometimes with a mission to expand national wood supplies, although more commonly, as in England, with the aim of enhancing the princely estate. Thus Hartlib called for an officer over the woods with regional deputies who could advise people on planting timber, enforce laws, provide for reafforestation, and negotiate with the navy. After all, had not Aristotle himself argued that the woods should come under the purview of magistrates, as was done in 'prudent *states*' like Venice?[81]

Hartlib's work was but one salvo in a barrage of news that thundered over England with the abolition of censorship (and the cheapening of paper that preceded it in the 1630s).[82] The network of correspondents, anchored by the astute compiler, became model practice for agricultural writing for the next century. In some cases the output was in the traditional, apparently single-authored volume, such as John Evelyn's *Sylva*. In other cases readers received a regular digest garnered from all corners of the world, such as the reports issued by John Houghton from the 1680s. Houghton gave vent to a great range of authors, sometimes anonymous, sometimes the acknowledged sage of some locality: Adam Martindale on Cheshire, Robert Plot on Staffordshire; while also reviewing and reminding readers of Markham, Evelyn or Worlidge. Houghton took the view that the years after the civil war were the turning point in 'improvement', 'when our gentry, who before hardly knew what it was to think, then fell to such an

the adventurers and planters in the fens and other waste and undisposed places in England and Ireland; whereunto are added some other choice secrets of experiments of husbandry; with a philosophical quere concerning the cause of fruitfulness, and an essay to shew how all lands may be improved in a new way to become the ground of the increase of trading and revenue to this common-wealth (London: Richard Wodenothe, 1653), p. 18.

[81] Hartlib, *Compleat husband-man*, p. 119.

[82] Michael Braddick, *God's fury, England's fire. A new history of the English civil wars* (London: Penguin, 2008); Tessa Watt, *Cheap print and popular piety 1550–1640* (Cambridge: Cambridge University Press, 1991).

industry'.[83] Half a century later William Ellis was doing the same with his agricultural columns. Through these lines of communication one could access knowledge and report of good practice elsewhere, such as Dr Meret's report on French forestry practices delivered to the Royal Society.[84] Of course, such wide networks of correspondents brought no guarantee of intelligibility; one of Houghton's respondents promised a bottle of wine to anyone who could answer his question 'in plain English'.[85]

Backwardness

Combinations of personalised networks, letter-writing and printed matter accelerated the movement of ideas and disseminated both the ethic of improvement, and specific techniques that might manifest it, across the country and indeed Europe. This was certainly a contributory factor to a sense of agricultural progress that became more confident over time. By the 1720s Bradley could assert that some (undefined) persons thought that 'improvement' had doubled the value of yields in Britain.[86] By the eighteenth century the continent-wide perception that the Flemings and Italians were the leaders in all things agricultural was being supplanted, and people began to look to Britain as the exemplar to follow. But from the perspective of determined improvers, change was not happening with the rapidity that one might expect, given the flow of information. This problem called forth more specific explanations for reluctance to change than a blanket condemnation of conservatism or a blind attachment to country ways.

Despite the national record of success, Bradley attested from personal experience that estates were reluctant to improve because of the expense of labour for acquiring dung, marl or chalk. A few decades earlier Blith had condemned rack-renting, that removed the profits of the tenant's investment from him; if allowed some of the returns from his investment, he was sure that the tenant farmer 'would act Ingenuity with violence as upon his owne, and draw

---

[83] Houghton, *Collection*, pp. 180–1; and cited in Thirsk, 'Agricultural innovations', p. 561; Slack, *Invention of improvement*, pp. 172–3.

[84] Houghton, *Collection*, p. 111.

[85] Houghton, *Collection*, p. 245.

[86] In introduction to Houghton, *Collection*, pp. i–ii.

forth the Earth to yeeld her utmost fruitfulnesse; which once being brought to perfection, will easily be maintained and kept up at the height of fruitfulnesse'.[87] In these cases backwardness came from a simple calculus of cost and benefit. Increasingly, it was recognised that a key aspect of encouraging higher output was providing a reliable vent for the produce of the land, without which no cultivator could recoup their investments. As Timothy Nourse wrote, 'little Profit may be expected from a Farm, be the Ground never so good, which lies not near to a good Market-Town, or which wants the Conveniences of good Roads, or of a Navigable River'.[88] Arguments about access and the inspiring power of markets were already being made about wood production, as we have seen in Chapter 2, though in the latter case more as a remedy to neglect than as a prompt to innovation. Up-to-date commercial information began to become of interest to farmers, not just merchants and speculators, as through more regular publications and increased volume of letter-writing the infrastructure of the information economy expanded rapidly in the second half of the seventeenth century.

As it became recognised that cost and risk factors inhibited the introduction of new techniques, so emerged – again, in a parallel development to thinking about woods – the first attempts to provide accounts of net profit in the printed literature. Certainly, for many decades private estate-owners and stewards had kept rough accounts, in imitation of techniques pioneered by manorial estates in late medieval times, along with merchants and bureaucrats (though in that latter case as much to provide transparency to auditors as to improve efficiency). In an account of the agriculture of Flanders penned by the exiled Royalist and long-standing and (by his own account) landlord Sir Richard Weston in the 1640s, balance sheets of the costs and returns to be expected by particular types of cultivation were provided. Weston did not publish his manuscript himself but passed it to his children; by 1649 it was in the hands of Hartlib who published it as an anonymous tract and drew on it for subsequent publications, eventually revealing Weston as the posthumous author. This tract was a model for subsequent writers. It is not perhaps surprising that the city merchant and writer on financial affairs John Houghton also paid a particular interest

---

[87] Blith, *English Improver*, f.4v.
[88] Nourse, *Campania foelix*, p. 14.

in the pecuniary returns to be hoped for from particular forms of cultivation.[89] Yet while such model calculations gradually found their way
into print, they did not become commonplace until well into the eighteenth century, and hardly *de rigeur* until the 1760s. Nevertheless, over
time demand rose for a more precise and rigorous way of assessing
the benefits of innovation. In his 1733 volume William Ellis took time
to respond to a reader of his first work on agriculture who was dissatisfied with his use of qualitative descriptions of amounts of crops
or yields, and on several occasions illustrated his points by using
farm accounts he kept in the early 1730s.[90] Farmers' accounts survive
from the seventeenth century and may have been quite widespread; in
this case the more measured economic sensibility over costs that was
entering the literature was, as indeed often was the case, behind events
on the ground.

The most vituperative and enduring debate over agricultural
improvement was, however, in regard to the commons and enclosure.
We have seen in Chapter 1 how arguments about enclosure became
embroiled in debates about the extent of tillage in the sixteenth century, and the broad consensus that associated enclosure with a pastoral
economy tended to inhibit the abolition of common rights. Enclosure
could not but be a political question, because it entailed the abolition
of jurisdictions, and in theory at least, certain legal steps and indeed
Parliamentary or royal assent. Much of the removal of common rights
over land that did go on was technically actually *approuvement* rather
than enclosure. Approvement was the right of the lord to claim his
share (usually understood to be a third) in the resources of the common
waste, removing it from common use. This procedure was perfectly
legal and supposedly uncontroversial so long as the commoners were
not impeded in taking resources necessary for their farms from the rest
of the common.[91]

Complete abolition of manorial jurisdiction, and the rights
attendant on being a tenant of the manor, was another matter. Enclosure

---

[89] Sir Richard Weston, *A discours of husbandrie used in Brabant and Flanders*
(London: Samuel Hartlib, 1650); Houghton, *Collection*, pp. iii–iv.

[90] Ellis, *Chiltern and vale farming*, p. 244.

[91] Bill Shannon, 'Approvement and improvement in the lowland wastes of early modern
Lancashire', in R. Hoyle (ed.), *Custom, improvement and the landscape in early
modern Britain* (Farnham: Ashgate, 2011), pp. 175–202.

of manors, or equally the widespread disafforestation of royal forests during the 1620s and later, that also abolished common rights previously exercised under the purview of the forest courts led to widespread unrest, riot and litigation.[92] These events brought sharply into focus the issue of whether improvement required a particular property rights regime. Generally speaking, improvers thought the more untrammelled the rights of the landholder, the more they were likely to improve their grounds. Those who resisted such enclosures, which were also part and parcel of great drainage projects that were implemented in fenland England such as Hatfield Chase in Yorkshire, and the Fens of Cambridgeshire, Norfolk and Lincolnshire, became the stereotypical standard bearers for backwardness, although examining such cases of resistance in detail shows they often touched upon issues of compensation and allocation of benefits rather than opposition to change per se.[93]

For much of the seventeenth century proponents of enclosure argued that commoning damaged, above all, the poor, because many commoners could not make adequate use of their commons in any case, and poor regulatory regimes meant that the lands were overstocked with animals by rich graziers.[94] Yet despite the (allegedly) obvious benefits of enclosure (handing the land out in parcels 'in severalty' to landholders who could use it as they wished with no reference to others), a combination of mutual suspicion, uncertainty as to results, lack of capital, and an unequal distribution of benefits all contributed to a reluctance to take the leap. As Blith argued, all of this was in itself quite reasonable:

> one sayes, I shall not have so great an Advantage by it as my
> Neighbour; and another he believes it will be good for present,
> but it will not last; and an another sayes, he hath not reason to
> beare so great a proportion of Charge, though he has as much

---

[92] See for example, Elly Robson, 'Improvement and epistemologies of landscape in seventeenth-century English forest enclosure', *Historical Journal* 60 (2017), pp. 597–632.

[93] Julie Bowring, 'Between the corporation and Captain Flood. The fens and drainage after 1663', in R. Hoyle (ed.), *Custom, improvement and the landscape in early modern Britain* (Farnham: Ashgate, 2011), pp. 235–61; Keith Lindley, *Fenland riots and the English revolution* (London: Heinemann Educational, 1982).

[94] Blith, *The English Improver improv'd*, p. 75; Hartlib, *Compleat husband-man*, p. 42.

> Land, yet he's not capable of so great an Improvement; & another saith. I could well be content to help on any publique worke, if others would, but for me to bestow cost and improve my Land, or commons, for others that will bestow none to eate and bite up my cost; much discourageth him, & indeed there is some Reason for his backwardesse.[95]

Reasonable; but somehow lacking in the stomach and vision of the virtuous improver. Or in the view of Sir William Dugdale in his history of wetlands and drainage of 1662 commissioned to justify the process, even lacking in civilisation: 'the most civilized Nations have by so much Art and Industry endeavoured to make the best improvement of their Wasts, Commons, and all sorts of barren Land'.[96] Thus it did not take much for some proponents of enclosure, even those who acknowledged the existence of good reasons to be cautious, to tip into more sweeping and contemptuous generalisations about their opponents, as was done frequently in regard to the 'lazy', 'barbarous' and 'unthankful' Irish, who had brought their fate upon themselves.[97] Part of the problem was perceived to be the kind of society that critics associated with the commons, which they thought were generated by the common lands themselves. Rather than alleviating poverty they were more a place to 'make poore, by causing idlenesse'. So thought Hartlib, who argued that there were fewest poor where there were fewest commons, a take on causation that could of course as easily have been reversed.[98] Evelyn pondered the need to coerce those who resisted enclosure into agreement or submission, and of course at this time the same logic was being applied to Ireland and the new American colonies.[99] A degraded state of the land and a degraded people seemed to go together in these accounts. Equally, how could the virtuous ever damage the land?

---

[95] Blith, *The English Improver improv'd*, p. 84.

[96] William Dugdale, *The history of imbanking and drayning of divers fenns and marshes, both in forein parts and in this kingdom, and of the improvements thereby extracted from records, manuscripts, and other authentick testimonies* (London: Alice Warren, 1662), f.3v.

[97] McCormick, *William Petty*, pp. 89–90, 191–2.

[98] Hartlib, *Compleat husband-man*, p. 42; similarly, the argument associated with John Aubrey or Thomas Fuller that landscapes fostered a 'particular genius' could also be applied less favourably. Slack, *Invention of improvement*, p. 21.

[99] Slack, *Invention of improvement*, pp. 35–6, 60.

Over the century there seems to have been a hardening of attitudes. Those who resisted such an obvious service to the commonwealth must in fact be its enemies, anti-improvers as much as anti-enclosers, who denied the national mission: 'many of them must be confess'd to be very rough and savage in their Dispositions, being of levelling Principles, and refractory to Government, insolent and tumultuous: What Gentleman soever than shall have the Misfortune to fall into the Neighbourhood of such Boors, let him never think to win them by Civilities, it will be much more easie for him to teach a Hog to play upon the Bagpipes, than to soften such *Brutes* by *Courtesie*'. So wrote Timothy Nourse, further expanding his contempt and condescension by observing that 'Such men then are to be look'd on as trashy Weeds or Nettles, growing usually upon Dunghills, which if touch'd gently will sting, but being squeez'd will never hurt us.'[100] In the Pyrennes, peasants were condemned by forester reformers as 'drunkards… strongly attached to their traditional privileges, and sworn enemies of all innovations from the smallest bagatelles because since they don't have much taste, everything makes them angry. The women are no less brutal.'[101]

In these seventeenth-century debates anti-improvers were portrayed not just as custom-bound clowns and boors, but people who lacked character and even basic decency: they were not improvers. Backwardness was a human failing, even if those who clung tenaciously to their common rights were sometimes seen as a rather limited, perhaps lesser kind of human – just as were those who resisted colonisation and 'improvement' overseas. The governance of the land (or as we might now say, the 'property regime') and the nature of the people who lived upon it became the cause of the land's miserable state, or even degradation. As Nourse hyperbolically proclaimed, 'A Common… is nothing but a Naked Theater of Poverty, both as to men and Beasts, where all things appear horrid and uncultivated, and may be term'd, not improperly, the very abstract of Degenerated Nature.'[102] We must

---

[100] Nourse, *Campania foelix*, pp. 15–16; see similar attitudes discussed in John E. Morgan, 'Flooding in early modern England. Cultures of coping in Gloucestershire and Lincolnshire', PhD thesis, University of Warwick, 2016, p. 87.

[101] Froidour, cited in Mukerji, 'Great forest survey', p. 245.

[102] Nourse, *Campania foelix*, p. 99; similar sentiments were expressed by Joseph Lee, a close neighbour of Walter Blith, in his *Considerations concerning common fields and enclosure* of 1654, followed up in 1656 arguing, 'The first and most that are fofended at Inclosure, are the ruder sort of people; which to speak truly, have most

remember that for Nourse improvement was the recreation of Eden, a godly task, and thus it was an easy matter to arraign the state of the land and the people who cultivated, or who did not sufficiently cultivate it, along an axis of salvation and damnation.

Of course, there were equally vituperative expressions on the other side, whether they took the form of hedge-breaking, physical assault or a tract in purple prose. The sixteenth-century condemnation of enclosure as a conspiracy that simultaneously gifted profiteering and reduced the supply of tillage died hard. It was hard to distinguish whose sin played the greater role, according to an apologist for the Caroline regime of the 1630s that for a few years had turned its head against enclosure: 'the *Forestaller* and *Ingrosser*, or the *Depopulator*, be the heaviest in the scale, both being the spawne of that blood-sucking *Cynomyia* covetousnesse'.[103] In this discourse enclosure brought depopulation, 'a strangling or chaoking of the wombe, and causing an utter sterility', an abrogation of Christian duties to 'The earth on which wee tread and walke, and must make use of the fruit and increase thereof, to sustaine and support our houses of clay.'[104]

Yet these analyses – from which I quote here admittedly extreme manifestations – shared a diagnosis of people's moral character as being culpable for the state of the land. The apparently bare and unproductive common, or unpeopled acreages of pasture, held a mirror to the society that allowed them to be so. Such narratives persisted across the Enlightenment period and beyond, but have deeper roots in the sixteenth and especially seventeenth centuries. At the end of the seventeenth century Florinus, writing in the *Hausvater* tradition of Germany, stated that 'an advantageous matter [meaning 'resource'] is, in the hands of a neglectful and ignorant owner, in most cases no different as a sharp knife, with which they could as well cut their nose from the face as a slice of bread from a loaf'.[105] Around 1800, for

erason... they live upon rapine and spoil of others, [and] daily make a prey upon their neighbours corn and grasse.' Joseph Lee, *Eutazia tou agrou: or a vindication of regulated Inclosure* (London: Thomas Williams, 1656), p. 29. See Thirsk, 'Plough and pen', p. 312.

[103] Robert Powell, *Depopulation arraigned, convicted and condemned, by the lawes of God and man a treatise necessary in these times* (London: Richard Badger, 1636), p. 4.

[104] Powell, *Depopulation*, p. 10.

[105] Florinus, *Oeconomicus prudens*, p. 825.

example, the leading liberal forester in Bavaria, Hazzi, framed the unimproved forest as a residual of 'chaos' left from the Creation and as yet uncivilised, and 'As cultivation [*Kultur*] reaches an ever higher level, so less of this chaos remains.'[106] Alexandra Walsham has shown how 'Protestantism reinforced the belief that nature was a sensitive barometer of moral disorder and a vehicle by which God habitually communicated by human beings.'[107] If 'when nature was defective'[108] it could be brought to a worthier state through industry and art, then failure to do so also became a living memorial of the Fall: 'cursed is the ground for thy sake; in sorrow shalt thou eat of it all the days of thy life'.[109] Whether cajoled, conquered or seduced, nature had no agency of its own, and thus could be raised up or cast down as easily as the Christians who lived from it.

Climes

But there was another way of thinking aside from that which ascribed the state of the land to moral failings. What if people, and what they could achieve, were in fact shaped by nature? What if circumstances made them as much, or perhaps more, than they made their circumstances? Such thinking on a local scale did not fit well with the idea of individual will and grace that infused the Christian tradition, and the application of such ideas seems to have been limited before climatic explanations became more widely wedded to racial explanations of destiny in the nineteenth century. However, such a strand of thinking did exist.

The possibility of a relationship between climate and character was a just a subset of a broader problem that troubled writers on husbandry (and indeed many other topics) long into the nineteenth century. Were discoveries about the influence of soils, manures or techniques of tillage upon harvests generally applicable, or could they only be replicated in the place they were first demonstrated? Could agricultural

---

[106] Cited in Richard Hölzl, *Umkämpfte Wälder. Die Gscichte einer ökologischen Reform in Deutschland 1760–1860* (Frankfurt: Klostermann, 2010), p. 47.

[107] Alexandra Walsham, *The reformation of the landscape. Religion, identity and landscape in early modern Britain and Ireland* (Oxford: Oxford University Press, 2011), p. 393.

[108] Dugdale, *History of imbanking*, p. 1.

[109] Genesis 3:17.

knowledge travel? 'Improvement' was a universal project, to be sure, but this did mean that one had to re-learn what improvement might mean in every locality, or was there a template that was efficacious across the world? If success was always located in the particular circumstances of each place, then it raised the possibility that what seemed unambiguously good in one spot may actually mislead and be damaging elsewhere, even if one was a virtuous Improver. If agriculture was local, and even more if people were formed by their locality, it raised the possibility that such destinies were set to such a degree that backwardness could never be transcended. This idea troubled thinkers despite the numerous examples of successful transplantations and acclimatisation of people, and animals and plant species around the globe. The debates and critique which we now associate with 'modernist' agriculture and 'one-size-fits-all' policy are not novelties of recent times.[110] But was movement of ideas or beings merely a precursor to degeneracy and failure?

Environmental determinism had a long and respectable pedigree. The fourth-century BCE tract attributed to Hippocrates of Kos, *Airs, waters, places*, explained the condition and health of the human body by the elements around it. Herodotus had diagnosed the struggle against an allegedly harsher environment as being the reason that the Greeks were so virtuous and hardy compared with their opponents from the Middle East.[111] This antique thinking was transmitted along various lines into early modern writing, perhaps most influentially in the treatise on statecraft written by the Italian Giovanni Botero in the 1580s (whom we met in Chapter 1), who suggested that the Reformation could be attributed to an inordinate love of freedom that the cold clear airs of the north inspired in higher latitudes.[112] Much more famous and controversial was Montesquieu's *Spirit of the Laws*

---

[110] For a prominent recent example of this, see James C. Scott, *Seeing like a state. How certain schemes to improve the human condition have failed* (New Haven, CT: Yale University Press, 1998).

[111] David Arnold, *The problem of nature. Environment, culture and European expansion* (Oxford: Oxford University Press, 1996).

[112] Glacken, *Traces on the Rhodian shore*, p. 369. In England, a discourse about 'airs' found first in chorographical works and then emerging into a revived Hippocractic medicine was generally related to health rather than character. Vladimir Jankovic, *Reading the skies. A cultural history of English weather, 1650–1820* (Chicago, IL: University of Chicago Press, 2000), p. 80; Jan Golinski, *British weather and the climate of Enlightenment* (Chicago, IL: University of Chicago Press, 2007), ch. 5.

published in 1748, a standard bearer for arguing that certain climates, through physiological effects on their inhabitants, created more flourishing and ideal forms of government.[113] The extensive temperate zone in which Europe lay allegedly created a relatively strong but restless set of peoples, but due to its constrained geography set competing strong states alongside each other which forced them in turn to achieve greater strength. Colonial and non-colonial encounters around the world also generated vigorous debate about whether geography and atmosphere might explain differences between polities, national character and races.[114] Before the second half of the eighteenth century the question of climate remained largely framed as one of defining indigeneity, and the degree of adaptability of the body and species to new climes. The shaping of character of whole regions or latitudes was approached first and foremost as a medical question of the influence of temperature and moisture on bodily sensibilities.[115] Savants wondered if a people raised in one place should also be fed and medicated by plants that grew in the same soil, and not 'outlandish' ones. The science of seeds had also made clear their sometimes extreme sensitivity to location, and possibly to the very form of the plant that emerged and inter-species transformations.[116]

[113] Montesquieu's line of reasoning was nevertheless well-established before he wrote. See Stephen Gaukroger, *The natural and the human. Science and the shaping of modernity 1739–1841* (Oxford: Oxford University Press, 2016), pp. 250–8.

[114] Charles-Louis de Secondat, Baron de La Brède et de Montesquieu, *De l'Esprit des Lois* (Paris: Barillot et fils, 1748), chs XIV–XVII; Golinksi, *British weather*, ch. 6; J. Hector St. John de Crèvecouer, *Letters from an American farmer* (London: T. Davies, 1782), II; on continued debates about links between climate and health, see Andrea A. Rusnock, *Vital accounts. Quantifying health and population in eighteenth-century England and France* (Cambridge: Cambridge University Press, 2002), pp. 137–75; Grove, *Green imperialism*, pp. 153–67, 205, 316.

[115] See for example, William Falconer, *Remarks on the influence of climate on the disposition and temper of mankind* (London: C. Dilly, 1781).

[116] As Alix Cooper and Brian Ogilvie have argued, this brought about a renewed interest and focus upon 'indigenous' species that dominated botanical practice, rather than what was brought or encountered overseas. Nevertheless, the transfer of plants and development of 'exotic' collections, often for medical reasons as well as prestige, with the associated challenges of acclimatisation, preoccupied some Dutch botanists and physicians especially. Cooper, *Inventing the indigenous*, pp. 21, 29–31, 35–8, 44–5, 47. Ogilvie, *Science of describing*, p. 58; Cook, *Matters of exchange*, esp. ch. 8; Lisbet Koerner, *Linneaus. Nature and nation* (Cambridge, MA: Harvard University Press, 1999), pp. 113–39. On seed, Elizabeth Scott, 'The secret nature of seeds. Science and seed improvement, c.1520–1700', PhD thesis, University of East Anglia, 2016, esp. ch. 4.

'Climate' was the word that was used the capture the panoply of influences that shaped each place's nature, and an interest in a comparative approach to 'the place's native style and habit'[117] was taken from classical authors and embedded in writing on husbandry from an early date. In the 1550s, Charles Estienne commented:

> As it is ordinarily seene that the complexions of people dwelling in the seueral provinces of one great region and countrie doe differ from one another according to the aire, or aspect of the Sunne which is called the climat they dwell in: so in like manner one may see the nature and fertilnesse of arable grounds to engender and bring form divers complexions and sortes of ordering of the same more in one place than another, according as the ground shall be moist and glib, grauelly consisting of fullers clay, brickie, stonie, or free and well-natured.[118]

Estienne's observation was neutral in tone but already in the early seventeenth century John Norden discussed how the 'climat' of woodlands and sea coasts bred stubborn and bad people (just at the time when his employer the Crown was attempting to increase revenues from changing management practices in the forests, and claim ownership over contested stretches of land that had emerged with changes in coastal morphology).[119] Gervase Markham, who as we have seen had foregrounded the importance of understanding the soil, remarked pointedly that 'It is to be vnderstood that Husbandry doth vary according to the nature and climats of countries; not one rule observes in all places, nor all places to be governed and directed by one rule.' He was also an enthusiastic user of the term 'climate'. His French contemporary Olivier de Serres presented his great work in the tradition of Estienne, with the words 'Here is simply represented the art of using and cultivating the earth in all its parts, according to its diverse qualities and climates.'[120]

---

[117] Virgil, *The Georgics* (London: Penguin, 1982), p. 58. See also Wilkinson, 'General introduction', p. 59.

[118] Estienne, *Maison rustique*, p. 527.

[119] Norden, *Surveyors dialogue*, p. 216; Joan Thirsk, 'The Crown as projector on its own estates, from Elizabeth I to Charles I', in Richard Hoyle (ed.), *The estates of the English crown, 1558–1640* (Cambridge: Cambridge University Press, 1992), pp. 298–352.

[120] Gervase Markham, *Markhams farwell*, p. 148; Olivier de Serres, *Du theatre d'agriculture*, front matter; see also on Markham and Gerard, cited in Margaret

Thus although they wrote for national or even international audiences, agricultural writers of the seventeenth and early eighteenth centuries spent a considerable amount of time considering regional variation and the specific properties of the land. Indeed, the injunction to know one's own land already rung loudly from the manuals of Varro and Cato. As well as knowing the soil, you had to know the weather. Around 1700 Timothy Nourse advised keeping a calendar of the local weather as being a more useful tool than astrology and prognostications, as 'upon the same Concurrence of Causes and Circumstances, we meet with the same Effects'. This was a universally valid law that could only be applied in with specific local knowledge.[121] Almanacs that were often used as weather diaries were among the best-selling forms of literature of the age. Extremely localised variations in climate have been put forward as a rationale to scatter plots around large common fields, to ensure that one's crops were not all struck by some misfortune. Writers were preoccupied with weather-related blights like mildew and the mysterious 'blasting', and the effects of proximity to woodlands and hedgerows that seemed to increase atmospheric moisture in lands divided by such barriers 'in severalty'.[122]

Thus while there was no shortage of starry-eyed certainty when it came to the benefits of improvement and enclosure, authors remained cagey as to precisely what one should do in any particular circumstance. This applied as much to below-ground as above-ground phenomena. When he came to recommendations on manuring the ground, Timothy Nourse restricted himself to opining that 'in all these Cases no definitive Rule can be given; forasmuch as the Natural Temper or Disposition of the Earth being in several Places very different, more or less help must be us'd'. He did reckon lime to be the best manure of all, and observed that it was increasingly replacing marling, possibly a result of the expanding availability of coal. Mortimer, in his compendium of agricultural writing published in 1707, similarly noted that different climates affected the outcomes from the same type of soil, and recorded the variable practices to be found in southern English

Willes, *The making of the English gardener* (New Haven, CT: Yale University Press, 2011), pp. 113, 162.

[121] Nourse, *Campania foelix*, p. 16.

[122] Donald R. McCloskey, 'The Prudent peasant. New findings on open fields', *Journal of Economic History* 51 (1991), pp. 343–55.

counties.[123] No-one was more sensitive to locality than William Ellis in the 1730s, who carefully described and explained the farming practices in different parts of his native Hertfordshire: 'every Farmer ought to make it his primary Study to inform himself of the several Sorts of Ground that often belong to his Farm, and that besides his own Judgment to consult his Neighbours, who as Natives on the Place may be able to let him know more than the Dictates of his own Reason, that formerly were more remote from the same'.[124]

So if Markham had talked of conquering nature by altering her, most adopted a much more modest patter by which one took nature's signs as a guiding hand as to which improvement would be most appropriate, a way of thinking that dominated agricultural thought throughout the eighteenth century. As Hale expressed this very common idea in 1758, 'Every soil has its natural produce: and so far as convenience will allow, that should be followed; for whatsoever is the growth to which a soil is fitted by nature, the same is that with which it will best succeed under the improvements of art.' One should, as Ellis recommended, consult with natives of the place, but in the end it is 'nature giving him the instruction'.[125] It was crucial to be attentive to the outwards signs of the soil's fecundity. These could be found directly, in its colour and texture, although here no one datum was terribly useful. The type of weed was useful, as of course was local experience of crops, or the height and straightness of trees that grew there. Cowslips were a sign of good pasture, according to Hale.[126]

It was clear to these authors that one could not waltz into a new place and expect very positive results from farming in ignorance of the climate. So much was already well-established in botany and horticulture, which had long relied on international networks and exchanges of plants and seeds, presenting problems of naturalisation in new climes.[127] The indisputable fact of local variation could also be held up against those who argued that all plant nutrition came from the air. For some this had been proven by van Helmont's famous experiment, related in England by Boyle and copied by Moses Cook, that growing

---

[123] Nourse, *Campania foelix*, p. 32; Mortimer, *The whole art of husbandry*, pp. 53–66.

[124] Ellis, *Chiltern and vale farming*, p. 48.

[125] Hale, *Compleat body*, pp. 7, 55.

[126] Hale, *Compleat body*, pp. 5–9, 24.

[127] Harkness, *Jewel House*, pp. 53–4; Cooper, *Inventing the indigenous*.

a tree in a restricted environment did not diminish the weight of the soil in which it grew, leading to the conclusion that it drew its sustenance from the air.[128] Francis Bacon had no very clearly stated view on the matter, but also thought that nourishment could be drawn directly from the air, on the basis of the fact that vegetables in storage, like onions hung up on a string, still sprouted, although elsewhere he stated that '*Plante* ex Terra & Aqua nutriuntur'.[129] If plants were entirely sustained from air, it was pointed out, there would be no differences between rich and poor lands. The advocates of the Helmontian view had a riposte: different soils did not absorb salt or nutritive juices from the atmosphere equally well, accounting for those differences. From such signs it was impossible to decide either way, accounting for the fact that the Paracelsian take on plants that there was an essential life-giving food did not supplant the 'humoural' Aristotelian explanation of the soil's properties until the late eighteenth century (see Chapters 1 and 6).

However, most authors seem to have taken a relatively all-encompassing view, as did Bacon, that did not rule out the possibility of multiple nutrients, such as air, water and 'oils' (a category as all-embracing as 'salts' that seemed to reside in the 'earth'), even if it remained an open question as to whether the specific life-giving element itself was nourished by these inputs to the body, or had to be part of the nourishment itself.[130] Moses Cook thought the food most

---

[128] Walter Pagel, *Joan Baptista van Helmont. Reformer of science and medicine* (Cambridge: Cambridge University Press, 1982), p. 53; Cook, *Manner of raising*, pp. 27–8.

[129] Bacon, *Sylva sylvarum*, p. 9; Francis Bacon, *Historia Vitae et Mortis* (London: Matthai Lownes, 1623), p. 103.

[130] Bacon's 'science' did not, in his own works, lead one only to strictly empirical observations of reality. His work was infused with references to 'spirits... that are in all *Tangible Bodies*... they are the most Actiue of Bodies', and indeed were used by Bacon as a major source of explanation, despite lack of any experimental evidence. Bacon opined that life was born of a combination of 'airy and flamey matter', that in turn had, respectively, water and oil as their main nutrients. Indeed in his *Historia Vitae et Mortis* he focused more on the *retention* of spirit inhibiting decay rather than the *source* of its life-giving power; but distinguished between a *spiritus vitales* and a *spiritus mortuales*, the latter found in all inanimate bodies, and the former that emerge, on the basis of the action of the *spiritus mortuales*, in animate matter. The overall schema is clearly derived originally from Paracelsus and was never fully elaborated in print or manuscript. It is impossible to know if Bacon ever reached a clear conclusion himself. Bacon, *Sylva sylvarum*, pp. 10, 31, 95; Francis Bacon, *Historia Vitae*, pp. 30–1; see Debus, 'Palissy, Plat and English agricultural chemistry',

likely a 'Spirit of the earth', having conducted van Helmont's experiment himself on the instigation of his employer, the Earl of Essex. But he conceded, 'for my part, I shall not contend whether [the food of plants] be Salt, Sulphur, or Mercury; or as some affirm, that 'tis Salt, Sulphur, Mercury, and Spirit: All, or any one of these that feeds the Plants of this Terrestial Globe; or if it be Fire, Earth, Water, or Air, as was formerly the opinion of the Learned; for Sulphur or Brimstone may answer to Fire, Salt to the Earth, Mercury to Water, Spirit to Air'.[131] This was not long after Hartlib had opined that 'salt is the seat of life and vegetation', but yet soon conceding he and others remained 'very ignorant of the true causes of fertility'.[132] The great majority, while possibly expressing a preference for a particular explanation, rested their recommendations on pragmatic grounds: 'it is in short adapting the proper plant to a proper soil, which promotes the husbandry that I would endeavour to recommend, and of which I have had long experience'.[133] As we shall see in Chapter 6, it took a revolution in the understanding of soil nutrition a century after Hartlib was writing to decisively shift attitudes to both the possibility of improvement, but also, of environmental degradation.

Thus for improvers, the current state of nature remained a divinely bestowed invitation to improve it. It was just that improvement had to take on adaptable, particular forms. If this was borne in mind, knowledge could travel well, and the virtuous person of the improver, at least, could also transcend their origins. The risks attendant on misjudging a locality also remained one-sided. A farmer could lose an investment, but could not fundamentally *worsen* the character of the land. The only way was up.[134]

pp. 74, 82; Gaukroger, *Francis Bacon*, p. 184; also on *spiritus* in Bacon and his probable source Telesio, see D.P. Walker, 'Francis Bacon and *Spiritus*', in Penelope Gouk (ed.), *Music, spirit and language in the Renaissance* (London: Variorum Reprints, 1985), ch. X; Graham Rees, 'Francis Bacon and *Spiritus Vitalis*', in Marta Fattori and Massimo Bianchi (eds), *Spiritus. IV° Colloquio internazionale del lessico intellettuale Europeo* (Rome, 1984), pp. 265–81.

[131] These categories are all derived from Paracelsus. Cook, *Manner of raising*, p. 27.
[132] Cited in Debus, 'Palissy, Plat, and English agricultural chemistry', p. 85.
[133] Bradley, *General treatise*, p. 126.
[134] Note Hales's contention that through effective dunging 'the worst soil… will thoroughly alter its nature, so that it never can relapse into its original barrenness again'. Hale, *Compleat body*, pp. 148–9.

Thus within nature's strictures there was best practice, and there was scope for experiment. Close observation of cause and effect was at the heart of the farming enterprise. This could proceed with little consensus on the theoretical explanations for why techniques were successful. Such a situation bred a kind of paradox; many writers on husbandry betrayed engagement with, and excitement about, an emerging botanical and chemical literature that might give them insights into what would provide greater yields. For their recommendations to be taken seriously, they felt they had to be legitimated with some reference to scientific endeavour that underpinned the miraculous effects of what they advised. But very few (Hugh Plat notwithstanding) could make the serious claim that litters early nineteenth-century works, that knowledge of chemistry was a prerequisite for state-of-the-art farming. And most readers were probably more impressed by the yield figures and testimony to experience that remained at the core of all agronomic authority.

Ellis noted little battalions of experimenters at work in his locality. A farmer in the Chilterns took peas and sowed them in three different ways in one field to test which worked best. Much of their performance turned out to rest on where they fell in the plough furrows, and where peas were sown.[135] Experiment had also discovered, against the principles of humoural thinking about the soil, that gravelly soils benefited from having chalk added, 'which at first, mov'd my Wonder, to see a warm, dry Soil dress a warm, dry Soil'. Ellis hypothesised that this was to do with texture rather than humoural qualities, and a 'third Nature' in the chalk of 'loose, and shattering Parts' benefited from the binding qualities of gravel.[136]

In many ways the period between Francis Bacon (d. 1626) and the florescence of the Scottish Enlightenment was one of great continuity in agronomic writing, despite it coinciding with the traditional dating of the 'scientific revolution'. True, experimental techniques, the media for disseminating agricultural novelty, networks and markets for obtaining plants, seed, animals and books were all hugely expanded and refined. Works on husbandry had become very much larger, on average, but also much more attentive to matters of detail, not least place. There were plenty of madcap theories and exaggerated claims in

[135] Ellis, *Chiltern and vale farming*, pp. 221–2.
[136] Ellis, *Chiltern and vale farming*, pp. 224–5.

circulation, but the standards against which an unschooled reader or inexperienced farmer might measure them were more widely known and accessible. In England, at least, crop yields were also undoubtedly higher, although the precise contribution of literature on husbandry is of course hard to gauge. There are other explanations that enter the mix, perhaps more convincingly: the slackening of population growth assisting a rise in income of the working population, urbanisation expanding markets and innovation, tenurial and labour-market shifts promoting efficiency. As well as the latest techniques being reported by prolific writers and publishers of correspondence like Bradley or Houghton, or in magazines and journals, the writings of antiquity were finally emerging in the vernacular with Columella translated into English in 1745. It is hardly the case that every farmer had a library, but we have come very far from Tusser's bestseller of the Elizbethan era that can hardly have contained anything that a competent farmer did not already know. And by the 1730s and 1740s, few would dispute that 'The farmer should perfectly understand his soil, before he enters on any other part of his profession; for it is the foundation of all.'[137] Perhaps this too had been a truism for cultivators for thousands of years. But now firmly established in the learned discourse of agricultural societies and landlords, the consensus around this proposition meant that when new theories of the soil emerged from the 1740s, the door was open for them to profoundly influence agronomic discourse and its wider impact.

[137] Hale, *Compleat body*, p. 19.

4 Paths to Sustained Growth, c. 1650–1760

States

By the middle of the seventeenth century it is possible to observe quite widely in Europe the idea that improved knowledge could allow people to make better use of the resources that were to hand, and also help in the discovery of new resources. The foci of such efforts were quite diverse and might relate to distinct problems: diffusing best agricultural practice to avert dearth, fostering new metallurgical knowledge, attracting artisanal expertise, instilling military discipline. In the case of maintaining wood supplies the strategies adopted were defensive rather than innovatory, providing for a legal regime to prevent ill-use as discussed in Chapter 2. The ethic infusing much of this thought was *expansionary*, in that the possibilities granted by divine providence were considered to be under-used. The attachment of such ideas to the figure of the 'improver' in England was a particularly striking and widely articulated phenomenon, but they were by no means unique to that nation.[1] A society's failure to avail itself of sufficient supplies of grain, or wood, or bullion, was seen above all else as an issue of character.

This view rested in part on an understanding of political relationships as fundamentally resting on the quality of a whole range of hierarchical interpersonal ties, each generating expected norms

---

[1] Although much in sympathy with the general approach, this is contrary to the view expressed in Paul Slack, *Invention of improvement*.

of behaviour. Correct behaviour would lead to better, providential outcomes. Yet optimism about enhanced *knowledge* seemed to offer the possibility of also enhancing the resources on which the polity relied (although there was no collective notion of 'resources' as inputs as we understand it today). At the same time, the demands of managing growing populations and fiscal and military pressures expanded the institutional reach of early modern rulers, tending to abstract the understanding of governance from personal ties. The effect of these changes was to promote a conception of the 'state' as an autonomous entity with which the fate of its people was bound up. In turn the success of the state could be imagined as related to the efficacy of its acquisition and distribution of resources. The idea of what constituted a desirable political order was being fundamentally reshaped. Nature, as the means to wealth, was integrated into the political order. This produced an altered view of both the destiny of states, and the destiny of nature. Sustainability as defined in this book emerged from acts of political as much as ecological imagination.

An appreciation of this change requires an examination of ideas of authority and political order in early modern Europe. The institutions that governed the continent's people took many forms. Some forms rested on 'vertical' ties, such as the prince's rule over his or her subjects, or the lord's paternalistic oversight of serfs, subjects, tenants and workers; others included more 'horizontal relationships' between members of guilds, village or urban communes, religious fraternities or indeed religious orders. Most people found themselves enmeshed in a variety of such relationships, some more, some less participatory; sometimes with no say at all. Then there were more intimate authorities, of masters over servants, heads of households (the great majority male) over those who shared their dwelling, and the nominal authority of husbands over wives.[2] In classical traditions, writers such as Plato and Xenophon had viewed the family as a model for the polity

---

[2] For general overviews, see for example, William Beik, *A social and cultural history of early modern France* (Cambridge: Cambridge University Press, 2009); Michael Mittrauer and Reinhard Siedler, *The European family. Patriarchy to partnership from the Middle Ages to the present* (Oxford: Blackwell, 1982); James Sheehan, *German history 1770–1866* (Oxford: Oxford University Press, 1989), pp. 14–41, 73–89; James R. Farr, *Artisans in Europe 1300–1914* (Cambridge: Cambridge University Press, 2000); Merry E. Wiesner, *Women and gender in early modern Europe*, 2nd edition (Cambridge: Cambridge University Press, 2000).

as a whole, and thus the prince wielded an absolute fatherly authority; to this way of thinking, the well-ordered household was a microcosm of the realm, giving a direct political interest in government promoting a hierarchical view of family life. Some early modern thinkers such as Bodin followed these precepts. Aristotle, on the other hand, had seen things differently; the *polis* was an association of peers, not a field of subordination. Citizens were lords in their own house, but in the street and the marketplace governance was an exercise in consultation.[3]

Amidst this varied experience of authority, political discourse recurrently utilised a relatively narrow array of terms to describe political actors, or indeed the idea of anyone who might legitimately act within the polity. German sources refer frequently and simply to the *Obrigkeit*, the 'authorities', clearly a moveable feast according to context. Appeals were made to the *gemein nutz* ('common good') or the 'common weal'.[4] When advocating the drainage of Sedgemoor in Somerset in the seventeenth century, for example, it was proclaimed beneficial for the 'commonwealth', for 'lawful commoners' and 'the Crown'. The change was supposed to ramify and cement the established order of relationships.[5] The 'common weal' was, in origin, the description of an experience, a blessing shared among inhabitants, but over time it came to describe the shared bounds of a polity itself; the 'commonwealth' being the collective entity which allegedly, at least, shared burdens and enjoyed benefits.[6] 'The Crown' meanwhile was that mysterious metonymy that embraced both the office and the person of the monarch, but that was evoked by anyone executing an action in their stead. In a case of a proposed enclosure, such as that in Sedgemoor, it

---

[3] Keith Tribe, *Land, labour and economic discourse* (London: Routledge & Kegan Paul, 1978), p. 22.

[4] Achim Landwehr, *Policey im Alltag. Die Implementation frühneuzeitlicher Policeyordnungen in Leonberg* (Frankfurt: Klostermann, 2000); Warde, *Ecology*, pp. 335–41; Lyndal Roper, '"The common man", "the common good", "common women". Gender and meaning in the German Reformation commune', *Social History* 12 (1987), pp. 1–22; Peter Blickle (ed.), *Deutsche ländliche Rechtsquellen* (Stuttgart: Klett-Cotta, 1977); Peter Blickle (ed.), *Landgemeinde und Stadtgemeinde in Mitteleuropa. Ein struktereller Vergleich* (Munich: Oldenbourg, 1991).

[5] Paul Slack, *From Reformation to improvement. Public welfare in early modern England* (Oxford: Oxford University Press, 1999), p. 69.

[6] Arguably it was itself an Anglicisation of the Ciceronian notion of *res publica*. Mark Knights, 'Commonwealth. The social, cultural, and conceptual contexts of an early modern keyword', *The Historical Journal* 54 (2011), pp. 663–7.

was thought important to distinguish between those people who might be currently exercising use of the resources of the moor, and the 'lawful commoners' who had a title that might stand up in court. But this also represented a more general view that political rights, or at least the claim that 'the authorities' had a responsibility to look after you even if you had no formal voice yourself, was itself contingent on obedience to the laws as determined by magistrates. As discussed in Chapter 1, the right asserted to have access to the necessary means to make a living according to one's station, the *necessitas domestica*, was seen as a constraint on the actions of those controlling the availability of such means, rather than the state of the means themselves.

These deceptively simple terms were used to describe a great range of relationships that encapsulated the dominant political ideals: of a political community in which members could expect benefits from membership, even though it was generally not voluntary; the idea of a point of sovereignty, a divinely ordained guarantor of order from which authority emanated; and a sense of mutual obligation that rights and rewards came with obeying the rules. Since late medieval times or before, 'public' bodies (as we might see them, somewhat anachronistically) were supposed to work for the welfare of members or subjects, and historians have become increasingly aware of how 'horizontal' ties of loyalty and shared experience were important in binding political communities together. This applied even when the exercise of authority in most of them was limited to privileged groups, whether the prince, nobility, patrician bodies of townsmen or wealthy farming families.[7] Public legitimation of authority heavily stressed the idea of authorities as the overseers of the common good. Whether this was a genuine ambition or not is of course an entirely different matter, never mind the small matter of mutually agreeing what was actually good for the commonality. As a sceptical pamphlet of the German Enlightenment put it, with a *non de plume* of 'Maria Machiavel' evoking the scandalous candour of the Renaissance author, 'No-one really believes that the sovereign's main concern is the welfare of his subjects.'[8]

---

[7] Katherine Lynch, *Individuals, families, and communities in Europe, 1200–1800. The urban foundations of Western society* (Cambridge: Cambridge University Press, 2003).

[8] Andre Wakefield, *The disordered police state. German cameralism as science and practice* (Chicago, IL: Chicago University Press, 2009), p. 11; T.C.W. Blanning, *The culture*

The evocation of the common good or 'weal' simultaneously dramatised what was most dangerous to order and welfare: *'eigen nutz'* or covetousness.[9] It was the turning of the individual's will to solely seek one's own benefit, without care to neighbours, that was seen to be the primary cause of social problems. Suffering was thus seen to be rooted, above all, in individual failings and sinfulness and the associated disregard for others. This view allowed, in some cases, everyday offences to be seen as a profound crime against all, and mandated legal precepts such that adultery, for example, could be treated as a crime of treason, a transgression of all authority. This was in part why the 'improvers' that we met in Chapter 3 drew such close connections between the development of technical knowledge, the virtues of the individuals who did so, and the benefits to be delivered to the wider polity. It also explains why the development of knowledge itself, aside from the practicalities of exchanging ideas, objects and information, were perceived as a fundamentally collegial activity. It explains too the fundamental shock occasioned by the publication of Bernard de Mandeville's *Fable of the bees* of 1723, with its argument that wealth came from pursuing self-interest.[10] There had certainly been many earlier expressions of the notion that people should dispose of their property as they willed (generally articulated in a very self-interested context), but to elevate this to, ironically, a virtue in promoting the wider welfare was a deeply transgressive step.[11]

Government was thus primarily viewed in the sixteenth and seventeenth centuries through a moral lens focused on individual wills, and the potential problem they presented. The emphasis of regulation was on restraint, discipline, good order and securing obedience. The goal of any change was 'Reformation', a matter both personal and political, thus also making the inner life politically charged and from which social order was expected to flow. The government's role

---

of power and the power of culture. Old regime Europe 1660–1789 (Oxford: Oxford University Press, 2002), ch. 6.

[9] Landwehr, *Policey im Alltag*, p. 63; Winifried Schulze, 'Vom Gemeinnutz zum Eigennutz', *Historische Zeitschrift* 243 (1986), pp. 591–625; McCrae, *God speed the plough*, pp. 23–79, 151–6.

[10] This was an expanded version of a text that previously had received little attention.

[11] For precursors, see Slack, *The invention of improvement*, pp. 142–69; Bernard de Mandeville, *The fable of the bees. Or, private vices, public benefits* (London: J. Tonson, 1724).

in providing order often emerged through '*police*', a French word soon taken up in English in the fifteenth century, and closely related to policy: that which the government does to produce order. In German the term '*polizei*' was applied in *Polizeiordnungen*, regulatory and disciplinary legislation passed in many states during the sixteenth century and later.[12] We have encountered in Chapter 1 a frequent preoccupation of these Renaissance governments in this context: the wish to secure tillage, accompanied by the fear that enclosure was covetous and would undermine order.

During the sixteenth century a new concept began to make headway: the 'state'.[13] This was an old word, having many applications just as it does today. It had Latin origins and part of its appeal, via the Italian *stato*, lay in the general enthusiasm for classical learning fired by the Renaissance. In Northern Europe the more frequent use of 'state' over time may also have emerged from the name of the complex of local and territorial assemblies that made up the polities of the Low Countries, and after the 1580s, the Dutch Republic: 'the States', the leading body of which was 'the States General'. These described a network of institutions that exercised sovereign power, yet were not the sovereign: the government beyond or without the prince. In Germany, this abstract beast was known as the *Wesen* in the sixteenth century,

---

[12] K. Härter, *Polizey und Strafjustiz in Kurmainz. Gesetzgebbung, Normdurchsetzung und Sozialkontolle im frühneitzeitlichen Territorialstaat* (Frankfurt: Klostermann, 2005); T. Simon, '*Gute Polizey*'. *Ordnungsleitbilder und Zielvorstellungen politischen Handelns in der frühen Neuzeit* (Frankfurt: Klostermann, 2004); M. Stolleis, 'Was Bedeutet 'Normdurchsetzung' bei Poiceyordnungen der frühen Neuzeit?', in R.H. Helmholz (ed.), *Grundlagen des Rechts* (Paderborn: F.Schöningh, 2000), pp. 740–57; Jürgen Schlumbohm, 'Gesetze, die nicht durchgesetzt warden – ein Strukturmerkmal des frühneuzetlichen Staates', *Geschichte und Gesellschaft* 23 (1997), pp. 647–63; K. Härter (ed.), *Policey und frühneuzeitliche Gesellschaft* (Frankfurt: Klostermann, 2000); André Holenstein, '*Gute Policey*' *und lokale Gesellschaft im Staat des Ancien Régime. Das Fallbeispiel der Markgrafschaft Baden(-Durlach)* (Epfendorf/Neckar: Bibliotecha Academica, 2003); Landwehr, *Policey im Alltag*; Achim Landwehr, 'Die Rhetorik der "Guten Policey"', *Zeitschrift für historische Forschung* 30 (2003), pp. 251–87; Warde, *Ecology*, pp. 161–223; Mark Raeff, *The well-ordered police state. Social and institutional change through law in the Germanies and Russia, 1600–1800* (New Haven, CT: Yale University Press, 1983).

[13] On the emergence of discourses situating the state, see Annabel S. Brett, *Changes of state. Nature and the limits of the city in early modern natural law* (Princeton, NJ: Princeton University Press, 2011).

but *Staat* became a term ever more frequently used by the middle of the seventeenth. Increasingly, it became popularised in usage by writers such as Thomas Hobbes, who neatly straddled the conceptual transition in evoking, 'that great Leviathan called a Common-Wealth, or State', describing an entity that channelled and exercised governing power and held the polity together, somehow more than the sum of its parts and that existed beyond and even despite them.[14]

Of course, the fact of an autonomous body of officials and courtiers who circled a monarch was not a new creation of the sixteenth century, although the work they did became more voluminous and more specialised during the early modern period. But the emergence of this conceptual differentiation was important, because it breathed life into the idea of a government that existed autonomously of the men who staffed it. While it might be essential for those men to be honest, ingenious, loyal and learned, it might also be the case that better government rested on how 'the state', the institution, *functioned*. In turn, over time, this drew the attention of political debate to the material, and we might say, environmental underpinnings of the polity, and hence becomes a crucial part of our story about sustainability. This idea of 'the state' arose hand in hand with the idea of an art of government and, in turn, made possible an art of producing the general welfare too, and the possibility that statesmen like Francis Bacon could contemplate making this a systematic process. Indeed, as is often the case at this time, the appearance of a literature advocating the unity of knowledge and government ran somewhat behind actual practice, because Bacon's contemporary William Cecil was active in such projects for state-directed industrial development during the reign of Elizabeth I.[15] Indeed, governors had been getting on with governing, regulating, allocating resources and policing forests for centuries.[16] However, the emergence of a permanently staffed bureaucracy extended the idea that government might not only act as a guarantor of justice, subsistence, security and the like by passing judgement on those who transgressed accepted norms, but was a body that could develop expertise, a means

[14] Thomas Hobbes, *Leviathan*, ed. R.Tuck (Cambridge: Cambridge University Press, 1996 [1651]), p. 9.
[15] Harkness, *The Jewel House*, pp. 163–74; Thirsk, *Economic policy*.
[16] For example, Appuhn, *A forest on the sea*; Elisabeth Johann, *Geschichte der Waldnutzung in Kärnten unter dem Einfluß der Berg-, Hütten- und Hammerwerke* (Klagenfurt: Verlag des Geschichtsvereines für Kärnten, 1968).

by which society, just like the rent of a plot of land or an agricultural technique, could be *improved*. Indeed, some of the more focused efforts on a general improvement of infrastructure and welfare, such as that pioneered by Henri IV of France at the beginning of the seventeenth century, drew on established techniques of managing great landed estates and applied them to the governance of the Crown's territory as a whole.[17]

At much the same time as the 'state' became popularised, people began to speak more of another medieval and ultimately Latin word, the 'public', and also the 'public good'. The distinction between the public and private was established in English by the mid-sixteenth century, but a little later began to take on the political sense that we associate with the Enlightenment: describing a body of consciously participating people, who have an especial associational quality because of what brings them together as a 'public'. In the long run this would allow consideration of how private interests were arbitrated in the public sphere in an analysis more subtle and morally flexible than the opposition of the 'common good' and 'covetousness'.[18] 'Public good' became suddenly and widely used in Jacobean England. Paul Slack sees it as a term more amenable to a centralising, sovereign monarch than the 'common wealth'. The older term was, he argues, both more inclusive and bore in it the suggestion of claims to a voice; it was collective but hierarchical, and certainly 'commonwealth' became irrevocably hitched to more radical thinking once applied to the regicidal regime of 1649. In contrast everyone could be construed as the monarch's 'public', but what brought them together as a public might not be what was 'common'.[19] Although historians often associate the idea of an emerging 'public' with more vigorous and inclusive debate, and the rise of a less fettered media in the Enlightenment, even in this later period it is recognised that the 'public' was frequently an entity summoned for

[17] Chandra Mukerji, *Impossible engineering. Technology and territoriality on the Canal du Midi* (Princeton, NJ: Princeton University Press, 2009), p. 13.

[18] One can find an early example of this in the arguments of Misselden in his *Circle of Commerce* of 1623 that 'Is not the publique involved in the private, and the private in the publique? What else makes a Common-wealth, but the private-wealth, if I may so say, if the members thereof in the exercise of Commerce amongst themselves.' Cited in J.O. Appleby, *Economic thought and ideology in seventeenth-century England* (Princeton, NJ: Princeton University Press, 1978), pp. 45–6.

[19] Slack, *Reformation to improvement*, p. 75; Slack, *Invention of improvement*, p. 62; Knights, 'Commonwealth', pp. 667, 679–80.

the convenience of speakers, an object one could claim to speak in the name of, an audience more than an actual interlocutor. Enlightenment thinking would wrestle with the question of whether the 'public' best described a plethora of voices out of whose conversation reasoned knowledge would emerge; or whether the public were the recipients of advice and instruction by experts tasked to make things better for them. The German philosopher Christian Wolff clearly articulated the second position, and the distinction between the two, in the 1730s: 'If all possessed the same degree of understanding and virtue, so would each contribute fully and voluntarily to the common welfare according to his powers and capacities: but unfortunately… the greater part of mankind possesses little of either.'[20]

Across the sixteenth and seventeenth centuries we can identify another broad and significant shift. Niccolò Machiavelli had courted controversy, and with his slim treatise *The Prince*, won fame and not a little admiration for inverting the usual advice about what made for a virtuous prince to examine what made for a successful one. Subsequent writers, often critics of Machiavelli, would come to argue that the rulers displayed their virtue by running successful states, and if one wanted to remain a Machiavellian, well then, the success of a ruler rested in any case on the success of a state. The particular virtues of princes were seen as less important over time, while knowledge of what they ruled and how they might rule rose in value.[21] A case in point was Giovanni Botero's *Reason of State* (*Della regio di stato*) penned in the 1580s and already translated into German by 1596: although as *staat* was not yet in fashion, the title referred still to '*polizei*'. As Bacon was to argue, the savant, the experimenter, the natural historian, could all be useful servants of the state. Yet such ideas were certainly much more widespread than the narrowly English circles that followed him, and built on traditions of humanism and practical government across the continent. Indeed, England and Bacon's projecting was marked by a notable failure to provide any institutional anchoring for such ideas.[22]

[20] Tribe, *Land, labour*, p. 31.
[21] A related, although distinct account was provided in Foucault's 'Governmentality'. Graham Burchell, Colin Gordon and Peter Miller (eds), *The Foucault effect. Studies in governmentality* (Chicago, IL: University of Chicago Press, 1991).
[22] Giovanni Botero, *Gründlicher Bericht von Anordnung der Policeyen Regiments auch Fürsten und Herren Stands sampt Gründliche… ung der Ursachen wodurch Stätt zu Auffnemmen und hochheiten komen mögen* (Strassburg: Zetzner, 1596); Slack, *Invention of improvement*, p. 45; Gaukroger, *Francis Bacon*, pp. 69, 162–3.

With the focus moving from the prince to what he or she governed, the question arose: what or who precisely were being governed? This was not just a matter of regulating human relations and seeing that each remained in their allotted places in the social and legal order (a 'society of orders' as historians have called it).[23] Such was a task that could be done without any overview of the whole. The new question was of how those humans were *distributed*, and asking could they be distributed more effectively? Equally, given that people and the fisc relied so much on agriculture, a ruler would have to know how the land was distributed, whether it was used as best it could, where were the mills, who controlled the waterways and the woods, etc.? The rather simple discourse around 'tillage' that we encountered in Chapter 1, predicated on fear of disorder resulting from dearth, shifted over a long period to considering land and people as units that could be shunted around to produce better results through the application of knowledge: a further application of what in England was being called 'improvement'.[24] We have already seen too in Chapter 2 how men like Arthur Standish were projecting reforms of wood production in England on the grand, indeed national scale in the 1610s. A decade later Adam Moore calculated that waste and common land could feed 1.5 million people if brought into cultivation. Improvement and enclosure was becoming an idea that did not pertain to a specific piece of ground and a single rental, but was a mission by which improving the productivity of one aspect of the territory could reap benefits across the whole.[25] Pieces of land would, late in the eighteenth century, become 'land', a factor of production. People would become a 'population'.[26]

In Germany, a determination to take inventories of the prince's whole territory emerged on a large scale in the second half of the seventeenth century. In many regards this was a continuation of previous

---

[23] Peter Burke, 'The language of orders in early modern Europe', in M.L. Bush (ed.)., *Social orders and social classes in Europe since 1500* (London: Routledge, 1992), pp. 1–13.

[24] Warde, 'The idea of improvement', pp. 127–48; Slack, *Invention of improvement*.

[25] Adam Moore, *Bread for the poor, and advancement of the English nation promised by enclosure of the wastes and common grounds of England* (London: Nicholas Bourn, 1653), p. 29.

[26] See also the more theorised considerations in Michel Foucault, *Security, territory, population lectures at the Collège de France, 1977–78*, ed. Michel Sellenart (London: Palgrave Macmillan, 2009).

bureaucratic practices and concerns emergent from the Reformation era. It created its own discipline, and its own set of university courses, named 'cameralism' – the science of the *Kammer* or princely treasury, and the first works in the field were written by men employed directly by princely administrations. In practice, cameralism stretched far beyond a narrow obsession with the princely fisc, because these writers usually viewed government revenue as being a function of the general state of the economy and society.[27] The growth and reputation of cameralism in Germany partly reflected the sheer number of polities within the Holy Roman Empire – this made for a lot of bureaucrats with similar functions in different administrations, and scale of personnel moving between administrations unmatched anywhere else in Europe. Equally, the claustrophobic nature of German politics, with so many principalities shoehorned into limited spaces, made for both an acute sense of the limits of local resources, and the belief that it was a realistic prospect to survey and account for all of those resources in an entire polity.[28] As agendas for government cameralist texts may have often remained rather optimistic, but they could also point to historical evidence of achievement in some of their ambitions; ambitions that remained far beyond the reach of rulers of much larger polities such as Britain, France, Russia or Spain at this time.

Picking up the pieces from the unparalleled destruction of the Thirty Years' War was another stimulus to taking stock and thinking about distributions.[29] Come 1648 and the Treaty of Westphalia, marked with banquets and splendid firework displays by the once antagonistic signatories in their neighbouring camps, the survivors cast an eye about them to see what remained. Across swathes of Central Europe the war had left over half the population dead or flown abroad, the same proportion of houses and barns demolished, burned or collapsed through abandonment.[30] What was left of the livestock, what meadows

[27] On the emergence of cameralism as an academic genre, and its extraction of economic consideration from an Aristotelian preoccupation with ethics, see Keith Tribe, *Strategies of economic order. German economic discourse 1750–1950* (Cambridge: Cambridge University Press, 1995), pp. 8–18.

[28] Indeed, this had already been achieved by some states in surveys undertaken long before the classic rise of cameralism or political arithmetic.

[29] Arguably, the initiatives of Henri IV in France also amounted to a post-war rebuilding program. Mukerji, *Impossible engineering*, p. 22.

[30] Wolfgang von Hippel, 'Bevölkerung und Wirtschaft im Zeitalter des 30 jährigen Krieges', *Zeitschrift für historische Forschung* (1978), pp. 412–48. All German social

were still mowed and fields sown? Authorities sought information on what they still ruled and what they might expect by way of revenue, comparing new surveys with those taken prior to the conflict. In the 1680s and 1690s parts of western Germany would endure much the same all over again as French armies and the putative protectors of the Empire steamrollered their way across the land in the Nine Years' War. These events were the context for the first classic of cameralism, Seckendorff's *Der Teutsche Fürsten Staat* of 1655. The author was yet a young man – a mere 29 – when he penned it, employed as a courtier and librarian in the mini-state of Gotha; his boss a scion of the ruling house of Saxony who had tired of war and claimed a tiny state as his inheritance in 1644, to settle down a build a peace-loving polity. Saxe-Gotha was however a miniscule territory with few resources, and the task Seckendorff set himself was to provide a blueprint for turning this into a renowned polity. He laid out all the things a ruler must know to astutely order his territory: topographical details of the land, the fertility of the soil, the classes of inhabitants, the jurisdictional rights over the grounds and resources.[31] The policies that Seckendorff advocated were in fact entirely unremarkable by late sixteenth century standards; what was novel was folding them together into a single programme for state action.[32]

Cameralist thinkers assumed that the ordering of the polity would be a matter for central and sovereign direction, perhaps a reasonable starting point given the condition of small territories that had been repeatedly ransacked during the war. Some of these 'states' were after all not much different from a very large private *estate*. During the war, leaders had increasingly come to appeal to the 'nation' (*natio*) or religious allegiances to mobilise their populations.[33] After the war, the claim, already long in place, that their sovereign role was to look after their people, became amplified; although given their abject failure to do

and economic histories of this period give some account of the destruction wreaked by the war.

[31] Veit Ludwig von Seckendorff, *Teutscher Fürsten-Staat* (Jena: Johann Meyer, 1737 [1655]) with additions by Hn. Andres Simon von Biechling (Geheimen-Rat in Sachsen-Meiningen); A.W. Small, *The cameralists. The pioneers of German social policy* (New York: Burt Franklin, 1909), p. 72; Wakefield, *Disordered police state*.

[32] Small, *Cameralists*, p. 90.

[33] Robert von Friedeburg, 'The making of patriots. Love of fatherland and negotiating monarchy in seventeenth-century Germany', *Journal of Modern History* 77 (2005), pp. 881–916.

so in the previous decades, they had some work to do. The mantra that to stay in power, you had to look after the population, echoed through cameralist texts. Thus, wrote the Austrian bureaucrat Schröder in 1686, while sovereign power is unlimited in theory, 'the prosperity and welfare of the subjects is the foundation upon which all happiness of a prince as ruler of such subjects is based'.[34] The emergence and ubiquity of these ideas was by no means confined to Central Europe, but was an international conversation. Schröder had travelled to England, was influenced by Hobbes, and was elected a Fellow of the Royal Society.[35] Political thinkers such as Hobbes, Grotius and Puffendorf had international reach. But the direct engagement of political thinkers with the day-to-day business of administration was rarer outside of Central Europe.

Eventually, 'cameralism' moved into the academy, its first lecturer being Simon Peter Gasser installed at Halle as chair of *Oeconomie, Policey und Cammer-sachen* in 1727. Nevertheless, he continued as a leading administrator, a task that took much more of his time than teaching.[36] As well as many governments, Germany had many universities, offering the opportunity for the proliferation of training in the cameralist mindset. At first the advance was slow. In 1755 there were still only five chairs in 'cameralist'-style subjects in Europe, one of which was in Åbo, the Swedish university in what is now Finland. It was only in the later decades of the eighteenth century that cameralism would thoroughly colonise the university world, and in consequence, many of the other subjects taught there.[37] There are straightforward enough political and institutional explanations of why eighteenth-century Germany or Sweden celebrated cameralism while British governments were far less dirigiste. British government was far less interested in inventorising its nation, although it came to closely monitor trade and colonies such as Ireland were a different case

---

[34] Happiness as a goal of government was regularly asserted in Britain and Germany. Small, *Cameralists*, pp. 172, 188–9; Slack, *Invention of improvement*, pp. 207, 253.

[35] Tribe, *Land, labour*, pp. 20, 42–3.

[36] Wakefield has recently stressed the lack of success of their ventures, but he takes a very small sample of cases. Wakefield, *Disordered police state*.

[37] Tribe, *Land labour*, p. 46; Koerner, *Linneaus*, p. 107; on the reception of cameralist thinking in Sweden, and particular the role of Andreas Berch, see in particular, Lars Magnusson, 'Comparing cameralisms. The cases of Sweden and Prussia', and other essays in Marten Seppel and Keith Tribe (eds), *Cameralism in practice. State administration and economy in early modern Europe* (Woodbridge: Boydell & Brewer, 2017).

(see Chapter 3). Some of its public servants, such as Charles Davenant, William Petty and Gregory King, took up the cause enthusiastically if, at times, rather speculatively, and with very modest influence on policy. These differences reflected long-inculcated habits of rule, and the lines of tension within them between different social groups and powerbrokers that emerged out of the tumultuous seventeenth century.

Nevertheless, variant viewpoints about the role of the state also were also linked to divergent ideas about fundamental aspects of social life that did not just split along national lines, but opened up lines of political disputation. This was most marked in arguments about property and its proper relationship with sovereign power. Those who imagined humans to have originally existed in some kind state of nature that permitted individual subsistence, but over time found mutual convenience and security in voluntarily contracting social bonds, tended to think that the social order was still reproduced through processes of negotiation where, in theory if not practicality, the individual commanded a moment of sovereignty. It was not to be assumed that social problems were automatically to be resolved by a collective agency or outside power. The right of property was conferred by labour; laws and customs let you keep it. This view was held by thinkers such as Grotius, Locke, Smith and later Ricardo. In contrast others, such as Puffendorf, scoffed at the idea that people could ever subsist by themselves. They were ineluctably bound to the collective from the beginning, and property and labour were subject from the outset to the state and the civil law. These ideas were championed by Hobbes, Montesquieu and Hume. We can see from these lists of names that the opposed positions did not translate into clear-cut political currents, but the second view was certainly among the intellectual armoury of the cameralists. For them, the subject of politics itself was the state, already assumed as an assembly of families established under a sovereign for their own happiness, its specific task 'finding the means by which the state achieves its purposes'.[38]

---

[38] Tribe, *Land, labour*, pp. 29–30; Fritzbøger, *A windfall for the magnates*, p. 28; Johann Friedrich von Pfeiffer, *Grundsätze der Universal-Cameral-Wissenschaft* (Frankfurt: Eßlinger, 1783); quote from Gottfried Achenwall, *Die Staatsklugheit nach ihren ersten Grundsätzen*, 2nd edition (Göttingen: Witwe Vandenhoeck, 1763), Inhalt, pp. A1r-v; writers did provide varying accounts of how this need for the estate arose; for Justi, it was the natural consequence of internal disagreements leading to a demand for wise counsel, arbitration and decision. Johann Gottlob von Justi, *Die*

Justifications for state regulation were also historical. Johann Heinrich Gottlob von Justi (1717–71) was perhaps the most prolific and renowned of the cameralists, indeed uninhibited in self-expression to the degree that one wonder at times if he ever failed to write down any of his thoughts. He argued that originally the forests had been the property of the emperor. At an early date, however, the emperor had alienated them to lords as there was no possibility of them generating revenue. Yet as property rights devolved down from an original right of the ruler, the government still retained final responsibility to ensure that the woods were well maintained. In any case, this right of *regal* over the forest was also drawn from the basic responsibility already frequently articulated in the sixteenth century that woodlands 'required the especial care of the government being an indispensible part of human life'. They were a 'collective necessity' (*gemeinschaftlichen Nothdurft*), a 'national necessity' (*Landesnotdurft*).[39] No ruler could ignore them. Thus by the early eighteenth century – and this is the crucial point – the concept of a 'state' was very widely established as a body that steered society through developing knowledge and expertise about that society, while in turn the endowment and condition of resources shaped the ability of the state to act. Increasingly, both in Britain and continental Europe, the 'happiness' of subjects underpinned the might of the ruler, while both happiness and might derived from access to material goods.[40] Wealth, rather than order, was becoming an overriding concern, and wealth required resources. Nature was swept up in a wider process of 'unification', as Eli Heckscher understood the development

Nature und das Wesen der Staaten als die Grundwissenschaft der Staatskunst, der Policey und aller Regierungswissenschaften (Berlin: Johann Heinrich Rüdiger, 1760), pp. 19–20.

[39] Johann Gottlob von Justi, *Staatswirtschaft oder systematische Abhandlung aller Oekonomischen und Cameralwissenschaftn, die zur Regierung eines Landes efodert [sic] werden* (Leipzig: Bernhard Christoph Breitkopf, 1758), pp. 206–7. For the most extensive account of the eighteenth-century understanding of the development of rights over the forest from Carolingian times, see Friederich Ulrich Stisser, *Forst- und Jagd Historie der deutschen* (Jena: Johann Friedrich Ritter, 1737).

[40] Craig Muldrew, 'From commonwealth to public opulence. The redefinition of wealth and government in early modern Britain', in Steve Hindle, Alexandra Shepard and John Walter (eds), *Remaking English society. Social relations and social change in early modern England* (Woodbridge: Boydell & Brewer, 2013), pp. 317–39; Paul Warde, 'Sustainability, resources and the destiny of states in German cameralist thought', in K. Forrester and S. Smith (eds), *Nature, action, and the future. Political thought and the environment* (Cambridge: Cambridge University Press, 2018).

of the idea of national economies at this time.[41] The state of nature thus also had to be a foremost area of a government's responsibility.

Resources

Nearly every person who turned their mind to such questions of development or improvement would have agreed with the judgement of Seckendorff: 'the greatest treasure of the country consists in the number of well-nourished people'.[42] This might come as a surprise to those schooled in the Malthusian tradition, who have noted that periods of rapid population expansion brought decreased income and more frequent crises to early modern polities while periods of low population growth, stagnation or the aftermath of crashes saw real incomes surge and in some cases, a degree of political equanimity prevail. Yet in the aftermath of cataclysmic falls in populations that had struck much of Central and Eastern Europe in the seventeenth century it was unsurprising that many rulers thought their subjects too few. Seckendorff wrote in 1655, when wide parts of Germany, Denmark and Poland were de-peopled and half-ruined. England, for different reasons, had a historically high proportion of unmarried adult inhabitants in the second half of the seventeenth century, and influenced by political arithmetic (see below), even passed a pro-natalist statute to levy a tax on the unwed, with rather little effect.[43] For most Enlightenment writers, it was evident that income was largely produced by the sweat of men and women's brows. As Julian Hoppit has noted, this claim was so ubiquitous as to be one of 'profound unoriginality'.[44] Mechanisation and capital endowment was limited in the vast majority of trades, where artisanry, reliability and physical strength were crucial to success. Thus more workers self-evidently meant more wealth, more consumers and larger markets encouraging commerce, leading in turn to more tax revenue, as well as a larger soldiery. After all, had God not

---

[41] In his classic work Heckscher identified these as 'mercantilist', the debate over which has often been confused by different definitions of the term. Eli F. Heckscher, *Mercantilism*, revised edn, ed. E.F. Söderlund (London: Allen & Unwin, 1955).

[42] Small, *Cameralists*, p. 104; see also p. 33.

[43] Slack, *Invention of improvement*, p. 181.

[44] Julian Hoppit, 'Political arithmetic in eighteenth-century England', *EcHR* 49 (1996), pp. 519–33.

instructed humankind to multiply and replenish the earth with people? Meanwhile, particularly in the eighteenth century, scholars conducted a long-running and lively debate over whether current populations were larger or smaller than those of the Roman Empire, and whether society was in a state of advance or decay.[45]

Nevertheless, Seckendorff had qualified his argument. The population should be *well-nourished*. Similarly, a century later Justi famously declared, 'A country in which subsistence and commerce flourish can never have too many inhabitants', and indeed he thought population densities could rise to three or four times the densities of the most populous states.[46] If Enlightenment economic thinkers regarded larger populations as desirable, they did not think that a growing population was in and of itself a route to wealth. Indeed, this important qualification with its attention to the need to provision people distinguished them from earlier commentators such as Bodin, Botero and Bacon who had commented favourably on large population.[47] The requirement of a florescence of food production and exchange was a stringent one in the conditions of eighteenth-century Central Europe. Nevertheless, there was no trace of the anxieties that would be expressed so forcefully by Malthus at the end of the eighteenth century: that the natural

---

[45] Rusnock, *Vital accounts*; Fredrik Albritton Jonsson, *Enlightenment's frontier. The Scottish Highlands and the origins of environmentalism* (New Haven, CT: Yale University Press, 2013), pp. 196–8; Carol Blum, *Strength in numbers. Population, reproduction and power in eighteenth-century France* (Baltimore, MD: Johns Hopkins University Press, 2002).

[46] Tribe, *Land, labour*, p. 65; the desirability of a greater population is found throughout Justi's works, and is seen as self-evident: 'should not every government have this wise intention?' *Die Grundfeste zu der Macht und Glückseligkeit der Staaten; oder ausführliche Vorstellung der gesamten Policey-Wissenschaft.* 1er Band. (Königsberg: Johann Heinrich Hartungs Erben, 1760), p. 81, *passim*; Ingrid Schäfer, *'Ein Gespenst geht um'. Politik mit der Holznot in Lippe 1750–1850. Eine Regionalstudie zur Wald und Technikgeschichte* (Detmold: Naturwissenschaftlicher u. Historischer Verein f. d. Land Lippe, 1992), p. 19.

[47] Slack, *Invention of improvement*, pp. 45–6; Jean Bodin, *The sixe books of commonweale* (London: G. Bishop, 1606); for an excellent discussion of the varied and developing understanding of 'population' in relation to situation and economic activities in seventeenth-century England, see Ted McCormick, 'Population. Modes of seventeenth-century demographic thought', in Philip J. Stern and Carl Wennerlind (eds), *Mercantilism reimagined. Political economy in early modern Britain and its empire* (New York: Oxford University Press, 2014), pp. 25–45. This theme runs throughout Nathaniel Wolloch, *Nature in the history of economic thought. How natural resources became an economic concept* (Basingstoke: Palgrave Macmillan, 2017).

tendency of populations was to expand, and this inevitably led to penury. Indeed, in contrast to Malthus, earlier writers could provide very clear empirical evidence as to whether a dense population was desirable or not. Andrew Yarranton had noted in 1681, 'where ever the Country is full of people, they are rich; and where thin, there the place is poor, and all Commodities cheap'.[48] Parts of southern England, the Netherlands and the Italian countryside exemplified the simple truth of this statement.

In the seventeenth century, no-one put more effort into accounting of people and resources than the colonial administrator, experimenter, economist and statistician William Petty. Initially inspired through work with the Hartlib circle discussed in Chapter 3, Petty soon, like the contemporary cameralist writers, cut his teeth on questions of distributing people and property in a devastated country: in his case, Ireland. Yet his pioneering works were also a response to the geopolitics of the 1660s and 1670s, and arguments about the relative strengths and virtues of England, France and the Netherlands. Despite the fact that the Netherlands had taken a greater battering in the wars of those decades than either of its rivals, it remained the economic powerhouse, and Petty stated bluntly at the beginning of his *Political Arithmetick* (penned in 1676 but not published until 1691, long withheld because of his embarrassingly low opinion of the state of France, an ally at the earlier date): '*A small Country and few People, may be equivalent in Wealth and Strength to a far greater People and Territory.*' More people was a good thing; but only if people were adequately supplied with resources and fertile soil. 'This part of the first principal Conclusion needs little proof', he continued, 'forasmuch as *one* Acre of Land, may bear as much Corn, and feed as many Cattle, as *twenty*, by difference of the Soil.'[49] Yet such immediate natural advantages were only part of the story. 'But the second and more material part of this Conclusion is,

[48] Yarranton, *England's improvement*, pp. 52–3; similarly, Daniel Defoe proclaimed, 'all that's valuable in a Nation... depends upon the number of its people'. Cited in Muldrew, *Food, energy and the creation of industriousness*, p. 310.

[49] William Petty, *Political Arithmetick* (London: Robert Clavel & Henry Mortlock, 1691), p. 1; see McCormick, *William Petty*, esp. pp. 8–9. These considerations also had a bearing on the relative importance of labour and land in producing wealth, as well as what was a desirable population, to which we will return in Chapter 7. See Andrea Finkelstein, *Harmony and balance. An intellectual history of seventeenth-century English economic thought* (Ann Arbor, MI: University of Michigan Press, 2000), p. 123.

that this difference in Land and People, arises principally from their *Situation, Trade*, and *Policy*.'[50]

Selective empirical observations backed up this point. Petty noted how it was possible to build a polity on relatively infertile lands, or where natural resources were comparatively scarce, and still prosper. Such observations were selective because they did not seek to take a broader view, by which it was obvious there were no wealthy societies, or indeed cities of any kind, in the frozen far north. Still, it was clear commercial acumen could transcend local limits: 'the matter is in itself as clear as the sun', wrote the Austrian bureaucrat Schröder after his peregrinations around Europe in the 1680s.[51] As early as 1613 the Italian writer Antonio Serra had set himself the task of explaining why Venice, isolated in its lagoon, was so much more commercially successful than Naples with its vast subject hinterland, in part because of Naples' persistent problems in its balance of payments. The answer was the Venetian focus on manufacture and commerce, on adding value to materials and specialising in what we might now call products with increasing returns. Much the same argument was made, with the approval of the head of the Dutch government and against the restriction of liberties by the Princes of Orange, by Pieter de la Court in 1662.[52] In England, John Keymer had observed in 1650 that although the wood resources lay in the east lands, 'the huge piles of Wainscot, Clapboards, Fir-deals, Masts and Timber, is in the Low Countries where none growth'.[53]

These views were something of a departure from the orthodoxy around the opening of the seventeenth century, which attributed

[50] Petty, *Political Arithmetick*, p. 2; a similar list was provided by Serra in 1613, but his tract was not known before the second half of the eighteenth century: Antonio Serra, [*Breve tratatto*] *A short treatise on the wealth and poverty of nations*, trans. Sophus A. Reinert (London: Anthem Press, 2011 [1613]), pp. 119–33; on the importance of situation, see also Pieter de la Court, *The true interest and political maxims of the Republic of Holland*, trans. John Campbell (London: J. Nourse, 1746), pp. 20–8. De la Court was also, like Petty, keen on the collection of quantitative data to illustrate his points, although rather less of an outlier and far less engaged with accounting than implied in Jacob Soll, 'Accounting for government. Holland and the rise of political economy in seventeenth-century Europe', *Journal of Interdisciplinary History* XL (2009), pp. 226–7 (although with a caveat on p. 229); see also McCormick, *William Petty*, pp. 169–75.

[51] Small, *Cameralists*, p. 160.

[52] Serra, *A short treatise*, pp. 133–55. De la Court, *True interest*, passim.

[53] Cited in Appleby, *Economic thought*, pp. 75–6.

potential economic success more to the inherent properties of the locality, and resources available to hand. Often such views were little more than a kind of local patriotism and bombast rather than anything more theoretical: take the Chancellor of France's boast in opening the Estates general of 1484, that 'this most prosperous kingdom has a greater number of provinces which, because of the beauty of the country-side, of the fertility of the soil, of the health-giving air, easily surpass all the countries of the earth', followed by much more in that vain vein.[54] However, as with any argument about climate, resources and economic success, such assertions did not take place in a vacuum, or some featureless theoretical space. Assertions that God had blessed particular places to be great were usually made out of a sense of frustration that people were *not* making the best of the hand they had been dealt. Thus the French king Henry IV's *controleur general du commerce* could survey the same land as his predecessor had more than a century previously and lament that 'Our French business men do not appreciate the priceless boon they have received from God when He caused them to be born in so rich and beautiful a country, with such mild skies and such fertile, smiling lands that it can bear and furnish even metals, raw materials, fruits, and the like; of which we do not know how to make good use.'[55] Men in government were particularly alarmed by this because it meant that scarce bullion was employed to buy in goods from overseas, whether these were allegedly superfluous luxuries like Italian silk stockings, or the sinews of power like naval stores and horses. These opinions have led to the erroneous belief among some historians that such 'mercantilists' (as so often, a retrospective and hostile appellation) mistakenly thought that wealth solely subsisted in precious metals and a positive balance of trade drawing them in. But the view, whilst often predicated on what looks retrospectively a weak grasp of economics, was a reflection of the monetary dilemmas faced by weak fiscal regimes dependent on scarce coin. As Montchrétien, coiner of the expression *oeconomie politique* in 1615, put it in a rather intemperate and xenophobic pamphlet calling for

[54] C.W. Cole, *Colbert and a century of French mercantilism* (Hamden, NY: Columbia University Press, 1939), p. 8; such general references to climate, as we have seen already in Chapter 3, can be found in authors such as Botero, but were not turned into any serious programme of government investigation and action. Botero, *Gründlicher Bericht*, p. 63.

[55] Cole, *Colbert*, p. 29.

the protection of domestic industries, 'It is not the abundance of gold and silver, the quantity of pearls and diamonds, which makes states opulent. It is the supply of things necessary for life and suitable for clothing.'[56] But he saw the export of bullion as investment lost to the mother nation.[57]

Yet this did not mean that economies could somehow float free of material necessities. It simply meant that it was possible to import them if you had something to exchange, and the means to achieve such exchange. Venice, as we have seen, still made sterling efforts to ensure that its acquisitions on *terrafirma* provided its arsenal and citizens with a ready supply of wood. As for the mighty Venetian trades, they still required the raw materials of someplace. Other economies, such as those of Scandinavia and Russia, were already conscious that in exporting raw materials to Britain and the Netherlands they commanded the part of the productive process that paid least, and sought to develop domestic industry. Considering the Dutch, Petty was not inclined to 'magnifie the *Hollanders*, as if they were more, and all other Nations less than Men… making them Angels, and others Fools, Brutes, and Sots' (and indeed he had spent time examining the cadavers of Dutchmen, studying anatomy in Leiden); 'I take the Foundation of their achievements to lie originally in the Situation of the Country, whereby they do things inimitable by others, and have advantages whereof others are incapable.'[58] For the Dutch, the natural advantage lay partly in a fertile soil but above all their access and use of water, facilitating trade. Thus argued Petty, that while other nations thought they could match the peerless Dutch, they knew they could never match their *situation*, placed at the gateway to the Baltic and dominating the great hinterland of the Rhine and Meuse. Access to resources was crucial, but they did not have to be produced domestically.

---

[56] Cole, *Colbert*, pp. 84, 86.

[57] This was equally a major theme in the famous English debate about the balance of trade and bullion in the 1620s, prompted by disruption to trade early in the decade. Here, not least because of suspicion of the granting of monopolies by the Crown, advocates of a more liberal trade policy emerged to argue that the resolution of imbalances was to increase exports. Appleby, *Economic thought*, pp. 36–45. A useful discussion of early thought, especially Italian, regarding commerce and trade is provided in Sophus Reinert, 'Introduction', in Antonio Serra, *A short treatise on wealth and poverty of nations (1613)*, ed. Sophus Reinert (London: Anthem Press, 2011), pp. 1–85.

[58] Petty, *Political arithmetick*, p. 10.

In the landlocked territories of the Holy Roman Empire, natural endowments, and wood in particular, loomed larger in political thinking. There could be no one-size-fits-all method of generating wealth, because God had chosen to distribute resources unevenly over the world ('to one land or empire this, to the other that heavenly blessing'), a deliberate way of inducing ingenuity and exchange.[59] So you needed people; you needed resources; and you needed knowledge. Indeed, this was very much in the tradition that we now think of as Baconian, already encountered in Chapter 3, by which the writing of natural history is a boon to the state and nature was a kind of 'factory in the earth' awaiting its ingenious workforce, as suggested by the Austrian cameralist Johann Joachim Becher and Saxon physician Urban Gottfried Bucher.[60]

It was also a problem that trade, even if feasible due to one's situation, left a nation vulnerable. Right down to the post-Napoleonic era the Baltic was frequently closed to the shipping of one nation or another, whether by accident of conflict among others making trade hazardous, or by the design of deliberate blockade. Exchange was subject to domestic events and the reactions they elicited, such as when Russia cut off the Archangel trade to Britain in 1649 as a response to the execution of Charles I.[61] There were consequently great incentives to ensure what we might call today 'resource security'. This could be done domestically, sometimes with the aid of mercantilist tariffs and restrictions on commerce that aimed to stimulate the productive use of raw materials at home. It could equally be achieved by drawing new colonies into the nation's orbit, both as sources of demand for domestic manufactures, but also to secure raw materials, and securing precedence or exclusivity in the shipping of goods, as England's Navigation Acts achieved after 1651. Both Britain and France's gains in North America were frequently advertised, for example, as substitutes for

---

[59] Carlowitz, *Sylvicultura oeconomica*, p. 64; see also Houghton, *Collection*, pp. 441–2.
[60] Cooper, *Inventing the indigenous*, p. 149; and see the general discussion pp. 140–51. Typically, such ideas were anticipated by Botero. See Slack, *Invention of improvement*, p. 33. Becher however very much focused on stimulating commerce and regulating market structures as a route to economic development. Johann Joachim Becher, *Politischer Discurs von den eigentlichen Ursachen deß Auf- und Abnehmens der Städt, Länder und Republicken* (Frankfurt: Johann David Zunner, 1668).
[61] J.T. Kolitaine, *Russia's foreign trade and economic expansion in the seventeenth century. Windows on the world* (Leiden: Brill, 2005), p. 108.

dependence on the 'Eastland trade' or Russia, securing supplies of timber, furs, ashes, iron, hemp and flax.[62] Indeed, the great questions of resources and trade came together above all in the need for shipping. It was this industry that provided a stimulus to colonisation, domestic tree-planting and protection, and in turn the development of a great merchant and military marine to keep the shipping lanes open. Oliver Cromwell declared to the English Parliament in 1658, 'If [the Dutch] can shut us out of the Baltic Sea, and make themselves masters of that, where is your trade? Where are your materials for your shipping?'[63] It came to be argued that good government rested on an itemisation and assessment of the territory's topography, natural history, population, agriculture, arts and commerce, as the list ran in Bern's *Oeknomische Gesellschaft* in 1762, itself working from precedents published in Sweden, Denmark, England, Ireland, Germany, Spain and France.[64] From attention to such things could greatness come, or as the younger Pitt argued in the 1780s, 'we owe our wealth and safety to an acorn'.[65]

Hans Carl von Carlowitz was born in 1645 only a relatively short distance from the Friedenburg castle in Gotha where Seckendorff penned *Der Fürsten-Staat*. When Carlowitz died 69 years later, he could look back on a long and distinguished life in the service of the Duchy of Saxony, in various roles overseeing the administration of mining, the metallurgical industries and forests. He had sustained a family tradition, as no fewer than seven of his ancestors, a well-established family of nobles, had held similar posts in the century before his birth.[66]

[62] Malcolm Gaskill, *Between two worlds. How the English became Americans* (Oxford: Oxford University Press, 2013).

[63] Cited in H. Zins, *England and the Baltic in the Elizabethan era* (Manchester: Manchester University Press, 1972), p. 3.

[64] Martin Stuber, '"dass gemeinnüzige wahrheiten gemein gemacht werden" – Zur Publikationstätigkeit der *Oekonomischen Gesellschaft Bern 1759-1798*', in Marcus Popplow, *Landschaften agrarisch-ökonomischen Wissens. Strategien innovativer Ressourcennutzung in Zeitschriften und Sozietäten des 18. Jahrhunderts* (Münster: Waxmann, 2010), pp. 126-7.

[65] E. Harries, 'A hint to the Minister of the Crown lands', *Annals of Agriculture* V (1786), p. 410.

[66] K. Hasel and E. Schwartz, *Forstgeschichte. Ein Grundriss für Studium und Praxis*, 3rd edition (Remagen-Oberwinter: Kessel, 2006), p. 318; Bernd Bendix, 'Zur Biographie eines Vordenkers der Nachhaltigkiet, Hans Carl von Carlowitz (1645-1714)', in Sächsische Carlowitz-Gesellschaft (ed.), *Die Erfindung der Nachhaltigkeit. Leben, Werk and Wirkung des Hans Carl von Carlowitz* (Munich: Oekom verlag, 2013), pp. 175-216.

He also, by the time of his death in 1714, produced what would turn out to be his own foundational text, the work now viewed as the first of its kind by many modern foresters: the *Sylvicultura Oeconomica*, penned during a final infirmity, published in 1713, and reprinted in 1732. This great tome summarised a lifetime's experience in the forests. It was also the first systematic attempt from a practical man of long experience in the woods to balance the demands of the state for resources, and the capacity of the woodlands to supply those resources.

Like all his early modern predecessors, Carlowitz saw his land as one tamed and stripped of trees by the progress of civilisation and growth of population. Once upon a time, he noted, Germany, Denmark, Sweden, England and Scotland had all been covered with woods set too thick to set foot in, as now could only be found in the colonial woods. At the time of Tacitus, Germany was blanketed by 'monstrous great woods' (*'ungeheuren grossen Wälder'*) of which only relics remained.[67] Nevertheless, the current distribution of woods was not only the result of historical events, but reflected the divine beneficence of a God who placed great reserves of fuel where the climate was coldest, hence explaining the great woods of the north.[68] In recent times, however, the growing shortage of wood, that familiar trope, presented a threat to the future progress of civilisation; for him, the wood ordinances of the sixteenth century were already historical evidence of this process. Carlowitz described future prospects in stereotypically hysterical fashion: without remedy 'poverty, distress and woe will groan, and suffer loss of sustenance, health and finally life'.[69] His particular concerns were very directly connected with his long employment by the state, although he was doubtless also conscious of addressing his employer, the Duke, and their shared interest in developing the duchy's key sources of income from mining, smelting and commerce. The production of the mines was 'through God's blessing inexhaustible', but 'wise men' had long been led to 'prophesying' that wood supplies could not keep up with the supply of metal, so that 'a future wood-shortage' would

---

[67] Carlowitz, *Sylvicultura oeconomica*, pp. 3–5, 43; Carlowitz, *Sylvicultura oeconomica*, 1732 edn, p. 99.
[68] Carlowitz, *Sylvicultura oeconomica*, p. 7.
[69] Carlowitz, *Sylvicultura oeconomica*, p. 44.

bring the mines into decline, and 'the flourishing commerce might be inhibited'.[70]

The elderly Carlowitz turned his energies against such possibilities. He was wiser than the wise men. There was no shortage of land so long as there was a 'careful cultivation of wood [*pflegilich Holz-Cultur*]', by which 'the poor subjects and our dear posterity may prosper through maintenance of their sustenance'.[71] Neither did he agree with those who argued that the state of local supplies were of no concern because there were so many woods yet unexploited in remote places. People no longer lived in the Garden of Eden where you did not have to work for your keep, he noted. Rather, there was a gross waste of resources close to home; many patches of ground where two or three trees stood that could house 20.[72] The problem was neglect; the problem was, as ever in early modern times, people. People thought, erroneously, that you could just rely on nature, 'as if this would always from itself proffer and furnish a superfluity of wood, without the application of people's industry and labour'. However, if industry and labour *were* applied one would not be able to describe the plenty of wood that could ensue. Carlowitz has been hailed as a prophet of sustainability today, but he was not arguing in the modern mode. Metal ores 'would not be used up... so long as the world exists' and wood was 'the inexhaustible treasure of our land' so long as people worked to tease it out of the ground.[73] He argued too against the thesis of the senescence of the Earth, that as it aged it would become more unproductive:

> It is mostly people who are themselves guilty, when infertility is found in the earth... ground and soil remain eternally able to harbour enough vegetation, if they are not neglected by people's lack of diligence, their carelessness, their inattentiveness, but appropriately worked, planted and cultivated, coming to the aid of a seemingly powerless Nature, and thus will the soil's

---

[70] He added the shortage, although Europe-wide, was particularly marked in the vicinity of mines, and also that the English had to import ship timbers from America at high prices. Carlowitz, *Sylvicultura oeconomica*, pp. 7, 44, 52–3.

[71] 'denen armen Unterthane und der lieben *Posterität* zur Erhaltung ihrer Nahrung *prospiciret* werden mag.' Carlowitz, *Sylvicultura oeconomica*, p. 5.

[72] Carlowitz, *Sylvicultura oeconomica*, p. 43.

[73] Carlowitz, *Sylvicultura oeconomica*, 1732 edn, p. 65.

perpetual and continually effective power be allowed to erupt in unending fertility.[74]

It is clear that Carlowitz and his cameralist contemporaries did not believe that, as some historians have believed of them, the economy of their time was a zero-sum game with fixed resources that set insurmountable limits to development. Protectionist policies, military competition or 'rent-seeking', using political power to cream off income rather than increasing productivity, were not the natural outgrowth of an assumption about the 'fixed' amount of wealth in the world.[75] Rather, they believed that local resources profoundly conditioned the starting point of each economy in a divinely ordained plan that enjoined the wise and pious to hard and ingenious labour. The rewards to such hard-working and knowledgeable men were, potentially, endless, both in this world and the next. 'The most savage wilderness, where hardly a sparrow can feed itself, can through good economics become the most wonderful land', exclaimed Linnaeus.[76] The husbanding and utilisation of resources would unlock the door to worldwide commercial expansion and exchange. As other places relied on grain, animals, fisheries or navigation, in Saxony it was wood. Natural resources were thus an essential basis for success, but were nothing without knowledge and expertise in how to use them, and how to exchange them. Equally, a successful state relied on the husbanding of resources into the future.

Thus Justi expressed the consensus of the age when he implied that larger populations were not a good in themselves, but

---

[74] Carlowitz, *Sylvicultura oeconomica*, p. 106.
[75] Although some statements, for example by Colbert, seem to bear in this direction, they were generally explicitly fixed on the short term and the exigencies of war financing. Colbert's famous memorandum to Louis XIV, for example, speaks of a fixed amount vessels carrying total trade, where 'it is easy to see that this number cannot be increased so long as the population in all countries and consumption are always equal'. Yet over the long term writers did not expect either of these conditions to hold. Many writers of the late seventeenth century were clearly preoccupied with the *relative* wealth of nations, and understood competition in commerce, and hence military might, in such terms. Terence Hutchison, *Before Adam Smith. The emergence of political economy, 1662–1776* (Oxford: Oxford University Press, 1988), p. 88; Heckscher, *Mercantilism*, pp. 22, 26. For a more varied and nuanced discussion of 'mercantilist' thought, see Philip J. Stern and Carl Wennerlind (eds), *Mercantilism reimagined. Political economy in early modern Britain and its empire* (New York: Oxford University Press, 2014).
[76] Koerner, *Linnaeus*, p. 102.

well-nourished and knowledgeable people were. Indeed, Carlowitz went on to praise the English for 'unending diligence, curiosity and industry', lauding along with the Dutch their famed efforts to conserve wood and provide shipbuilding timbers 'for themselves and their descendants'. This was not a very accurate description of what those maritime nations were actually doing, with their much greater propensity to increase imports rather than sow the land with trees, but speaks loudly of the values and associations that Carlowitz wished to see in Saxony.[77] The more perceptive observers of the time understood that far from inevitably leading to the destruction of the woodlands, industrial demand could provide a stimulus to husband resources and increase yields.[78] Indeed, just as the improvers of seventeenth-century England, cameralists understood well that states suffered from *under-exploiting* forest resources that were too remote from centre of demand. It was imperative to open up transport links; and if it was not possible to access the necessary waterways, then industry should be transferred to the forest to ensure revenue was not lost and precious specie spent on imports.[79] There was scope for specialisation too, as proposed by the Uppsala professor Anders Berch in 1759, so 'each county could have its main occupation, one grow grains, another keeps cows, butter and cheese, leather, a third takes care of sheep, a fourth horses'.[80]

The material world was thought to impose unavoidable constraints of *situation*, but the use of wit and knowledge to make the best of what was God-given could still navigate a path to enduring prosperity. Nevertheless, some resources were undeniably better than others. Justi pondered in the 1750s – as had Arthur Standish almost a century and a half before – whether coal was a viable alternative to firewood, an idea already being encouraged in several German states. His answer, given the clear evidence of British dependence on the mineral fuel, was affirmative. Justi did not think in terms of energy, but instead noted 'a northern land which has much mineral coal will

---

[77] Carlowitz, *Sylvicultura oeconomica*, 1732 edn, pp. 55–6, 65. These impressions were possibly gathered in his years of foreign travel and reading Evelyn's work that appeared only shortly before he arrived in England.

[78] Johnan Gottlob von Justi, *Politische und Finanzschriften über wichtige Gegenstände der Stattskunst, der Kriegswissenschaften und des Cameral- und Finanzwesens* (Kopenhagen und Leipzig: Rothenschen Buchhandlung, 1761), p. 441.

[79] Justi, *Politische und Finanzschriften*, p. 462.

[80] Cited in Koerner, *Linnaeus*, p. 98.

always, in relation to its other natural endowments, be able to be far more peopled, than another, that is not provided with these subterranean goods of nature, which take up no space on the surface'. Peat did not confer the same advantages of coal because it required large areas of the surface, and, so he claimed, was not so productive per unit of area. Yet for all the efforts of Prussia and other states during the eighteenth century to encourage the use of coal, it remained a minor fuel in comparison to wood, because the infrastructure was lacking that permitted it to be more widely employed. Coal seams were too remote, too difficult to mine, and nobody had any notion of the size of the reserves. Justi also observed that in cities where coal firing was widespread, such as London or Halle, it had detrimental effects on health.[81] He did not know that he was laying out some of the dominant features of life over the next two centuries.

Balance

So, a successful state needed commerce; and commerce needed resources. Yet if commerce or population expanded, could resources keep pace? For the authors I have cited so far the yield extracted from the earth was so meagre compared to its potential that this concern was hardly worth worrying about. It was not space or trees that were lacking, but the human capacity to make best use of them. True, there were some uses of trees that were so demanding of the raw material that only vast areas of land with precious few other demands on them could ever realistically provide for them, such as the production of tar, pitch or potash which caused 'a great ruin to the woodlands'. These products were best left to the Russians, or perhaps North America.[82]

There was no dismal law of diminishing returns in this world. Petty assumed that originally the number of people was in proportion to the land that it inhabited, and if not, this must be attributable to

---

[81] Justi, *Politische und Finanzschriften*, p. 442; Justi, *Die Nature*; On Prussian efforts more generally, see Rolf-Peter Sieferle, *The subterranean forest. Energy systems and the Industrial Revolution* (Knapwell: White Horse Press, 2001); Schäfer, '*Ein Gespenst geht um*', p. 19; Winifried Schenk, *Waldnutzung, Waldzustand und regionale Entwicklung in vorindustrieller Zeit im mittleren Deutschland* (Stuttgart: Steiner, 1996), p. 101.

[82] Justi, *Politische und Finanzschriften*, p. 464.

their 'situation', that is, some extraordinary capacity in the soil, or their ability to capture trade.[83] When he noted that London was seven times larger in his day than under the rule of Elizabeth I, he wondered aloud before the Royal Society in 1682 what the consequences of it becoming seven times larger again (and thus enjoying 4,960,000 inhabitants) might be. Would there be a sufficiency of 'bread and drink-corn... fruits, garden stuff, hay, timber', coal? His answer was affirmative, although he less sanguine as to whether his calculation of a future where a million sermons were preached in England each year, 'Composed by so many Men, and of so many Minds and Methods, should produce *Uniformity* upon the discomposed understandings of about 8 Millions of Hearers.'[84] He anticipated limits on the city's expansion, but these were imposed by the necessity of having a labour force sufficiently large to provide food for the metropolis, and given that by his projected rates of growth the population of London would very nearly match that of the rest of England by 1842, 'Then it follows, That *London* will be at its highest growth, and eight times as great as now, *Anno* 1800. That the *Growth* of *London* must stop before the said Year 1842, as aforesaid, and must be at its greatest height *Anno* 1800.' The whole world had a little longer; at Petty's estimate of 320 million around 1680, and this population doubling every 360 years, there were two full millennia before humankind being reduced to having two acres per head in the 'habitable parts' of the Earth. 'And then, according to the *Prediction* of the *Scriptures*, there must be *Wars* and great *Slaughter*, &c.' This might seem a gloomy assessment, but it is striking that Petty did not imagine the diminishing per capita extent of the 'habitable Earth' as being an issue until that final cliff edge was reached; in a providential universe, the story of population growth could be conveniently closed by the Last Judgement. In the meantime, resources could keep step with population. More cheerily, Petty also calculated the number of people that had ever lived, and then how much material might be required to constitute the resurrected bodies of the total of the Quick and the Dead should the Last Judgement be visited upon the Earth in the 1680s.

---

[83] Petty, *Political arithmetick*, p. 3.

[84] William Petty, *Another essay in political arithmetic, concerning the growth of the city of London; with the measures, periods, causes and consequences thereof* (London: Mark Pardoe, 1683), pp. 31, 34–5.

He was able to refute contemporary sceptics who fretted whether the whole globe could provide the substance for this great host; in fact, it would only take a one-foot thickness of turf pared from the surface of one-fifth of Ireland.[85]

The view of Malthus a century later regarding wealth and population was no different from the earlier consensus:

> The reason that the greater part of Europe is more populous now than it was in former times is that the industry of the inhabitants has made these countries produce a greater quantity of human subsistence. For, I conceive, that it may be laid down as a position not to be controverted, that, taking a sufficient extent of territory to include within it exportation and importation; and allowing some variation for the prevalence of luxury, or of frugal habits; that population constantly bears a regular proportion to the food that the earth is made to produce.[86]

A population would eventually encounter, of course, those limits we now call 'Malthusian', and to which we will return in Chapter 7. But the impression derived from the previous course of history was that food supplies responded to rising population, and the presence of more hands to till the soil would reap their reward. Malthus was, perhaps, not entirely consistent in his 1798 thesis. Certainly the 'power of population', its growth in a 'geometrical' (exponential) ratio, would always eventually outstrip the mere arithmetical expansion of food supplies. He took evidence of mortality crises in Germany provided by Süssmilch as an indication that this absolute threshold was close. Yet historically the problem had been more one of co-ordinating supply and demand over time.

> In a country where all the fertile spots have been seized, high offers are necessary to encourage the farmer to lay his dressing on land, from which he cannot expect a profitable return for some years. And before the prospect of advantage is sufficiently great to encourage this sort of agricultural enterprise, and while

---

[85] He overestimated the current population of England and Wales by around two million. Petty, *Another essay*, pp. 16–19, 44–7; for other projections in a similar vein, see Slack, *Invention of improvement*, p. 197.

[86] Malthus, *An essay on the principle of population*, p. 22.

the new produce is rising, great distresses may be suffered from the want of it.

Malthus presents the *historical* experience of dearth as arising not so much the fundamental capacities of the soil and labour applied to it, but the slow investment cycle in the agricultural sector. History had hitherto shown that agriculture, for all the temporary distress, caught up.[87]

Indeed, as Petty first set out with clarity in the seventeenth century, the potential of the division of labour to enhance productivity would lead to the expectation of greater resources per person, not lesser, as markets grew:

> the Gain which is made by *Manufactures*, will be greater, as the Manufacture it self is greater and better. For in so vast a City *Manufactures* will beget one another, and each *Manufacture* will be divided into as many parts as possible, whereby the Work of each *Artisan* will be simple and easie; As for Example. In the making of a *Watch*, If one Man shall make the *Wheels*, another the *Spring*, another shall Engrave the *Dial-plate*, and another shall make the *Cases*, then the *Watch* will be better and cheaper, than if the whole Work be put upon any one Man.[88]

Writing after Petty's argument had been given greater substance and approbation by Adam Smith, England's powers of commercial attraction and extraction, drawing in resources to its new looming dark mills, its shipyards, grocers, clothiers, soapboilers and furnaces, made Malthus view the prospect of raw material shortages with equanimity. 'It should be remembered always that there is an essential difference between food, and those wrought commodities, the raw materials of which are in great plenty. A demand for these last will not fail to create them in as great a quantity as they are wanted.'[89] Yet on the narrow ground of a particular village, smelting works or district the problem of balancing needs and supply came more clearly into focus. What if the demands of commercial expansion, or that utilising one resource (such as metal-smelting) put on another (such as fuel), created a great

---

[87] Malthus, *Essay*, p. 30.
[88] Petty, *Another essay*, pp. 36–7.
[89] Malthus, *Essay*, p. 30.

disparity in supply and demand? How to respond? Most authors were dimly aware of the issue. It was, after all, inscribed in laws and bye-laws across Europe in one particular form: too many immigrants into rural communities put the supply of goods from local woods and common lands at risk; if immigrants or the misfortunate became resource-poor in other ways, and incapable of labour, they placed demands on the purse or charity of their neighbours. Seckendorff briefly dwelt on the issue and noticed that, of course, the population of a village is constrained by the land available to it.[90]

Such concerns arose particularly in relation to the mining and metallurgical industries. As well as devouring huge quantities of wood, they were essential to the commerce of several states, especially upland and landlocked ones in the 'Ore Mountains' of Germany and around the Alps. These had been precocious in the extent of forestry regulation in the early sixteenth century, and we cannot be surprised that they were important locations for the development of forestry literature in the middle of the eighteenth.[91] It was typical of the sixteenth and seventeenth centuries that the proximity of wood reserves and demand for fuel for extractive industries was seen as a manifestation of God's providence and benevolence. As a report on the salt industry of Reichenhall in the northern foothills of the Alps put it in 1661, 'God has provided the woodlands for the salt [sources] so that they may continue eternally as Him, therefore humans should make sure, that before the old [woods] run out, the young should already be grown ready for felling again.'[92] The need for human hands to ensure that the woods rejuvenated properly was simply to walk the path that the divine creation clearly signposted.

In essence, the issue of balance had haunted sixteenth-century debates about tillage, but imbalance was blamed on covetousness. By the early eighteenth century a few foresters had adopted a more sophisticated take on the problem. The issue of balanced growth lay at the heart of Carlowitz's work, and the subsequent emergence of 'scientific forestry' as it emerged in eighteenth-century Central Europe. Rapidly rising fuel prices were a clear sign of imbalances in supply and

---

[90] Small, *Cameralists*, p. 98.
[91] Johann, *Geschichte*; Hasel and Schwarz, *Forstgeschichte*, p. 317.
[92] 'Gott hat die Wäld[er] für den Salzquell erschaffen auf daß sie ewig wie er kontinuieren mögen, also solle der Mensch es halten, ehe der alte ausgehet, der junge bereits wieder zum Verhacken hergewachsen ist'. Radkau, *Holz*, p. 97.

demand in the argument of the *Sylvicultura oeconomica*, and its author argued they should spur people on to consider what was causing them. Economic growth could lead to as much wood being consumed within the coming years as had taken centuries to grow. The 'all too strong consumption' had overwhelmed earlier efforts of careful forefathers who had predicted shortage and sought to encourage re-growth and thrifty habits. Carlowitz pondered the processes of consumer demand that led, sometimes through a 'feedback' effect as we would now say, to scarcity. The 'commonest and greatest cause' was the grubbing up of woodlands for fields and meadows that had restarted in the aftermath of the Thirty Years' War. It was 'a general scourge', that men preferred to possess agricultural holdings over wood, but new cultivators could neither provide themselves with enough food without having to purchase it, nor earn money working in the forest because of the increasing shortage of wood. This was especially the case in lands that were in any case dependent on manufacturing to pay for imports of corn.

This insight into the emergence of systemic pressures on resources in an organic economy was not pursued, however. Instead we find this passage followed by a typical listing of kinds of wasteful consumption, in building (taking the stone buildings of the south as a sign of wood scarcity); the northern practice of heating animal fodder; the large and poorly insulated chambers of rich and poor alike; and inefficient stoves.[93] There were also 'lazy and wicked inhabitants' who neglected agriculture and who lived off selling the wood they felled, 'not considering from where their descendants will get their wood, thinking of it as a *Fructus naturals*', and not even spending wisely the money they earned thereby. This critique of 'frontier expansion' and the kind of society that becomes associated with the free and uninhibited use of resources remains familiar today and would be widely evoked by critics of agricultural practices and neglect of the soil by writers in nineteenth-century America.[94] Carlowitz reverted in part to the traditional argument that the risk that people ran was forgetting to do godly work.

Yet it was also in was in the midst of arranging and assessing these various forces that were propelling the whole of Europe towards wood shortage, that Carlowitz set out his famous formulation of

---

[93] Carlowitz, *Sylvicultura oeconomica*, 1732 edn, pp. 44–9.
[94] Carlowitz, *Sylvicultura oeconomica*, 1732 edn, p. 50; see Chapter 8.

what we in retrospect call 'sustainability'. Or more correctly, that some modern authors have argued is a first definition of sustainability, although he never, in fact, used the word *Nachhaltigkeit*. 'If the annual output is fixed against the re-growth with sowing and planting, namely so that can be amply replaced, and the woods are treated with care, then no wood shortage will ensue... and if this precaution, and all devisable means are not applied such that a balance between growth and re-growth, and the output of the woods, ensues, then there is no doubt that this enterprise [*Wirtschaft*] will fail.'[95] To the modern mind, schooled in the assumptions of Thomas Malthus, such a pious formula cannot evade the reality that with population growth demand will eventually outstrip supply. But Carlowitz was not focused on such an issue, despite the occasionally broad sweep of his rhetoric. His framing was the particular needs of forest industries and communities, the possibility that limeworks or blast furnaces would cause localised shortages, leading to the demise of these industries, and the loss of thousands of jobs. The primary goal of Carlowitz – and what retrospectively is seen as his principle of sustainability – was to supply the metallurgical industries to allow 'continual, consistent and sustainable [*nach haltende*] use'.[96] In his mind, balance could be maintained with expanded production by the use of the best sylvicultural techniques. One such strategy had been in practice in some parts of Europe since the fourteenth century; if wood supplies were not keeping up with demand, then plant faster-growing trees.[97]

Carlowitz did, however, answer the charge that with expanding production, 'the land [would] not bear it... or at least it would over-cultivate the ground and soil and make it lean'.[98] His reply required some sense – or observational knowledge – of what made trees grow.

[95] Carlowitz, *Sylvicultura oeconomica*, 1732 edn, pp. 48–50.
[96] Carlowitz, *Sylvicultura oeconomica*, 1732 edn, pp. 50, 65.
[97] The very first artificial plantation of conifers established near Nürnberg in the 1360s by Peter Stromer had been to provide for his mines and smelting works. L. Sporhan and W. Von Stromer, 'Die Nadelholzsaat in Nünrberger Reichswäldern zwischen 1469 und 1600', *Zeitschrift für Agrargeschichte und Agrarsoziologie* 17 (1969), pp. 79–106; see also the development of coppicing strategies in response to the market in medieval France in Richard Keyser, 'The transformation of traditional woodland management. Commercial sylviculture in medieval Champagne', *French Historical Studies* 32 (2009), pp. 353–84; Radkau, *Holz*, p. 103; Carlowitz, *Sylvicultura oeconomica*, p. 72.
[98] Carlowitz, *Sylvicultura oeconomica*, p. 68.

He had been fired by an enthusiasm for horticulture and the successful dissemination of plants and techniques around Europe by the literature and networks of expert practitioners we examined Chapter 3, and on the basis of this he pondered what the biological basis of tree growth might be. He looked to 'experiments' to provide the answers, but conceded honestly that plant nutrition remained a process whose 'essence' (*Wesen*) remained an 'inscrutable matter' of some kind of 'elemental fire'. Minerals, water and heat combined through the roots, each seed preferring 'its particular climate', although he also noted experiments and arguments that some invisible quality of the air was important too.[99] In the end, forestry was a practical enterprise, and he recommended applying the same kind of rooted wisdom that could be found in husbandry manuals. While virtually all sorts of ground could support trees, the qualities of different earths gave different trees different amounts of nutrition, about which 'no certain rules can be found, other than that it will follow the climate and other circumstances'.[100] Soils could generally be judged by the outward appearance and vigour of the plants that grew upon them, although one could also suspend them in water to investigate its 'temperament', going by 'appearance', 'texture', 'taste' and 'smell'.[101] Yet most importantly, one did not have to worry about replenishing the soil, because 'careful Nature answers [this objection] herself, namely that every tree bears and contributes, and then casts forth from itself its annual manure, namely the leaves, shoots, twigs, blooms, bark, *tangeln* and oils that are washed from it by rains and snows and by which the ground and soil are improved'.[102] In this matter at least Carlowitz trusted to the generosity of nature as much as those who pillaged the woods without replenishing the stock.

Already in the late seventeenth century in the Harz mountains, however, voices did wonder 'to what extent the usage [of the woodlands] could have to be adapted to the growth'. That this was presented as an issue of *policy* underlines the distinction we must maintain between the problem of sustainability as a political issue, and the existence of sustainable practice. In the context of local firewood supply, bye-laws stipulating limits to the annual extraction from coppiced woodland

---

[99] Carolowitz, *Sylvicultura oeconomica*, pp. 21–3; 1732 edn, pp. 83, 105.
[100] Carlowitz, *Sylvicultura oeconomica*, 1732 edn, pp. 98–9.
[101] Carlowitz, *Sylvicultura oeconomica*, 1732 edn, p. 101.
[102] Carlowitz, *Sylvicultura oeconomica*, 1732 edn, p. 68.

were long-established in many European villages and towns.[103] Yet the presence of the same problem in an intensely industrialised district, where the hope of future expansion was entertained, put things in a different context. Indeed there, worry about the pressure expanding demand exerted on wood supplies was not entirely new (as we have also seen in Chapter 2). In the 1580s one observer there had declared that anyone who thought the level of wood consumption presented no problems 'speaks of it as the blind speak of colour'. By 1724 a leading mining official, the *Vice-Berghauptmann* von Heimburg, floated the idea that 'the business and running of mining and smelting may have to order itself according to the current situation of the forest and woods, and not the economy [*Haußhaltung*] of the forest after the business and running of the smelting-works'. Such suggestions were not unique to the Harz.[104] When even carefully husbanded resources of particular industrial works proved inadequate for an affordable supply, the question arose of how to maintain over time a balance (*Gleichgewicht*) between what the furnaces consumed, and what the woods provided.[105] Not everyone judged the capacity for an expansion of supply elastically as did the great Saxon author of the *Sylvicultura Oeconomica*.

Whatever one's views on the potential for expansion, establishing a theoretical balance in the present or the future required *information* on supply and demand. The wood economy consequently had to become part of the information economy of the cameralist thinkers. It was essential that the authorities, remarked Justi in the 1750s, gathered details on how much wood was consumed in town and country. He expected people to exaggerate their actual consumption to appear more prestigious! Equally, one needed to know 'how much wood could annually be felled sustainably, economically and without ruin to the woodlands', which was a job for foresters. By combining these two pieces of information, one can ensure that 'no more wood is annually felled and consumed than will annually grow back', thus advancing Carlowitz's formula to the level of the polity.[106] The burden of maintaining this balancing act remained however on

[103] P.-M. Steinsiek, *Nachhaltigkeit auf Zeit. Waldschutz im Westharz vor 1800* (Münster: Waxmann, 1999), p. 97.

[104] Steinsiek, *Nachhaltigkeit*, pp. 69, 77, 99; See also Radkau, *Holz*, p. 155.

[105] See Steinsiek, *Nachhaltigkeit*, p. 103.

[106] Justi, *Politische und Finanzschriften*, pp. 443–4; also Pfeiffer, *Die Grundsätze*, p. 158.

the purveyors of the wood – and thus remained the responsibility of foresters. Thrifty, economical consumption (*Sparkunst*) was of course to be encouraged, not least because Justi followed the French physiocrat Mirabeau in blaming some of the rise in demand to a new taste for luxury, including fripperies like stoves on the stairs and maidservants with their own rooms having both heat and light.[107] Alternative fuels should be employed if possible, particularly coal-mining as being less wasteful of space than peat.[108] Yet when the wealth and power of a state rested on commerce, no-one could expect commercial activity to permanently limit itself to what current wood production would bear, even if commerce might have to apply the brakes to particular activities if wood became more expensive. Justi reckoned that 'it is obvious, that from day to day wood is in decline', and 'a sure evidence of its decline' was 'this extraordinary price rise of wood', sixfold in terms of silver in the past century, four times more than grain.[109] But his contemporary, cameralist writer and lecturer (typically, after a previous career in official service), Georg Heinrich Zincke, provided a checklist of everything that had to be achieved to ensure *both* a sustainable (*nachhaltig*) supply of wood to the ruler's subjects, and the growth of commerce in wood: 'Use of all available state and private woodlands that is sustainable and serviceable to improvement, and especially in these times both a continual new plantation of wood, and bringing into use ever better means of economizing on wood, and after this, a good cultivation and peopling of the towns and villages and the flourishing of those activities which have need of wood and forest products.'[110] In other words, there remained an expectation of being able to supply more of everything, but sustainably.

The task that foresters set themselves in response to this challenge was to deliver as much wood as possible, but in such a way that future supplies would be just as high. Heinrich Cotta, the doyen of Saxon forestry a century after Carlowitz, expressed this goal as being to 'sustainably win from the woods in relation to requirements the greatest possible and most appropriate usage with the lowest possible

[107] Justi, *Grundfeste*, p. 82.
[108] Justi, *Grundfeste*, pp. 78–80.
[109] Justi, *Staatswirtschaft*, p. 212; Justi, *Grundfeste*, p. 86.
[110] Georg Heinrich Zinck, *Anfangsgründe der Cameralwissenschaft worinne dessen Grundriß weiter ausgeführet und verbessert wird. Part II* (Leipzig: Carl Ludwig Jacobi, 1755), pp. 596–7.

costs'. The most renowned definition of the task to be taken into hand came from Cotta's contemporary and theoretical rival, Georg Hartig, who eventually came to direct forestry in Prussia: 'Every wise forestry administration must take the measure [*taxieren*] of the woodlands, indeed as high as is possible, but seek to exploit them such that the subsequent generations [*Nachkommenschaft*] can draw at least so much advantage from them, as currently living generations appropriate.'[111] Within the overall set of expectations that characterised cameralist thinking, what was implicit in this vision of a balanced forestry was actually a far more intensive exploitation of forested land. It would prove to be not a vision of restraint, but of transformation. It was also a vision that was deeply implicated in the ambitions of the fiscal state.

This did not mean that there was to be *no* restraint. We noted above how the unhappy thought of limits had already occurred to industrial enterprises. In an earlier age, governments had banned the felling of woodlands and in some places even sought to arrest the expansion of tillage or vineyards to preserve wood supplies. As Malthus's moment loomed, a French observer travelling in the Duchy of Berg in the 1790s – soon to be one of Germany's industrial heartlands – noted that the woods had slowly been made 'light' by the rapidly increasing number of people.[112] Yet the burden of imposing restraint fell upon the institutions that managed resources, not the pressures that generated demand. Perhaps the idea made explicit by Malthus, of the constancy of the passion between the sexes, was too obvious a truism for most to bear any further thought.[113] Equally, the problem of balance was now understood within a more dynamic vision. It was the goal of cameralism, and economic endeavour more generally, to increase population, to increase commerce, to increase wealth. It was

[111] Hasel and Schwarz, *Forstgeschichte*, pp. 335, 341; interestingly it was the camerliast Pfeiffer who presented the task of forestry as the 'lasting [*fortdauernder*] and highest possible use of the woodlands', but neglected to worry about costs. Pfeiffer, *Grundsätze*, p. 155.

[112] Burkhard Dietz, 'Wirtschaftliches Wachstum und Holzmangel in bergisch-märkischen Gewerberaum vor der Industrialisierung', www.lrz-muenchen.de/~MW?Hardenstein/Dietz/htm, p. 9.

[113] It was however disputed by Malthus's rival Godwin, who argued that 'propagat[ion]' would decline with the cultivation of the mind; a notion with a long tradition in Hippocratic thought. Rolf Peter Sieferle, *Bevölkerungswachstum und Naturhaushalt. Studien zur Naturtheorie der klassischen Ökonomie* (Frankfurt: Suhrkamp Verlag, 1990), p. 84.

not good enough simply to call a halt to exploitation of some resource, as previous generations of authorities had sought to do in particular localities. Obviously that could not work; only a halt to *everything* would produce the necessary balance. But surely the problem of 'light woodlands', and the gap between yield and consumption, could be redressed by a forestry regime that determinedly sowed lands and applied the best knowledge, as the forester Peter Kling proposed in a lecture to the Mannheim Academy of Sciences in November 1790.[114] Nevertheless, in Kling's state, the Palatinate, various regimes did find it necessary to resort to the old-style prohibitions outlined in Chapter 2. In 1803 and with the Restoration government of 1814 they ordered that felling should not be 'beyond the limits of the sustainable yield of the woods', an instruction that nominally at least applied to privately owned lands as well.[115] This was, however, only one step along a road already mapped towards a profound transformation in the management and yield of wood resources, to which we turn in the next chapter.

[114] Grewe, *Der versperrte Wald*, p. 11.
[115] Grewe, *Der versperrte Wald*, pp. 66, 70.

5 Nature Translated, c. 1670–1830

Survey

It is easy to forget that sixteenth-century governments were almost entirely reliant on other people telling them what their polity was like. They had virtually no documentary evidence on the land or population they ruled, and the even those records that began to be systematically taken (such as baptismal and burial registers, tax assessments, or account books of revenues and expenditure) were not aggregated into useful summaries and were difficult to consult. No early modern finance minister could produce a budget as we would understand it. Accounting was largely done to combat fraud, not to produce material that could feed into the making of policy. Most governmental paperwork consulted by historians has probably lain unheeded and unloved for all the years since its making. It was one thing to declare the necessity of providing an inventory of all of the wealth and natural resources of the realm, but quite another thing to achieve it.

Nevertheless, despite such obstacles, we have seen in Chapter 4 how the idea that government could steer society towards prosperity was becoming widely articulated among elites by middle of the seventeenth century. This was partly shaped through the incremental experience of managing assets of the Crown or collecting taxes, and partly shaped by new currents in intellectual life. But managing resources on a grand scale meant equally grand aspirations to know where and what those resources were; otherwise any aspiration to balance, or a tax policy that favoured desirable trade and a positive balance of payments, or maintained the woods, was no more than groping in the dark. One could think of the state as a kind of estate, but it was one thing to keep track of a small manor's tenants, and at a stretch the assets they husbanded; quite another to do so for a whole polity. As we have already seen, the earliest cameralist works, and to a lesser degree those of political arithmetic, saw inventorisation of the land, topography and resources contained therein as a first step towards their wise distribution and enhancement.

This chapter describes the first, rather episodic and variably successful efforts towards providing these means to rule more effectively. They sought to make the land 'legible', in the words of anthropologist J.C. Scott, who took the development of German forestry in the eighteenth century as the paradigmatic case of a central state attempting to both assess and transform the land that it ruled. In Scott's account, this is an aesthetic as much as a practical vision, and led eventually to the policies of 'high modernity' imposing reductive and socially and ecologically damaging policies on the land. There is much to be said for Scott's account, and the risks of reductionism. In the struggle to make a polity legible, one may end up creating what one wishes to see – a pattern of taxable and controllable assets.[1] Yet by itself this account is also reductionist. Foresters, for example, were often intensely interested in the natural world that they governed, and were often well aware of how the desire for 'legibility' presented complex demands to those on the ground. And as well as offering the means to effect transformations, which certainly had major ecological impacts, new techniques of quantification and record-keeping would also, crucially for this story, provide evidence for the existence of *degradation* of the environment in a form legible to the powerful. As usual, history is replete with ironies. Above all, this period saw the development and institutionalisation of new techniques and languages for describing and understanding nature. The major consequences of adoption of these new languages lay further in the future, and should not be treated as inevitable; they offered varied possibilities. It was a case of Nature being translated, rather than transformed.

It does seem to have been the case that these developments advanced the furthest, and had the greatest impact, in forestry. Chapter 2 has laid out how state government of the forests was already

---

[1] Scott, *Seeing like a state.*

highly developed in its juridical claims and administrative apparatus by the sixteenth century. However, the origins of technologies of legibility lay not in princely states but cities, and above all the rural properties of landlords. Efforts to record particular assets, generally for taxation purposes, had occurred episodically from late medieval times. They were most complete in the case of urban centres where the population was contained and the basic form of the asset easier to assess than qualities of land.[2] On a smaller scale, private and especially monastic estates kept records of their holdings; the manorial accounts of medieval England were a major tool of administration for large agglomerations of properties, although they tended to record expenditure and transactions rather than being cadastres. Thus the aspiration to gather such information on a larger scale did not necessarily entail, at first, any conceptual shift, or new expertise. Men with surveying expertise had existed since medieval times, and became more professionalised, with greater geometrical knowledge and the emergence of a dedicated literature during the sixteenth century.[3] The difficulty lay in marshalling such men, having the means to process the information they provided, and most challenging of all, utilising it to shape policy.

For the most part, early surveying had concerned itself with relatively small parcels of land, usually cultivated in some way. Husbanding a wood supply presented greater problems, especially if the wood lay distant from the estate centre and was of large extent. Where was the woodland, how could the bounds be recorded and protected, and how could you keep track of what was within them? Such tasks were rather easier for private owners and communities to complete than more distant bureaucrats who dreamed of a well-ordered and monitored state. Identifying a boundary in a wood is never a simple matter, and nor is

---

[2] For example, Wolsey's surveys of the 1520s and those associated with the dissolution of the monasteries and chantries in England and Wales in the subsequent two decades. Slack, *Invention of improvement*, p. 44. However, this kind of record-keeping was most advanced in the Italian cities.

[3] Heather Falvey, 'Marking the boundaries. William Jordan's 1633 pre-enclosure survey of Duffield Frith (Derbyshire)', *Agricultural History Review* 61(I) (2013), pp. 1–18; Andrew McCrae, 'To know one's own. Estate surveying and the representation of the land in early modern England', *Huntington Library Quarterly* 56 (1993), pp. 332–57; such advances were not always received well by tenants who feared more accurate surveying would lead to higher rents or expropriation. Slack, *Invention of improvement*, p. 26. On France, see Mukerji, *Impossible engineering*.

keeping an inventory of what is in it – especially where that woodland regenerates naturally rather than through deliberate planting and clearance of 'weed' species. Such problems did not just relate to the generation of data on a large scale. Without a clear inventory, how could you prove that someone was illegally felling timber unless they were caught in the act? How could you allocate timber wisely and judge whether felling was judicious or nor, particularly if one had responsibility for a large area and visited it only infrequently?

Thus making it a legal requirement to properly demarcate woodland space was the key preoccupation (though unnoticed by most historians) of Henry VIII's woodland legislation in 1543, and also formed the primary theme of the first two books devoted to forest matters published in Europe in 1560 and 1576 by the German jurist and bureaucrat Noé Meurer.[4] Much early writing on woodlands was about jurisdiction and access, and over time, one of the major activities of foresters was to simply record and measure what they could see. But even if woodlands could be demarcated, mapped and inventoried, they were not easy places to police. In many cases multiple users held use-rights over them: landlords, commoners, princes, naval officials, foresters. They were the habitats of numerous species, who (including those controlled by people, game animals such as wild boar and deer, or herds of cattle, sheep and pigs) could wander far and wide with unpredictable effect. Even when seasonal entry bans were in force on parts of the woodland, it was impossible to either have personnel constantly on station to enforce them, or provide the labour and material for fencing. The ban might be indicated by hanging up a bale of hay or some mark on a trunk – a signal easily ignored.

Boundary-setting was at first a bodily, not a documentary exercise, a practice perfectly adequate for local purposes, but not the kind of legibility demanded by more distant owners or rulers. Communities had long 'beaten the bounds' or practised 'rogations' of parishes and fields as a group so that elders could inform youngsters of where their assets lay and to prevent the encroachments of neighbours.[5]

---

4 Statutes of the Realm 35 Hen. VIII c.17, p. 977; Noé Meurer, *Vom forstlicher Oberherrligkeit und Gerechtigkeit* (Pforzheim: Georg Rab, 1560); Meurer, *Jag und Forstrecht*.
5 On legibility, see Scott, *Seeing like a state*; Nicola Whyte, *Inhabiting the landscape. Place, custom and memory, 1500–1800* (Oxford: Windgather, 2009), pp. 59–90; Warde, *Ecology*, pp. 38–41; Nicola Whyte, 'An archaeology of natural places. Trees

Often prominent trees were used as markers. Sometimes the 'beating' was a literal cuff round the ear so the information was not forgotten. The Duchy of Zweibrücken's forest ordinance of 1568 made communal beating of woodland bounds mandatory, expanding to the polity typically local habits.⁶ The limits set by such bodily habit were both physical and temporal. First, one marked where the wood was in one's memory by standing at its edge, and perhaps leaving behind mark-stones. If part of the object was to preserve the woodland, it was no good simply saying that the wood was composed of the trees. What if the trees were felled? One had to be present and make that presence a future witness to how things had been. Boundaries depended on testimony.⁷

On top of the basic challenges of limiting space were the shifting seasonal demands on land. Mast for pigs came in the autumn, and so swineherds were permitted entry to woodlands at that time. The stewards of game demanded a 'fence-month' in the summer to ensure that breeding deer were not disturbed. More generally, it became quite common for territorial forest ordinances or local by-laws to limit days when people could go and cut wood, whether barring access altogether at some times, or more frequently, making it a crime to carry any tool that might be used to fell a tree or hack off a branch (the gathering of deadwood was more generally permitted). In the Venetian oak reserve of Montello, carrying a cutting edge without permission could even become a capital crime.⁸

In these early rules and regulations, the issue was access to the trees, and woodland space was simply where the trees and other resources were. The concern was to get best value out of individual

in the early modern landscape', *Huntington Library Quarterly: Studies in English and American History and Literature* (2013), pp. 508–16; Nicola Whyte, 'Landscape, memory and custom. Parish identities, *c.* 1550–1750', *Social History* 32 (2007), pp. 166–86; Allmann, *Der Wald in der frühen Neuzeit*, pp. 162–70; Bob Bushaway, *By rite. Custom, ceremony and community in England 1700–1880* (London: Junction Books, 1982), pp. 81–8.

⁶ For this and other examples of surveys and boundary marking, see Allmann, *Der Wald in der frühen Neuzeit*, pp. 72, 100, 162–76; Andy Wood, *The memory of the people. Custom and popular senses of the past in early modern England* (Cambridge: Cambridge University Press, 2013), pp. 188–219.

⁷ Whyte, *Inhabiting the landscape*, p. 67.

⁸ Appuhn, *A forest on the sea*, p. 108; Christoph Ernst, *Den Wald entwickeln*, pp. 68–9, 87.

trees, even when laws prompted fear about the enduring provision of many trees into the future. One could not yet talk of a *silviculture*, or conceive of an overall productivity of the woodland that might wax or wane. Woodlands were assuredly shaped by human hands, but in this literature there was no grand strategy as to craft them en masse even though coppicing, as we have seen, was already ancient practice. The earliest English works of husbandry and surveying by Fitzherbert in the 1520s discussed the plashing and cutting of hedgerows, or the pollarding of trees to ensure enduring regrowth of small diameter wood for the hearth, fencing, hurdles and tools.[9] Fitzherbert briefly gave the kind of advice that was a staple for husbandry manuals thereafter, recommending when tasks such as felling and selling should be done, and proffering advice on the shredding of trees for browse and provision of fencing.[10] The closest practice to a modern silviculture was dividing the woodland into the 'coupes', 'compartments' or 'fells' that were cut each year as coppice, leaving, as Walter Blith reminded readers, enough space between the coppice stools to get your cart in and out.[11] In much the same way, delineations of cultivated land were primarily concerned with access and use rights, not assaying productivity, and hence boundaries were often given as simply the abutting land of the neighbours, with no greater precision or comment on the land's qualities.

Yet from tentative beginnings, the art of the survey took hold, and the land took shape on paper. The foundations of a more abstract and planned estate management or forestry were laid. The major impetus beyond the profession of surveying came from private estates who wished to keep track of tenancies, assets and measure their output. Leonard Digges's surveyor's guide of 1556 also included detailed instructions of measuring the dimensions of felled timber. These developments complemented the keeping of local property cadastres, usually to smooth property transactions and reduce disputation. As a state, Venice was ahead as usual, providing a cadastre of community forests in Friuli in 1507, and developing the practice more widely in

---

[9] Fitzherbert, *Boke of surveying*, f.xlvi.v; John Fitzherbert, *Boke of Husbandry* (London: Thomas Berthelet, 1540), ff.52–4.
[10] Fitzherbert, *Husbandry*, ff.52–4; Markham, *Markhams farwell*, pp. 153–7.
[11] Blith, *The English Improver Improv'd*, pp. 155–6.

1530s.[12] The Duke of Württemberg demanded and got a survey of every woodland under his rule in 1556, and a copy of each local survey was retained for reference by forest officials. Queen Elizabeth I of England, at once so much greater but so much more distant from her subjects, restricted herself to a survey of royal woodlands in 1565, carried out by Roger Tavernor and covering 20 counties and listing tree species and coppice. This could be used for comparison with later surveys.[13] Basic boundary-setting and the appointment of a forest surveyor to every region was one of the primary activities of Colbert's famous forest surveys after 1669, intended simply to give a rough vision of the woodland area, rather than imposing a tool of abstract management. This was in fact an extension of requirements already articulated for royal domanial woodlands under Charles IX in the 1560s but only widely applied by the end of Henry IV's reign in 1610. All woodland boundaries in the Duchy of Württemberg were mapped during the 1680s.[14]

Simple as these early surveys were, they present a key moment in woodland history and aspirations to resource management. They provided the institutional means to assess a forest over time, and instilled the idea that a desirable state of the wood could not only be *replicated*, as coppice-systems already achieved, but could be *calculated*. One could now lay the very best plans. On 22 March 1606 Christopher Forde delivered his to the royal government of England:

> That there be an equal number of the decayed trees yearly cut
> for fewell and profit for his majesty so that the same number
> may endure yearly to be cut for one hundred years. And that the
> coppice woods may be so divided that they may be all cut over in
> twenty years except some special coppices which may be reserved
> to stand thirty or forty years for some other uses.
> ...

[12] Leonard Digges, *A boke named Tectonicon briefelye shewynge the exacte measurynge, and speady reckenynge all maner lande, squared tymber, stone, steaples, pyllers, globes* (London: Felix Kyngston, 1556); Appuhn, *Forest on the sea*, pp. 153–9.

[13] Warde, *Ecology*, pp. 228–42; Morrison, 'The Stuart forests', p. 21; Pettit, *Royal forests*, pp. 99, 110–11.

[14] Chandra Mukerji, 'The great forest survey of 1669–1671. The use of archives for political reform', *Social Studies of Science* 37 (2007), pp. 230–1; Corvol, *L'homme et l'arbre*, p. 18; Corvol, 'Les communautés d'habitants'; Andreas Kieser, *Alt-Württemberg in Ortsansichten und Landkarten, 1680–1687* (Stuttgart: Theiss, 1985).

Admit the wood containeth... 100 acres

That in every acre there be 20 trees which is in the
whole wood... 2000 trees

Whereof sound timber in every acre 10 trees and
decayed 10 trees.

For profit you may cut every year for the space of
100 years 10 trees which will be well worth £4 6s 8d yearly

In place of these 10 trees let there be 2 acres of
ground inclosed with underwoods, as with the Loppes of
thornes hollins and such like, and the first year plant that
ground with acorns setting in every goad being 28ft in length
9 akorns, 6ft distant the one from the other, which will be
in every acre 1440 plants in 2 acres 2880 plants, so that
in this 100 acres of wood in 100 years the King may make
£333.6.8 & instead of 2000 decayed trees there will be 2880
young timber trees which being generally used in all the kings
woods with the good preservation of all the Kings coppices
will yield sufficient Timber Firewood and coals for the Kings
provision and bring unto his Highnesses Exchequer the sum of
£6000 yearly and almost treble the number of trees that shall
be cut.[15]

In practice, governments found it extremely hard to produce surveys
that gave truly useful data, or indeed plan on budgetary matters in a
way that made such foresight relevant. Most of the information about
even the Crown or princely woodlands was still obtained from the
local woodwards. In England in 1612 a sample of questions set to these
relatively lowly royal officials ran thus.

How many coppice woods and underwood and thickets were in
the said forests... what were their said names.

... how many coppice woods and underwoods and
thickets have been felled since you have been the keeper...

... whether the said coppice etc so felled were left
standing and growing sufficient standells and stores in every acre
according to the statute... whether the said standells or store
have been preserved since the felling thereof... [and] have been
sufficiently fenced and the springs thereof sufficiently kept and

> preserved from destruction of cattle for the space of 9 years after
> every felling according to statute...[16]

Such information could produce a general sense of the quality of management and the state of the wood, were the answers honest. Yet it was
far from the detail desired by enthusiastic projectors. Surveys could
however claw towards a surer knowledge, to both contemporary observers and later historians, of the state of things: 'In the late Surueyes and
Sales of diuers of his Maiesties Copies and Woods wherein I found lam-
entable scarcitie, and exceeding abuses (which I feare to be vniuersally
as wel ouer the Realme, as in the said particular places).'[17] The men
who gathered these details could put names to the woods that were
being felled; John Norden noted those in the Weald that had fallen to
glassworks, and saw grubbing up a particular problem in Middlesex
as the booming market of London stimulated the expansion of cultivation, with coal imports compensating for losses to fuel supply.[18]

Great Venetian surveys of woodlands resources had already
begun in 1586, and provided the means for a tree-by-tree comparison in 1602, covering all those over 18 ft tall. By 1604 officials
had catalogued 750,000 oaks in 800 woodlands.[19] English surveyors
counted over a million trees in royal woodlands, but without information on size, this had little predictive value (the surveys distinguished
between useful 'timber' trees and 'dotards' good only for firewood).[20]
An alternative to detailing potential supply was to tightly regulate
consumption, which could generate its own data. In Lützelstein in
south-west Germany in 1592, all building wood could only be felled
with official approval. Since 1560 every subject was required to enter
the building wood they needed in a register. Trees selected for felling
were marked for the carpenters and cartwrights, just as naval officials
marked trees to be reserved for the fleet all over coastal Europe.[21]

Across the seventeenth century we see both expanded attempts
at calculation demanding detailed information, and a growing habit
of survey. Often this incipient attention to detail came before the

[16] BL Add MS 38444.
[17] Church, *An old thrift*, p. i.
[18] Norden, *A surveyors dialogue*, pp. 214, 217.
[19] Appuhn, *Forest on the sea*, pp. 183–4.
[20] BL Add 38444.
[21] Allmann, *Der Wald in der frühen Neuzeit*, p. 108.

development of political arithmetic and studies of disease that are more familiar to historians who concern themselves with the history of quantification. It is easy to perceive with hindsight that these processes would shape the future of forestry, and condition the idea of the improvability or sustainability of the woods. Yet the courtship between surveying and forest management could not be consummated until later. A correspondent of John Houghton in 1693 suggested a good manager should rate the value of the land per acre, then the price of wood in the place, and what an acre of young wood affords at various ages: 'at fourteen years for *cord-wood*... One *acre* will bear twenty *cord*, a stack eight foot long, four broad, and four high, every stick at least three inches about. And after fourteen years the body or stem increases slower, the boughs more and many small *trees* are destroyed by the dropping of the more prosperous.'[22] It was understood that calculating potential profit, and thus choosing the best way to manage the land, required an accurate view of acreage and yield. Yet continuously monitoring the latter was still beyond the projectors, especially as the tree aged and an increasing number of contingencies could affects its condition. 'But it were good if one could tell the yearly improvement of a *tree*', sighed Houghton's correspondent.[23]

Statistics

Writers on agriculture and forestry were not the only people to become gradually more enthused as to the possibilities of quantification during the seventeenth century. Many authorities were keeping better accounts and inventories, partly to clamp down on fraud and embezzlement (probably with relatively little success), partly to devise more reliable means of assessing taxation. There was an expansion of accounting of all kinds, of forest surveys and government commissions, of customs accounts, registers of births, marriages and deaths; in London, the famous 'bills of mortality' that were initially introduced to provide warning of the onset of plague.[24] These records of the causes of death led John Graunt to his historic 1662 work *Natural and*

---

[22] Houghton, *Collection*, p. 100.
[23] Houghton, *Collection*, p. 103; see also Turner, 'Natural philosophers'.
[24] Rusnock, *Vital accounts*.

Political Observations, adapting the practice of mercantile accounts and using public registers to produce a founding text of demography and statistics.[25] It is revealing that while the title juxtaposed 'natural' and 'political', they were considered fundamentally intertwined phenomena that were amenable to quantitative investigation.[26] His ever-present friend and networker William Petty was soon to give air to 'political arithmetic'.[27]

To the political arithmeticians, it seemed that numbers would reveal the interconnections by which land and people produced revenue and welfare. To understand this process one needed overviews of the whole; for them, the polity was composed of aggregates, not just many sets of individual moral relations. In turn, the state was the body that could manage aggregates and shape their inter-relations: indeed, it had of course a direct interest in doing so given that one of its major tasks was to collect the revenue it required for its own operations, and those demands grew very considerably in that century. Tax was a direct interest of early political arithmeticians such as William Petty and Gregory King. The latter, for example, constructed his famous 'social tables' in the early 1690s in order to calculate likely tax incomes from different groups of people, and so the categorisations he made and that were subsequently used by generations of historians were defined with this very specific problem in mind (equally, his famous distinction between those increasing and those draining the wealth of the kingdom). Much of the thinking in Petty's *Political Arithmetic* was drafted in the early 1660s as part of his *Treatise on Taxes*. The balance of trade was a common preoccupation of early modern political debate and from the 1660s customs figures were used to attempt a more accurate accounting of it in England. These methods were then imitated in France.[28] There was actually a great deal of continuity

---

[25] John Graunt, *Natural and political observations made upon the bills of mortality* [1662], in Peter Laslett, ed., *The earliest classics* (Farnborough: Gregg International, 1973); Judy L. Klein, *Statistical visions in time. A history of time series analysis 1662–1938* (Cambridge: Cambridge University Press, 1997), pp. 25–47.

[26] Rusnock, *Vital accounts*, pp. 15–16.

[27] For a brief general introduction, see Theodore M. Porter, *The rise of statistical thinking 1820–1900* (Princeton, NJ: Princeton University Press, 1986), pp. 18–39.

[28] Tom Arkell, 'Illuminations and distortions. Gregory King's Scheme calculated for the year 1688 and the social structure of later Stuart England', *EcHR* 59 (2006), pp. 39–59. McCormick, *William Petty*, pp. 135–47; Slack, *Invention of improvement*, pp. 180, 185, 192, 246. BL Add MS 36785 fols 4–5, 91–2.

between the two halves of the seventeenth century in the manner in which quantitative data were gathered, for all the claims to originality of the 'arithmeticians'. Historians of economic thought have simply been unaware of how much surveying and census-taking was being gradually, haltingly, built into the everyday practice of many European states, not having worked on the manuscript evidence. Indeed, part of the reason why the work of Petty and King stands out is that they were simply much better informed, and hence more adept at manipulating data, after decades of gradually accumulated information, than precursors of a similar mind such as Bodin or Gerard Malynes.[29] Similarly, in Austria at nearly the same time as Gregory King was making his jottings, the cameralist official Schröder was writing his chapter 'Whether a Prince Can Know How Much Each Citizen Earns or Might Earn, in Order that He May Know How the Money is Distributed'.[30]

The expectations of this literature were set out by Shelborne in the introduction to Petty's volume when it appeared in 1691. '*It was by him stiled* Political Arithmetick, *in as much as things of* Government, *and of no less concern and extent, than the* Glory *of the* Prince, *and the* happiness *and* greatness *of the* People, *are by the* Ordinary *Rules of* Arithmetick *brought into a sort of Demonstration.*'[31] Petty, heir of the ambition of his one-time mentor Hartlib, also appealed to the panoptical view of the state as a collator and clearing house of information that could assist development: 'Nor would it misbecome Authority it self, to clear the Truth of those Matters which private Endeavours cannot reach to.'[32] Later, this would become widely recognised as a fundamental duty of the state, not only for its own ends. Petty's *Political Arithmetick* was in fact an exercise in comparison intended to make a geopolitical argument about the relative strengths of the north-west European powers, covering estimates of the value of land, housing, shipping tonnage and population. Of course, Petty did not have comprehensive data on such things; but as well as contributing

---

[29] Slack, *Invention of improvement*, pp. 49–50; Gerald Malynes, *Englands view, in the unmasking of two paradoxes with a replication unto the answer of Maister Iohn Bodine* (London: Richard Field, 1603); esp. pp. 135–6; on information gathering, see Fox, 'Printed questionnaires', pp. 593–621.

[30] Small, *Cameralists*, pp. 163–4.

[31] Petty, *Political arithmetick*, dedication.

[32] Petty, *Political arithmetick*, 'Preface', f.5r.

to the idea that such things were desirable, he was also establishing a tradition of estimating them anyway even if data did not yet exist. He had already employed the technique of estimating the number of one thing by estimating its ratio in regard to a better-known quantity in calculating the assets of Ireland in the 1650s.[33] In this he anticipated the modern, rather than the original, meaning of *statistics*. As this term emerged in English in the early nineteenth century, it referred to the collection of information (preferably numerical) of use to the state. Petty demonstrated that one could produce proxies for comprehensive data out of fragmentary or indirect information, and how meaning or significance could be inferred from numbers gathered for some other purpose, or that did not convey that meaning explicitly: much more in line with what the discipline of statistics has done since the late nineteenth century. Again, this was not entirely novel, as earlier efforts had been made to calculate populations on the basis of extrapolating limited information by the use of multipliers, using for example the available count of the number of households and multiplying by an estimated number of people per household, or attempting to calculate the mortality rate and come thereby to a figure for total population by using the available counts of burials.[34]

Petty's work presented his information as self-evident, if novel; a simple and reliable truth, in much the same way that modern politicians still grasp at the straws offered by cost–benefit analysis that appear to supply a sturdy bridge between the blurred complexity of the world and a desire to appear to make only rational, 'evidence-based' decisions. In Petty's words, 'The Method I take to do this, is not yet very usual; for instead of using only comparative and superlative Words, and intellectual Arguments, I have taken the course (as a Specimen of the Political Arithmetick I have long aimed at) to express my self in Terms of *Number, Weight*, or *Measure*; and to consider only such causes, as have visible Foundations in Nature; leaving those that depend upon mutable Minds, Opinions, Appetites, and Passions of particular Men, to the Consideration of others.'[35] Mathematics, or even simple accounting, could provide order, even if it was blind to

[33] Webster, *The great instauration*, p. 443.
[34] Rusnock, *Vital accounts*, pp. 38, 192–206.
[35] The famous comment on number, weight or measure in fact directly mimicked Bacon and Malynes. Petty, *Political arithmetick*, 'Preface', ff.3v–4r; Webster, *The great instauration*, p. 351; on Petty in Ireland, see McCormick, *William Petty*, pp. 84–118.

the sense of the questions which it was pressed to answer. It allegedly provided a truth beyond mutability and dispute. Some of the most striking early applications of such methods were in medicine, where for certain diseases one could plot a relatively straightforward relationship between location and mortality, or inoculation and morbidity. It was also, it might go without saying but should be said, a technology of power.[36] Numbers were a way of making the ruled more legible, as James C. Scott has argued, and nearly always linked to the suggestion of grand plans for steering populations in a particular direction, making them more industrious, better generators of revenue, or more resilient in war. Almost immediately after Petty's *Treatise on taxes* was drafted, the indefatigable Jean-Baptise Colbert was at work reforming French governance and commissioning a range of studies on the trade and administration of the Dutch state, at that time perceived as the model to emulate in terms of economic success.[37] Petty had established his reputation in government, as seen in Chapter 3, by his efficient organisation of the survey and expropriation of Ireland, facilitating colonisation and the Protestant Ascendancy that was not finally swept away until independence in the 1920s. The cool diffidence that Petty claimed was not necessarily a weapon in the hands of colonisation or the improving landlord scorning the rage of the dispossessed. But all too often this is precisely what it was.[38]

Wider enthusiasm for mathematics had been building from the sixteenth century, when it was a respected but second-tier university subject. Mathematics was considered to have a strong practical orientation, not least because of the military and navigational uses of mechanics and geometry.[39] The seventeenth century saw major advances in its prestige and use, becoming foregrounded in the influential Jesuit schools of Europe, and being associated with new discoveries in astronomy and physics, and probability theory, the apogee of which was of course Newton's explication of the theory of gravity.[40] By these

[36] The fact that statistical techniques could themselves be disputed and lead to a new politics of risk is discussed in Jean-Baptiste Fressoz, *L'apocalypse joyeuse. Une histoire du risqué technologique* (Paris: Seuil, 2012).

[37] Soll, 'Accounting for government', pp. 235–7.

[38] Rusnock, *Vital accounts*, pp. 31, 43–106; Hacking, *The emergence of probability*, pp. 104–5.

[39] Gaukroger, *Francis Bacon*, pp. 20–5; Harkness, *The Jewel House*, pp. 113, 119–20; Webster, *The great instauration*, pp. 349, 351, 358.

[40] McCormick, *William Petty*, pp. 26–7; Hacking, *The emergence of probability*.

standards nothing 'political arithmeticians' or indeed foresters would apply was very sophisticated, but a significant context for the development of resource management was that mathematical approaches were viewed as cutting-edge and, during the eighteenth century, became widely taught in Central European universities.[41] A key figure in encouraging training in maths and geometry within German academia was a leading light of the Prussian and Pietist university at Halle, Christian Wolff (1679–1754). Wolff had been trained as a mathematician and in physics, but after his arrival in Halle he began to turn to more philosophical topics. Eventually he would come to write highly influential texts across a vast range of fields in what we now separate into the sciences and humanities, most famously the *Vernünfftige Gedanken* of 1720. He bore with him from his early days a conviction that mathematics was the best route to certainty in any question, and sought to apply mathematical and deductive techniques to all kinds of reasoning. Famously, his faith in the independent power of human reason brought him into dispute with his Lutheran colleagues. He argued that Chinese Confucianism could through reason, and without the revelation of a Christian God, achieve true moral precepts. This inflamed the mercurial temper of the monarch Frederick William I, who believed Wolff's notions opened the door to the rational individual conscience usurping hierarchy and especially military command. Wolff was given his own marching orders and fled to Marburg in 1723. But in 1740 he would triumphantly return to Halle under the patronage of the austere but more intellectually sceptical and irreligious Frederick the Great, cementing his position as the undisputed eminence of German intellectual life. Although one eminent modern commentator has described Wolff's particular oeuvre as being that 'he ruthlessly bores', he nevertheless did more than anyone to establish mathematical training as a desirable requisite for general intellectual endeavour.[42] In April 1741,

[41] Shapiro, *A culture of fact*, pp. 154–60; Stephen M. Stigler, *Statistics on the table. The history of statistical concepts and methods* (Cambridge, MA: Harvard University Press, 1999), pp. 203–73; Ivo Schneider, 'Mathematisierung des Wahrscheinlichen und Anwendung auf Massenphänomene im 17. und 18. Jahrhundert', in Mohammed Rassem and Justin Stagl (eds), *Statistik und Staatsbeschreibung in der Neuzeit vornehmich im 16.–18. Jahrhundert* (Paderborn: Schöningh, 1980), pp. 53–66.

[42] Christian Wolff, *Vernünfftige Gedancken von den Kräfften des menschlichen Verstandes und ihrem richtigen Gebrauche in Erkäntnis der Wahrheit* (Halle: Renger, 1713). Many issues of this work, appeared, along with excerpts and variants of *Vernünfftige Gedancken* focusing on particular subjects. He also authored the

soon after his return to Halle, Wolff provided an enthusiastic preface to Süssmilch's famous work on demography, which had been inspired by Petty and Graunt and would provide much of the raw material for Malthus's first work.[43]

Yet grand projects for the production of statistics remained largely beyond reach, even if there were some notable achievements such as the more rigorous compilation of trade figures, or the 1676 Crompton Census of religious affiliation in England.[44] Various German territories assembled detailed statistical data on districts within them, but even as demands for surveying were ratcheted up and rolled out in some polities, the collection of *national* data proved episodic and the information could soon become redundant. Examples include Denmark's complete land survey in its absolutist reconstruction after wars with Sweden the 1680s, or the efforts by Bourbon Spain, rather akin to much earlier projects in England and Venice, to count every tree in the realm in the 1740s. More promising was the great Milanese land survey, but it took nearly four decades between 1718 and 1757. Nehemiah Grew sought to improve on Petty and other's estimates of the size of England in order make people 'universally engag'd to Inclose, and to Improve, every Foot of our Land', although it is hard to see that efforts had much impact in practice.[45] Thus while it should be remembered that on a local level, often in efforts to limit legal disputes and stabilise knowledge of property, municipalities and local government had been producing registers of people and property since late medieval times, at the level of the whole state initiatives like Grew's still

oft-printed *Anfangs-Gründe aller mathematischen Wissenschaften* (Halle: Renger, 1710); Keith Tribe, *Governing economy. The reformation of German economic discourse 1750–1840* (London: Cambridge University Press, 1978), p. 16.

43 Johann Peter Süßmilch, *Die göttliche Ordnung in denen Veränderungen des menschlichen Geschlechts* (Berlin: Buchhandlung der Realschule, 1741), pp. 9–12.

44 Hoppitt, 'Political arithmetic', pp. 517–18. The excellent English trade data gathered from 1697 can be found in The National Archives, CUST 3. See also Peter Buck, 'People who counted. Political arithmetic in the eighteenth century', *Isis* 73 (1982), pp. 28–45.

45 Thomas Munck, *Seventeenth century Europe 1598–1700* (Basingstoke: Palgrave Macmillan, 1990), p. 346; Erich Bauer Manderscheid, *Los montes de España en la historia* (Madrid: Ministerio de Agricultura, Pesca y Alimentación, 1991), pp. 122–47; Peter Jones, *Agricultural Enlightenment. Knowledge, technology, and nature, 1750–1840* (Oxford: Oxford University Press, 2016), p. 38; Nehemiah Grew, 'A demonstration of the number of acres contained in England, or South-Britain; and the use which may be made of it', *Philosophical Transactions* 27 (1710), p. 269.

expressed an aspiration, as if the unimproved spaces were a vacuum that improvers would inevitably fill once appraised. Further inspiration came from statistically minded men who utilised data gathered for other purposes, such as records of baptisms, marriages and deaths: the endlessly energetic polymath Benjamin Franklin in America (who also designed a successful wood-conserving stove among his myriad achievements), or Süssmlich in Germany. It was these men, above all Süssmilch's compendious work, who provided the empirical underpinnings to the seminal demographic work of Malthus in its first edition of 1798.[46] Parallel efforts towards data collection went on in the sciences, such as the work at botanical gardens, or the field trips of Linnaeus, themselves legitimated as part of a national itemisation of resource potential (if not actually a count of resources as such).[47] The capacity of central governments to generate fairly reliable and universal surveys of some resources and populations was only to be fully realised, and then for a few countries during the nineteenth century.[48] But imagining that this could be done was a critical step in this direction and began to shape how the world was to be governed.

Early statistics did not contain the matter at the heart of its modern practice: a theory of probability. To the Enlightenment savants these issues were overwhelmingly matters of 'fact', not likelihood.[49] In that sense they were not tools for prediction; while in theory providing grounds for decisions, they were not employed to outline possible futures. Despite the emergence of theories of probability over the seventeenth and eighteenth centuries, such thinking remained largely isolated from matters of governance, where instead people retained

[46] Malthus, *An essay on the principle of population*, p. 38; 'For further information on this subject, I refer the reader to Mr. Sussmilch's tables. The extracts that I have made are sufficient to shew the periodical, though irregular, returns of sickly seasons, and it seems highly probable, that a scantiness of room and food was one of the principal causes that occasioned them.' These developments were also aided by the emergence of the idea of 'population' as a quantifiable entity with its own, somewhat autonomous dynamics. See McCormick, 'Population'; Süßmilch, *Göttliche Ordnung*.

[47] Koerner, *Linnaeus*.

[48] Theodore Porter, *Trust in numbers. The pursuit of objectivity in science and public life* (Princeton, NJ: Princeton University Press, 1995); Silvana Patriaca, *Numbers and nationhood. Writing statistics in nineteenth-century Italy* (Cambridge: Cambridge University Press, 1996).

[49] Although Graunt certainly used rates of probability to estimate life-tables. Shapiro, *A culture of fact*; Hacking, *The emergence of probability*, pp. 23, 108–10.

great faith in the idea that information would deliver the means to correct action.[50] It remained as it had for Francis Bacon, among many others at his time and since: demonstration was the guarantor of truth. Indeed, people had not yet widely learned to doubt their own eyes, even if in some realms, most notably the heliocentric theory of Copernicus, reason had eventually trumped commonsensical observation. There were exceptions, of course. Hobbes stated quite clearly that '*experience concludeth nothing universally*', anticipating the scepticism of David Hume. But in a world of profound information scarcity – at least as it seemed to those who aspired to rule and improve the world – some kind of facts seemed much closer to the truth of things than none at all. 'Mathematical proofs' or *a priori* reasoning could thus provide the empirical grounding for the development of political theory, according to the mid-eighteenth-century German writer (and also, at times, financial bureaucrat, advisor to the Hanoverians, and professor), Gottfried Achenwall. He distinguished carefully between areas where *a priori* and *a posteriori* reasoning could safely be applied, praised the value of historical example as well as the possibilities offered by 'the logic of probability', and insisted on the truth that changed circumstances could always alter the applicability of any rule.[51] Nevertheless, Achenwall could write with the benefit of decades of work by the arithmeticians and others who had made a step towards modern probability theory. The idea that the frequency of phenomena and their observed associations were grounds for averring causal relationships took hold, banishing the older idea that something was 'probable' because it was stated by a revered authority. Truth – supposedly – could be found in numbers.[52]

Metrics

For all the aspirations to compile the means to an arithmetic of state, the collection and use of quantitative data, and mathematical technique and notation, remained very limited for much of the Enlightenment. Applied mathematics was also largely confined to a few areas of

[50] On probability, see Hacking, *The emergence of probability*.
[51] Achenwall, *Die Staatsklugheit*, pp. a4v-5r, b3r.-v, 7v-8r., c1v-3r.
[52] Hacking, *The emergence of probability*, pp. 44, 48.

engineering, mechanics and navigation, and almost entirely absent from what we now know as the life sciences and chemistry. It found only very limited, if retrospectively renowned, applications in medicine. Yet if we peer ahead a little to the close of the enlightened century, there was one discipline where an aspiration to measurement, exactitude and prediction had become dominant, at least in terms of professional training and prestige if not as yet everyday practice. That discipline was forestry. By the end of the eighteenth century, the combination of the ambitions of foresters, most especially in Central Europe, their institutional reach through state forestry administrations and the mission of cameralists, had produced *Forstwissenschaft*, or 'scientific forestry'.[53] This was the discipline in a form recognisable to modern practitioners. In the 1790s German forester G.U. Däzel set out both the ends and means of this endeavour:

> If improvement of the condition of the forest is our purpose, and the cultivation of trees [*Holzzucht*] the means to this purpose; thus is the annual sustainable yield the ground for determining the manner of cultivation. If this is larger than the highest possible removal [*Absatz*], that scarcely is the case in the German provinces, then the rejuvenation of the forest can be left to Nature alone; in the opposing case one must support it through artificial means [*Kunst*].[54]

Yet what would a 'sustainable yield' (*nachhaltigen Holzertrag*) look like? 'No rational use of the woods can be thought of', declared the Prussian 'classic' forester Georg Hartig in one of his early writings in 1795, 'without having by the most reliable means possible estimated or calculated: how much and what kind of wood the forest can yearly provide, if it always should remain in as good a condition as possible'.[55]

---

[53] Beckmann, who first employed the term, seems to have meant it initially in the more limited sense of having a deep and systematic knowledge of the forest. J.G. Beckmann, *Gegründete Versuche und Erfahrungen der zu unsern Zeiten höchst nöthigan Holzsaat, zum allgemeinen Besten* (4th Auflage, Chemnitz: Johann Christoph Stößel, 1777 [1755, 1759]), p. 13.

[54] G.U. Däzel, *Ueber Forsttaxierung und Ausmittelung des jährlichen nachhaltigen Ertrages* (Munich: Joseph Lindauer, 1793), p. 1.

[55] Georg Ludwig Hartig, *Anweisung zur Taxation der Forste oder zir Bestimmung des Holzertrags der Wälder* (Giessen: Heyer, 1795), p. i.

This relatively simple declaration bore within it a series of ambitious requests: to inventorise all the kinds of wood that might be produced in a forest, their growth rates, and a determination of what kind of balance of species and ages made for the greatest 'good'. The last was perhaps the most demanding task of all, for the best condition of the wood was determined both by the ecological characteristics of the woodland itself, and the demand for particular products that people wanted from it. It was a step change from the vague legal prescription that had previously been enforced in most German states, that woodland owners could limit woodcutting rights so that 'they may not cut more wood than the woodland suffer'.[56] Hartig set the ambition that the yield should be as 'high' as possible, within the parameters of sustainability. But the yield of what? Volume of timber? Value to the consumer? If the forest produced many types of wood, how would these become aggregated together? How can one produce a balance of things when there are not, in fact, just two sides to the scales but many things that might be measured that might not even be of the same kind? What might at first seem a simple balancing act soon turned into a high-wire performance of dizzying complexity – unless some order could be imposed upon the whole. Over three decades later the forestry textbook published by Hundeshagen defined scientific forestry as 'the scientific principles for the most perfect and secure satisfaction of our present needs in raw products of the woodlands'.[57] His solution was to imagine an extended present in terms of demand and match the woodland to it. The fact of a dynamic economy that changed its size and demands over time, set against this elastic present of the foresters, would continually create tensions within the discipline.

One needed to organise the data and decide what was important, and this demanded systematic techniques. The result was the emergence of a series of practical tools in forestry to visualise and distribute information and generate applied knowledge. Hence 'sustainability', as demanded by this new forestry discipline, would be shaped, for a time, by the information that fitted these tools. One such

[56] Legal norm cited in Christoph Donauer's notes to Florinus, *Oeconomus Prudens*, p. 784.
[57] J.Ch. Hundeshagen, *Encyclopädie der Forstwissenschaft* (Tübingen: Heinrich Laupp, 1821), p. 1.

emergent tool in the organisation of resources was a deceptively simple one: the table. Tabulating information in rows and columns was a relatively old procedure in accounting, and facilitated the taking of surveys by estate stewards and government officials, although it was by no means a standard technique in the seventeenth century.[58] Seckendorff used and recommended tables in *Der deutsche Fürsten-Staat* to collate information in a way that made the condition of, and connections between, different elements within the table visible at a glance (his long career eventually took him to the rectorship of the University of Halle in 1692, at the heart of the early German Enlightenment, although he died after only a few weeks in office). The success of tables was by no means instant and universal; they are extremely rare in eighteenth-century literature by comparison with modern policy advice. However, they offered a simple device both for the relatively uninitiated to comprehend large amounts of data, and a means by which processes could be standardised and followed through simple steps. Its use was developed in forestry, above all, by Georg Hartig.

The tabular tradition was first established in cameralist writing, with the demand that the occasional tables produced to categorise tax assessments, cadastral and customs records should be harnessed to provide more comprehensive knowledge of the state. Already in the seventeenth century, the well-travelled Austrian writer Schröder proposed the tabulation of data related to manufactories for their potential to enhance population and commerce. These tables would be the '*Staatsbrille*', literally the 'spectacles of state', through which the polity would be viewed and comprehended. There was a purely practical aspect to some of this: as Zincke noted in 1755, 'those who deal with the carrying out of forestry matters, accounts etc. should prescribe appropriate and various formulae, tables and schemas for their work, because it is impossible that everything can be done in the same form in every place, and equally the work of the Treasury is greatly eased'.[59] Some cameralists such as Heynitz with his *Tabellen über die Staatswirtschaft* of 1775 made them the centrepiece of a system of economic intelligence, while others, whilst not employing

---

[58] Rusnock has noted this earlier history, and the use of tables by Graunt and Petty, which in fact post-dated Seckendorff's work. The uses of the table were also expounded by Bacon who, typically, did not make much use of them himself. Rusnock, *Vital accounts*, pp. 16–24; Gaukroger, *Francis Bacon*, p. 142.

[59] Zinck, *Anfangsgründe der Cameralwissenschaft*, p. 625.

them widely in their writings, suggested their efficacy in the demand
for information-gathering.[60] Through the use of tables, the chair in a
prince's study could become the panopticon by which the polity was
observed, or as Rößig put it his *Versuche über Oekonomische Policey*
in 1779:

> These *Policeytabellen* are the most seemly tapestry in the cabinet
> of a ruler; what is more proper for him than when those things
> which instruct him on the internal condition of his land are
> constantly before his eyes; without these he cannot know it, and
> how should he make it happy, if he does not know it?[61]

Once such information had been gathered, the governing mind could
start to consider in what direction policy might push the figures, and
mathematics could provide the tools by which it could be modelled.
Historians of economic thought will at this point think of the famous
and much-debated *tableau economique* of François Quesnay, conceived
in 1758 and developed in various forms over the 1760s. However, the
origins of this work appear to lie in a different tradition of hydraulic
machinery, and possibly Quesnay's preoccupations as a physician with
circulation of blood and fluids.[62] In truth, his table bore little resem-
blance to the *Tabellen* of the cameralists, and neither was Quesnay
much of an enthusiast for mathematics or geometry. We will return
to his work – and the attitudes of the French 'Physiocrats' and other
practitioners of political economy in relation to the products of the
soil – in Chapter 7. In practice, such initiatives only very slowly took on
a more systematic form, and even with the compilation of works like
The Statistical Account of Scotland begun by Sir John Sinclair in 1791,
county surveys in England and Denmark, or stuttering efforts under
the Napoleonic regime. They did not move that far beyond surveys
of districts or natural histories already to be found in the German

---

[60] Tribe, *Governing economy*, pp. 20, 33; Wakefield, *Disordered police state*, p. 33.
[61] Tribe, *Governing economy*, p. 33.
[62] Loïc Charles, 'The visual history of the Tableau Économique', *The European Journal
of the History of Economic Thought* 10 (2003), pp. 527-50. Quesnay's work became
available in English in 1766 through the translation of Mirabeau's explication of his
ideas: Marquis du Mirabeau, *The oeconomical table, an attempt towards ascertaining
and exhibiting the source, progress, and employment of riches, with explanations*
(London: W. Owen, 1766).

territories in the seventeenth century or aspired to by the Royal Society (see Chapter 3).[63]

For the cameralists and foresters of the mid- to late eighteenth century the issue at hand was achieving a balance of supply and demand at a high level of productivity, and providing the means to optimise production. Yet although Carlowitz justified the need for his silviculture as a counter to wood shortages, the *blame* for those shortages was attributed to backwardness and the lack of best practice in the woods. In other words, the fundamental problem to be overcome by new forestry techniques was not an existential crisis brought on by *overuse*, but rather *underuse*. This was despite the fact that these eighteenth-century authors also lambasted wastefulness and what they felt to be superfluous consumption, although the critique of luxury in heating and cooking was much less pronounced than found in relation to other consumer goods. Waste was, in principle, a negative factor for the industrious Improver, and to be reduced as far as possible. But the real challenge was to universally raise yields to what they could be. Woodland management moved from the primarily juridical approaches we saw outlined in Chapter 2 (without ever abandoning them), which focused on natural regeneration within parameters set by long-standing human use of the woods, towards a more interventionist stance guided by aspirations to improvement and innovation. Degradation of the environment was not an issue in this discourse, and any localised waste and barren patches could be remedied through the application of professional knowledge. In turn, the avoidance of either superfluous costs caused by the *oversupply* of timber or the threat of shortage from neglect and *undersupply* required information on balance. 'Where a sure balance of forest use', declared Hartig, 'based on mathematics and natural philosophy, is lacking, wood will always be over- or under-utilized.' Data collection and collation provided the means by which one could be 'sure', at first characterised by an appeal to detailed and systematic empirical knowledge of the ground and what grew from it. From the 1770s we find a shift towards a more abstract ambition of employing mathematics to bend the very substance of the

[63] Jones, *Agricultural Enlightenment*, pp. 21–2, 67, 218; Jonsson, *Enlightenment's frontier*, pp. 54–6. Plenty of district-level survey data of animals, food requirements, woodlands, etc. was already being compiled in Württemberg in the sixteenth and early seventeenth century, although it remains doubtful what use was made of it. Warde, *Ecology*, passim; Warde, 'Subsistence and sales'.

trees themselves towards the techniques thought most amenable to their management.[64]

It was one thing to say or write such things – quite another, as we have so often seen, to implement them. For a start, one needed the trained personnel. We have also seen how the development of the survey on both the private estate and within forestry entailed the emergence of a cadre of personnel schooled in geometry. But only a small minority of forest administrators and officials had such training, and more broadly, the first professor formally appointed to combine mathematical knowledge with the practice of Ökonomie was only appointed in 1736, at Göttingen in central Germany. Works on forestry, such as those of Noé Meurer or John Evelyn, had focused on juridical or arboricultural matters, not the technical knowledge required to accurately survey land. In Germany, the first volume devoted to applied geometry for surveying was the Praxis geometriae of J.F. Penther in 1729, running to eight more editions over the next six decades. In later editions Penther specifically expounded the benefits of geometry in being able to calculate the division of areas of coppice-wood into coupes to ensure an equal output each year, a practice of course well-established on a more rough-and-ready basis for many centuries.[65] The widespread application of such techniques could only occur after a long and painstaking

---

[64] The necessity of assessing the area and stock of wood was already made by Moser in 1757. Moser, Grundsätze, pp. 93, 96; H.E. Lowood, 'The calculating forester. Quantification, cameral science and the emergence of scientific forestry management in Germany', in T. Frängsmyr, T.L. Heilbronn and R.E. Rider (eds), The quantifying spirit in the 18th century (Oxford: Oxford University Press, 1990), pp. 330–9; on parallel developments in Austria, shaped in particular by Carato and closely aligned with the interests of the mining industry, see Heinrich Rubner, Forstgeschichte im Zeitalter der industriellen Revolution (Berlin: Duncker & Humbolt, 1967), pp. 72–3.

[65] This is sometimes called the first book on geometry for foresters, but actually it is for land surveying more generally. In practice too, geometrical techniques were familiar to surveyors, architects and cartographers. Johann Friedrich Penther, Praxis geometriae worinnen nicht nur alle bey dem Feld-Messen vorkommende Fälle, mit Stäben, dem Astrolabio, der Boussole, und der Mensul, in Ausmessung eintzeler Linien, Flächen und gantzer Revier, welche, wenn deren etliche angräntzende zusammen genommen, eine Land-Carte ausmachen, auf ebenen Boden und Gebürgen, wie auch die Abnehmung derer Höhen und Wasser-Fälle, nebst beygefügten practischen Hand-Griffen, deutlich erörtert, sondern auch eine gute Ausarbeitung der kleinesten Risse bis zum grösten, mit ihren Neben-Zierathen, treulich communiciret werden (Augsburg: Jeremias Wolffs Erben, 1761); Hasel and Schwartz, Forstgeschichte, p. 327; A.F. Schwappach, Handbuch der Forst-und Jagdgeschichte Deutschlands (Berlin: J. Springer, 1886), p. 557.

dissemination of knowledge through the academy and on the ground. And as is so often the case, it was only at the *end* of this process when a fulsome account of the necessary practices could be given in the great 'classics' of forestry such as the works of Georg Hartig already cited.

The spread of information required access to texts, to teachers, and the administrative competence to survey, map and process information. The emergence of cameralist literature in some ways embodied this combination, as the core texts were very frequently, as has been shown by Keith Tribe, based on university lectures or drawn directly from them (accounting for their sometimes peculiar and repetitive style). There was a great proliferation of this literature from around 1770, and earlier examples both in cameralism and forestry were pathbreakers that ran rather ahead the existence of a suitably educated cadre to implement their proposals. Individual rulers helped foster a wider 'scientific' culture by taking a direct interest in such efforts, such as Markgraf Karl Friedrich of Baden who travelled to Paris in 1771 and 1776, engaging with Physiocratic thinkers, before introducing reforms at home.[66] The tradition of itinerant bureaucrats peddling their expertise around the myriad courts of the Holy Roman Empire and its neighbours was also a key part of this process, as it already had been in the emergence of the *Forstordnungen* of the sixteenth century: men like *Oberjägermeister* Langen who refined mapping techniques in a career that took him from Germany to Danish-ruled Norway, and back to provide extensive surveys of the woods of Brunswick and Stolberg-Wernigerode in the 1740 and 1750s. Especially from the 1770s this was compounded by a denser network of journals devoted to agronomy, forestry and general improvement, which we will see more of in Chapter 6.[67]

Geometry had to be applied not just to the ground, but to the volume of the tree itself, first calculating its height accurately, and then translating this into volume, an accurate understanding of which required an appreciation that trees are cones, not cylinders. This 'Practical proof, that mathematics provides an indispensible service to

---

[66] Tribe, *Land, labour*, pp. 16–17, 94–8; Marcus Popplow, 'Von Bienen, Ochsenklauen und Beamten. Die ökonomischen Aufklärung in der Kurpfalz', in Marcus Popplow (ed.), *Landschaften agrarisch-ökonomischen Wissens. Strategien innovativer Ressourcennutzung in Zeitschfiften und Sozietäten des 18. Jahrhunderts* (Münster: Waxmann, 2010), pp. 181, 192.

[67] Hasel and Schwarz, *Forstgeschichte*, p. 319; Hölzl, *Umkämpfte Wälder*, pp. 133–8.

forestry', as the literal but none too pithy title of his 1765 volume put it, was provided by Christoph Oettelt.[68] By these means the science of 'stereometry' emerged, of measuring wood volumes, translated from a centuries-old literature on how to calculate solid volumes of felled timber to taking measures on the stump.[69] The apogee of this approach would be G. König's *Forstmathematik* of 1835, which facilitated these techniques developing as a distinct disciplinary specialisation within forestry.[70]

It took decades of work even to survey and map the ground of the princely woodlands of most European states, and the governments of many European countries maintained a rather fuzzy view of how much woodland there actually was within their borders before the arrival of satellite mapping at the end of the twentieth century. Measuring the number and extent of all of the trees was recognised by clear-headed thinkers as impossible, and some method had to be devised for using the new expertise in a practical fashion. The constraints of time meant that the quick eye of the forester and the rough categorisation of trees into classes which could be tabulated and assessed became the preferred way. Abstraction and mathematisation did not, thus, *demote* the role of the personnel on the ground with local knowledge. Rather, it made greater demands on them than ever before. Johann Gottlieb Beckmann, a forester in Saxony, gave his staff bags of coloured nails, and they would proceed through a stand of trees placing the colour-coded nails in trees of particular sizes. A count of the nails left in the bags at the end would give a count of the number and approximate age of trees in the stand.[71]

To be able to balance felling rates with re-growth one needed to know, however, the rate of re-growth. This preoccupation was not only a German one. Richard Bradley suggested in England in the

---

[68] Christoph Oettelt, *Praktischer Beweis, dass die Mathesis bei dem Forstwesen unentbehrliche Dienste tue* (Eisenach: Georg Ernst Witterkindt, 1765); see also the *Neueröffnete Jägerpraktika* of H.W. Döbel (Leipzig: Johann Samuel Heinsii Erben, 1746), and Johann Ehrenfried Vierenklee's *Mathematichsche Anfangsgründe der Arithmetick und Geometrie für Forstleute* (Leipzig, 1767).

[69] See Lowood, 'Calculating forester', p. 328.

[70] Hasel and Schwarz, *Forstgeschichte*, pp. 329, 346; in the typically narrow and semi-dynastic development of forestry, König was Heinrich Cotta's son-in-law. Rubner, *Forstgeschichte*, p. 128.

[71] Lowood, 'Calculating forester', p. 325. On local knowledge and surveying, see Mukerji, *Impossible engineering*, p. 33.

1720s that if the growth rate of trees could be calculated, so could the enhancement of their value over time, echoing the daydreams of John Houghton's correspondent three decades previously (as foresters realised later, this could only be done if relative prices remained stable for many decades).[72] Fears of wood shortage in France communicated to the French Academy of Sciences led to the commissioning of experiments and works by Buffon and Duhamel that soon found their way across the Channel, just as these authors were themselves reading English works of husbandry. They focused, however, in a rather traditional style on methods of setting and cultivating individual trees to improve growth, rather than managing them en masse.[73] Equally, the established official habit of taking a snapshot survey of trees could not resolve this problem. For how could you know the rate of future advance of 'perfect young stands' when you only had the example of 'imperfect old copses' to go on? The solution recommended by Georg Hartig at the end of the century was to find and categorise areas of consistent growth within each woodland, and then organise a planting regime around these micro-environments that allowed greater predictability.[74] Once an old stand and had been cleared and a new stand planted on land that was expected to give predictable patterns of growth, the tiresome empirical work of ocular assessment could be laid to one side. The method would be all the more reliable the more consistent in form the trees were, and the better the local conditions were known: a preference for what Henry Lowood calls 'minimum diversity' in the quest for sustainability.[75]

It would thus be wrong to characterise the rise of metrics and mathematics as a withdrawal from close and empirical engagement with the woodland. On the contrary, the new methods required intimate knowledge of highly local environments. G.U. Däzel, a Prussian, in 1792 wrote a guide for and led reform of Bavarian forestry, drawing extensively on new laws and practices that were set up in Prussia in the preceding years.[76] For Däzel, what really distinguished the new from the old was not the forester's academic distance from the ground. Rather, it was his capacity to use formal tools to transform what he found.

---

[72] Bradley, *General treatise*, pp. 9–10.
[73] Hartley, 'Exploring and communicating', pp. 237–8.
[74] Hartig, *Anweisung zur Taxation*, pp. i–ii, 78–80.
[75] Lowood, 'Calculating forester', p. 328.
[76] Däzel, *Ueber Forsttaxierung*, pp. i–ii.

The chief failing of the 'mere practical man, the empiricist' is that he 'achieved his knowledge only through the passage of time and mechanically', and hence without understanding its underlying principles he is incapable of adapting to change or innovating.[77] Thus Däzel insisted on the necessity of theory and the relative poverty of experience as a guide to action; he argued that a formal education was essential to his legitimacy and expertise, dismissing in one fell swoop the accumulated wisdom of most of his colleagues, perhaps especially those who acquired office as inheritance or a comfortable, state-funded sinecure. What was now required to maintain a balance between the supply and demand of wood was a new kind of survey that did not simply account for things as they were, as was the common practice, but that could predict the future. If all trees were identical, noted Däzel, this could be done easily. The problem of recording and comprehending the diversity of woods was old, and he listed the various methods proposed by others to calculate the stock of wood from sampling with an emphasis on making the labour efficient. But Däzel argued that the only truly reliable method of prediction was to fell and measure sample trees at all stages of growth, identifying districts of homogeneous growth patterns which would be managed accordingly. Where there were insufficient trees of the full age range available to calculate growth patterns, this would be done with more limited samples and applying logarithms.[78]

Even with the tools for sampling and estimation that were developed, an important strand within German forestry nevertheless remained sceptical of the capacity for reforms to be universally implemented, and of the possibility of accurate projections of yield. And it was equally the case that the forester never retreated to the library or the office. Work in the field and the personal wielding of an axe remained markers of prestige, authority and expertise long into the twentieth century.[79] In the words of Wilhelm Pfeil, who headed the leading forestry school at Eberswalde in Prussia from the 1820s to

---

[77] 'der bloße Praktiker, Empyriker, der nur durch die Länge der Zeit und maschinenmäßig zu seinem kenntnissen gelangt ist'; Däzel, *Ueber Forsttaxierung*, p. vi; see also similar comments by Walther, in Hölzl, *Umkämpfte Wälder*, p. 116; and W.G. Moser, *Grundsätze der Forst-Oeconomie* (Frankfurt and Leipzig: Heinrich Ludwig Brönner, 1757), pp. 10–11.

[78] Däzel, *Ueber Forsttaxierung*, pp. 2–8, 17–35.

[79] Foresters persisted in arguing that one had to personally know the ground to be able to make sensible predictions of yield. Moser, *Grundsätze*, pp. 156, 223.

1840s, 'We lay great value on the observation of Nature, on the study of trees and their natural behaviour, of the careful consideration of all circumstances under which one works [*wirtschaftet*].' And: 'Ask the tree, how it wants to be raised; it will teach you better than the books can.' Being an 'exact observer of Nature', and choosing her as one's 'chief guide' was the 'first and most important rule' for any forester, according to Zanthier. This view gained rapid ground in the second generation of 'classical' foresters, when empirical work introduced a 'sobering' of the wilder ambitions for a complete ordering of the woods, but the purveyors of the new forestry had always insisted on the importance of being active managers, as did writers on agricultural matters. In the case of forestry it was nearly always true. This still involved consulting their subordinates as to the particularity of local conditions. At the inception of modern forestry, Moser was careful to argue in 1757 that 'An old woodcutter has often noticed much better what assists this or that spot to such fine growth, or what has stopped or hindered the same, than any bureaucrat or forester.' Nevertheless, as complete local knowledge was impossible, some principles were required.[80] Thus did foresters place themselves in strategic command of the paths by which society managed its key resource, even if their gatekeeping varied in form. Only a long, hands-on and intimate education in woodsmanship and close observation of the natural world could confer the authority to properly manage a forest. Yet at the same time, anybody who *only* had that experience to draw on could not adapt to the demands of the future, for which the apparatus of cameralist university lectures, or later training at a private or state forestry school was required. 'In these times whoever as a student wants to come to be called a cameralist or an economist [*Oekonomen*], should be ashamed if they are afraid of algebra.'[81] Däzel was implying the same applied to foresters in 1793, and much later such a view would incorporate all of the environmental as well as many of the social sciences. 'Epistemic credibility' in forestry came to derive *both* from experience in the field

---

[80] Hasel and Schwarz, *Forstgeschichte*, pp. 343–4; indeed Pfeil was a critic of more extreme abstractions of forest planning such as Hundehagen's '*Normalwald*' that he viewed as an 'unachievable ideal'. Rubner, *Forstgeschichte*, pp. 126–8. Quotation on woodcutter from Moser, *Grundsätze*, pp. 12, 18; H.D. von Zanthier, *Abhandlungen über das theoretische und praktische Forstwesen. 2e Sammlung* (Berlin: C.W. Hennert, 1799), pp. 13–14; see also examples in Radkau, *Wood*, p. 194.

[81] Däzel, *Ueber Forsttaxierung*, p. ii.

and a technical training that allowed one to at least make use of the tools of surveying and categorisation developed by mathematically schooled thinkers.[82]

Plans

It was thus through forestry that sustainability was established in public language as a concept, initially in German, and emerged as a practical necessity backed by the state. This in turn required an earlier history of concern over resources, inquiry into the nature of the economic development of states, and incipient forms of accounting. Yet it is important to remember that this pertained only to wood resources. To talk of the need for a sustainable wood supply, or imagine a sustainable forest, did not mean that the same logic was applied to society or the environment more generally. Some may today look back to foresters as founders of a modern environmental sensibility, not least foresters themselves, but they are mistaken. The advocates of the new forestry did not articulate a general argument about sustainability in relation to the environment as a whole. They did not fear that development might degrade the Earth. They only provided an early model for one way to approach the problem.

We have seen in Chapter 2 how at an early date thinking about wood resources turned minds towards the future. Sowing trees was for the long term; never mind classical antecedents, was Abraham not already to be found planting trees in the Book of Genesis? When Hans Carl von Carlowitz decried the bare or barely treed groves of Saxony in 1713, he argued that the work of replenishing them was urgent, because a shortage of wood was not like a dearth of grain that could be resolved by the next good harvest, but could hardly find remedy in a century.[83] The logic of forestry, increasingly so with the tools that became available to it, was to plan: not in a general way, aspiring for an eventual increase in wealth, or a more godly society, but with exactitude, with definitive results to be achieved at predetermined dates.

[82] The term 'epistemic credibility' was borrowed into history from philosophy by Chandra Mukerji in her study of the construction of the Canal du Midi. Mukerji, *Impossible engineering*, ch. 3.
[83] Genesis XXI. Carlowitz, *Sylvicultura oeconomica*, 1732 edn, pp. 68–9.

Debates about best forestry practice would consequently move into debates about what institutional framework was capable of delivering plans far into the future. This became more and more significant as woodland management moved away from coppicing for fuel and agricultural uses, in favour of stands of mature timber for construction, pit-props and railway sleepers.[84]

Carlowitz wrote at the end of a long and distinguished career. However, the 'scientific forestry' of the eighteenth century and its preoccupation with the future was mostly a young man's game. Often important works were written as spin-offs from courses of lectures by new appointees, whether as a summation of their content, or essentially collections of the lectures themselves.[85] Wilhelm Gottfried Moser (1729–93) published his *Grundsätze der Forstökonomie* when only 28 in 1757, the most substantial contribution to the genre since Carlowitz; Johann Beckmann's *Grundsätze der Landwirtschaft* appeared when he was 30 in 1769. Thanks to another Beckmann, Johann Gottlieb (1700–77), there was a new term to describe this branch of knowledge: *Forstwissenschaft*.[86] It was immediately taken up by other authors, staking a claim to a novel and particular expertise that went beyond the remit, so it implied, of traditional foresters and woodwards. While Moser was determined to frame his work as part of the cameral sciences (*Cameralwissenschaften*), he was equally determined to set forestry on its own two feet as a separate discipline, and especially distinguish it from the treatment of forestry as a subsection of the *Hausväterliteratur*.[87] *Forstwissenschaft* is commonly translated as 'scientific forestry', although its original sense was to capture the idea of forestry as a systematic branch of knowledge, a discipline as we might say, rather than an activity subject to the rules and expectations we associate with 'science' in modern English. This new nomenclature coincided, as we have seen, with the rising prestige of mathematics within forestry literature (if only to a very limited degree among foresters), and equally, the proliferation of cameralism itself as a taught discipline within the universities. But most writers on forests

---

[84] Grewe, *Der versperrte Wald*, p. 225.
[85] Tribe, *Land, labour*.
[86] Moser, *Grundsätze*; Beckmann, *Gegründete Versuche*; Hasel and Schwarz, *Forstgeschichte*, p. 317.
[87] Moser, *Grundsätze*, pp. 6–7.

of the mid-eighteenth century still had a background in legal studies, as did Moser.[88]

By the 1750s the body of forestry literature was sufficient for debates over good practice to emerge, and indeed one now finds extended complaints about rivals, precursors of battles over the best way to judge sustainable yield – by area or by volume produced, or revenue? – that would characterise and bedevil classical forestry for much of nineteenth century.[89] The 1760s saw accelerated attempts to systematically organise the exchange of knowledge, which was still heavily dependent on the movement of individual foresters (or cameralist officials), and the haphazard acquisition of books and journals. Johann Friedrich Stahl founded his *Forst-magazin* in 1763, part of a coterie of efforts by this forestry and hunting official to develop education in Württemberg.[90] Like most of the many agricultural journals founded at this time, it was short-lived, being highly dependent on its driving personality, and had folded by 1769. Much innovation emerged from the small polities of central and mountainous Germany, where forestry was crucial to the mining and smelting industries. In these lands the cameralist enthusiasms of particular rulers strongly shaped local practices, employment of officials and financial support. Stahl's journal was able to attract significant contributors in his crusade to disseminate best theory and practice: Justi, the foresters Moser, Zanthier and Oettelt, and from abroad, the Comte de Buffon and Duhamel du Monceau.[91]

By the 1780s forestry was established as a theme among university-trained cameralists. Now that the idea of a formal discipline of *Forstwissenschaft* was embedded among men of university training, more autonomous and formal courses could be established. Trunck was the first cameralist to give lectures directly to foresters, as opposed to students seeking a more general training, at Freiburg in 1787. This was in the context of a new forestry ordinance for the Outer Austrian territories (located in the far south-west of Germany alongside the Rhine)

---

[88] Hasel and Schwarz, *Forstgeschichte*, p. 316.

[89] See for example Beckmann's spat with Döbel; Beckmann, *Gegründete Versuche*, pp. 2–7.

[90] Isabelle Knap, 'Die Anfänge "wissenschaftlicher" Frstleuten am Beispiel des *Allgemeinen oeconomischen Forst-Magazins* (1763–1769)', in Popplow, *Landschaften*, pp. 61, 65.

[91] Knap, 'Anfänge', pp. 66, 70–5.

the previous year that for the very first time required a formal examination for foresters, and the requirement to attend lectures: obviously fulfilment of the law required such lectures to be held![92] G.U. Däzel, whom we met above, set up the first Bavarian forestry school in 1787, and in the following year, questionnaires were sent out to ascertain the full extent of the duchy's woodlands. Having set up the infrastructure to apply juridical control over the forests in the sixteenth century, in common with many European states, these German principalities now moved precociously to lay down the preconditions for their 'scientific' management through providing the (often uniformed) workforce to achieve this. Yet attaining these goals was still very far off: Max Emanuel Graf von Larosée commented in 1795 that in Bavaria, 'reading and writing are the rarest talents of forest officials'. According to Simon Rottmanner in 1780 these foresters were 'as ignorant as a peasant'.[93] This period also saw more engagement with French writing about forestry, via inquiries by Reaumur in 1710 (published in 1721), Buffon in 1739, and by far the most comprehensive, the work of Duhamel de Monceau published in 1764 (and rapidly translated into German). In France the influence of an experimental natural history was stronger, with a more theoretical approach to the physiology of plants. In contrast, the gentlemanly tomes of Evelyn and his imitators seemed rather dilettantish with no real grounding in economic realities.[94] Such exchanges also prepared the ground for the French reception of a more systematic and planned forestry from Germany, with opening of their first forestry school at Nancy in 1824. As elsewhere, an enduring theme among French discussions was simply that foresters were corrupt and unreliable, particularly as there men could purchase

---

[92] Hasel and Schwarz, *Forstgeschichte*, pp. 326–7.

[93] Martin Knoll, *Umwelt – Herrschaft – Gesellschaft. Die landesherrliche Jagd Kurbayerns im 18. Jahrhundert* (St Katharinen: Scripta Mercaturae, 2004), pp. 117, 194–6. Nevertheless, 1795 was a key year in Bavaria with the appointment of Johann Peter Kling at the head of a new department of forestry, who drove forward the measurement and planning of Bavarian forests, an area then greatly augmented by acquisitions at the end of the Napoleonic wars. Hölzl, *Umkämpfte Wälder*, pp. 37–8, 144–7, 157.

[94] M. de Buffon, 'Memoire sur la conservation et le retablissement des forests', *Memoires de l'Academie Royale* (8 Apr. 1739), esp. p. 148; Henri-Louis Duhamel du Monceau, *De l'exploitation des bois. 2 vols* (Paris: H.L. Guerin, L.F. Delatour, 1764); see also Henri-Louis Duhamel du Monceau, *The elements of agriculture*, trans. P. Miller (London: Vallaint & Durham, 1764).

the office; while reforms of 1661 attempted to deal with this malady, by the end of the 1680s the status quo had been restored. French forestry practice, hampered by the venality of office, remained behind German aspirations and achievements (as measured by the foresters) both intellectually and on the ground, despite the continent-wide renown that authors like Duhamel du Monceau might attain.[95]

Nevertheless, the higher ranks of forestry administrations were increasingly populated by men educated in law, mathematics and the sciences who believed they now had the capacity to plan the most desirable – and sustainable – woodlands far into the future. Trainees could avail themselves both of specialist texts on particular aspects of forestry, and compendious handbooks that ranged from the physiology of trees to sowing practices to remedies against pests, with readings lists appended.[96] The leading figures in this movement around the turn of the eighteenth century were Georg Hartig and Heinrich Cotta. Like so many, Hartig came from a forestry family, and after an education in cameralism, obtained his first post in 1786. He followed what would become a stereotypical path for these 'classics': formal education, elevation to early responsibility, and the publication of a forthright and confident volume laying out prescriptions for a model forestry, in Hartig's case, his *Anweisung zue Holzzucht für Förster* in 1791.[97] Now that the discipline was more established the years of itinerant wandering in the service of various lords, and the transition to formal teaching, became much shorter. Stahl, who set up his *Forst-magazin* in 1763, had blazed a trail: born in the tiny Württemberg town of Heimsheim in 1718, he had followed an interest in cameralism and forestry to Saxony, the Harz and Bohemia before returning home and eventually founding his journal in his forties, and then lectured in forestry from 1772 at Württemberg's military school at Solitude, a barracks and hunting palace ensconced in woodlands north of Stuttgart.[98] This followed the model of Zanthier's very first forestry school founded in the Harz in

---

[95] Corvol, *L'homme et l'arbre*, pp. 3–4; Whited, *Forests and peasant politics*, pp. 28, 33; Matteson, *Forests*, pp. 50–105.

[96] For example, Johann Leonhard Späth, *Handbuch der Forstwissenschaft worinnen der praktische Betrieb der Waldungen, ihre mögliche Erhaltung, Verbesserung und cammeralistische Benutzung abgehandelt wird* (Nürnberg, 1801).

[97] Hasel and Schwarz, *Forstgeschichte*, pp. 336–8.

[98] Knap, 'Die Anfänge', p. 66.

1763.[99] Hartig in contrast set up his first school at Dillenburg within his first decade of service. The prestige of his teaching and above all publications would lead him into Prussian service by 1811, and the erection of the famous forestry school that settled at Eberswalde by 1830 (then under the direction of Hartig's often contrary and equally prolific pupil, Wilhelm Pfeil).[100] Similarly, Hartig's peer in the pantheon of classical foresters, Heinrich Cotta, moved from a private forestry school based at Zillbach, to a larger Institute at Tharandt near Dresden which was granted state funding by the Saxony government in 1816. His textbook provided for an education beginning with mathematics, plant physiology, chemistry (of increasing importance as we will see in Chapter 6) and natural history, before moving to practical forestry.[101] This was also the highpoint of idealised plans, when Hartig lobbied for a form of sustained yield based on planting forests designed and anticipated to deliver repeated and consistent volumes of timber, requiring a forest compartmentalised, sown and felled accordingly (known as *Massenfachwerk*). His opponent Cotta argued that this ideal was unachievable and instead that it was sufficient to design a forest where it was simply the compartments, not the growing timber in its entirety, that were managed systematically, with the equivalent areas expected to give roughly equivalent yields. Indeed. Hartig's plans proved too complex to realise and were abandoned after his death, and in the long run neither method brought the precision hoped for. Yet their principles transformed the forest nevertheless.[102] What such methods also required was the formal categorisation of all woodlands according to age and type, which established enduringly the vocabulary and metrical definitions of modern forestry. Woods were divided into *Niederwald* (underwood), *Mittelwald* (coppice with standards in English; tellingly, no single definition was ever developed by the insular laggards in forestry) and *Hochwald* (high forest). *Niederwald* was first used by Cotta 1804, followed by Hartig in 1809; while it has since been used

---

[99] Lowood, 'Calculating forester', p. 319; Rubner, *Forstgeschichte*, p. 118.

[100] Hasel and Schwarz, *Forstgeschichte*, p. 341.

[101] Heinrich Cotta, *Grundriß der Forstwissenschaft. 2 Auflage* (Dresden: Arnold, 1836), p. vi, passim. Hasel and Schwarz, *Forstgeschichte*, pp. 338–40.

[102] Heinrich Cotta, *Grundriß der Forstwissenschaft. 2 Auflage. Bd.2.* (Dresden: Arnold, 1838), p. 3; Hasel and Schwarz, *Forstgeschichte*, p. 338; Grewe, *Der versperrte Wald*, pp. 237–8.

retrospectively to describe coppices, in actual fact a range of local terms of varied meaning had previously been used.[103]

Men like Hartig were schooled in the expectation that the state would drive forward innovation and best practice, whether through education, sponsorship or granting privileges to entrepreneurs, or taking management of resources directly in hand. This was in the tradition of the powerful forestry administrations of Central Europe established in the sixteenth century. The mix of policies developed by early modern states, especially in Central Europe, also gave rise to opportunities for rent-seeking (that is, living off monopoly rents that could be charged by those holding the privilege to do so, rather than having to run efficient and competitive businesses). There were plenty of examples of the worst excesses we expect from the unchallenged access to state largesse: corruption and powers of persuasion leading to the funding of fantasists and pipedreams (although with the latter two the private sector was no less vulnerable). Economic historians often operate with pre-established assumptions about the virtues or vices of such institutional arrangements. Those more sympathetic to state ownership have viewed these monopolistic and patronage-based strategies of resource management as the necessary condition for promoting growth in poorer and backward economies. Others more inclined to the free market have asserted equally strongly that such institutions were profound hindrances to the economic liberties that would allow enterprise to blossom and bear fruit. We do not have to adjudicate between these views here (or indeed decide whether any view was consistently true), but should note that living in the long shadow of Carlowitz, university-educated foresters of the late Enlightenment were convinced that nearly all users of the woodland under-utilised the resource,[104] and while some argued in favour of deregulating the market and controls over the land, most were convinced that the proper long-term planning they believed requisite to maximising wood production would never be achieved without government intervention. This is despite the fact that as early as the 1750s it was noted that through careful maintenance of

[103] Matthias Bürgi, 'How terms shape forests. "Niederwald", "Mittelwald" and "Hochwald" and their interaction with forest development in the canton of Zürich, Switzerland', *Environment and History* 5 (1999), p. 328.

[104] It was important to remove wood from the forest, argued Moser, because otherwise it inhibited growth; hence one should remove an amount equivalent to that which annually grew. Moser, *Grundsätze*, p. 100.

accounts the return from woodlands could be used to impute a return on capital which could then be used to compare its value as an asset to other investments, although a high return was probably a sign of unsustainability.[105]

Views on forest planning were initially propagated through private forestry schools that were set up alongside the offices that foresters held in princely administrations, but also through leading lights of cameralism in Germany, such as the self-professed 'anti-physiocrat' Johann Ludwig von Pfeiffer, who decried the 'physiocratic dream of unbounded freedom' when only the 'welfare of the state' could decide on the best use of the woodlands and allocation of wood.[106] However, private schools were fairly rapidly able to win support and be absorbed as publicly supported institutions. They were, after all, largely training individuals for public service. The necessity of this move was rationalised in the same way that the same problem had been addressed in the seventeenth century. Men's lives were too short, and most failed to perceive or care about the importance of benefits that would only be enjoyed long after they were gone. It was one thing to express this as a general observation on the fact that it took longer than a lifetime to produce good-quality timber, but the new tabular plans that men like Hartig produced stipulated tasks that would have to be observed for a century or more. Who could guarantee such actions so far ahead? 'Only the state', declared Heinrich Cotta, 'manages for eternity.'[107] It was later in the nineteenth century that Roscher spoke of 'the eternal character of the state', but early modern foresters would have understood his imputation very well. 'The state', declared the French forest code of 1827, 'is taking over control of communal woods only in order to assure their perpetuation...'[108] By that time, the experience of peremptory privatisation of woodlands or the release of private holdings from supervision by royal foresters during the Revolution had shown a

---

[105] Moser, *Grundsätze*, pp. 76–7. Moser also thought that it was unlikely a private owner could accumulate the long experience needed to assess the growth-rates of trees in any locality; but he was a young man; p. 95. Beckmann used examples of his planting work begun in the 1720s to demonstrate potential profit rates, even claiming that hardwoods brought a greater return than arable farming. Beckmann, *Gegründete Versuche*, pp. 52–4.

[106] Pfeiffer, *Die Grundsätze*, p. 164.

[107] 'Nur der Staat wirtschaftet für die Ewigkeit'; Rubner, *Forstgeschichte*, pp. 121–3.

[108] Radkau, *Holz*, p. 143; Whited, *Forests and peasant politics*, p. 35.

widespread proclivity to cash in on timber assets as quickly as possible, contrary to liberal expectations that it would promote conservation.[109] Arguments for the urgent need to intervene were stoked by fears of wood shortage, a recurrent theme but one that reached new heights of intensity in Central Europe during the eighteenth century. Rather than such anxieties merely occurring simultaneously in many places, a more international market in literature allowed direct influences and citations across borders, as Geutebrück in 1757, for example, quoted Buffon's 1739 tract on the fact that wood was becoming scarce for basic needs, although he hardly lacked for equivalent German claims and indeed swiftly moved to a discussion of local prices.[110] The argument was present and correct in the seminal text of Wilhelm Gottfried Moser, whose 1757 work really set the frame for the genre of *Forstwissenschaft* from that date: 'In our times… if timely counsel is not taken, the wood shortage may press even harder than the bread shortage in various regions of our a Fatherland, and eventually draw after it the decline and decay of entire settlements.'[111] A variety of causes was blamed, sometimes rather indiscriminately: above all the wastefulness of the peasants, but also 'wood-devouring' industries, population growth or an inordinate taste for luxury, such as ordinary people wanting hot drinks and heated rooms for themselves.[112] As in earlier periods, this rhetoric was employed pervasively throughout the social order, and sometimes accompanied by local calculations of supply and need. In Saarbrücken, for example, the needs of iron production were assessed in 1750 and by the 1770s surveys revealed that demand was outstripping the sustainable supply. In this region of western Germany rising prices and fears of shortage were equally reflected in a rise of inter-community disputes over access to and rights in woodlands, along with largely ineffective attempts by the governments to encourage the use of coal.[113] Publications highlighted the threat of wood shortage

---

[109] Matteson, *Forests*, pp. 115-25.

[110] Carl August Geutebrück, *Kurze Anweisung wie mit dem Anbau des Holzes, zu gedeylich anzuhoffenden Anwuchs desselben zu Werck zu gehen?* (Erfurt: Johann Friedrich Weber, 1757), p. A2.

[111] Moser, *Grundsätze*, p. 5; Beckmann, *Gegründete Versuche*, pp. 8–9.

[112] The list was already established by Carlowitz and altered little thereafter. Moser, *Grundsätze*, pp. 30–1; Hölzl, *Umkämpfte Wälder*, pp. 71–9.

[113] The most detailed survey of the varied experience of regions in western Germany is surely that of Uwe E. Schmidt, *Der Wald in Deutschland im 18. Und 19. Jahrhundert. Das Problem der Ressourcenknappheit dargestellt am Beispiel der*

were especially prevalent between the early 1770s and around 1810, that probably reflected both the widespread institutionalisation of the new scientific forestry at precisely this time, but also the despoliation of the woodlands attendant on the Revolutionary and Napoleonic wars, although institutional reorganisation and the nationalisation of Church property also stimulated reform.[114] By the end of the eighteenth century in both Germany and France the possibility of deforestation causing climate change was added to the list of woes.[115]

Warfare prompted a call to arms in the woods. England's naval losses during the Seven Years' War led to the publication of *Heart of oak. The British bulwark* by Liverpool shipwright Roger Fisher, who took testimony about the exhaustion of timber from shipwrights and purveyors around the nation. The nature of the argument was very different than the German case, however, in that there was no use of statistics, and authority came from the status of Fisher and his interlocutors as wood merchants: 'I will not join in the publick clamour concerning the decrease of oak timber merely from hear-say; but will relate what, by *ocular demonstration*, I know to be fact, and what I have had from others *whose testimony is undeniable.*' He saw Britain falling behind the diligence shown in replanting in France, or access to colonial reserves by Spain; although he feared relying on Britain's own American colonies, despite cautiously stating 'far be it from me, to accuse our plantations of disloyalty'.[116] Fisher knew that there were plenty of statutes running back to Henry VIII little enforced, but his remedy went no further than the seventeenth-century call for more law and more patriotism from landowners to 'immediately take into consideration the means of establishing a royal navy for the year 1850'.[117]

Waldressourcenknappheit in Deutschland im 18. und 19. Jahrhundert – eine historisch-politische Analyse (Saarbrücken: Conte, 2002), pp. 49–51, 72, 76–81, 170–1, 269–71. An overview is provided on pp. 275–301. See also Schäfer, *'Ein Gespenst geht um'*; Sieferle, *The subterranean forest*, pp. 162–4; Steinsiek, *Nachhaltigkeit*, p. 56.

114 Whited, *Forests and peasant politics*, pp. 24–5, 30.

115 Schmidt, *Der Wald*, pp. 313, 338–41.

116 Roger Fisher, *Heart of oak. The British bulwark* (London: J. Johnson, 1763), pp. 8, 76, 80; the same arguments regarding naval timber were carried by the Portuguese government into Brazil by the 1790s. José Augusto Pádua, '"Annihilating Natural Productions". Nature's economy, colonial crisis and the orgiins of Brazilian political environmentalism (1786–1810)', *Environment and History* 6 (2000), p. 274.

117 Fisher, *Heart of oak*, p. 87.

Interestingly, he argued that the commercial logic of shipbuilders was detrimental to resource management, as ships were being deliberately mothballed after the war to generate business for the yards with new construction. 'Posterity has no place in the breast of our modern planners.'[118] The Crown and parliament would not respond until the Commissions of Land Revenue around 1790, and then focusing on Crown estates.[119] Otherwise, advice in Britain and Ireland was focused, as with the works of the seventeenth century and the husbandry literature, on improving landlords and the value of raising trees to estates.[120]

For the 'classics' like Hartig and Cotta in Germany it was fidelity to new techniques and plans that brought a sustained yield and maximised the output of forestry. Focused on timber production, and in particular softwoods (often reflecting demand from the mining industry), they desired stands of trees managed on relatively long cycles, and to the exclusion of other interests in the woods. Brought up amid the panics about wood shortage that grew ever more intense over the eighteenth century, the ultimate goal was the highest possible sustained yield, and the development of methods to produce the wonder, to paraphrase the giant king Bobradigil in Swift's *Gulliver's Travels*, of two trees where one had stood before – or indeed much greater ratios of success. These plans, it hardly needs underlining, were focused on the supply-side. But some thinkers imagined a greater co-ordination between all aspects of supply and demand, with the state as the co-ordinating body ensuring a match between the annual forms of production in all their diversity, and the very disparate needs of the polity we have met in Chapter 2. Moser stated as a commonplace that the state had 'the right to determine the applications and usage of wood'.[121] Certainly such co-ordination had taken place since the sixteenth century where forest ordinances in some German

---

[118] Fisher, *Heart of oak*, p. 89.
[119] Sheila Lambert, ed., *House of Commons sessional papers of the eighteenth century. Vol. 76. George III. Reports of the Commissioners of Land Revenue 1–7. 1878–1790* (Wilmington, DE: Scholarly Resources, 1975); see also Edward Harries, 'General observation on the state of oak timber. &c.', *Annals of Agriculture* XV (1791), p. 556.
[120] See this approach exemplified on both sides of the Irish Sea in Batty Langley, *A sure method of improving estates* (London: Francis Clay & Daniel Browne, 1728); and S. Hayes, *A practical guide to planting and the management of woods and coppices* (London: Allen & West, 1794).
[121] Moser, *Grundsätze*, p. 28.

states had required purchasers to present a list of what they wanted to foresters by set days who would then decide on the size and location of allocations according to the state of the local reserves. But to do this on a regional or territorial scale was an altogether different endeavour, as suggested by the prescriptions of Pfeiffer for achieving this very goal:

> Aside from the general wood consumption in towns and in the countryside, one also has particular, and in part very valuable economic branches that have to be supplied with sufficient wood and charcoal; and one wants no less wood for trade, for shipping, and for the encouragement of many fire-devouring factories. It is however not possible that this great quantity of things can be continually satisfied in timely fashion with the requisite goods, never mind fulfilling the forestry plans [*Forstetat*], if forestry matters do not have one man at their head, who can give to one forest and take from another, and who can see the closer, further or more convenient location for removing wood; the more expensive or better value transport; the distribution of forests over all areas of the state; the export prices; the composition of neighbouring forests, the multiple uses of wood; shipbuilding; indeed understands how to manage everything with wise intent.[122]

One wonders where such a presiding genius, with this information at his fingertips, might be found in the 1780s. Contrary views emerged among those men captivated by the new political economy that emerged from Scotland and England, which we shall see more of in Chapter 7. The core of this incipient liberal analysis rested on how men came to value things through exchange, and how people esteemed the products of each other's labour; although here too an alternative strand of thought argued for a 'civic cameralism' that would stimulate afforestation, especially of the larch.[123] For liberals inspired by Scottish political economy, such as foresters Pfeil in Prussia or Hazzi in Bavaria, 'wood shortage' and the attendant high prices would induce better management and more investment in forestry when people sensed the possibility of future profit. High prices would also restrain the less profitable

---

[122] Pfeiffer, *Die Grundsätze*, pp. 161–2.
[123] Jonsson, *Enlightenment's frontier*, ch.6.

aspects of demand through the discipline of the market.[124] Foresters would respond to others' needs as communicated through the price mechanism. Faster growing poplars or conifers would supplant sentimental attachments to oak or beech, although they also had the effect of ruining the grazing, which achieve the same end as abolishing common rights by more costly legal process. The contrasting interests of graziers and foresters were an enduring source of tension as foresters sought to transform woodland space. This was not least because, as Moser noted, 'the wood shortage is presumed to press on our descendants, but the loss of pasture is a burden upon the living'.[125] Opposing views among foresters emerged in explosive arguments over whether forestry should seek to maximise the net yield of *timber* or *money* in the 1850s and 1860s.[126] Those who preferred the former might be attracted to state ownership that reduced the pressures of having to pay market rents and provided a buffer against shifts in demand and exchange rates, while others argued that there was little point in producing a high level of output for which there was insufficient demand to cover costs, although arguably this latter opinion was the conceit of an age confident in its ability to satisfy demand.

As we have seen, foresters had already been prognosticating on the longevity of wood supplies for centuries by the time Hartig and Cotta were writing. Basic surveys too stretched back to the sixteenth century. Most of this anxious prediction was rather vague, with exceptions such as the figure of 16–17 years until exhaustion given for the mining regions of the Harz in 1643 (this was as it turned out hugely overly pessimistic).[127] Johann Peter Kling introduced more detailed

---

[124] These views were in a distinct minority, perhaps only one-twentieth of publications of the theme, as estimated in Schmidt, *Der Wald*, p. 313; Radkau, *Holz*, p. 142; Hölzl, *Umkämpfte Wälder*, p. 75; Rubner, *Forstgeschichte*, p. 142.

[125] Radkau, *Holz*, pp. 42–3; Moser, *Grundsätze*, p. 119.

[126] Known as *Waldreinertragslehre* and Preßler's rent-focused *Bodenreinertraglehre*. Radkau, *Holz*, p. 170. Radkau has even suggested, without any clear evidence, that foresters encouraged long cutting cycles to give themselves a job far into the future, although it is unclear why any single forester should be in favour of this any more than a landowner would care about the return to succeeding landowners. The notion of trees as 'capital' providing an interest payment that had to both sustain the size of the capital itself and an additional 'use percentage' (*Nutzungsprozent*) was developed by Hundeshagen, a bridge towards comprehending the forest in purely monetary terms. Hundeshagen, *Encyclopädie der Forstwissenschaft*; Rubner, *Forstgeschichte*, pp. 121, 143–4.

[127] Steinsiek, *Nachhaltigkeit*, pp. 115, 119.

surveying of woodlands in the Palatinate and Bavaria, building on the principles laid down from the sixteenth century, and one-third of the former's woods had both surveys and plans for their future management (*Nutzungspläne*) by the 1780s. In these surveys conifers were defined and recorded by their age, pointing to the new era of forestry and the amenability of these species to more exact prediction and management. Beech was simply recorded as being suitable for felling or not and oaks by possible use, exactly like any sixteenth-century survey, although oak dimensions were also recorded (as the Venetians had done 200 years before). By the 1820s the principles of the Bavarian forestry administration were clearly set out as 'To achieve on the smallest possible area the highest and greatest possible material yield, and to use the sustainable yield to the greatest advantage.'[128] The famed surveys of France instigated by Colbert in 1669 had mostly focused simply on boundaries and jurisdiction, with very little on the actual trees at all, even if detail gradually was added over subsequent decades. In this regard, though widely cited by historians, Colbert's proposals fell far short of what would be needed for a sylvicultural reform as proposed by the German foresters a century later. In France, the practice of charging fees to peasant communities who were compelled to have their own woods surveyed only compounded resistance. Even basic surveys only became the norm after a century of enforcement; as Andrée Corvol noted three decades ago, the reform of 1669 was only 'one step on a long path'.[129]

Nevertheless, we should not overstate the rapidity with which this transformation in *thinking* was realised on the ground. It produced neither an autarchic, 'sustainable' wood supply in the major European states, nor a universal transformation of the forest to match the foresters' ambitions. The history of the woodlands of the Palatinate in western Germany set out by Bernd-Stefan Grewe shows how halting and gradual the actual realisation of such plans was, even where forestry was (in its own terms) most advanced. The surveying of the state woods begin in the 1770s and 1780s was no more detailed than that

---

[128] 'auf der geringsten Fläche den höchsten und bestmöglischsten Material ertrag mit dem mindesten Aufwand zu erzielen und den nachhaltigen Ertrag auf das vorteilhafteste zu verwenden'; Grewe, *Der versperrte Wald*, pp. 221–2, 229.

[129] Corvol, *L'homme et l'arbre*, New pp. 8, 13–16, 646; see also Hamish Graham, 'Fleurs-de-lis in the forest. "Absolute" monarchy and attempts at resource management in eighteenth-century France', *French History* 23 (2009), pp. 311–35.

achieved in the Duchy of Württemberg in the 1550s and 1580s. The real difference was of intent: these surveys were actually used, albeit haltingly. The ambition of producing even-aged stands that would be managed on cycles of many decades according to the newly minted 'classic' model of scientific forestry was only firmly established as policy in 1840, as part of a wider Bavarian forestry reform that finally set out to systematically generate long-term plans across the polity from the mid-1830s, and only fully unified its operations in 1852. Before this date the general run of forestry owed more to techniques described by Carlowitz than Hartig. Yet even in the 1860s the surveys that could establish areas of homogeneous growth and demarcate the stands for long-term planning applied only rough calculations of equivalently yielding areas into which to compartmentalise the forest.[130] Application of more regular coupes and felling patterns in the Hunsrück under the Archbishopric of Trier, initially to the state-owned woods from 1760 and then to communally owned woods from 1790 did fairly rapidly reap reward in higher yields, although it is not clear these were sustainable in the long run.[131] In the Prussian provinces of Rhineland and Westphalia, the finance ministry only took in hand systematic reform across the whole woodland space with a series of commissions established in 1834.[132] It took Prussian rule to effect that switch to plantations of conifers in Saarbrücken from 1821, although wood shortage and the need to balance supply and demand had been a subject of discussion for a century.[133] Equally, the example of the Austrian administration in making the formal examination of foresters a *requirement* for office, and exclusion of such officials from privately profiting from the wood trade, was only properly implemented during the 1840s.[134] It is perhaps not a surprise that it was also this decade, with the widespread implementation of very long cutting cycles which inevitably reduced the availability of wood in the short run, that also witnessed the shrillest condemnations of wood shortage, and the breaking of a vast and seemingly unstoppable wave of wood theft. One young activist, philosopher and journalist who took up his pen to

---

[130] Grewe, *Der versperrte Wald*, pp. 229–30, 240; Hölzl, *Umkämpfte Wälder*, pp. 155–6; Hauptstaatsarchiv Stuttgart A59 Bü 13.
[131] Ernst, *Den Wald entwickeln*, pp. 95, 152–4.
[132] Dietz, 'Wirtschaftliches Wachstum', pp. 14–15.
[133] Schmidt, *Der Wald*, pp. 55–6.
[134] Grewe, *Der versperrte Wald*, pp. 77–8, 82.

condemn these events in typically both vitriolic and analytical terms was a certain Karl Marx.[135] And by the time the efforts of 'scientific forestry' truly came to fruition, by the 1860s, Germany had for the first time become a land with net imports of timber.[136]

[135] Grewe, *Der versperrte Wald*, pp. 245–7, Lowood, 'Calculating forester', p. 339; Warde, 'Fear of wood shortage', pp. 28–57; on France, see Whited, *Forests and peasant politics*, pp. 40–3.

[136] Hölzl, *Umkämpfte Wälder*, p. 32.

6 Theories of Circulation, c. 1740–1800

Life

Previous chapters have offered an account of the increasing integration of the state, the economic fortunes of society, and the need to have access to, and manage, resources during the early modern period. This took place above all on the conceptual level, rather than the practical, but was manifest most strikingly in state intervention to encourage wood supply, and also endeavours to promote colonial natural history.[1] Agriculture also remained the largest sector of the economy everywhere. Fuel and the raw materials of most industries were also organic matter. This was, in the words of Tony Wrigley, an 'organic economy', 'bounded by the productivity of the land'.[2] Nevertheless, economic thinkers remained highly optimistic that this productivity could be significantly raised. Yet during the second half of the eighteenth century, the combination of autonomous developments in what we may, appropriately, call the 'life sciences' were combined with the technologies of quantification and accounting to bring a new perspective to the essential place of agriculture. Among those seeking to establish ways to raise

---

[1] On colonial natural history, see Drayton, *Nature's government*; Spary, '"Peaches which the patriarchs lacked"'; Grove, *Green imperialism*; Cook, *Matters of exchange*; Londa Achiebinger and Claudia Swan (eds), *Colonizing botany. Science, commerce, and politic in the early modern world* (Philadelphia, PA: University of Pennsylvania Press, 2005).

[2] Wrigley, *Continuity, chance and change*. For a more elaborated quantification of what this meant, see Kander et al., *Power to the people*.

the productivity of the land, the fear emerged that there might also be a systemic logic of *decline*. The nature of the balancing act between resource supply and economic growth was shifted, with failure being seen to put society as a whole in peril. The story of these developments will be traced over the next three chapters, but begins in an unexpected place: the understanding of life itself.

What is life? How would one go about answering such a question, and its corollaries: what is death? And what is the absence of life? If one cannot be sure what it is that makes a thing living, then neither is it so easy to discern what distinguishes those things that do not live. This categorical problem helps explain why some early modern botanists treated the mineral kingdom alongside animals and plants. It was, perhaps, possible to distinguish sufficient features to define the kingdoms themselves, but it was less easy to determine whether they were fundamentally different in their inner workings. Indeed, Buffon, the great French natural historian and superintendant of the *Jardin du Roi* in Paris, noted that the interior organs of animals appeared to be fundamentally similar; it was in their exterior features that a multitude of differences arose.[3] Simple observation could record that stones appeared to emerge on the Earth's surface in unlimited supply, leading to the postulate that they had an endless property of self-generation (a view any gardener might be tempted to believe).[4] If the capacity to reproduce appeared to be a common feature of animals and plants, did this mean that stones were also alive? Soils could grow and diminish in an imperceptible fashion, and many thought, optimistically, that seams of metal could also regenerate themselves deep in the earth. Crystals, after all, certainly did grow. It was hard to find anything that was clearly 'inanimate'. Earlier thinkers, such as Cesalpino in 1583, had distinguished animals and plants by attributing different 'souls' to them, a pleasingly non-verifiable strategy that lasted long into the Enlightenment although rejected by Cartesian thinkers.[5]

---

[3] Comte de Buffon, *The Natural History of Animals, Vegetables and Minerals with the Theory of the Earth in general* (hereafter NH), vol. ii, trans. W. Kendrick and J. Murdoch (London: T. Bell, 1775), pp. 299–301; the great forester Heinrich Cotta was still worrying about this issue as late as 1830. Cotta, *Grundriß der Forstwissenschaft. Bd. I.*, pp. 41–7. For earlier variants on this concern, see Webster, *The great instauration*, p. 331.

[4] Evelyn, *Philosophical discourse.*

[5] Cartesians were only prepared to attribute an animating soul to humans, and explained all other species by mechanical means. Stephen Gaukroger, *The collapse*

These questions were not theological, or merely the strange preoccupations of men and women of science. Growth, organic and economic,
depended on generative power, and thus when men turned their minds
to its explanation, eventually their arguments came to have bearing
on the prospects for development – or survival – of both individuals
and society as a whole. If life was sustained by other forms of life,
what limits might this set? This would be a very different route to
thinking about sustainability than that which preoccupied foresters
and cameralists, with their metrics of supply and demand for wood as
a commodity.

Even in the case of animals and plants one could ponder
whether these things were truly different in kind, or merely in some
superficial properties, such as their powers of motion.[6] The discovery
that plants, for example, were also sexual beings (and were so described
with a degree of metaphorical abandon by Linnaeus, albeit in the context of innumerable little marriages) suggested that there was a fundamental unity, that all of life was branches on a single tree, although
not one characterised by sequential development, or 'evolution' as we
have come to call it.[7] All of these debates touched, of course, upon

of mechanism and the rise of sensibility. Science and the shaping of modernity 1680–
1760 (Oxford: Oxford University Press, 2010), pp. 189–90. This went against a more
widespread view, influenced by Paracelsus, that some vital animating spirit had a
material basis. See Allen G. Debus, 'Chemistry and the quest for a material spirit of
life in the seventeenth century', in Debus, Chemistry, X. Also Chapter 3.

[6] Palissy, whom we met in Chapter 1, believed that rocks must grow or otherwise
the world would be depleted as the old ones decayed. Buffon distinguished clearly
between minerals on the one hand, and animals and plants on the other, but was more
circumspect in arguing for more of a continuum between animals and plants, where
the former, while in a state of sleep, could be viewed as similar to the latter: 'An oyster,
which appears to have no external movement, no external sense, is a being formed to
sleep for ever. In this sense a vegetable is merely an animal that sleeps; and in general
the functions of every organised being, which is destitute of sense and of movement,
may be compared to the functions of an animals, which, by its nature, is doomed to
a perpetual sleep.' Buffon, NH, II, p. 296. Also, 'there is no absolutely essential and
general difference between animals and vegetables, but that nature descends by steps
and by imperceptible links from an animal, which is the most perfect to that which
is the least, and from the latter to the vegetable. The water polypus then forms the
line where the animal creation ends, or where that of plants begin.' Buffon, NH, IV,
p. 113; Gordon L. Davies, The Earth in decay. A history of British geomorphology
1578–1878 (London: Macdonald & Co., 1969), pp. 2, 21–2.

[7] For an extended discussion of issues of classification of form, see James L. Larson,
Intepreting nature. The science of living form from Linneaus to Kant (Baltimore,
MD: Johns Hopkins University Press, 1994).

God's intentions for his Creation, and on a recurrent discussion about whether that Creative act was singular and complete, or ongoing. The latter proposition elicited the uncomfortable prospect for some that creation could proceed without the invisible hand of the Almighty, or alternatively, implying that God had created a world which required his constant, unblinking attention and intervention. If the creative act was a permanent, infinitely extended one, and every happening a little miracle, what space or purpose was left for those miracles recognised by Church authorities?

Thus across the Enlightenment scholars debated whether creatures or plants had been bestowed with their own powers of generation, where each new animate thing was itself an act of creation, or whether on an infinitesimal scale all created things had been formed at the beginning of time, and their apparent conception and growth was simply an extension of these tiny but perfect forms into their full destiny. Mechanistic explanations of the origins of life required that every movement must be a proportional response to some original motion, and thus saw the embryo as a pre-formed entity buffeted into life by exterior forces in the womb. Such thinking was challenged by obvious (to us) objections. If all creatures were pre-formed at the Creation, which implied that the germ of the later individual could only reside within one of the father or the mother, then how come people took on the features of both of their parents?[8] But the death knell to biological mechanism came from experimental results, when observations of polyps in the 1740s by the Swiss investigator Abraham Tremblay revealed that they could regenerate from dismembered parts and that an entire polyp could be re-grown from any part. Suddenly it appeared irrefutable that the powers of life and generation resided in every part of an organism, although eventually this would lead to fierce debate still ongoing in the twentieth century as to why organisms ended up as the ordered, consistent entities that they did, and whether the information to produce an organism was distributed equally throughout.[9] Experiments with electricity, muscle action and chemistry also seemed to show that forces were not a proportional reaction to a motive force

[8] As asserted by Maupertuis. Gaukroger, *Collapse of mechanism*, p. 361.
[9] Gaukroger, *Collapse of mechanism*, p. 358, Peter Hanns Reill, *Vitalizing nature in the Enlightenment* (Berkeley, CA: University of California Press, 2005), pp. 56–61; Gregg Mitman, *The state of nature. Ecology, community, and American social thought, 1900–1950* (Chicago, IL: University of Chicago Press, 1992).

acting upon them; a muscle spasm, for example, could be far stronger than the slight stimuli that prompted it into action.[10] Life could not be reduced to a gargantuan and eternal game of pinball as the mechanistic explanations dominant since Descartes had implied. But what was it?[11]

The precursors of modern botanists and zoologists had worked across the sixteenth, seventeenth and eighteenth centuries to categorise and order the animals, plants and minerals they collected; the most important contributions made by the retiring English collector John Ray, and the brilliant, somewhat mercurial and self-promoting Swedish botanist, Carl von Linné, generally known as Linnaeus. Their clear principles of taxonomy, while still displaying limitations even in their own era as to how many species could be convincingly categorised, made formally manifest what must have been commonsensically apparent to many: a very large number of species shared common characteristics, whether the limbs, eyes or organs of animals, or the sexual differentiation and reproductive habits of plants and animals. Rather than the 'tree' metaphor for the organisation of life, with for moderns its implications of historical evolution, many early modern scholars rather ranked species along a 'Great Chain of Being' where the most developed species (humans, of course) shared all of the characteristics of the more primitive species, but emerged from these not after an immense period of evolutionary transformation, but within the very process of germination and embryonic development. In this view, every creature recapitulated the history of life on Earth in its emergence, and as all life had been created at the same time, each single life was a re-enactment of the original act of Creation. The more perceptive realised that none of the questions of classification, function and relatedness could be given clear-cut answers. As Buffon wrote, one could only 'approximate the truth, by the means of probabilities' – although he did not assign specific values to these.[12]

There were, however, other ways to attack questions of identity and difference; if what produced life itself remained elusive,

---

[10] In Scotland this notion was made popular by the work of Edinburgh Professor of Medicine, Robert Whytt, in 1751. Gaukgoger, *Collapse of mechanism*, p. 397.

[11] See the discussion in Gaukroger, *Collapse of mechanism*, pp. 394–402.

[12] Buffon, *NH*, II, p. 302; see also Reill, *Vitalizing nature*, p. 41.

one could examine the *conditions of life*. This is where the apparently abstruse story of largely forgotten scientific debates finds itself running alongside the history of 'sustainability'. If, after all, the object of 'sustainability' as we now understand it is to create the conditions for a preferred kind of life to flourish, what are those conditions? What does life need to live? Hence we return, again, to the question that had preoccupied the writers on husbandry: what is the food of plants? Is it the same as the food of animals? Where is it found, how can it be enhanced, can it be depleted? Such questions provided an empirical route to identifying the particular forms of life that flourished in different parts of the Earth, and different niches within each locality: although, as we can see, assumptions about the core characteristics of life shaped analysis of its conditions at least as much as the reverse. Towards the end of the nineteenth century these questions would be brought together under the title of ecology, examining the life of organisms in an environment, at first as a means of explaining plant physiology.

We have seen in Chapters 1 and 3 that agricultural writing was largely practically orientated in the early modern period. Even if some gave their work a theoretical gloss, and argued that soil chemistry was a key to good husbandry, very few ventured explanations of final causes. Even those writers who made great play of the theoretical foundations of their husbandry, such as Jethro Tull (1674–1741), were providing an essentially post hoc justification for systems of farming that had impressed them in action (in his case, the methods of vinedressers in the Mediterranean).[13] By the end of the eighteenth century, there were plenty of theoretical explanations of the growth of crops to choose from. As late as 1799, James Hendrick writing in the British *Annals of Agriculture*, was citing the now ancient 1610 experiment of van Helmont as the authority that water was 'the principal nutriment which plants draw from the earth'; although he then conceded, 'It is more easy to mark the changes produced upon soils by working and manures, than to investigate the reasons why such changes render them more productive.'[14] Although Headrick could also

---

[13] See G.E. Fussell, *Jethro Tull. His influence on mechanized agriculture* (Reading: Osprey Publishing, 1973), pp. 43–50.
[14] J. Hendrick, 'Effects of manures in the production of plants', *Annals of Agriculture* XXXIII (1799), p. 275; see also Houghton, *Collection*, p. 23. No consensus existed

cite Boyle, Duhamel du Monceau, Bonnet and Chaptal, distinguished scientists all, he seems to have missed the fact that his predecessor Tull and even more distinguished contemporary chemist Humphry Davy noted that van Helmont's theory of water being the food of plants was disproved as long ago as 1691 by Woodward.[15]

The indefatigable farmer and writer Arthur Young declared in 1786 the foundation of his experimental agriculture to be:

> observations on vegetation, and the circumstances that accelerate or retard it – On the component parts of soils and manures – On the form, penetrating, and imbibing powers, &c. of the roots and leaves of plants... To discover, by experiment, the food of plants, and the component parts of all soils: that is may be known on what fertility depends, and what are the true means of remedying evils, and supplying deficiencies.[16]

Yet despite centuries of explanation, from Palissy, Plat, van Helmont, Markham and many others, there was not even consensus over whether there were one or more foods that provided the essential nutrition of a plant.[17] The renewed enquiry into this still open question, despite a

on the matter by the end of the eighteenth century and some authors, self-declared practical men, equally argued that so long as farming was effective such knowledge did not matter. George E. Fussell, *Crop nutrition. Science and practice before Liebig* (Lavenham: Tortoise Shell Press, 1971), p. 158.

[15] As most of this work was reported by Duhamel du Monceau, it may well be that Headrick had not actually read the earlier authors. The idea was also rejected by Ray, who thought that water played no role in nourishment save as a vehicle. Young would still print the experiments of others that he decried, such as the Fleming de Beunie who claimed that soil 'was to be fertile in proportion as they contained... clay'. The Reverend Edward Holmes wrote about the role of 'phlogisticon' in feeding plants although conceding 'that I pretend to no chymical knowledge', but having read Stahl. Fussell, *Crop nutrition*, p. 276; John Ray, *The wisdom of God manifested in the works of Creation*, 3rd edition (London: Sam Smith & Benj. Walford, 1701), pp. 96–7; Duhamel du Monceau, *Elements of agriculture*, pp. 48–9; Humphry Davy, *Elements of agricultural chemistry* (London: Longman, Hurst, Rees, Orme & Brown, 1815), p. 12; Jethro Tull, *Horse-hoeing husbandry; or, an essay on the principles of vegetation and tillage*, 4th edition (London: A. Miller, 1762); J.B. de Beunie, 'Annalysis of soils', *Annals of Agriculture* II (1784), p. 229. Rev. Edward Holmes, 'On the food of plants', *Annals of Agriculture* VI (1786), p. 185.

[16] Arthur Young, 'On the conduct of experiments in agriculture', *Annals of Agriculture* V (1786).

[17] Bradley, *General treatise*.

lack of clear consensus, would however have profound implications for the understanding of the fate of 'organic economies'.

Chemistry

The commonest early eighteenth-century view was that a mixture of air, water and some essential ingredient – a salt, or 'nitre' – worked in combination to promote plant growth. John Houghton, who was no agriculturalist but an avid and wide-ranging correspondent and reporter, reflected these opinions in his collected essays of the 1680s and 1690s. The fact that plants seemed to extract food from 'mould' (soil) was no indication that this was the origin of that food, because when the very same mould was dug back into the earth and rested, after a period of years it was perfectly capable of bringing forth plants again. As nothing else had been imbibed by it, he argued that only air could have been the source of this nutritive element. He suspected that the beneficial effects of lime were, in the absence of moisture, to suck nitre from the air into its pores, which 'becomes a food fit to be suckt up by the *plants*'. The heat of the sun, too, dried the land and caused nitre to be drawn from the air, and manures had a similar effect as receptacles of aerial nitre.[18] Such a view could be reconciled with the old humoral theory, because there was no shortage of nitre in the air, and it was qualities of heat and cold, or moisture and dryness, that served to draw that nitre out into certain soils. This argument also permitted one to be highly optimistic about the capacities of the earth to support improvement.

But other authors, such as the first Cambridge professor of botany Richard Bradley, who collected Houghton's writings and wrote an adulatory preface, nevertheless took a different view: crop rotation was evidence that different plants had different foods. Thus 'the earth can never be rendered unprolific, unless she is constantly constrained to feed one kind of herb or plant'.[19] This was repeated in generic fashion by the German agronomist Germershausen in

---

[18] Houghton, *Collection*, pp. 36, 24, 175, 223–4; for other examples, see Adolphus Speed, *Adam out of Eden or Asbtract of divers excellent experiments touching the advancement of Husbandry* (London: Henry Brome, 1658), who was an enthusiastic follower of Hugh Plat; on the alchemical origins of this idea, see Allen G. Debus, 'The Paracelsian Aerial Niter', in Debus, *Chemistry*, IX.
[19] Bradley, *General treatise*, 41, 97; Bradley, in Houghton, *Collection*, vii.

1783: 'Through continual experience and satisfactorily tested foundations', provided by crop rotation, 'each kind of plant has its own particular kind, oils and salts, that it draws to itself, leaving behind others salts to other plants.'[20] Duhamel du Monceau, one of the agronomists read most widely in his day, and a friend and business partner of Buffon, was not so sure. If this was the case, why did plants apparently compete for food and moisture? For him, the fallowing included in crop rotations suggested that plants must have a common food, which was why the ground benefited from resting! He was both liberal and uncertain enough to offer a variety of conflicting theories to his readership.[21]

So many agricultural writers evoked chemistry, and yet barely any could lay any reasonable claim to be a chemist. This changed in the late 1740s, and the change came in Scotland. The men who effected this shift – William Cullen, Francis Home and to a lesser extent Cullen's pupil Joseph Black – all belonged to the tightly knit intellectual circles of Glasgow and Edinburgh that brought together in everyday society, learned associations and economic projects, university men, medical practitioners, experimentalists, noble improvers, philosophers and government agents. As often as not men stepped easily across several of these roles, whether sequentially or simultaneously. Both Cullen (1710–90) and the younger Home (1719–1813) had stints as surgeons overseas, trained primarily as medical men, and spent much of their careers as physicians (Cullen both to David Hume and Adam Smith).[22] Edinburgh was and remained a great centre in which the study of botany, training of apothecaries, chemical experiment and interest in agricultural improvement easily intermingled. The physicians and chemists rubbed shoulders and exchanged letters with Adam Smith, David Hume, Lord Kames, Adam Ferguson and other luminaries of that world that easily bestrode urbane scholarship

---

[20] C.F. Germershausen, *Der Hausvater in systematischer Ordnung* (Leipzig: Junius, 1783), pp. 520–1; see also Ellis, *Chiltern and vale farming*, p. 373.

[21] Duhamel du Monceau, *Elements of agriculture*, pp. 51, 60, 62–4; he was a more sceptical follower of Tull (see below), who argued strongly for a single and universal food of plants. Tull, *Horse-hoeing husbandry*, p. 20. See also Francis Home, *The principles of agriculture and vegetation* (Edinburgh: G. Hamilton & J. Balfour, 1757), pp. 104–5; on Duhamel and Buffon, see Emma Spary, *Utopia's garden. French natural history from Old Regime to Revolution* (Chicago, IL: University of Chicago Press, 2000), p. 22; and Gillispie, *Science and polity*, pp. 337–56.

[22] Margaret Schabas, *The natural origins of economics* (Chicago, IL: University of Chicago Press, 2005), p. 65; Jonsson, *Enlightenment's frontier*, pp. 17–18.

and teaching, genteel improvement and vast imperial horizons.[23] Many of them had a hand in the Honourable the Society of Improvers in the Knowledge of Agriculture in Scotland, founded in 1723, or one its cognate or successor organisations.[24] They collectively generated an ethic that Fredrik Albritton Jonsson has appositely called 'civic cameralism', a search for an institutionalised ethic of knowledge collection, information-sharing and 'improvement' that unlike its Central European counterpart was only intermittently given support from the state.[25]

Both Cullen and Home were deeply embedded in the milieu of civic cameralism. In 1748 Cullen was delivering 'Chemical lectures and experiments directed chiefly to the Arts and Manufactures' at Glasgow University, including talks on agriculture that provided the inspiration for an outlined but never-completed book on the topic. Home produced his *Vegetation and the Principles of Agriculture* of 1757 as a direct response to a prize essay competition of the Edinburgh Society for Encouraging Art, Science, Manufactures and Agriculture.[26] But Cullen was also a farmer (or at least a landowner). He corresponded with Duhamel du Monceau at this time not just as a curious intellectual, but as a man who wanted to grow better vegetables. Cullen began his lectures with axioms of his study, which should be 'Vegetation & Chemistry United'; that 'The business of agriculture is to promote the Vegetation of Plants. Art promotes this by furnishing the proper quantity of nourishment or directing the proper application of it.' He was of the most widely accepted opinion, that plants all had a common food.[27] His manuscripts show him working through and developing ideas for his planned 'Principles of Agriculture' that never got beyond being a set of lectures.[28] He had carefully read a range of British and French writers on chemistry and agriculture, including Tull and Duhamel du Monceau, who at that time was captivated with Tull's controversial

---

[23] Emma Rothschild, *The inner life of empires. An eighteenth century history* (Princeton, NJ: Princeton University Press, 2011); Jonsson, *Enlightenment's frontier*.

[24] Charles W.J. Withers, 'William Cullen's agricultural lectures and writings and the development of agricultural science in eighteenth-century Scotland', *Agricultural History Review* 37 (1989), p. 144.

[25] Jonsson, *Enlightenment's frontier*.

[26] Withers, 'William Cullen', p. 149; Charles A. Browne, *Thomas Jefferson and the scientific trends of his time* (Waltham, MA: Chronica Botanica Co., 1944), p. 117.

[27] Glasgow University Library (GUL) MS Cullen 435/1, pp. 1r-2r, 4v; also in GUL MS 435/2.

[28] GUL MS Cullen 435/1–435/8.

prescriptions for husbandry that argued manuring could be dispensed with altogether. Cullen's ideas varied as he worked on the problem, but he came to conclude that:

> 1. That there is quantity of matter fit to constitute vegetables &
> which I name the vegetable matter dispersed in different places
> under different forms. Now in the Body of living vegetables,
> sometimes in the bodies of animals... 2. the collection of this
> vegetable matter in the earth is the principal point in view of the
> husbandman & if the several forms under which it may be collected
> are not all equally proper for the nourishment of plants he must
> farther have in view the preparation & fit or the conversion of the
> improper forms into the one peculiarly fit for being applied to the
> nourishment of plants.[29]

In other words, 'we need to seek for the nourishment of vegetables no where else than in the destroyed matter of Vegetables themselves'.[30] Plants were recycled plants, although it remained a question as to how that recycling was achieved.

He was not the only person who was struck by this thought in the 1740s. It was as revolutionary as it now seems banal. Cullen's emphasis on the recycling of plant matter may have come from encountering the experiments conducted by Buffon and his colleague Daubenton, and the English naturalist Needham, although Buffon did not publicise them widely until his essay 'De la reproduction en général' of 1749. These authors argued that all matter was divided into 'organic' and 'inorganic' molecules, a thesis that remained controversial among naturalists, and that Buffon himself refined over time to argue that 'organic' molecules had been created by particular forces of heat and attraction.[31]

---

[29] GUL Cullen MS 435/5.

[30] Withers, 'William Cullen', pp. 151–2; Fussell appears to be in error in his description of Cullen's views; Fussell, Crop nutrition, p. 131; Duhamel proceeded to test Tull's arguments experimentally, with rather dismal results leading to more flexibility in his arguments. Gillispie, Science and polity, pp. 362–4; André J. Bourde, The influence of England on the French agronomes 1750–1789 (Cambridge: Cambridge University Press, 1953), pp. 50–2.

[31] Buffon, NH, II, pp. 466–7. '[O]rganic matter, universally diffused in all animal and vegetable substances, which alike serves for their nutrition, their growth and their reproduction. Nutrition is performed by the intimate penetration of this matter in all parts of the animal or vegetable body.' Buffon, 'Of nutrition and growth', extract from On the generation of animals, p. 182, and also 'Experiments on the method

Buffon did not claim that *only* organic molecules could feed organic matter, but nevertheless he implied that these organic molecules passed between different living things over time. Buffon himself was primarily interested in the question of reproduction and definition of species:

> There exists... a determinate quantity of organic matter which nothing can destroy; there exists, at the same time, a determinate number of moulds capable of assimilating it to themselves, which are every instant destroyed, every instant renovated... proportioned to the quantity of living matter.[32]

It was also in 1749 that Isaac Biberg, student of Linnaeus, published the doctoral thesis usually attributed to the illustrious supervisor: *Oeconomica Naturae* ('Economy of Nature'). In this a brief passage discusses the decay of dead plants to produce fresh mould from which new plants draw their nutrition, although the extension of plant roots is seen as a means by which the soil at their disposable continually *expands*. The origin of this additional 'mould' that the roots draw from is unclear. The authors noted, 'fertility remains uninterrupted: whereas the earth would not make good its annual consumption, if it were not constantly recruited by new supplies'. Linnaeus did not develop the idea, but the notion of recycling plant matter as of essence is clear.[33] A new paradigm emerged that focused on the

---

of generation', p. 187. Trans. J.S.Barr, in J. Lyon and Phillip R. Sloan, *From natural history to the history of nature: readings from Buffon and his critics* (Notre Dame, IN: University of Notre Dame Press, 1981), p. 182; J.H. Eddy Jr, 'Buffon, organic alterations, and man', in *Studies in the History of Biology* 7, eds William Coleman and Camille Limoges (Baltimore, MD: Johns Hopkins University Press, 1984), pp. 7–9; Spary, *Utopia's garden*, p. 105. See also Buffon, *NH*, II, pp. 450–1, 465.

[32] Buffon, 'Recapitulation', in Lyon and Sloan, *From natural history*, p. 207.

[33] Carl Linnaeus and Issac J. Biberg, *Oeconomica Naturae* (Uppsala: na, 1749), pp. 23–4. The work was translated by Benjamin Stillingfleet in his *Miscellaneous tracts relating to natural history, husbandry, and physic. To which is added the calendar of flora*, 2nd edition (London: R. & J. Dodsley, S. Baker & T. Payne, 1762), pp. 77–8; and from here found its way into husbandry manuals such as John Mills, *A new system of practical husbandry, Volume 1* (London: J. Johnson & B. Davenport, 1767), pp. 252–3; and likely from that source into *The Complete Farmer Or a General Dictionary of Husbandry In All Its Branches, Containing the Various Methods of Cultivating and Improving Every Species of Land*, 4th edition (London: Longman, Law, Robinson, Robinson, Cadell, Baldwin, Otridge and Lowndes, 1793), p. 529.

movement of such matter between living things, which also defined their 'living' qualities. It would become a dominant, although not the only, explanation of the fortunes of agricultural systems by the end of the century.[34]

Francis Home was no farmer. 'I don't intend the following remarks to settle facts, or teach the practical part of farming', he declared. 'That I leave to farmers. My design is only to sketch out the great outlines of this art, and show, that it is capable of being reduced, like others, to a regular system.'[35] Home wrote amid a flurry of interest in the agricultural application of chemistry in mid-1750s Edinburgh, in the very years that Cullen was installed as professor of chemistry in that city and lectured on 'the Chemical History of Vegetables'. Home was also an avid reader of Duhamel's work, although he only encountered it after writing his own treatise.[36] Some of Home's comments were directed at the English agronomic star, Jethro Tull, but by implication Cullen too. Home acknowledged that the earth must *contain* the food of plants, but he objected to further inference of Tull that 'earth' *was* the food of plants. Tull had drawn the conclusion on observing hoe-based Mediterranean agriculture and argued that what one needed was not manure, but breaking the soil into a very fine tilth to accelerate its assimilation into plants' roots. 'Had Tull been a chymist', rejoined Home, 'he would have known, that mere earth makes but a small part of all plants... Whence the salts and oils of plants? These are objections which the favourers of his system never can answer.'[37] Home saw that resolving plants into the materials that composed them was now something chemists were able to achieve in the laboratory with far more refinement. What constituted the body of a plant, and what fed it, was no longer a matter of inference from observing how a plant behaved when certain substances, whether from the soil, water, light or heat, were supplied or excluded from it. Their composition could be resolved by experiment, and hence the sources of these substances identified. These methods did however put the focus firmly back on

---

[34] In Cullen's case he also developed an attack on mechanistic approaches in medicine. Reill, *Vitalizing nature*, p. 122.

[35] Home, *Principles of agriculture*, p. 5.

[36] Gillispie, *Science and polity*, p. 365.

[37] Home, *Principles of agriculture*, pp. 8, 107.

the earth rather than the air and water.[38] But Home was adding more than just another twist to this old debate: he was stating chemistry to be the foundation for agriculture.

Home's answer to the conundrum of plant nutrition was that it was the consequence of a chain of chemical reactions, to which many substances contributed; the traditional elements of earth and water, the salts that had assumed a prominent position in seventeenth-century thinking, but also oil and fire in a 'fixed state'.[39] Rotted plant matter provided nourishment to the next generation of plants, both directly when reduced to sufficiently 'small parts... as to be capable of entering the minute vessels of plants', and also through processes of volatisation, so the oils and salts therein were 'carried up into the air, and descend again to fructify the earth, which was lately robbed of them. Corruption, then, is the parent of vegetation.' This process was achieved by the combination of a nitrous acid in the air with particles (antacids) in the ground. The particles were especially prevalent in putrefying matter, which attracted the acid and created a neutral salt (or 'nitre'). The nitre also volatised oils and made them available for absorption by plants.[40] Earth was thus 'enriched' by the air. Use of other manures such as lime accelerated this process of 'putrefaction'. Putrefaction was key: 'it provides for our future nourishment, and carries on that beautiful circle, which nature is commanded, by her author and constant supporter, to move in'.[41] His story is more sophisticated than that provided by Cullen, but again he foregrounded the essential role of recycling plant matter, by which further chemical processes were triggered that provided the full range of food to plants, alongside essential moisture.

Home's chemistry itself was not for the most part very original. As is so often the case its radical effect was translating knowledge onto

[38] Although Home's objection to the kind of theory advanced by writers such as Houghton does not itself stand scrutiny, as Home's proof of its falsity does not, in fact, refute Houghton's argument. 'That plants thriving better in some soils than in others, and in proportion as these soils are manured, shows the ground to be the principal pasture of plants; the air being the same in grounds adjoining one another.' Home, *Principles of agriculture*, p. 108.

[39] Home, *Principles of agriculture*, pp. 130–1.

[40] Home, *Principles of agriculture*, pp. 132–3.

[41] The air's contribution was to produce a 'nitrous acid' from a vitriolic acid found in aerial nitre which combined with oils in the putrefied matter of the earth. Home, *Principles of agriculture*, pp. 37, 57, 59, 67, 118–21; Home is discussed in Fussell, *Crop nutrition*, pp. 117–20.

a new object. He owed much to the work of the preceding decades, above all that of Georg Ernst Stahl, a Saxon physician who eventually came to serve the royal court in Berlin, but whose greatest influence lay in a reformulation of chemistry in a series of works published from the 1697 to the 1730s. In the cameralist tradition he sought to bring science to the service of society, focusing his early studies on how improved methods of making alcoholic drinks could reduce imports, and later researching ore-smelting processes.[42] In his *Opusculum Cymico-Physico-Medicum* of 1715 Stahl firmly argued that one had to chemically analyse the substance of animals and plants to understand why they grew, concluding that the nutritious substance was the same in both cases and that this was drawn from earth combined with water.[43] Stahl was responsible for the idea of the 'organism' based on a circulatory system connecting various bodies.[44] Moreover, Home owed much to Stahl for his account of putrefaction, that key process that volatised salts and oils in plant matter and the soil, and permitted their chemical combination with aerial acids. This was triggered by an 'elementary fire' that all matter contained, called 'phlogiston' by Stahl and his tutor Becher, which combusted and released heat, in turn creating motion among the particles and volatising oils and salts.[45] To their minds phlogiston performed almost the opposite function to that which we now know oxygen to do. As putrefaction was a self-generating process, it could explain the particular efficacy of animal dung as manure, because this was already in an advanced state of putrefaction. At the same time the ideas of Cullen and Buffon's 'organic molecules' suggested that specifically life-giving matter was required for this cycle of putrefaction and growth.[46]

---

[42] Reill, *Vitalizing nature*, pp. 76–7; M. Teich, 'Circulation, transformation, conservation of matter and balancing of the biological world in the eighteenth century', *Ambix* 29 (1982), pp. 17–28.

[43] Browne, *Thomas Jefferson*, p. 101; on his related medical doctrines, Reill, *Vitalizing nature*, pp. 126–7.

[44] Gaukroger, *Collapse of mechanism*, p. 394.

[45] This work was translated into English in 1730, from an original work of 1723. George Ernest Stahl, *Philosophical principles of universal chemistry; or, the foundation of a scientifical manner of inquiring into and preparing the natural and artificial bodies and the uses of life*, trans. Peter Shaw (London: Osborn and Longman, 1730); Home, *Principles of agriculture*, pp. 76–88; Fussell, *Crop nutrition*, pp. 96–7.

[46] Home, *Principles of agriculture*, p. 88; also the discussion in Browne, *Thomas Jefferson*, pp. 134–5.

Chemistry and natural history, perhaps rather more than agronomy, were advanced by international networks. Although notably the works of Tull, Duhamel du Monceau, and towards the end of the century, Arthur Young won international renown, relatively few works out of the very many published on husbandry crossed linguistic boundaries. In contrast, chemical works were rapidly disseminated. Home's work was translated into French, for example, as early as 1761.[47] This broader intellectual movement perhaps also explains coincidences, such as the publication in Sweden by Wallerius and Gyllenborg of their *Agriculturae Fundamenta Chemica* in 1761, so very close in time to the prize-chasing volume of Home, although there is no evidence of a direct connection. This work was found in English by 1770, by which time more works focused explicitly on agricultural chemistry were appearing.[48] Wallerius had become a professor of chemistry at Uppsala in 1750, and conducted numerous experiments on the chemical properties of soil and effects of vegetative growth, arguing that the 'active principle' of fertilisers was animal fats, an organic interpretation.[49]

The greatest work of natural history of the age, both in reach and size, was Buffon's *Histoire naturelle*, co-written with his colleague Daubenton and eventually stretching to 36 quarto volumes between 1749 and 1788. The piercing and clear prose, the accessibility of a text mostly comprising reportage, facts and description spliced with (for the age) relatively pithy theoretical reflection, made it far more accessible and entertaining than most contemporary science. It won a large, sometimes somewhat worshipful following. As the decades from the appearance of the first volume stacked up it increasingly came under criticism as unscientific, as too imaginative, too fantastical. Still, it remained one of the most widely owned books in Europe, and the touchstone for natural history until Darwin's celebrity (perhaps its massive run of volumes helped the chances of a genteel library holding at least one of them).[50] Indeed, one cannot imagine many contemporary natural historians or chemists also writing a *Discourse*

---

[47] Francis Home, *Les principes de l'agriculture et de la vegetation* (Paris: Prault, 1761); see also Bourde, *Influence of England*, p. 170.
[48] Fussell, *Crop nutrition*, p. 120; George Fordyce, *Elements of agriculture and vegetation* (London: J. Johnson, 1771).
[49] Spary, *Utopia's garden*, p. 119.
[50] Spary, *Utopia's garden*; it was the third most frequently held book in private libraries in France. Gaukroger, *Collapse of mechanism*, p. 366.

on Style. In the first volumes, published in 1749 and translated into English in 1775, Buffon declared, 'Nature is herself perpetually alive, herself a work-woman perpetually active, with full ability to turn every thing to her own use, and who, always acting upon the same fund, far from exhausting it, renders it inexhaustible.'[51] Matter was alive simply because it was alive: the logic of this tautology was that a fund of living matter had been created that went on to make up all subsequent living matter. 'Organic molecules are the active principles which she employs for the formation and the development of organised beings.'[52]

In fact, Buffon was reheating an argument of Stahl, that itself drew on ancient traditions. The German physician's account of chemical transformations was a major step away from mechanistic explanations of the universe that had become the orthodoxy since Descartes, but in a similar fashion to the need for mechanists to distinguish clearly between the immaterial soul and the material world (thus saving the will as a phenomenon), Stahl too found he had to draw a distinction between the material relations he described, and an '*anima sensitiva*' that permeated living matter and breathed life into it. But unlike the soul that presided in a mechanistic world, Stahl's *anima* provided an energy by which living processes became materially different from non-living ones, which distinguished, for example, mere fermentation from digestion.[53] This doctrine became known as 'vitalism', and while it may seem tautological and abstract to the modern reader, it represented a step away from attempts at metaphysical or universal explanations that had prevailed when mechanistic thinking was the fashion, towards a more phenomenological and empirical approach. Buffon would be its most widely read exponent, although Stahl's theory was taken more seriously by his scientific peers.[54]

Yet the vitalist concepts of 'organic molecules' propounded by Buffon, and the un-organic chemistry of salts and oils in vegetable matter elaborated by Cullen, Home and others, or latterly the recognisably modern system of elements, pointed in a similar direction.

---

[51] Buffon, *NH*, II, p. 457.
[52] Buffon, *NH*, II, pp. 450–1.
[53] Browne, *Source book*, p. 104; Reill, *Vitalizing nature*, p. 81.
[54] Spary, *Utopia's garden*; indeed, although Buffon was perhaps the most widely read of eighteenth-century writer on natural history, he was repeatedly called into question by other researchers. See Larson, *Interpreting nature*, passim. On vitalism more widely, see Gaukroger, *Natural and the human*, pp. 101–10, 127–40.

Living things were sustained by the rags and remnants of previously living things, and their capacity to assimilate other necessaries, such as limited amounts of earth or water, or to fix substances from the air, was predicated upon the availability of vegetable matter (with animals being viewed as largely composed at least in their brute physical substance from what had once been vegetable matter, to which they would return). Only dung was 'the true food of plants'.[55] The constituent parts of plants could be isolated by chemical analysis and as these were diminished in processes of combustion or respiration this required a constant stream of the same elemental inputs. Managing nature and her products thus became a question of managing flows.

Circulation

In the long period before this chemical revolution, as we have seen, the melioration and management of the soil was explained as a balancing of the elements and humours; in the Paracelsian-inflected version, this balance influenced the take up of salts that were the plants' essential nourishment.[56] A similar belief in balance could be found in some of the few thinkers who bent their thoughts towards geomorphological processes, such as denudation which might eventually wash all the soils away from uplands. This was imagined either as a providential service to relocate soil to fertile lowlands, or was thought to be somehow restored through rather vaguely specified atmospheric processes. This was the argument of the deist geological thinker (and another friend of Joseph Black, Adam Smith and the Edinburgh crowd of the 1770s and 1780s), James Hutton. His pioneering *Theory of the Earth* was published in succinct form in 1788, although conceived two decades earlier, and then reissued as two grander volumes in 1795, in which

---

[55] Johann Friedrich von Pfeiffer, *Vermischte Verbeßerungsvorschläge und freie Gedanken über verschiedene, den Narungszustand, die Bevölkerung und Staatswirtschaft der Deutschen, betreffende Gegenstände* (Frankfurt: Eßlinger, 1778), p. 22. Pfeiffer saw non-organic manures as improving the texture of the soil and enhancing the absorptive capacity of plants.

[56] There is perhaps no better illustration of the state of affairs than the rather rambling account of the food of plants provided by Moses Cook, clearly influenced by Paracelsus and Bacon, and in discussion and experiment with his patron the earl of Bedford, who end up concluding their true food is 'the Spirit of the Earth'. Cook, *Manner of raising*, pp. 20–8. For the Baconian view of Spirit, see Chapter 3, note 130.

he imagined the earth as a kind of machine, 'so contrived, as either to have those parts to move without wearing and decay, or to have those parts, which are waiting and decaying, again repaired'. In other words Hutton, who as a farmer was familiar enough with the soil, argued that its loss to erosion must be compensated by wearing of rocks or accumulation elsewhere.[57] Linnaeus offered an equally vague confidence in regard to the balance of numbers of creatures and species in his 1749 work, *Oeconomia naturae*.[58]

Another strand of thinking won brief prominence in agricultural thinking, if less influence in practice, with the 'horse-hoeing husbandry' of Jethro Tull whom we have had occasion to meet above. Tull argued that earth, plain and simple, was the food of plants and the heart of good farming was producing a tilth so fine that this earth could enter in the pores of plants. Salts and water merely accelerated the motion of this earth towards the roots. Publishing his famous work in 1731, but already pondering the importance of the fineness of tilth in the 1690s having observed the habits of vinedressers in the south of France, Tull continued in many ways a seventeenth-century focus on the soil, and was a close reader of John Evelyn on the topic.[59] But he began his book, admittedly a post hoc justification of his enthusiasm for the seed drill and repeated ploughing, in the style of the dawning era. How did plants live? Their food was earth, the means of acquiring food must be the roots, and hence it was the degree to which roots could penetrate and access the earth that determined yields. 'And this artificial Pasture ['pasture of plants', as Tull called the tilled ground] may be increas'd in proportion to the Division of the Parts of Earth, whereof it is the Superficies, which Division may be mathematically infinite.'[60] This panglossian take on improvement was equally more in step with the seventeenth century than Tull's successors. The value

---

[57] Davies, *The Earth in decay*, pp. 156–60, 171–2.

[58] On Hakewill, Woodward and Ray in this regard, see Davies, *Earth in decay*, pp. 114–17. Hakewill, in the alchemical tradition, called this 'circular progress', but it was not related to any clear model of circulation of material that was developed in eighteenth-century thought. Carl Linnaeus, *Oeconomy of Nature*, in *Miscellaneous tracts relating to natural history, husbandry and physic*, ed. Bernard Stillingfleet (London: J. Dodsley, S. Baker & T. Payne, 1791).

[59] Tull, *Horse-hoeing husbandry*. From Evelyn (among other earlier authors such as Grew and Papin), pp. 30–1, 35; on Tull's career and writing, see Fussell, *Jethro Tull*, pp. 5–42.

[60] Tull, *Horse-hoeing husbandry*, p. 29.

of dung was not for what it contained, but the effects of its fermentation, as the gassy bloating of the excrement compressed and shattered
clods of earth into more desirable finer textures (an idea advanced by
Columella).[61] When Thomas Hale wrote in the mid-1750s, perhaps
unaware of the new thinking emerging in a few corners of Europe, he
was still under the spell of Tull; the benefit of dung lay in its fermentation in the soil, 'puffing it up and rendering it lighter', like yeast in
dough: 'This is the natural and real use of dung.'[62]

Ironically, given his adherence to Tull's theory, Hale provided
one of the prescriptions that would become a centrepiece of the 'new'
new husbandry of Arthur Young, Albrecht Thaer and a range of
reformers who sought support for their agricultural prescriptions from
chemistry. 'There should always be a proportion preserv'd between the
pasture and the tillage land; that the dung of one be enough to supply
the other.' For Hale, this particular balance was nothing to do with a
flow of nutriment, but simply to ensure a sufficient mass of dung to
do work of loosening the soil. 'The dung does not directly nourish the
crop, but makes the earth more fit to nourish it, by breaking and dividing the earth.'[63] Cropping the land clearly did leave it 'drain'd of this
its natural richness'.[64] Yet –as could have been written a century and
half before – as the ensuing 'barrenness... depends on the abundance
of some one ingredient, there is scarce any one kind that may not serve
as manure for some other'.[65] In other words, as the problem was one
of imbalance, it could as well be seen as the product of superfluity of
something as scarcity of another. 'Nature succeeds by a mixture of several ingredients; which might, of themselves, be called unfruitful. The
due proportion is the great matter.'[66]

Only two years after Hale's largest and most comprehensive
tome appeared in 1758, an anonymous 'Farmer' published in London
and Glasgow *An essay on the theory of agriculture, intended as an
introduction to a rational system of that art.* Farmer the author may
have been, but the short book was written by someone familiar with
Columella, Stahl, Stephen Hales and, one must suspect, the recent work

---

[61] Tull, *Horse-hoeing husbandry*, pp. 29–36.
[62] Hale, *Compleat body*, pp. 135–6.
[63] Hale, *Compleat body*, pp. 136, 51.
[64] Hale, *Compleat body*, p. 17.
[65] Hale, *Compleat body*, p. 107.
[66] Hale, *Compleat body*, p. 107.

of Home. In a genre generally far more marked for its adulation of field experience than theoretical knowledge, it is rather startling to see the author 'observe, that chemistry may contribute more to our knowledge of soils, and their productions, by its several operations, than all the attempts hitherto made by practice and observation'.[67] 'Farmer' follows Home closely, if without acknowledgement, in arguing that alkaline salts combined with aerial acids to produce a neutral salt delivered back to the earth by rain and dew, assisted by the action of 'fire'. His further observation that the denser air of winter accelerated the entry of both salts and sunbeams into the soil may have been his own elaboration.[68] Although the quality of tilth was important, and dung accelerated chemical reactions through its heat, the most important step in the process was the putrefaction of dung. 'To talk further of the nourishment of plants is needless, the principles necessary to this are best discovered by the chemical analysis of plants.'[69]

'Farmer''s work disappeared into complete obscurity, while Thomas Hale is recorded by historians as a representative if unoriginal author. But that short passage of years at the end of the 1750s marked a changing tide, and it was the anonymous author who was the herald of a new age. At the end of the Napoleonic wars, the pre-eminent British chemist Humphry Davy could survey the new dispensation with the authority of innumerable experiments conducted by chemists across the continent.

> The exhaustion of soils by carrying off corn crops from them, and the effects of feeding cattle on lands, and of preserving their manure, offer familiar illustrations of the principle; and several philosophical enquirers, particularly Hassenfratz and Saussure, have shewn by satisfactory experiments, that animal and vegetable matters deposited in soils are absorbed by plants, and become part of their organized matter… The soil is the laboratory in which the food is prepared. No manure can be taken up by the roots of plants unless water is present; and water or its elements exist in all the products of vegetation. The germination of seeds does not take place without the presence

---

[67] Farmer, *An essay on the theory of agriculture, intended as an introduction to a rational system of that art. By a farmer* (London: T. Becket, 1760), p. 5.

[68] Farmer, *Essay*, pp. 21–2, 24.

[69] Farmer, *Essay*, pp. 36. 39.

of air or oxygene gas; and in the sunshine vegetables decompose
the carbonic acid gas of the atmosphere, the carbon of which
is absorbed, and becomes part of their organized matter, and
the oxygene gas, the other constituent, is given off; and in
consequence of a variety of agencies, the oeconomy of vegetation
is made subservient to the general order of the system of nature.[70]

The system of nature was a circulatory system, now with the knowledge
of photosynthesis grafted onto the circulation of vegetable matter via
simple decay, or traversing the alimentary tracts of animals to return
as dung to the fields. Yet these were just circles within circles. Stephen
Hales had discovered the transpiration of water in plants, published in
the *Vegetable Staticks* of 1727, and this insight had led to the linkage
of foliage cover with the greater hydrological cycle.[71] Now the living
world could be seen as part of a greater set of flows in which animals
and plants were bound together in mutual exchange:

Water is raised from the ocean, diffused through the air, and
poured down upon the soil, so as to be applied to the purposes
of life. The different parts of the atmosphere are mingled
together by winds or changes of temperature, and successively
brought in contact with the surface of the earth, so as to exert
their fertilizing influence. The modifications of the soil, and the
application of manures are placed within the power of man, as
if for the purpose of awakening his industry and calling forth his
powers.[72]

The grand panorama presented by Davy had already been
articulated as part of the grand vision of the Comte de Buffon. He
expressed this circulating fund that gave life in the form of 'organic
molecules'.

The body of each animal, or of each vegetable, is a mould in
which are indifferently assimilated the organic molecules of all
the animals or vegetables which have been destroyed by death,
and consumed by time... the organic parts, still subsisting, are

---

[70] Davy also listed gypsum, salts and alkalis as the food of plants that constituted their
stiffer parts analogous to 'bony matter'. Davy, *Elements*, pp. 14, 17.
[71] Grove, *Green imperialism*; Fussell, *Crop nutrition*, p. 95.
[72] Davy, *Elements*, p. 15; see also Spary, *Utopia's garden*, pp. 144–6.

resumed by organised bodies. At first imbibed by vegetables, and afterwards absorbed by the animals which feed on vegetables, they contribute to the development, the maintenance, and the growth of both; they constitute their life, and, circulating continually from body to body, animate all organised beings.

Indeed, for Buffon, life on Earth was a fixed quantity. 'There exists, therefore, upon the earth, in the air, and in the water, a determinate quantity of organic matter which nothing can destroy.'[73] Buffon did not draw serious consequences for agriculture from this claim. He saw that the world was full of dismal, untamed spaces that gave plenty of scope for cultivated lands to expand and increase output even though the total fund of life was fixed.

The authoritative version of the circulatory system underpinning agriculture was developed by the tireless English traveller, experimenter and scribbler Arthur Young, who dedicated his life to agricultural improvement and won renown in his lifetime and posthumously as the foremost agricultural authority in Europe of his day. Young was initially apprenticed to a merchant in the town of King's Lynn, and may have acquired there his habits of bookkeeping by which he sought to give his advice a sure foundation in yield ratios and demonstrations of profit or loss. Switching to farming in the 1760s he soon began to issue a great series of reports on his own experience ('In numerous incidences, I have been a very bad farmer') and commentary on practices observed in a series of journeys across England and the near continent in the 1770s and 1780s.[74] As a young man he condemned all his predecessors for some kind of failing, whether lack of experimental rigour, or a failure to report their findings accurately, declaring in 1770, somewhat disarmingly for the modern observer, that 'If one tenth of the books published on this art had consisted only of the *record of cases*, agriculture, by this time, would have received the same perfection as medicine',[75] a measure of perfection we would hardly

---

[73] Buffon, *NH*, II, p. 466.

[74] Arthur Young, *A course of experimental agriculture* (London: J. Dodsley, 1770), pp. v–vi. John G. Gazley, *The life of Arthur Young 1741–1820* (Philadelphia, PA: American Philosophical Society, 1973).

[75] Young, *Experimental agriculture*, p. xv; see also the more intemperate remarks in Arthur Young, *Rural oeconomy; or, essays on the practical parts of husbandry... To which is added, The rural Socrates: being memoirs of a country philosopher* (London: T. Becket, 1770), p. 4.

wish upon anyone. Two decades later his views on other writers had tempered somewhat and in the 1799 'Essay on manures' he provided a careful survey of different kinds of manure, past writers on them, and chemical explanations fully apprised of the latest writings for their effects, having conducted and reported on many experiments over the years.[76]

Whilst his writings were certainly not narrow in scope, Young's essential theorem was that it was necessary to recycle the material bodies of plants via animal manure to maintain yields. This was an organic cycle that depended on the circulation of mucilage (as the organic matter was called) and the process of putrefaction that made old living matter accessible to the new. Crucial was thus finding 'a peculiar *proportion* between the parts', starting with balancing the arable and pasture. 'If any of the proportions are broken, the whole chain is affected... so much does one part of a well-arranged farm depend on the other.'[77] He increasingly perceived a problem that on the wider stage of a market society, and especially with the growth of cities, foodstuffs were withdrawn from the place of production and their matter lost into the guts and middens of consumers; even worse, with water closets, would be flushed into the sea whilst the collection and spreading of 'night soil' had at least added to the fertility of land near cities. Given these losses, 'All the ensuing management depends upon the quantity of straw and stubble, or litter, being large... The farm-yeard manure depends on the consumption of hay and straw', as these both contained organic matter from the crop, and acted as the binding material for dung. Individual farms could be improved by purchasing fodder for large herds, but the system as whole was closed.[78] At the same time, eliminating weeds was crucial to optimising such flows.[79]

By the 1790s these arguments took on more refined forms as chemistry advanced. The Irish chemist Richard Kirwan, for example,

---

[76] Arthur Young, 'An essay on manures', *Annals of Agriculture* (1799), pp. 577–620; Young's experiments can be found reported very frequently throughout the *Annals*. Young expressed strong regret for headstrong assertions of his younger days. Gazley, *Arthur Young*, p. 16.

[77] Young, *Rural oeconomy*, pp. 7, 12.

[78] Young, 'Essay on manures', p. 579; Young, *Rural oeconomy*, p. 30.

[79] Young, *Rural oeconomy*, p. 58.

saw the essential circulatory substances being compounds of carbon: 'Hence we may understand how soils become effete and exhausted, this effect arising... from the gradual loss of the carbonic principle, deposited by vegetable and animal manures, and from them passing into the growing vegetables, and also from the loss of fixed air contained in the argillaceous part of the soil, which is decomposed by vegetables, and from the calcinations of the ferruginous particles contained in the soil.'[80] It is true that the theory of organic circulation was not universally held; Young's peer and to some degree rival, William Marshall, self-proclaimed 'SCIENTIFIC FARMER', held that 'the value of Land does not depend more on the soil, or vegetative stratum, than it does on the sub-soil'.[81] But generally the doctrine of recycling via manure took hold, and the idea that low yields were the consequence of soil-mining: 'every means of exhausting the soil are taken, but none of replenishing it'.[82] So high do Young's arguments tower over subsequent agricultural writing that he has all but obliterated any detailed memory of earlier anglophone writers, Tull perhaps excepted, with many subsequent agricultural historians assuming that his preoccupations stand for those of pre-industrial agriculture as a whole. Indeed, the clarity of this system has perhaps disguised the degree to which Young's own opinions vacillated over the years as he attempted a long stream of experiments on the food of plants. Nevertheless, he managed to bring new development in atmospheric chemistry back into line with his convictions about the vital properties of dung, arguing that if 'inflammable air', or phlogiston, was the true food of plants as appeared might be the case in the mid-1780s, it 'undoubtedly resides in that portion of animal and vegetable substances, which forms the *mould*, the *humus*, the extraneous particles, which I contend are always found proportionally to the fertility of the soil'.[83]

---

[80] Richard Kirwan, 'What are the manures most advantageously applicable to the various sorts of soils? And what are the causes of their beneficial effect in each particular instance?', *Annals of Agriculture* XXIII (1795), p. 105.

[81] William Marshall, *Experiments and observations concerning agriculture and the weather* (London: J. Dodsley, 1779), pp. 2, 110.

[82] Young, *Rural oeconomy*, p. 59.

[83] In the mid-1780s Young and others were captivated with the notion that 'inflammable air', or phlogiston, was the true food of plants, in parallel with the interest in Priestley's work in chemistry, drawing originally on Stahl, and especially Cavendish's discovery of hydrogen, which he named 'inflammable air' and assumed at this moment to be identical with phlogiston. This certainly did not undo organic

The implications of this thinking were already clearly articulated by the anonymous 'Farmer' of 1760: 'Nature has fix'd bounds to fertility beyond which we cannot proceed, however prompted by avarice.'[84] Home gave reason for optimism, and before the French Revolution the finite magnitude of life-giving nutrients does not seem to have been a course for alarm: 'The earth, though exhausted, attains again, under proper management, a great degree of fertility.'[85] Yet conditions for success were becoming more stringent; as no less a luminary than Thomas Jefferson proclaimed on reading Young, 'it is only by increasing cattle that you can increase wheat permanently'.[86] This meant of course that the reverse was also possible, and if one part of this system failed, the whole was put – systemically – at risk. By 1824, it was even to be found in an American school textbook that exhaustion of the soil was going to require a more systematic replacement of nutrients by recycling, 'to make plants grow with their former luxuriance. This may be called THE ERA OF SYSTEMATIC AGRICULTURE.'[87]

Good management, flows, circulations; some of this was the bread and butter of cameralism, of keeping the fuel flowing to the furnaces that smelted the metal that oiled the wheels of commerce. But it must also remind us of a new world of circulatory flows that was taking form at the same time, and nowhere had greater influence on this than Scotland. 'The increase in the quantity of useful labour actually employed within any society', wrote Adam Smith, 'must depend altogether upon the increase of the capital which employs it; and the

---

or vitalist theories, but suggested that phlogiston was an animating force which had to be encouraged by introducing matter (such as dung) with a chemical affinity for it. It was during the 1780s that Lavoisier's work would establish the role of oxygen and explode phlogiston theory. Arthur Young, 'On the air expelled from earths, &c.', *Annals of Agriculture* VI (1786), pp. 265–324; Arthur Young, 'Experiments on the food of plants', *Annals of Agriculture* VI (1786), pp. 442–52; Mr Pitt, 'Miscellaneous observations', *Annals of Agriculture* VIII (1787), p. 147; Arthur Young, 'Experiments on expelling air from soils', *Annals of Agriculture* XII (1789), pp. 393–4, 407.

[84] Farmer, *Essay*, p. 47.
[85] Home, *Principles of agriculture*, p. 2.
[86] Thomas Jefferson, *The works of Thomas Jefferson*, federal edition (New York and London: G.P. Putnam's Sons, 1904–5), vol. 7, ch.: NOTES ON ARTHUR YOUNG'S LETTER 1 J. MSS.
[87] Cited in Steven Stoll, *Larding the lean earth. Soil and society in nineteenth-century America* (New York: Hill and Wang, 2002), p. 48.

increase of that capital again must be exactly equal to the amount of the savings from the revenue, either of the particular persons who manage and direct the employment of that capital, or of some other persons who lend it to them.'[88] Yet despite the affinities in these ways of thinking, as we will see in the next chapter the political economy of Adam Smith would not unite the system of value and the system that we now call ecological.

Communication

The new chemistry had a further implication: the finite quantity of circulating matter was, in principle, quantifiable, and even if not directly measurable could be proxied by a concern for proportion between contributory elements (meadows, animals and crops). As we have seen in the previous chapter, this was entirely in tune with the spirit of the age. Accounting was nothing new to estate management, but was conducted increasingly widely and had become a central aspect of the proposals for improvements advanced in cameralism and forestry. Balancing the parts of a farm could move beyond issues of local knowledge and nous, to a more formal kind of calculation related to chemical experimentation and calibration. The goal for some, although certainly with many doubters about its feasibility, was a precise science. As Young put it, 'To discover, by experiment, the food of plants, and the component parts of all soils: that is may be known on what fertility depends, and what are the true means of remedying evils, and supplying deficiencies', a sentiment striking in some ways for the failure to move beyond the aspirations of Hugh Plat in the 1590s, yet now seen as full of enlightened promise from the toast of the continent's agronomists.[89] Nevertheless, prophets of ever newer husbandries faced challenges in demonstrating even basic facts. Young followed up the previous statement with an article replete with experiments, particularly on the role of carbon dioxide ('fixed air') in plant nutrition. Yet his results 'have been from the beginning contradictory', he noted, sorrowfully concluding, 'Time may render them more interesting than they appear at present.'[90]

---

[88] Smith, WN, II, p. 143.
[89] Young, 'On the conduct of experiments', p. 37.
[90] Young, 'Experiments on the food of plants', pp. 532, 535.

An enthusiasm for accounts and metrics in agriculture became widespread across Europe from the middle of the eighteenth century; albeit among that tiny minority of writers on the theme who leave a trace of their ideas. A more precise arithmetic of farming seems to have been more prevalent in the German-speaking lands, where as we have seen in Chapter 5, cameralist training and the latest forestry laid stress on such techniques.[91] Such calculations were already to be found in the German economic thinker Pfeiffer who thought that working out a balance between livestock and land to be manured was also a means to calculate profits. His ideas were disseminated in the *Berliner Beyträge* after 1770 to a broader audience.[92] Suggestions as to 'the appropriate number of livestock for the arable' became commonplace, understood now as part of a system of circulation, beyond an earlier and continuing concern simply to make sure there was enough fodder for the herd.[93] Eckhardt's *Experimentalökomonie* suggested a demesne (*Vorwerk*) of 64 *Hufen* (one *Hufe* was around 30 acres) of arable should have 300 acres of 'good meadow', 100 *Hufen* of pasture, 384 head of cattle, 1,000 sheep, 50 draught beasts and three *Schock* of pigs. The oxen used for ploughing or dung-carting were also calibrated according to their hours and rate of work actually harnessed, as was the extent of sheepfolding. In turn, this was reckoned to give an exact harvest which could be transformed by the animals into a set amount of dung, with the diet of the animals carefully stipulated. Of course, it goes without saying that other authors offered slightly different proportions, sometimes taking into account the variability of the quality of the ground.[94] These numbers could be displayed in neat tables, and indeed the animals were converted into standardised units of manure production to be expected under particular fodder regimes.[95]

---

[91] For England, by way of contrast, see Fussell, *Crop nutrition*, p. 176.

[92] Steffi Windelen, 'Die vollkommene Landwirtschaft, der vernünftige Landwirt und die Erdflöhe. Die *Berliner Beyträge zur Landwirtschaftswissenschaft* (1771/74–1791)', in Popplow, *Landschaften*, pp. 87–9.

[93] Germershausen, *Der Hausvater*, p. 306. Section 'Die dem Acker angemessene Zahl des Viehes', both for draught power and manuring; recommendations continued in the latter tradition, as found for example in a report on the regulations for managing the estates of the Graf von Sweerts in Bohemia from 1767, reported in the *Leipziger Intelligenzblatt* 12 (24 Mar. 1770), p. 113.

[94] Germershausen, *Der Hausvater*, pp. 308–15.

[95] Germershausen, *Der Hausvater*, pp. 658–95.

Perhaps the apogee of this systemisation came with the work of Albrecht Thaer (1752–1828), born into a court physician's family and who, residing in Hanover, was ideally placed to absorb arguments arriving from England, with their shared Georgian sovereigns. From 1804 with state support he developed an experimental farm and worked closely with the chemist Einhof. He advised on liberalising economic reforms in the Prussian state in 1807 and between 1810 and 1812 published his *Principles of Agriculture*, a towering work in German agronomy.[96] According to Thaer:

> The principle article which contributes most to the formation of plants which we cultivate, which causes them to grow and bear the seed which is destined for their reproduction, is manure, or the mould produced by its decomposition. The quantity and quality of the plants which we propagate depends, therefore, the quantity of and richness of the manure which we can afford them.[97]

Manure was far more important than the original quality of soil. Thaer and Einhof developed a system of nutrient accounting of 'degrees' of fertility, such that a load of manure contained 2, a bushel of rye harvested contained 5, and so on, by which ratios for the whole farm could be calculated, 'the great balance-wheel of every well-regulated agricultural undertaking'.[98] 'The greatest portion of produce can only be obtained when the soil, the manure, the labour, and the kind of grain sown, are in their relative proportions to each other.'[99] This system of accounting and mathematical calculation to promote soil fertility and prevent exhaustion was most fully developed by Thaer's pupil, Carl von Wulffen.[100]

---

[96] Albrecht D. Thaer, *The principles of agriculture*, trans. William Shaw and Cuthbert W. Johnsson (London: Ridgway, 1844), pp. i–xiii, 233–4; Marion W. Gray, 'From the household economy to "rational agriculture". The establishment of liberal ideals in German agricultural thought', in Konrad H. Jarausch and Larry Eugene Jones (eds), *In search of liberal Germany. Studies in the history of German liberalism from 1789 to the present* (New York: Berg, 1990), pp. 46–7.

[97] Thaer, *The principles of agriculture*, p. 130.

[98] Thaer, *The principles of agriculture*, pp. 24, 138–9, 141, 144–6, 161.

[99] Thaer, *The principles of agriculture*, p. 142.

[100] For example, Carl von Wulffen, *Die Vorschule der Statik des Landbaues* (Magdeburg: Wilhlem Heinrichshofen, 1830), especially from p. 42 onwards; also the later *Entwurf einer Methodik zur Berechnung der Feldsysteme* (Berlin: Veit und

The wider emergence of a prescriptive literature on balance in agriculture raised anew questions of the applicability of results found in particular locations, and the need for experiment to discover what was locally appropriate: a refinement of issues around climate and acclimatisation that we saw in Chapter 3, and that rumbled on into twentieth-century agronomic debates. The issue was discussed in the first editions of both the *Berline Beyträge* and the British *Annals of Agriculture*, in the latter case by the luminary Arthur Young.[101] Some authors refuted the idea that any experiment could have general applicability, given that 'each soil requires a particular knowledge of the different modes of cultivation, according to the nature, the situation, and the climate where they are situated... we can justly decide nothing but from experiments made on the spot'.[102] Humphry Davy was careful to explain that local variations in soil type and rainfall could mean that a technique beneficial in one place could be destructive in another; and drawing on developments in geology he observed that as soil was created by the erosion of rocks there could be as many types of soil as the various combinations of rock and stones exposed at the surface.[103] A modest resolution was proposed by Germershausen in Germany, to proceed carefully on the basis of one's own and predecessors' experience, and to try out innovations initially on a small scale, 'so that not too much is risked'.[104]

Yet even more pressing was getting the message out at all. During the eighteenth century, and with increased frequency after 1750, efforts to reach wider audiences proliferated, especially in the British Isles, France and Central Europe. The husbandry manuals of an earlier age had predominately been purchased or inherited by gentlemen, while other information was spread via networks of correspondents and nurserymen. In England the network of

Comp., 1847). On the reception of his work, initially published in 1815, see Peter Jones, 'Making chemistry the "science" of agriculture, c. 1760–1840', *History of Science* 54 (2016), p. 180.

[101] Windelen, 'Vollkommene Landwirtschaft', p. 86; Young, 'Observations', pp. 111–12; see also Arthur Young, 'Experiments on manures', *Annals of Agriculture* II (1784), pp. 17–32.

[102] Monsieur Mouron, 'Observations on agriculture', *Annals of Agriculture* III (1785), p. 7; for Swiss debates, see Stuber, '"dass gemeinnüzige wahrheiten"', pp. 140–1.

[103] Davy, *Elements*, pp. 166–7, 178.

[104] 'die Versuche nur erst im Kleinen bestehen lassen, damit man nicht zu viel wagen dürfe'. Germershausen, *Der Hausvater*, p. 521.

agronomically engaged landlords was sufficiently dense that when upper-class devotees got to hear of experimenters like Jethro Tull – himself a university-educated man – they descended on his farm and eventually persuaded him to write up his findings.[105] The most renowned work of agronomy in early eighteenth-century France was still Estienne's *Maison rustique*, which we met back in Chapter 1, and that had long ago found influence in English gentlemanly libraries through Richard Surflet's translation. From the late 1740s travellers' reports and contemplation of a geopolitical rival made England the fashionable exemplar for progress in France in works such as Diderot's *Encyclopédie*. At this moment the idea of great improving lords transforming their estates and through that the nation may well have appealed as a route to improvement that did not challenge the social order.[106] There was a huge expansion in French, anglophone and Swedish publications on husbandry from the 1750s, just as germanophone works on forestry and cameralism proliferated at this time.[107] Enlightenment literary culture also fostered efforts towards much more inclusive societies for improvement (albeit still reaching only a minority of those farming the land) and the emergence of journals. In the wake of this literary enthusiasm, the foundation of an Agricultural Society in Rennes in 1757 was followed by their appearance 'everywhere' in France.[108] How easily knowledge could be translated between different environments and cultures became a regular matter of concern. Clergymen appeared, as well as estate managers, as nodes in this culture of communication, recipients of advice from afar and purveyors of information about local agricultural practice, weather and natural history. Clerics were frequent contributors to the *Annals of Agriculture*, although more frequently directing their advice towards the upstanding gentleman, the old

---

[105] Fussell, *Jethro Tull*, pp. 24–5.

[106] On French thinking c. 1750, see Bourde, *Influence of England*, pp. 18–27. Indeed, two of the major works on husbandry published in France by Liger at this time paid due homage to Estienne in deliberately evoking the slighty modified authority of the old: *Oeconomie générale de la champagne ou nouvelle maison rustique* (Paris: Claude Prudhomme, 1701); and *la nouvelle maison rustqiue* (Paris: Claude Prudhomme, 1721).

[107] Indeed, this literature is really beyond the capacity of any one individual to read. Bourde, *Influence of England*; Jones, *Agricultural Enlightenment*, pp. 59–64.

[108] Bourde, *Influence of England*, pp. 194–7.

figure of the improver, than farmers.[109] Old hierarchies found new justification as purveyors of modernity and progress that could be portrayed as matters of information and technology, rather than wealth and power.

The most famous examples of such initiatives are the French *Société Royale d'Agriculture de Paris* of 1785 and English *Royal Society of Arts* of 1754, followed by more focused bodies such as the *Committee on Agriculture* and eventually the *Board of Agriculture* founded in 1793.[110] But similar societies for the promotion of applied knowledge were founded in, for example, Edinburgh in 1723, Dublin in 1731, Florence in 1753, Bern in 1759, Sweden in 1766 and Copenhagen in 1769. These comprised an international network of exchange, the Bernese society translating works from English, French, Latin and Swedish, whilst the north German *Celler Landwirtschaftgesellschaft* of 1764 set out to imitate the Royal Society in its ambition to promote well-founded experimentation.[111] 'One country is ignorant of the methods which enrich another', declared Young, but efforts were well under way to provide remedy by the time he wrote this, with journals sometimes having regular sections devoted to news from abroad.[112] Some of these initiatives stemmed from like-minded bourgeoisie and landowning gentlemen, while others appeared at the behest of reforming princes, such as the *Société Royale d'Agriculture* of France, Denmark's Agrarian Commission of 1757, or under the influence of Physiocratic thought (see Chapter 7), the *Gesellschaft der nützlichen Wissenschaften des gemeinen Besten* (Society for Useful Knowledge for the Common Good) established by the Markgraf Karl Friedrich of Baden in 1765. They would appear

[109] See for example, Rev. Mr Kedington, 'On the proper husbandry for a gentleman', *Annals of Agriculture* VI (1786), pp. 11–17; Pfeiffer, *Grundsätze*, p. 367. On the collection of especially meteorological data, see Rusnock, *Vital accounts*, ch. 5; Bourde, *Influence of England*, p. 56 esp. n.1.

[110] Jones, *Agricultural Enlightenment*, pp. 68–72.

[111] Stuber, 'gemmeinnüzige wahreheiten', pp. 123, 124; Erland Mårald, *Jordens kretslop. Landbruket, staden och den kemiska vetenskapen 1840–1910* (Umea: Umea Universitet, 2000), p. 27. The Bern society also published *Flugschriften* for popular consumption; Hölzl, *Umkämpfte Wälder*, pp. 119–25.

[112] Arthur Young, 'Hints to the correspondents', *Annals of Agriculture* I (1784), p. 133. He added, 'The present imperfection of agriculture does not arise from a want of experiments, but from the backwardness of gentlemen taking any care to make known those which are every day tried.'

somewhat later in the United States, between the 1810s and 1830s, often organised at the level of states by local politicians, editors and farmers, with a relatively broad social base in comparison to European counterparts.[113] These organisations often became the seat of publications that in an earlier era had proceeded more from individual initiative, and matters of interest for farming often appeared in journals such as the pioneering *Wöchentlichen Frag- und Anzeigungs-Nachrichten* of Frankfurt, the *Hannoverischen Anzeigen*, the *Leipziger Intelligenzblatt*, or in England the *Gentleman's Magazine* and *Philosophical Transactions*. Such publications could present however a somewhat bewildering miscellany rather than a practical tool of reference. Liberal use was made of translations; the French *Journal Oeconomique*, for example, had sections devoted to short reports on, or translations from, Germany, 'Holland and the north' and England.[114] Book reviews and summaries further disseminated ideas about both agriculture and forestry; in later editions of his *Investigations and Experiences into the urgently needed sowing of trees* first published in 1755, forester Johann Gottlieb Beckmann thanked the publicity bestowed on him by articles in the *Leipziger gelehreten Zeitungen* and *Dresdnischen wöchentlichen Frag- und Anzeigen*.[115] There was also plenty of repetition, which could generate biting cynicism: 'I read little or so to say even nothing more of economic writings; because everything that emerges from them, is pure warmed up coals, one book plagiarised from another. One would get more use from the paper on which it was printed if it were used to manure the fields, than from all that bumph that is supposed

---

[113] The encouragement of the French Crown was however also connected to a desire to nullify debates on agricultural policy among civic associations and societies from the 1770s. Popplow, 'Von Bienen', pp. 181–3; Spary, *Utopia's garden*, pp. 110–1, 124; Jones, *Agricultural Enlightenment*, pp. 19–20, 43, 47. Such initiatives also spread to Russia under Catherine the Great. 'Encouragement of agriculture by the Empress of Russia, extracted from Mr Coxe's travels', *Annals of Agriculture* II (1784), pp. 233–7; Margaret W. Rossiter, *The emergence of agricultural science. Justus Liebig and the Americans, 1840–1880* (New Haven, CT: Yale University Press, 1975), p. 9; Benjamin R. Cohen, *Notes from the ground. Science, soil and society in the American countryside* (New Haven, CT: Yale University Press, 2009), p. 52.

[114] *Journal Oeconomique*, passim.

[115] Beckmann, *Gegründete Versuche*, pp. 8–9; on journals, see Hölzl, *Umkämpfte Wälder*, pp. 133–8.

to make a farmer rich.' An English author suggested the material was actually a subsidy to the paper and printing industry.[116]

Nevertheless, as every educationalist knows, repetition has its virtues. Societies and rulers sponsored model farms, gave subsidies and premiums, prizes, and exhorted subjects to plant orchards, trees and take up new crops. In turn, there was a renewed stimulus to the systematic gathering of information of the kind we had encountered in Chapter 5. Giuseppe Galanti trekked across southern Italy and Sicily assembling his pioneering 'statistics' between 1786 and 1794, and such efforts were given a more bureaucratic stamp under the occupation of the French imperial regime although the Neapolitan project was in many ways more complete and rigorous than efforts in France itself. Sir John Sinclair in Scotland adopted the highly successful method of securing reports from correspondents in the parish clergy.[117]

It was Sinclair who laid out the conditions of possibility for improvement:

> There are three points on which the prosperity of agriculture must depend. 1. Upon giving the famer and opportunity of acquiring, with as little trouble and expence as possible, full information respecting the best and most advantageous methods of managing his farm. 2. Upon exciting a spirit of industry and experiment among that description of men. 3. Upon the farmer having a sufficient capital of credit to carry on his operations.[118]

The initiatives described above related to the first point. It remained a point of debate whether the second point would flow naturally from people being better informed, or it whether it would be stymied by institutional barriers, the lack of commercial incentives, or (as we have seen in Chapter 3) cultural backwardness. From the 1770s governments generally signed up to the argument that the presence of

[116] Marcus Popplow, 'Die ökonomische Aufklärung als Innovationskultur des 18. Jahrhunderts zur optmierten Nutzung natürlicher Ressourcen', in Popplow, *Landschaften*, p. 30; Jones, *Agricultural Enlightenment*, p. 70.

[117] Stefania Barca, *Enclosing water. Nature and political economy in a Mediterranean valley, 1796–1916* (Cambridge: White Horse Press, 2010), pp. 20–1, 39–43; Jones, *Agricultural Enlightenment*, pp. 74–6; Fox, 'Printed questionnaires', pp. 620–1.

[118] John Sinclair, 'Plan for establishing a Board of Agriculture and Internal Improvement', *Annals of Agriculture* XX (1793), p. 205.

common property was inhibiting a 'spirit of industry', and the process of enclosure and privatisation accelerated, often superintended by state commissions staffed by men who saw such changes as a prerequisite for innovation – and of course, greater profit.[119] The greater emphasis on sharing information at the middle of the century gave way, without in any way being abandoned, to a stress on the primacy of correct property relationships in permitting change.[120] Nearly all reformers desired the state to intervene and reform property rights and abolish commons, to provide incentives for innovation, sponsor agricultural research and disseminate knowledge, yet at the same time would accede to the principle that, in Thaer's words, 'It is in free and unrestricted conversation where the best interchange of ideas and opinions is effected... These conversations ought to be encouraged and rendered frequent by every possible means.'[121] But the majority of tillers of the soil were seen as targets for propaganda rather than participants in debate.

An image was formed of an agricultural reformer: someone who went beyond the exemplary character of the virtuous improver and more actively sought out his fellows (and, of course, also female landowners, although they were not explicitly mentioned). 'It is a duty incumbent upon every individual to contribute as much as possible to the benefit of society, and a good man will ever feel his internal satisfaction increase, in proportion as he renders himself more extensively useful', declared the Reverend H. Close as he pronounced upon best practice in the cultivation of potatoes in the *Annals of Agriculture*.[122] Doubtless for most innovators the bottom line remained the greatest inspiration, but Arthur Young pronounced dissemination a higher calling beyond the profit motive: 'And even the exertions of a spirited husbandry, if they aim no further than to unite the receipt of the landlord with the profit of the farmer, is but a paltry intention, that manifests rather an

---

[119] Popplow, 'Ökonomische Aufklärung', p. 23; see also Popplow, 'von Bienen', p. 228 for the case of the Bavarian Academy directly promoting the application of chemistry in agriculture; Hölzl, *Umkämpfte Wälder*, pp. 118–38; Gillispie, *Science and polity*, p. 335.

[120] Bourde, *Influence of England*, pp. 82–9, 96–7; Clemens Zimmermann, *Reformen in der bäuerlichen Gesellschaft. Studien zum aufgeklärten Absolutismus in der Markgrafschaft Baden 1750–1790* (Ostfildern: Scripta Mercaturae, 1983); Stefan Brakensiek, *Agrarreform und ländliche Gesellschaft. Die Privatisierung der Marken in Nordwestdeutschland 1750–1850* (Paderborn: Schöningh, 1991); Jones, *Agricultural Enlightenment*, pp. 35–9, 50–1.

[121] Thaer, *Principles of agriculture*, p. 14.

[122] Rev. H. Close, 'Experiments on potatoes', *Annals of Agriculture* I (1784), p. 397.

illiberal than a respectable principle.'[123] Historians have called this a 'georgic' ethic, harking to Virgil's *Georgics*, and indeed we may hear the echo of the *Hausväterliteratur* discussed in Chapter 1, but applied in a more egalitarian (if hardly equal) social context.[124]

The flip side of dissemination was, of course, the collection of information, and Young was also an indefatigable traveller, gathering facts about farming and environments across Britain and the continent in a number of journeys leading to his renowned travelogues. At the same time, the Scottish Board for Annexed Estates was sponsoring rather similar journeys and surveys to ascertain the potential for improvement of the Highlands.[125] More than ever, this reformer was also a man of science, although it remained the case that the influence of science was less in the development of experimental and novel techniques than providing a new justification for the systematic ordering of traditional practices. Agriculture had progressed to new crops and higher yields in an ad hoc manner through adoption and adaptation for many centuries. New avenues of communication could accelerate these processes, but equally lead to the association of progress with particular social strata and property relationships, such as enclosed land. In farming, where initiative in the end devolved upon landowners and tenants, the framing of the mission was rather different than in forestry where much greater emphasis was laid on professionalisation and, if necessary, coercive restraint of a wider populace. However, views of the wider populace were somewhat variable among reformers. The German writer Medicus thought that the peasantry would adopt better methods through sensible economic calculation: 'among this great class of people there are a mass of thinking heads, and their number will greatly grow, when the situation of their households is steadied by greater cultivation of fodder crops...'[126] In contrast, a correspondent of the Bernese society argued that the best away to disseminate good practice was to distribute literature to the local clergy, and when their innovations showed themselves as successful, the surrounding peasantry would 'follow like apes' in adopting them.[127] It is doubtful that

[123] Arthur Young, 'Conclusion', *Annals of Agriculture* I (1784), p. 467.
[124] Cohen, *Notes from the ground*, pp. 20–39.
[125] Jonsson, *Enlightenment's frontier*, pp. 47–8.
[126] Popplow, 'Von Bienen', p. 201.
[127] The same argument echoed through forestry texts. Stuber, 'gem meinnüzige wahreheiten', p. 144; Beckmann, *Gegründete Versuche*, p. 28.

new arguments about the source of life and fertility weighed much in the minds of cultivators who could see for themselves whether change brought improvement. But the insulation of these debates into the heart of agricultural reform would provide a powerful and all-embracing argument about why things could go wrong, as we will now see.

7 Political Economies of Nature, c. 1760–1840

Wealth

In 1696 John Asgill declared, 'What we call commodities is nothing but land severed from the *soil*... Man deals in nothing but earth. The merchants are the factors of the world, to exchange one part of the earth for another.'[1] Contrary to Asgill's asssertion, the fertility of the earth has played only a very marginal role in modern economics. Some might argue that economics has severed commodities from the earth. Nevertheless, previous chapters have shown how during the early modern centuries, resources such as food, timber and fibres, products of the organic economy all, were viewed as essential to maintaining the social order. As fears mounted regarding wood shortage, or new considerations emerged regarding the management of circulatory flows in agronomy, one might expect those writing on the political economy of the age to pay close attention. Writers in this school of thought were supposedly well aware of the limits imposed by the organic economy. Land featured prominently as a factor of production in their analysis. It has been viewed as ironic that Adam Smith wrote at precisely the moment when the Industrial Revolution was pointing towards a new type of growth based not on the limited area of land, but technology and fossil fuels.[2] The explanation for the subsequent detachment of

[1] John Asgill, *Several assertions proved, in order to create another species of money, than gold and silver* (London: E. Curll, T. Jauncy & W. Boreham, 1720 [1696]), p. C2.
[2] This is the position taken by Tony Wrigley. Wrigley, *Energy and the English Industrial Revolution*. See also Wolloch, *Nature in the history of economic thought*.

economics from the earth can in this account be seen as a parallel movement to the liberation allowed by fossil fuels from the 'photosynthetic constraint' on energy supplies. Latterly of course we have encountered new constraints in pollution, biodiversity loss and climate change.

This chapter will argue that in fact a different irony was at play. Rather than arriving at the dusk of the 'organic economy', hidebound to the assumptions of limits attendant on that world, classical political economy emerged precisely at the time when such limits were *first* becoming a matter of concern – and yet barely considered them. The idea that 'Man deals in nothing but earth' was not considered a serious constraint to economic development, still less the idea that the earth could become *less prolific*. Such possibilities took up but a few pages in the many thousands written in the genre. When problems associated with land featured more prominently, they did so in regard to two specific issues: the rate of increase of food production (Malthus) and their differential yield (theory of rents). Unsustainable usage, and even limits to growth, barely garnered a flicker of interest.

This is not to say that political economists harboured a fantasy of *no limits*. Rather, the idea of the limit was not seen as very relevant to the issues that did preoccupy them. This makes the continuities between economics ancient and modern seem rather greater. The first two sections of this chapter will devote considerable attention to the place of land within the thinking of the Physiocrats and Adam Smith, to explain a fact that seems surprising with hindsight: they did not worry about limits. Political economists did indeed engage with the new breeds of improver, agricultural chemists and model farmers who proclaimed the need for the management of flows and balancing of the elements of life. For the most part however, the interchange of ideas between such groups, sometimes bound in a tight web of interpersonal connections as we have seen, provided new means by which a further enhancement of power and wealth could be imagined by applying best practice to raise yields. This apparent insouciance poses the question of how ideas about the finite capacity of the soil eventually appeared as a systemic threat to the wealth of nations. It will be argued that the framing of political economy, once integrated with new theories of the soil, *did* permit the identification of a new systemic risk: the degradation of the land. But this argument was not advanced by the economists, but by men working in agronomy who had also become preoccupied with making their work relevant to the wider polity.

At a very basic level the justification for studying husbandry or forestry was simple. One needed food in one's belly, one needed timbers to build ships, one needed fuel to smelt ores. These were surely all required for wealth. But it had been recognised for a long time that there were problematic and complex relationships between such physical needs and the way in which they were valued in exchange. Plentiful resources did not instantly translate into wealth. Those polities best endowed with natural resources were not necessarily those that were richest or more powerful. The Dutch, who combined ingenuity and *situation*, were the favoured case to illustrate this point. It was frequently observed that merely having a rich supply of raw materials did not make one rich. Possibly the contrary was true. Many writers suggested that relative poverty of resources stimulated effort and innovation, a trope already found among the ancient Greeks and that would be transplanted to explain the allegedly greater industry of Europeans as opposed to the lackadaisical inhabitants of the luxuriant tropics.[3]

As well holding the idea that a poor soil might actually be the nursery of virtues, theories of wealth contended with the problematic relationship between the value of a good to individuals who used it, and the value it attained in exchange. Arguing that certain resources were required for military success, to build wealth or spread happiness might imply that this value was reflected in the price one paid for them. Yet when economic thinkers examined the price mechanism, and how values were actually determined in the market, it was far from obvious how the particular inputs that went into making a useful good were reflected in what someone else was prepared to pay for it. And when 'wealth' came to be assessed, it was precisely these money values that mattered. Early political economy was thus, as much as anything, a *moral* question, about how (or whether) the social interactions that determined prices reflected and respected needs and the true sources of value. Adam Smith occupied, as is frequently pointed out, a chair in moral philosophy, and later generations of economists would be

[3] See Wolloch, *Nature in the history of economic thought*, passim; Arnold, *The problem of nature*, pp. 158–62.

preoccupied with psychology as a discipline that could explain the wants expressed in the marketplace.[4]

An examination of contemporary arguments about the determination of value and prices, and thus the basis of wealth, can help us see why the canonical thinkers in political economy paid relatively little attention to natural history and technical work about the bounty of the land. An exemplary early case is John Locke, who made a crucial linkage between property rights and the value things acquired in exchange.[5] He proposed that both were related to the *labour* invested in the transformation of nature. Thus the explanation for wealth emerged from behind the immediate signs of it: the wealth one could see, smell, taste, touch and could consume became a secondary phenomenon for Locke, part of a semiotic chain that gave glimpses of the true system of wealth-generation of which they were part. It was *labour* that gave one property rights in the product of one's labour. Exchange became a mutually agreed mark of the esteem with which the buyer accorded the quantity and quality of labour that the seller had put into a good. The stock of capital that could put more labour to work was itself a kind of embodied labour devoted to allowing more work rather than immediate consumption.

William Petty, the polymath and expropriator of Ireland whom we have encountered several times in the course of this book, also foregrounded labour as the explanation for the relative price of goods. Petty asked why a certain quantity of grain could buy a certain

---

[4] This traditional approach is still very apparent in Marx, while an interest in the underlying psychology of demand is still prominent at the beginning of works by Jevons and Marshall. Only in the twentieth century did older distinctions between needs and luxuries come to seem relative and subjective. In modern economic practice, an old question has been reversed. Market prices express the agreed results of a negotiation of values between seller and buyer, and thus to conduct economic analysis there is no need to delve into *how* the morals that assign values are expressed in prices. This is not because economists are amoral (in the main!) but because prices are considered a suitable proxy for agreed values. If 'externalities' such as environmental damage or public goods are problematically left out of prices negotiated in the marketplace between individuals, then a justification is identified for intervening to adjust the price to the 'correct' level to reflect values. This is in marked contrast to the early modern preoccupation with whether prices *could* express a desirable morality. Psychology's influence on economics has revived, but more in regard to behaviour than values, although questioning rational choice models in economics implicitly questions the reasoning that links market prices to values in neoclassical economics.

[5] Wolloch, *Nature in the history of economic thought*, p. 29.

quantity of silver, and his answer was that once the subsistence needs (however defined) of the workers who produced the grain and silver had been met, they exchanged at a rate determined by the surplus amount that remained of each commodity that had been produced by a set amount of labour in a specified period of time (which Petty also equated with the rent).[6] If, for example, two groups of 100 full-time labourers in one year each produced, over and above their subsistence, 400 units of grain and 100 units of silver, then the ratio of exchange would be 4:1. In this very simple economy, with only two goods available, the relation was manifest: grain could only be exchanged for silver. It implied that value was determined by the relative input of labour per unit (net of subsistence costs). This did in practice not address many problems in the real-world economy, not least the experience of choosing between many, many goods, and the issue of varying preferences between those goods.[7] In another work, Petty implied that the average food consumed daily by a labouring man could be a common unit of value.[8]

If price, the value that denominated wealth, was simply a function of the relative inputs of labour, then how could resources (or 'land') find a place in economic analysis? For Locke the wise application of labour was the essential issue.

> I think it will be but a very modest computation to say, that of
> the products of the earth useful to the life of man, nine tenths are
> the effects of labour: nay, if we will rightly estimate things as they
> come to our use, and cast up the several expences about them,
> what in them is purely owing to nature, and what to labour,

---

[6] William Petty, *Treatise of Taxes and Contributions* (London: Edward Poole, 1662), pp. 12–25; Also cited in Alessandro Ronacglia, *The wealth of ideas. A history of economic thought* (Cambridge: Cambridge University Press, 2005), pp. 70–1; see also Finkelstein, *Harmony and the balance*, pp. 117–18.

[7] Smith sought to resolve this problem by introducing the idea of variable 'esteem' for different labour. Smith, *WN*, I.6.3. There is some implication that the skill itself was acquired by the input of a certain period of labour-time in training, so labour pure and simple remains the measure, but Smith is not very clear on this point. Petty's example seems to ignore the basic problem that the grain-grower is already producing their own subsistence, while the silver miner cannot deduct their subsistence from their output before they trade, but must use some of their total output to make a bargain for food.

[8] Cited in Finkelstein, *Harmony and the balance*, p. 117.

we shall find, that in most of them ninety-nine hundredths are wholly to be put on the account of labour.[9]

However, this did concede that the availability of the 'products of the earth' made some difference. Petty referred to labour as the 'father and active principle of wealth', and land as 'the mother'. He recognised that land may have some role in generating value beyond the labour invested in it, and speculated that such a value could be determined working out the additional food derived from a calf left by itself for a year on an area of pasture. This could be compared with the food won from the same area by a labourer working on it.[10] Of course, the calf and the labourer were not actually producing a standard good, and arguably this is a comparison of a labourer's work with the metabolic work of the calf, rather than an intrinsic value of the land. Petty was interested in the question because he wanted to design a tax system that correctly assigned liabilities to the true sources of value, but was unable to come up with a satisfactory system. Thus from the beginning, despite the recognition that an economy needs a material base, the land does not enter into questions of the determination of value. The contribution of the 'mother', as so often, is taken for granted.

In the 1720s the Irish banker and economic thinker Richard Cantillon (c. 1680-1734), fairly typically for the time, named both land and labour as the progenitors of wealth (without gendering them) and sought to take Petty's calculations further, reckoning that the ratio between the value of land and labour was set by the amount of food required to feed a labourer, which in turn could be related to an average area of productive land. However, Cantillon recognised that the recompense of a labourer in food and raiment was socially determined and was the product of cultural norms, and so there could be no fixed and intrinsic ratio but only ones that held for certain times and places. Even in this case the 'intrinsic price' was subject to market fluctuations.[11] We

---

[9] Locke: John Locke, Second treatise, V. 40; see also Muldrew, Food, energy and the creation of industriousness, pp. 310-12.

[10] See Hutchison, Before Adam Smith, pp. 34-5.

[11] Richard Cantillion, Essay on the nature of trade in general, ed. and trans. Henry Higgs (London: Frank Cass & Co., 1959), I.IX-I.XV. Later, while also believing that the wage level would tend towards subsistence, Malthus acknowledged in the second and subsequent editions of his Essay that different societies set very different levels of subsistence, which was in practice a cultural norm. Thomas Malthus, An Essay on the Principle of Population, Or a View of Its Past and Present Effects on Human

might still ask whether the value of the food feeding the labourer was really attributable to land, or simply the work of another labourer on a specified area of land needed to supply the food.

It was the insight of Locke that stuck. In his abstract world, an original labourer on virgin soil won the natural right to property in the fruits of his labour. This labourer did not take any of those fruits and thankfully return them to the land.[12] Nature did not enter into a system of payments, and therefore could not be accounted for as a progenitor of wealth. The fact that the labourer could appropriate a part of nature and barter his harvest with other people had its origins in his actions alone. Value was attendant upon property, and property was the reward for labour.

Political economy was, in this conception, derived from sociability. Property was an exclusive claim, and without other people the Lockean labourer would have no need for property. In turn, property and exchange were only possible because of his invested labour. Yet it was precisely this insight regarding sociability that the French school of Physiocratic thought, strongly influenced by Cantillon whose unpublished manuscript was available in Paris, would turn on its head to argue that the land was the wellspring of value after all.

The Physiocrats, or 'economists' as they called themselves, clustered around the royal physician Francois Quesnay (1694–1774) who published his most famous work, the *Tableau economique*, in 1758.[13] The *tableau* portrayed the economy as a circulatory system of production and consumption. Within this Quesnay famously distinguished between the 'productive' class, which comprised agriculture, and the 'sterile' class of commerce and manufacturing. This division would be attacked by Adam Smith, although the habit of dividing the economy between productive and unproductive classes was well-established and indeed was applied by Smith himself.[14] The Physiocrats

---

Happiness; with an Inquiry Into Our Prospects Respecting the Future Removal or Mitigation of the Evils which It Occasions, 2nd edition (London: J. Johnson, 1803), passim.

12 Although historically many religions had done precisely this.

13 See Schabas, *Natural origins*, pp. 45–50; Liana Vardi, *The Physiocrats and the world of the Enlightenment* (Cambridge: Cambridge University Press, 2012).

14 Gregory King made use of it in his own social tables that were inspired by Petty's early work. Smith relegated servants to the unproductive class, meaning that they did not produce any commodities that could be further exchanged. See Gregory King, *Natural and political observations and conclusions upon the state of England*

adhered to the view, as expressed by the statesman Turgot (1727–81), that 'The husbandman is the only one whose industry produces more than the wages of his labour. He, therefore, is the only source of all wealth.'[15] In exchanges for goods, Turgot argued, the most a labourer receives is 'the wages of his toil', whether this is 'limited to his wants' (i.e. a subsistence wage) or 'a conditional valuation of the price of his day's work' (one might say, the value of the esteem accorded to his labour in an exchange of goods). No-one can achieve a surplus above the mutually agreed value of their labour. This social bargain must be struck for exchanges in all sectors of the economy – save one. The labour of the husbandman who works the land is not, in the initial process of production, subject to the rigours of an agreed exchange: 'Nature does not bargain with him, or compel him to content himself with what is absolutely necessary.' There is no question of a farmer's wage being driven down to subsistence level in a competitive labour market, for example, because what the farmer obtains is 'independent of any other man, or of any agreement… It is a physical consequence of the fertility of the soil.' Thus a husbandman could draw from that fertility a value greater to that which he could in any other sector where he would be constrained by others' valuation of his toil.

This argument could in fact be applied to anyone who transformed the raw materials of nature, not just farmers, although at the time most inputs to the industrial sector came from agriculture. The principles are equally true of mining or fishing (the primary sector). According to Turgot, in manufacturing, commerce and other trades, everyone receives the just wages of their labour, as determined by the bargaining process. In contrast, the relationship between husbandman and soil (or the miner and silver) is asocial; the husbandman does not attribute any needs to nature, which is not paid for what it delivers, just as what nature delivers is entirely indifferent to the self-esteem of the husbandman or the miner. What nature bestows are gifts, a 'first advance… which by their circulation [sic], animates the labours of

___

(London, 1696), and 'The LCC Burns journal', a manuscript notebook containing workings for several projected works (composed c. 1695–1700) in Peter Laslett (ed.), *The earliest classics* (Farnborough: Greggs International, 1973); Adam Smith, *An Inquiry into the Nature and Causes of the Wealth of Nations* (subsequently *WN*) (W. Strahan & T. Cadell, 1776), II, ch. 3.

[15] A.R.J. Turgot, *Reflections on the formation and the distribution of riches*, trans. William J. Ashley (New York: Macmillan, 1898 [1770]), ch. 7.

society'; but every subsequent exchange within the economic system between people is a socially determined wage.[16]

Did the bounty of nature, and his ability to sup at the wellsprings of value, render the farmer rich? Of course, all the evidence pointed against this. Peasants were not the wealthiest in society by any stretch of the imagination. This was because in practice the payment the husbandman received corresponded to the costs of production (including, with Turgot, an acceptable rate of profit). In other words the farmer, just like everyone else, only worked and exchanged the products of their labour if they received the costs of their reproduction – a payment corresponding to the physical and psychological wants that had to be met if they were going to turn up for work the next day. Yet they tended to receive no more than this. Quesnay distinguished a *bon prix*, the price that had to be paid to get the farmer to work, and the *prix fondamental* that was the bare costs of production. The gap between the two was what the farmer could command for selling the products of his labour, but on the assumption that the *prix fondamental* was the subsistence wage, anything on top of that was the result of he or she obtaining a free gift of nature. However, in Quesnay's model, the payments for this 'gift' did not go to the husbandman, but to those who had legal power over the land, who used the scarcity of land to appropriate the greater share of the surplus: landlords. Indeed, the landlord class commonly took between a third and half of the harvest as rent.

Thus according to the Physiocrats, wages always tended towards subsistence (or the minimal acceptable for a certain station in life), while the fund generated by the fertility of the soil was a *rent*. It was really the distribution and expenditure of *rents* that could heave any person's income above subsistence levels. This created a surplus both for demand for other products, and for taxation, a crucial interest of Quesnay's. Decades later, the political economy of Thomas Malthus would also specify the importance of rents that drew upon soil fertility, 'a bountiful gift of Providence', in his refutation of his friend Ricardo's theory of rent and labour theory of value. For Malthus, the crucial virtue of this bounty was that it always called forth its own demand in the shape of hungry consumers, a problem that efficiency improvements through mechanisation could not, in his view, resolve. Malthus insisted that 'wealth' should only be defined in terms of material goods, not

---

[16] Turgot, *Reflections*, ch. 53.

services, making the economic role of rent derived from the material products of the soil all the more important.[17] The originary power of nature did get a payment after all, but it was appropriated by the landlord.

What the Physiocrats described, in the end, was the dependence of the economic system on biophysical flows for whose reproduction humans had to perform no work, but they did not discuss the nature of the biophysical flows themselves.[18] The whole of human labour was sterile without raw materials provided by Nature. 'The earth was ever the first and the only source of all riches.'[19] As all other exchanges only covered the reproductive needs of workers (in the broadest sense, in that it 'reproduced' their readiness to labour for the next economic cycle), only the fund of rent could actually be used to expand economic activity. The Physiocrats drew the conclusion that it was thus essential to expand the agricultural sector, and remove any impediments to development there, in order to expand this fund that animated all of the 'sterile' parts of the economy. They argued that fixed maximum prices of food and burdensome rents were a disincentive to farmers to expand that fund, and it was these liberalising ideas that Turgot tried and failed to introduce during his career as finance minister in the 1770s.

One might expect the Physiocrats to be highly sympathetic to concerns about the capacity of nature to sustain economic development. Their work did provide a welcome political context to the burgeoning of agricultural societies in France, although this was a continent-wide phenomenon (see Chapter 6).[20] Quesnay, in his first major publication on 'farmers' as a contribution to the famous *Encyclopédie* in 1756, stated unequivocally that 'It is the wealth [*richesses*] of the

---

[17] Thomas R. Malthus, *Principles of political economy, with a view to their practical application*, 2nd edition (London: William Pickering, 1836; first edition 1820), pp. 48, 54, 112–16.

[18] Indeed, the lack of clarity and variation in analogies applied by both Quesnay and his followers has allowed historians to posit a very wide range of 'inspirations' for both the animating force and the operation of circulations in the *Tableau Économique*. See Vardi, *The Physiocrats*, pp. 52–67.

[19] Turgot, *Reflections*, ch. 53.

[20] Richard Grove calls Pierre Poivre's work on Mauritius 'physiocratic conservationism', although he makes a case that Poivre developed the detail of his thinking from his travels and experiences on the island, rather than in France. Grove, *Green imperialism*, p. 259.

farmer which fertilises the land, that multiplies the livestock, attracts and maintains the rural population and keeps it in the country, and which is the strength and prosperity of the nation.' He backed up his analysis with numerous calculations on profits in farming and of national population, food supply and income in the manner of political arithmetic. Farming's virtues were opposed to the baleful influence of the city: 'The decadence of empires has often closely followed a flourishing commerce.'[21] Quesnay's discussion focused, however, on the lack of capital investment in agriculture, which would also benefit from economies of scale where horse-ploughing teams could be employed, rather than the fragmented and capital-poor holdings of peasants. Manufacture and commerce diverted investment funds from farming. In other words, Quesnay's initial analysis was of *institutional* barriers to a flourishing agriculture, and the threat to society came not from an over-extended agriculture, but a misallocation of funds into commerce, price fixing to favour urban consumers and the fact that land taxes were too high. In the accompanying article 'Grains', Quesnay argued that it was in any case the fund of rent that provided the main source of demand for domestic manufactures, which argued for more investment in farming to provide demand for manufactures.[22]

Land did feature in the considerations of political economy and Physiocratic thought. Yet the focus was not on 'nature', but rather on the allocation of labour and investment. This was the real conundrum to be solved: unleashing the productive capacities of well-resourced farmers to provide an animating source of rents. Nature's powers were, as usual, considered under-utilised and rather taken for granted. Quesnay illustrated the reasonableness of his arguments by comparing the returns to different modes of farming, to show how far below best practice most still languished. In turn, his critics would not dispute that providing more capital to farming was a good investment, but rather whether it was the *only* truly productive investment on which the others depended. Most prominently in the work of Adam Smith, value was treated not in relation to a point of origin in the land or labourer, but as something added across the operation of a system.

---

[21] François Quesnay, 'Fermiers', in *Oeuvres économiques et philosophes de F. Quesnay, fondateur du systéme physiocratique*, ed. August Oncken (New York: B. Franklin, 1969 [1888]), p. 189.

[22] François Quesnay, 'Grains', in *Oeuvres économiques*, pp. 193–249.

Systems

Adam Smith rightly condemned those thinkers who thought that workers who merely covered the costs of their own reproduction[23] were not adding to the nation's wealth, because manifestly the economy was larger for them having laboured rather than not, even though their earnings only amounted to what they consumed, while the farmer produced both her or his own earnings and a rent. At the same time, the expansion of the fund provided by nature was not restricted to agriculture. Knowledge and technology applied outside the agricultural sector could effectively increase the size of that rent ('add value' in modern terms) by using the produce of the land more efficiently. Thus it was not true that the surplus or rent of agriculture was the sole source of value, nor that other sectors were 'sterile'.

In practice everybody agreed that the treasure house of nature was required as an originary source of inputs into the economy.[24] True, an increase in productivity in one branch of manufacturing (assuming manufacturers did not consume all their own products) did not bring any personal long-term gain if it simply cheapened your product relative to the goods you wanted to buy. But *someone* gained thereby, possibly the farmer who got more for her free gift of nature. And in the short run, more productive manufacturers could capture market share off rivals.

This was the argument advanced by Smith. The original source of value might be foodstuffs, but the division of labour in manufactures and incentives to improvement in agriculture subsequently allowed production to expand far beyond that amount. Indeed, there were great incentives to do so because:

> The desire of food is limited in every man by the narrow capacity of the human stomach; but the desire of the conveniencies and ornaments of building, dress, equipage, and houshold furniture, seems to have no limit or certain boundary. Those, therefore, who have the command of more food than they themselves can

---

[23] Although this included an average rate of profit and hence the possibility of savings.
[24] This can also be found in early nineteenth-century writers like Say and McCulloch although they extended the idea of a bounteous nature to inputs to the industrial sector, as in imitation did Marx. See Wolloch, *Nature in the history of economic thought*, pp. 158-80.

consume, are always willing to exchange the surplus, or, what is the same thing, the price of it, for gratifications of this other kind. What is over and above satisfying the limited desire, is given for the amusement of those desires which cannot be satisfied, but seem to be altogether endless. The poor, in order to obtain food, exert themselves to gratify those fancies of the rich, and to obtain it more certainly, they vie with one another in the cheapness and perfection of their work. The number of workmen increases with the increasing quantity of food, or with the growing improvement and cultivation of the lands.[25]

The Physiocrats considered 'the earth... the source of all riches' because their circulatory system had to pass through the bottleneck of the narrow ground. But for Petty, and even more for Adam Smith, this did not seem much of a constraint. There was still plenty of land, and everybody agreed that there was plenty of fertility to be tapped into. What was in short supply was time, as Benjamin Franklin noted so evocatively. Time was money! And so productivity was raised by the division of labour, because the division of labour essentially bought more time. This was the message of the 'frivolous' model of the famous pin factory that Smith borrowed from Diderot's writing in the *Encyclopèdie* to illustrate the division of labour in the *Wealth of Nations*.[26] By specialising in particular tasks, the same number of people could do much more work in a given day, although there was no drop in the amount of raw material required per unit of output. Smith's was essentially an argument that labour was at heart of the value-creating process because having more raw materials available could not induce the same amount of labour to produce more goods, but effectively expanding the amount of labour (or labour-time) by reducing the period it took to perform a specific task could increase productivity per labourer. This in turn stimulated more demand for other goods in exchange. Time had been the great constraint.

Stimulating a division of labour could overcome this constraint, possibly because cultural habits or lack of markets (that is, the relative abundance of the gifts of Nature relative to demand) had induced idleness. This was argued by Francis Hutchseon: 'If people have not acquired an habit of industry, the cheapness of all the necessaries of

[25] Smith, *WN*, I.11.59.
[26] Smith, *WN*, I.1.3.

life rather encourages sloth. The best remedy is to raise the demand for all necessaries; not merely by premiums upon exporting them, which is often useful too; but by increasing the number of people who consume them; and when they are dear, more labour and application will be requisite in all trades and arts to procure them...'[27] The bounty of the land did not automatically turn into rents, but was actually stimulated by generating neediness that prompted a more effective use of time to harness that supply. In the traditional agricultural economy, there had been no stimulus in the direction of more effective labour. Work patterns had been wasteful of large portions of the day, which encouraged inefficiency:

> A man commonly saunters a little in turning his hand from
> one sort of employment to another. When he first begins the
> new work he is seldom very keen and hearty; his mind, as they
> say, does not go to it... The habit of sauntering and of indolent
> careless application, which is naturally, or rather necessarily
> acquired by every country workman who is obliged to change
> his work and his tools every half hour, and to apply his hand in
> twenty different ways almost every day of his life; renders him
> almost always slothful and lazy, and incapable of any vigorous
> application even on the most pressing occasions.[28]

In contrast to the arguments of seventeenth-century improvers, who had imagined that the cultivation of virtue would produce more and did not worry much about a vent for these goods, in the emerging political economy a lack of *demand* had inculcated bad habits among the workers. In truth, the remedies of the Physiocrats were similar. Their stress on the agricultural sector was not because of some premonition of ecological dependency and limits, but because they felt that institutional barriers diminished the profits of farming and prevented the productive class of farmers from gratifying a demand that could be met from the free gift of nature, and that would in turn enhance the stock of materials to be worked on by everybody else.

The produce of the land was limited not by the powers intrinsic to that land (although these differed between different places), but

---

[27] Francis Hutcheson, *System of moral philosophy*, vol. 1 (London: A. Millar & T. Longman, 1755), pp. 318-19.
[28] Smith, *WN*, I.1.7.

according to the amount and quality of labour it was thought worth investing in it, argued Smith:

> farmers and country labourers can no more augment, without parsimony, the real revenue, the annual produce of the land and labour of their society, than artificers, manufacturers and merchants. The annual produce of the land and labour of any society can be augmented only in two ways; either, first, by some improvement in the productive powers of the useful labour actually maintained within it; or, secondly, by some increase in the quantity of that labour.[29]

However, labour did not labour alone, hence the reference to 'parsimony'. The productive powers of labour could be augmented by increasing use of capital, and capital was the product of investments generated by savings from some share of the surplus of product above subsistence. This was the circulatory system that formed the basis for modern economics: the flow between production and consumption leading to more production along the low road, supplemented by the high road of savings and investment that augmented the powers of labour to produce.

Smith's anti-Physiocratic stance, and his attribution of value-creation to labour, left some issues unaddressed. If the productive power of labour was, in fact, augmented by capital, why was it not also augmented by resources?[30] If one used the same amount of labour, for example, to dig coal rather than to fell and hew firewood, clearly the return of energy was much higher in the former case. This was much the same as using some better bit of technology that raised productivity. Technically one could call this a 'rent' as in modern resource economics, and the nature of the resource clearly affected the return to labour. Resources were not, however, abstracted in a way that could easily

---

[29] Smith, WN, IV.9.34.
[30] This was a point made implicitly by Jean-Baptiste Say who criticised Smith's discussion of value-creation and cited with approval another author of 1776, Browne Dignan: 'The class of reproducers includes all who, uniting their labour to that of the vegetative power of the soil, or modifying the productions of nature in the processes of their several arts, create in some sort a *new value*, of which the sum total forms what is called the *annual reproduction*.' Jean-Baptiste Say, *A treatise on political economy*, trans. C.R. Prinsep (Philadelphia, PA: Lippincott, Grambo & Co., 1855 [1803]), note 21.

identify a fact that is now apparent to us. They were goods extracted from the 'land' by labour, materials subject to processes that turned them into commodities, rather than materials that provided services themselves. If anything, resource abundance was reckoned to induce sloth among workers. The role of a particular resource in making labour more productive of a particular service (such as heat from fuel) was not included in the schema. The abundance of coal, for example, was examined in terms of the resultant *cheapness* of provisions, not the *productivity* of coal miners. The expectation was that any super-fluous produce of the land would be captured by the owners of the land in rents, although a counter-example staring him the face was in fact recorded by Smith, who noted that rents for coal mines were actually rather lower than those for farmland if they afforded a rent at all.[31] This implied that the 'rent' of the abundant natural resource was being captured by consumers rather than mine owners. With a focus on the history of agriculture, Smith assumed that a low rent indicated low labour productivity, rather than a high elasticity of supply of the resource, easy conditions of entry to the market and a low oppor-tunity cost (land has many alternative uses; seams of coal do not). The labour used in mining coal would thus appear relatively unproductive judged by his assumption about rent, and as not contributing greatly to wealth, despite the fact that elsewhere Smith noted that the cheap heat provided by mineral coal was recognised to be an important deter-minant of the location of economic activity.[32]

What is almost entirely absent from these debates in polit-ical economy, despite the ubiquity of references to land, is a discus-sion of by what processes the free gift of Nature was brought forth. This was considered a technical question of secondary interest to the incentives for cultivators to devote more and better labour to the fields. Productivity, and crucially the right to assert property in the products of one's labour as the basis of economic exchange, was seen in terms of the circulation of value derived from labour, even if land was a neces-sary condition for labour to do its thing.

By the 1770s, the contours of the systems thinking that would dominate subsequent decades were becoming clear. For political economists, there was a system of labour, capital (embodied labour)

[31] Smith, WN, I.11.62–74.
[32] Smith, WN, V.2.157.

and land that operated through the circulation of goods produced by an expanding input of labour. Adam Smith published the great statement of this view in 1776, with his *Inquiry into the causes of the wealth of nations*. In the emergent agricultural chemistry, there was a system by which life-giving, vital properties circulated through and quickened plants, animals and people, but had to be channelled in the correct amounts to maintain yields and future fertility. And at the larger scale of thinking about the balance or 'oeconomy' of nature, all the way from Linnaeus's *Oeconomae Naturae* of 1749 to the geologist Charles Lyell's *Principle of Geology* in the 1830s, the interaction of species was imagined as a system of adaptation by which niches were filled and in the long run food was to be found thus bringing 'perfect harmony'. Or as the Swiss naturalist Charles Bonnet declared, 'Everything in the world's edifice is systematic. Everything is in connection, in relation, in combination and precise conjunction.'[33] All of these ideas inhabited an analogous conceptual universe, and arguably made individual thinkers more receptive to each form of systems thinking, but they were created rather autonomously and far from integrated into a single worldview. Indeed, despite their apparent homology we must be careful not to assume that they represent a world of shared concerns and constraints. For the most part, they formed worlds in parallel; close by but never meeting. Any intersection was episodic and partial.

Indeed, there were very definite differences in the nature of these systems, as becomes clear by examining the animating forces within them. Adam Smith's system famously rested in 'truck and barter', social interactions that demanded sympathy with the interlocutor (in the sense of the capability of becoming aware of their needs and how they might be met), which also involved the development of cultivation of a range of sentiments. These might be founded in needs and desires, but also a negotiation of the 'esteem' accorded to each person's labour, and a sense of right conduct in dealing with others. As we have also seen, for Turgot the distinction between the farmer and all others lay in a requirement (or lack of) for sociability in meeting wants. Smith had been examining the moral and motivational basis for human relations since his first lectures in Glasgow in the 1740s, and repeatedly stressed in his works how sympathy for the condition of others was a key element in directing behaviour, and itself a manifestation of

[33] See Schabas, *Natural origins*, pp. 29–33.

self-interest. The system made people social beings, a shape-shifting circulation which argued for virtues of a society of free individuals in conversation because they tended to know their own wants best, but also had the capacity to come to know others.

Nevertheless, the consistent abstraction of these sociable people into 'labour' ran the risk of stripping the interactions by which value was determined of the relations of power. In reality people did not negotiate esteem on a level playing field, in much the same way that talking only of 'land' obscured the specific properties of resources. Dukes and drudges did not enjoy equal capacities in an argument, just as the ingenuous 'improver' who gave out instructions as to how his or her estate was to be managed won rather more play in the *Annals of Agriculture* than the cleverest smallholder. Adam Smith certainly had plenty to say about power, but this was largely to condemn institutions that prevented people from just being themselves. Once so liberated, they could proceed to bargain out contracts and exchanges that by definition secured the mutual satisfaction of needs. Thus while a person could be covetous in themselves, once liberated from the dead hand of another's interest, they could only serve a common good in the moment of exchange, by which they would necessarily be meeting another's needs. This was because according to Smith the mutuality embodied in exchange meant that each would extract the greatest benefit for themselves, and the sum of these maximised the general welfare. The old clear distinction between *eigen nutz* and *gemein nutz* that we met in Chapter 4 dissolved in a more thorough way than the famous appeal of Mandeville earlier in the century to the virtues of vanity in promoting consumer demand in *The Fable of the Bees*.[34]

If the sum of exchanges established the value of the collective wealth, the origin of value for Smith was a process of *rapprochement* and sentiment that reflected a mutually agreed assessment of the esteem of labour. People and resources feature in Smith's analysis, but he was not interested in suggesting ideal distributions of these. Rather, the implication of the model of relations chosen was that one should facilitate the relationships by which people gain what they each coveted and won through effort. 'The annual labour of every nation is the fund which originally supplies it with all the necessaries and conveniences

---

[34] On Mandeville and associated debates, see Gaukroger, *The natural and the human*, pp. 270–7; Slack, *Invention of improvement*, pp. 208–12.

of life which it annually consumes', with the per capita level of consumption regulated in turn, 'by the skill, dexterity, and judgment with which its labour is generally applied' and 'by the proportion between the number of those who are employed in useful labour, and that of those who are not so employed. Whatever be the soil, climate, or extent of territory of any particular nation, the abundance or scantiness of its annual supply must, in that particular situation, depend upon those two circumstances.' Labour is itself a response to identifying mutual needs, and in entering a system of exchange people will, by that famous 'invisible hand', distribute their efforts according to the demand for the commodities they exchange.[35]

Thus was the logic of Adam Smith's system, and the focus of his writings. But if Smith dismissed the Physiocrats, he nevertheless lived in the milieu of the New Husbandry and rubbed shoulders with the prominent promoters of agrarian improvement in Scotland, among them the purveyors of new chemical theory at his own university in Glasgow. Smith did not ignore these currents; it would be fairer to say that he was simply not much preoccupied with the potential constraints of the environment, rather than claiming that he thought there were none at all. He was acquainted with the natural history literature of the day and writing on husbandry.[36] He had clearly absorbed the notion, indeed the new orthodoxy, that there should be a balanced relation between the fertility of the arable land and the application of manure: 'the quantity of well-cultivated land must be in proportion to the quantity of manure which the farm itself produces; and this again must be in proportion to the stock of cattle which are maintained upon it'.[37] Indeed, this need for the manure of cattle is how Smith justifies the argument that the price of labour required to cultivate a given amount of corn 'in every state of society, in every stage of improvement' remained static because the improved productivity of labour over time simply called forth the need for more manure that raised the price of cattle.[38] Two years later Henry Home, Lord Kames, the improving writer and patron of many Enlightenment projects and thinkers, extended these

[35] Smith, WN, I.1.1 and IV.2.9.
[36] Jonsson, Enlightenment's frontier, p. 130.
[37] Smith, WN, I.11.197.
[38] Smith provides no justification as to why the improved productivity of labour and the higher price of cattle should be proportional, save for the implication that they operate within a closed system that must balance output and inputs.

thoughts by noting that the export of provender to feed the animals concentrated around the city led to a loss of dung in the wider hinterland where it would have a greater relative effect, being 'a loss to the nation in general'.[39] Here was a moment when the two systems were almost brought in concert. Yet in *The Wealth of Nations* Smith was not interested in the question of whether this limitation restricted the capacity of the economy as a whole to expand, but rather what made it worthwhile to keep the cattle to fertilise the land. Thus for him the problem was the insufficient demand for cattle, which in turn was a function of the limited size of the market, low degree of specialisation and low earnings in towns.[40] In these circumstances 'the farm' was 'much under-stocked in proportion to what would be necessary for its complete cultivation'.[41] Here, he remains in the long-standing improving tradition that the fundamental agrarian problem was underuse, although his solution focuses more on the stimulating effects of demand and the freedom to exercise it.

Adam Smith was concerned above all with *relative* values. As with most writers of political economy before him, he was preoccupied with the ratios of exchange, and his core interest lay in the process of exchange. Changes in prices create an incentive to apply more or less labour; or an alteration from the 'natural rent' causes more or less land to be made available. The rapidity or scale of these transitions, or indeed the knowledge required to achieve them, is barely addressed. He could make blithe predictions such that 'The quantity brought thither will soon be sufficient to supply the effectual demand.'[42] For all his later adherents have been called out on a naïve belief in the 'optimising' properties of the market, this was actually something Smith disowned; he did not seek the perfect system, a rejection manifest in his critique of physical metaphors to be found in the work of Quesnay:

> Some speculative physicians seem to have imagined that the
> health of the human body could be preserved only by a certain

[39] Henry Home, Lord Kames, *Sketches of the History of Man Considerably enlarged by the last additions and corrections of the author*, vol. II (London: W. Strahan & T. Cadell, 1778), ch. XI.
[40] Smith, *WN*, I.11.197.
[41] Kames, *Sketches*, XI.
[42] Smith, *WN*, I.7.14.

precise regimen of diet and exercise, of which every, the smallest, violation necessarily occasioned some degree of disease or disorder proportioned to the degree of the violation. Experience, however, would seem to show that the human body frequently preserves, to all appearance at least, the most perfect state of health under a vast variety of different regimens... Mr. Quesnai, who was himself a physician, and a very speculative physician, seems to have entertained a notion of the same kind concerning the political body, and to have imagined that it would thrive and prosper only under a certain precise regimen, the exact regimen of perfect liberty and perfect justice... If a nation could not prosper without the enjoyment of perfect liberty and perfect justice, there is not in the world a nation which could ever have prospered. In the political body, however, the wisdom of nature has fortunately made ample provision for remedying many of the bad effects of the folly and injustice of man; in the same manner as it has done in the natural body, for remedying those of his sloth and intemperance.[43]

In this statement it becomes clear how very different the political economy of Adam Smith was from the optimising and exactly specified circulation of nutrients suggested in the work of Arthur Young and made explicit in the writing of Thaer and other agrarian vitalists (see Chapter 6).[44] In the mind of the naturalist Bonnet, the universal and systematic connectivity of all nature also remained too complex and occult to be grasped by anything but intuition.[45] System took many forms, and indeed in Paris the compiler of the *Encyclopédie* d'Alembert distinguished clearly between two ideas of system. One was the 'spirit of system' and closure, the other a 'systematic spirit' of investigation.[46] Buffon and Smith were kindred spirits in this regard; both could think of Nature as a closed and finite circle, but there was sufficient room for manoeuvre within it that the magnitude of current changes was not a major issue. They told stories of adaptation and sympathy, and were personally resistant to over-systematisation and abstract theory, although they provided tools by which this could re-emerge in new

[43] Smith, *WN*, IV.9.28.
[44] On this point, see also Sieferle, *Bevölkerungswachstum*, pp. 50–1.
[45] Reill, *Vitalizing nature*, p. 136.
[46] Larson, *Interpreting nature*, p. 21.

forms.[47] Agricultural thinkers also adopted a great variety of positions, but the most influential in the history of sustainability were those that adopted that spirit which tended towards *closure*, and hence the likelihood of failure within closed systems. For all the links between political economy and developments in natural history and ideas of improvement, there remained distinct strands within them which should not be conflated, as Fredrik Albritton Jonsson has rightly warned.[48]

Limits

In 1763, not long after his ennoblement, and in the final year of his service to the Swedish Academy of Sciences he had helped found, the great Swedish naturalist Carl Linnaeus declared, 'nature's economy shall be the base for our own, for it is immutable, but ours is secondary. An economist without knowledge of nature is therefore like a physicist without knowledge of mathematics.'[49] This was not an injunction to which political economists paid much heed. But Smith did imagine the endgame of economic development:

> In a country which had acquired that full complement of
> riches which the nature of its *soil* and climate, and its situation
> with respect to other countries allowed it to acquire; which
> could, therefore, advance no further, and which was not going
> backwards, both the wages of labour and the profits of stock
> would probably be very low. In a country fully peopled in
> proportion to what either its territory could maintain or its stock
> employ, the competition for employment would necessarily be
> so great as to reduce the wages of labour to what was barely
> sufficient to keep up the number of labourers, and, the country

---

[47] Reill, *Vitalizing nature*, pp. 31, 40; Buffon's critique of system was in part directed at Linnaeus and a source of tension between these two grand figures of mid-eighteenth-century natural history. Larson, *Interpreting nature*, pp. 9, 12–13, 15. Emma Rothschild highlights a particularly striking comment of Smith: 'the man of system… seems to imagine that he can arrange the different members of a great society with as much ease as the hand arranges the different pieces upon a chess-board. He does not consider that… every single piece has a principle of motion of its own.' Cited in Rothschild, *Economic sentiments*, p. 49.

[48] Jonsson, *Enlightenment's frontier*, p. 125.

[49] Koerner, *Linnaeus*, pp. 103–4.

being already fully peopled, that number could never be augmented.[50]

Yet the precise nature of such a limit was not a focus of Smith's work, nor of most of his British successors. Indeed, it is perhaps too easy to gloss over key aspects of this statement: his stress on 'the situation in respect to other countries', suggesting a 'full complement' can always be enlarged so long as a trading frontier exists; and the preoccupation with the relative scale of wages and profits. There was indeed a limit. Elsewhere he was explicit on this point: 'Both productive and unproductive labourers, and those who do not labour at all, are all equally maintained by the annual produce of the land and labour of the country. This produce, how great soever, can never be infinite, but must have certain *limits*.'[51] But it was not necessarily one that societies were near.[52] After all, as Smith pointed out, a country like the Netherlands is not so different from towns that produce no foodstuffs, 'yet draw to themselves by their industry such a quantity of the rude produce of the lands of other people as supplies them, not only with the materials of their work, but with the fund of their subsistence'.[53] Indeed, this point was made quite explicitly in regard to the apparently 'stationary' situation of China, whose riches 'may be much inferior to what, with

[50] Smith, WN, I.9.24. He had already made a version of this argument in his *Letters on jurisprudence*, and he implied the same elsewhere in other sections of *The wealth of nations* in ascribing the effects of a ban on trade or high taxes to being isolated in a country with poor soils.

[51] Smith, WN, II.2.3.

[52] Equally, Smith noted the importance of fertile soils and a favourable geographical position for allowing societies to embark on growth in the first place, without ever examining in detail when or if this would hinder development irrespective of the qualities of labour, writing of the 'circumstances [that] are absolutely necessary to bring about this improvement in the arts of life amongst a people in this state. The *soil* must be improveable, otherwise there can be nothing from whence they might draw that which they should work up and improve. That must be the foundation of their labour and industry. It is no less necessary that they should have an easy method of transporting their sumptuous produce into foreign countries and neighbouring states... if their be no such opportunity of commerce, and consequently no opportunity of increasing their wealth by industry in any considerable degree, there is little likelihood that they should ever... produce more sumptuous produce than will be consumed within the country itself... Tartary and Araby labour under both these difficulties.' Adam Smith, *Lectures on jurisprudence*, ed. R.L. Meek, D.D. Raphael and P.G.Stein (Indianapolis, IN: Liberty Classics, 2005), Thursday 24 Feb. 1763, IV.61–2.

[53] Smith, WN, IV.9.37.

other laws and institutions, the *nature* of its soil, climate, and situation might admit of'. Smith did not, however, expand on what it was about the soil and climate that set limits, and the signs of the endpoint approaching are described only in terms of factor prices, that is, low returns on labour and capital. When in a more historical mood, Smith implied that pressure exerted by a population on resources is actually a stimulus to expansion, rather than a limit. As noted above this was a very conventional view. The transition from hunter-gatherer to cultivator was prompted by a swelling population.[54]

Smith may have been familiar with the early volumes of Buffon's *Histoire naturelle*; he had read the travelogue of Linnaeus's student Per Kalm; and he wrote and revised the ideas in *The wealth of nations* at the time when Francis Home was publishing and teaching in Edinburgh and Glasgow, and Arthur Young embarked on his career of writing and experimentation.[55] Smith knew well energetic improvers of the Scottish Enlightenment, such as Henry Homes, Lord Kames. But there is not much evidence of this in his published work. And we should remember that the emerging set of arguments about the nutrition of plants and manure-based recycling had by no means won universal consent. As late as 1799 Headrick, a contributor to the *Annals of Agriculture*, scoffed at 'the absurdity of those theories concerning the food of plants with which so many volumes are stuffed; where it is frequently represented as a great magazine, or *pabulum vitae* originally created by the Supreme Being, and distributed in various proportions over the different districts of the globe. The alarms which these authors have attempted to excite lest this vegetable subsistence should, by the exportation of provisions, be exhausted in a particular country.' Certainly some solutions to this potential problem, such as 'salts raised in vapour from the sea, or of chilling blasts from the frozen regions of the north', were, as Headrick said, 'curious and ridiculous'. Headrick was more sanguine, in fact, because he held to the now antediluvian theory of van Helmont that water was the food of plants, and given the extent of the oceans, 'The multiplication of vegetables has no other bounds than the labour and ingenuity of man to prepare the earth for their reception.'[56] Followers of Smith could point more prosaically

---

[54] Smith, *WN*, I.9.15.
[55] Schabas, *Natural origins*, p. 83.
[56] Headrick, 'Effects of manures', pp. 278-9.

to the benefits of trade, to which one could equally apply labour and ingenuity. Providential arguments also remained alive and well, blaming any deficiency on human failings: 'God never made mouths, but that he found bread, is an adage as important in its principal, as it is universal in its truth; and nothing but the constant perversion of man in the wickedness of his heart, ever could counteract it in fact.'[57]

But by 1799, a tumultuous decade of revolution had put a different gloss on arguments about the capacity for improvement. Events in France had brought both the first male universal franchise, and the Terror. Enthusiasm, reaction and censorship in Britain shifted the public reading of Smith from being a radical advocate for what was becoming 'the left' to being a wise and restrained voice for conservatism.[58] Harsh weather and war sent prices spiralling upwards, and England conducted a national debate on the advisability of reforms to poor relief. This was the context for the most famous Cassandra of limits, Thomas Malthus, and his dismal theory of crisis elaborated in its first incarnation in his *Essay on the Principle of Population* of 1798. Yet even Malthus was not a prophet of unsustainability, as defined in this work. Like his great peers Smith and Ricardo, he was not swept up with concern for the degradation of the Earth and the loss of soil fertility, because as we have already touched upon in Chapter 4, his great argument was something altogether different, and more akin to those found in cameralism and early *Forstwissenschaft*: the issue of differential rates of growth.

Malthus had been agitated by what he saw as the panglossian theories of Marquis de Condorcet (1743–94), who had breezily dismissed the view, expressed occasionally throughout the previous century, that population growth could outstrip resources. (By the time Malthus was writing, the revolutionary leader was already four years dead, having never returned from a prison into which he was cast on the orders of his erstwhile comrades.) Condorcet conceded the theoretical possibility of limits, but replied, 'There is no person who does not see how very distant such a period is from us; but shall we ever arrive at it? It is equally impossible to pronounce for or against the future realization of an event, which cannot take place, but at an æra,

---

[57] Governor Pownall, 'On the necessity of regulating the making and selling of flour, and on the bread assize', *Annals of Agriculture* IX (1788), pp. 557–627.

[58] Rothschild, *Economic sentiments*.

when the human race will have attained improvements, of which we can at present scarcely form a conception.'[59] This set Condorcet along-side Smith in his scepticism regarding an excess of political arithmetic, and especially predictive political arithmetic. Petty, for example, had a century earlier projected current growth rates in population to estimate the future size of London. He performed similar exercises for England and the whole habitable world, using one simple metric of two acres being required per person, which would allow the English to number nine million. The world had two thousand years before reaching a limit, and neither France nor England were 'overpeopled'.[60] According to Condorcet, progress meant that all bets were off.

Malthus chose to answer Condorcet with an equivalently open-ended proposition. 'It has been said', he began, 'that the great question is now at issue, whether man shall henceforth start forwards with accelerated velocity towards illimitable, and hitherto unconceived improvement; or be condemned to a perpetual oscillation between happiness and misery, and after every effort remain still at an immeasurable distance from the wished-for goal.' The proposition with which he memorably answered this question was 'that the power of population is indefinitely greater than the power in the earth to produce subsistence for man'.[61] The grandiosity of this rhetoric – of eras, the perpetual, the illimitable, the immeasurable, and the inconceivable – is a sign of how detached the core of this debate was, in its initial form, from the careful computation and experiment that had become the rhetorical style in agronomy and forestry. These were arguments about and for forever, at the same time as being an instant judgement on contemporary politics. 'Population, when unchecked', continued Malthus, 'increases in a geometrical ratio. Subsistence increases only in an arithmetical ratio. A slight acquaintance with numbers will shew the immensity of the first power in comparison of the second. By that law of our nature which makes food necessary to the life of man, the effects of these two unequal powers must be kept equal.'[62]

This is not to say that Malthus was uninterested in empirical data. He took Jefferson's (originally Franklin's) estimates on

[59] Cited in Malthus, Essay, p. 46.
[60] Petty, Political arthimetick, pp. 70, 73. The population of England and Wales reached 8 million around 1789!
[61] Malthus, Essay, pp. 9–10.
[62] Malthus, Essay, p. 10.

the doubling of the American population from 1751 as evidence of a maximum rate of growth in a population that faced no restraint, and used Süssmilch's study of mortality crises in Prussia to suggest that limits may already have been reached. In later editions of his magnum opus he greatly expanded the content.[63] But the logic of his argument was not dependent on such information. Agricultural production could perhaps increase at the rate of population, although it was unlikely in the extreme. 'In a few centuries it would make every acre of land in the Island like a garden.'[64] And hungry mouths would still, eventually, outstrip the supply of food. In thought experiments like these, however, Malthus did not closely investigate, and indeed did not need to, the actual potential for agricultural expansion, or what might be the limiting factors to that, beyond a general commonsensical observation. There is no doubt that Malthus was minded to interpret rising mortality in his own day as evidence that the limit of a recent upward oscillation was being reached. He did not, however, have recourse to the knowledge of natural history or chemistry to demonstrate the physical truth of his mathematical reasoning.

In this Malthus also distanced himself from earlier authors such as Robert Wallace, who reckoned population numbers were much lower than ancient times, a result of an addiction to luxury rather than the scarcity of subsistence. A return to simple virtue would in his view see a rejuvenated populace. Wallace, a prolific author and savant on the Edinburgh scene of the 1750s and 1760s, is now almost forgotten, not least because many of historical estimates and future projections turned out to be entirely wrong. Yet he stated clearly that 'mankind would increase so prodigiously, that the earth, would at last become overstocked and become unable to support its numerous inhabitants', but with the proviso that this would only happen under a 'perfect government' that restricted luxury and ran an efficient economy. Yet he was one of the few authors inclined towards political economy, if of a rather unsystematic kind, who would explicitly proclaim that 'Limits' existed 'to the fertility of the earth', echoing Buffon. Malthus simply did not consider such a concern significant for his argument about relative rates of progression. 'No limits whatever are placed to the productions

---

[63] Malthus, *Essay*, p. 12.
[64] Malthus, *Essay*, p. 13.

of the earth', he proclaimed. What could be clearer?[65] Just before
Malthus wrote, Joseph Townsend's *Dissertation on the poor laws* had
used the parable of goats and dogs on a desert island to explain how
'some check, some balance is therefore absolutely needful', to restrain
human numbers, 'and hunger is the proper balance'.[66] Curiously,
Townsend's Robinsonade did not achieve the same fame as Malthus's
stern geometrics, as perhaps did no tale of this kind until Garret
Hardin's 'Tragedy of the commons' two centuries later (which was also
a parable about population and welfare).[67] People do not seem to have
been struck by the idea that the world was like an island.

The fact that political economists did not draw on the evidence of agronomy or chemistry to examine the nature of limits in
any detail is all the more explicable when we observe that many natural historians and chemists often remained highly optimistic as to
the scope for future improvement. Buffon imagined a quite rational
observer of nature declaring:

> Brute Nature is hideous... Let us dry up these marshes... let
> us form them into rivulets, into canals; let us destroy all these
> rank weeds, these withered and useless trees which encumber
> the ground. These things accomplished, instead of the noisome
> productions of the earth, of which the toad composes his venom,
> the fields will be adorned with the renunculus and the trefoil,
> with every pleasant and salutary herb; flocks of bounding
> animals will tread on these grounds, hitherto deemed unpassable;
> from them will they obtain a copious subsistence, will they find
> an ever-renovating pasture... By our hands will a second Nature
> be produced.

His was a vision of cultivated nature beautified, near beatified by
improvers: 'All the flowers, all the fruits of the earth, perfected, and

---

[65] Robert Wallace, *A dissertation on the numbers of mankind in antient and modern times; in which the superior populousness of Antiquity is maintained* (Edinburgh: G. Hamilton & J. Balfour, 1753); and Robert Wallace, *Various prospects of Mankind, Nature and Providence* (London: A. Millar, 1761), cited in Jonsson, *Enlightenment's frontier*, pp. 22–4; Malthus cited in Foster, *Marx's ecology*, p. 93; see also Sieferle, *Bevölkerungswachstum*, pp. 72–3.

[66] Sieferle, *Bevölkerungswachstum*, pp. 76–7.

[67] Garrett Hardin, 'The tragedy of the commons', *Science* 162 (13 Dec. 1968), pp. 1243–8.

multiplied to an infinity; all the useful species of animals transported from their native climates, propagated, augmented without number, and the all noxious ones reduced, confined, banished.'[68] Buffon held a positive view of the transformatory powers of human labour in the world, despite the importance of his theory of finite organic molecules, and one rather more positive in regard to the human impact on nature than his contemporary and admirer Jean-Jacques Rousseau. In the 1830s Lyell argued that humans did not create 'a larger quantity of organic life' by cultivating the Earth, but gave no reason to think that humanity faced limits in its capacity to appropriate more of that life.[69]

Even when the exhaustion of soil and finite supplies of plant nutrition were being isolated and documented, this did not translate into general limits. 'When cattle are fed upon land not benefitted by their manure, the effect is always exhaustion of the soil', commented Humphry Davy in his lectures on agricultural chemistry, extending the problem that the fertility of arable land could not be maintained without inputs of manure to the same being true of the land where the beasts were de-pastured.[70] And yet, problems such as this were in his view no more than rallying calls to improvers. Davy continued by valorising a future man where 'By the accidents which interfere with his efforts, he is made to exert his talents, to look farther into futurity, and to consider the vegetable kingdom not as a secure and inalterable inheritance, spontaneously providing for his wants; but as a doubtful and insecure possession, to be preserved only by labour, and extended and perfected by ingenuity.'[71] This is a very fine example for historians of the dangers of cherry-picking quotes, because every clause could be cast in a very different light without its neighbours. Thus was the initially negative note soon supplanted. 'Nothing is impossible to labour, aided by ingenuity... the soil offers inexhaustible resources, which when properly appreciated and employed, must increase our wealth, our population, and our physical strength.'[72] Thus for all the developments of the eighteenth century, many natural historians could have still joined the clarion call of Linnaeus, of an earlier age, that 'The

[68] Buffon, *NH*, II, pp. 252–3.
[69] Spary, *Utopia's garden*, p. 32; Schabas, *Natural origins*, p. 33.
[70] Davy, *Elements*, p. 319.
[71] Davy, *Elements*, p. 238.
[72] Davy, *Elements*, pp. 331–2.

most savage wilderness, where hardly a sparrow can feed itself, can through good economics become the most marvellous land.'[73]

Similarly, the proud farmer and opponent of Malthus, James Anderson, asserted in 1800 that far from failing to keep up, agricultural output had largely kept in step with population growth during the eighteenth century and only waste prevented it from continuing to do so. Animal manures were left scattered and unutilised all over the kingdom, of which the manure of the 'immense population' of London currently wasted 'does not amount to one hundredth part of the total loss'.[74] More efficient use of these would ensure a continued rise in yields. 'The earth is an indulgent mother to all her children, ever ready to yield her stores in abundance to all those who know properly how to draw them from her.'[75] Anderson had attended Cullen's lectures and had been an assiduous experimental farmer, but had certainly drawn no lessons regarding limits.[76]

Neither developments in knowledge of plant nutrition, nor the habit of inventorising the resources of the state, nor the circulatory theories of political economy, nor the cacophony of claims about wood shortage led yet to a general theory or debate about the sustainability of society. Yet placing an analysis of the sources of wealth on a more systematic footing gave room to the possibility that the circulation of value could be linked to the circulation of nutrients: a new kind of

---

[73] Koerner, *Linnaeus*, p. 102.

[74] James Anderson, *A calm investigation of the circumstances which have led to the present scarcity of grain in Britain, suggesting the means of alleviating that evil, and of preventing the recurrence of such a calamity in future* (London: John Cumming, 1801), pp. 73–8. Whilst John Bellamy Foster draws attention to the important fact that Marx read Anderson, he selectively quotes from the latter and gives the impression that Anderson thought generally that proper application of wastes could 'sustain the "*soil for ever after*, without the addition of any extraneous manures"'. But Anderson states that the manure from 1,000 of London's inhabitants would be applied to one acre, so his calculation only relates to 700 x 365, or 255,500 acres, although proper expansion of recycling could allow this acreage to expand as further manure was brought from London. Anderson does not comment at all on the situation of those soils from which London drew its foodstuffs, and thus he does not, as Foster asserts, seem to claim that the separation of town and country *caused* a lack of agricultural output, but avers that use of urban manures could be an important part of its *remedy*. Elsewhere Anderson argued that advantages given to manufactures were prejudicial to improvement. He was certainly very optimistic about the prospects for improvement. Foster, *Marx's ecology*, pp. 144–7.

[75] Anderson, *A calm investigation*, p. 5.

[76] Jones, 'Making chemistry the "science" of agriculture', p. 173.

coupled thinking became possible. The 'classical' founders of political economy found that they did live in a limited world, but specified it in such abstract terms that it remained for the most part only a dim, dark bank of cloud on the horizon, with little sense of whether society was sailing closer to its dangers. And it was not entirely clear why those limits were not, in fact, surmountable. It was a reminder to hunker down and not to engage in too many flights of fancy. In contrast, for leading figures among those who made the natural world their object of study, for all the elaborations of the need to keep farms in balance, to relate cattle to tillage, and provide accounts of flows of 'succulent juices', any general limits were very far off, localised barriers simply invitations to application and innovation.

Yet such concerns were being brought into a narrower orbit, and their gyrations became closer still in the work of the eastern German landowner Johann Heinrich von Thünen, who first published his classic *The isolated state* in 1826, when he was in his early forties. Thünen is now considered the founder of economic geography, and the book is remembered for developing a theory of why particular land uses would emerge in particular locations around a centre of consumption, in its most abstract version a perfectly flat terrain where transport costs played the decisive role. As well as managing his own estate, he was well-versed in the work of Albrecht Thaer and also wrote in the wake of the publication of the English economist David Ricardo's theory of rent. Ricardo had argued that rents were determined by a 'margin of production', that is, ground that could either be farmed in such a way to deliver only bare subsistence, or where no landlord had the power to assert property rights. The highest rent could only ever represent the gap between that margin, where zero rent was charged, and the yield of the most fertile land. Assuming the most fertile land was cultivated first, rents would then diminish towards the margin of production as extracting the same amount of value from the land became progressively more costly.[77] Whilst focused on land as a factor of production, this aspect of Ricardo's work did not focus on the properties of the ground itself. He was interested in why rents became fixed at a certain level, adhering to a labour theory of value.

[77] David Ricardo, *On the principles of political economy and taxation* (London: John Murray, 1817).

In some ways Thünen shared this interest in a theory of *diffe-rence*, and he equally noted that the kind of theoretical knowledge he purveyed was not actually necessary to the success of farming, 'other-wise the race of men would have starved'.[78] Nevertheless, he declared the uses of modern learning: 'No rational farmer can any longer do without with the knowledge of chemistry.'[79] Thünen devoted a very considerable share of *The isolated state* to considerations of crop fer-tility and the recycling of nutrients, and hence the determinants of yields that partly underlaid his economic geography. He spoke abstractly of the 'richness' (*Reichtum*) of the soil that could be quantified in degrees, and developed a detailed accounting of the inputs of labour, stocks of beasts and flows of manure required to maintain these degrees of soil fertility. This was derived from his reading of Carl von Wulffen, the devoted pupil of Albrecht Thaer, in turn the translator and system-iser of Arthur Young's work in Germany (see Chapter 6). Thünen also noted that the absorptive capacity of the land was limited, in that there were diminishing marginal returns to further inputs at a certain level.[80] Thus while highlighting that 'Cattle are to be viewed as an indispens-able machine, by which straw and dung are transformed...' in the cycle of production, Thünen also noted that:

> Clarity is gained in the matter when we assume another separate factor in the effects of previous cropping and labour – that is, for that which first and foremost stands in the power of the farmer; to consider this activity as a quality inherent in the ground.[81]

Thus, 'R (Richness) = H (Humus content) x Q (Quality)', where 'H' should be understood as the quantity of organic matter.[82] Thünen then expended considerable effort in relating the degree of richness to actual practice in balancing the distribution of labour, animals and crops,

---

[78] Johann Heinrich von Thünen, *Der isolierte Staat in Beziehung auf Landwirtschaft und Nationalsökonomie* (Rostock: G.P. Leopold, 1842 [1826]), p. 77.

[79] Thünen, *Der isolierte Staat*, p. 78.

[80] Thünen, *Der isolierte Staat*, p. 66. Before its famous formulation in the Ricardian theory of rent, various theorists had noted the likelihood of diminishing returns to labour as one moved to cultivate less fertile ground, without providing any detailed account of why, or indeed deploying the natural sciences in inquiry. See Sieferle, *Bevölkerungswachstum*, pp. 132–5.

[81] Thünen, *Der isolierte Staat*, pp. 243, 65.

[82] Thünen, *Der isolierte Staat*, p. 56.

drawing on Thaer and other writers in the later eighteenth-century tradition of agrarian cameralism.[83] To develop a quantitatively robust model he had to assume that 'Q' in any given place remained constant, but examined the different agricultural regimes that might exist given variable qualities of land, and by which 'R' could be maintained or raised. Linked directly to a framework for explaining the spatial distribution of production and consumption, this was a model that could pose the question of optimising the circulation of nutrients not only on a single farm but across the hinterland of a city or, indeed, an entire nation. It also suggested limits to the absorptive capacity of the ground. Already, by a new edition that appeared in 1842, Thünen was grappling with further developments in soil chemistry that were to transform it over the rest of the nineteenth century, and lead to a full-blooded theory of how civilisations relied on soil: the revolutionary work of the chemist Justus Liebig.

Revolution

Chemistry had not stood still. In the latter decades of the eighteenth century, rapid strides were made in the identification of elements and an appreciation of plant respiration. Arthur Young developed 'Experiments to ascertain how far, and in what form, Phlogiston is the food of plants', and kept up a correspondence with Joseph Priestley, the leading figure in phlogiston theory who would later discover oxygen.[84] Others seized upon 'fixed air' (what we now call carbon dioxide) as part of the story, which was discovered in the 1750s by a series of experiments by Cullen's pupil and successor to his chairs both in Glasgow and Edinburgh, Joseph Black.[85] The latter part of the eighteenth century saw a spectacular revolution in chemistry: it must have

---

[83] Such as the Prussian estate-owner and statesmen Karl Friedrich von Benekendorf, also an important source for Thaer and August Karbe. Thünen, *Der isolierte Staat*, pp. 88, 188, passim.

[84] Arthur Young, 'Experiments to ascertain how far, and in what form, Phlogiston is the food of plants', *Annals of Agriculture* I (1784), pp. 139–89; Browne, *Thomas Jefferson*, p. 142.

[85] See for example, Rev. Swayne, 'Reply to Mr. Holmes' queries on lime', *Annals of Agriculture* 4 (1785), pp. 37–47; and James Headrick, 'Effects of manures', p. 285.

been hard for the most avid gentleman farmer to keep up, as the previous ethereal world of nitrous acids and elemental airs and fires dissolved in the face of a new language of elements: oxygen, hydrogen, charcoal (carbon) and azote (nitrogen). Over these years the Dutch physician Ingenhousz's experiments in London and Vienna discovered – as we now realise – photosynthesis, and demonstrated to his mind that plants emitted oxygen that was consumed by animals, while in turn animals produced the carbon dioxide or Black's 'fixed air' which was absorbed by plants.[86] For Ingenhousz this was evidence that air contained the real nourishment of plants. His work would help draw a stronger line between the nature of plants and animals, that demarcation called into doubt by Buffon and others in the middle of the century.[87]

On the other side of this chemical revolution stood Humphry Davy. As unquestionably the foremost English chemist of his day, he was invited to give lectures on agricultural topics by the Board of Agriculture from 1802, and in 1815 they finally appeared bound as his *Elements of Agricultural Chemistry*. Allegedly this would supply the farmer with 'simple and easy experiments for directing his labours, and for enabling him to pursue a certain and systematic plan of improvement'. Here such a farmer could find answers for the perplexing sterility of his soil. 'Are any of the salts of iron present? They may be decomposed by lime. Is there an excess of siliceous sand? The system of improvement must depend on the application of clay and calcareous matter. Is there a defect of calcareous matter? The remedy is obvious. Is an excess of vegetable matter indicated? It may be removed by liming, paring, and burning. Is there a deficiency of vegetable matter? It is to be supplied by

---

[86] Charles A. Browne, *A source book of agricultural chemistry* (Waltham, MA: Chronica Botanica Co., 1944), pp. 145–7; John Ingenhousz, *Experiments upon vegetables discovering the great power of purifying the common air in the sun-shine it and of injuring it in the shade and at night* (London: P. Elmsly & H. Payne, 1779). He drew directly upon the discoveries of Joseph Priestley, while the German pharmacist Scheele discovered oxygen around the same time whilst working in Sweden; see also Teich, 'Circulation', pp. 19–21.

[87] This is despite the fact that Ingenhousz actually provided an early formulation of 'the law of the minimum'; Fussell, *Crop nutrition*, p. 152; made famous by Justus von Liebig, whilst paradoxically arguing for a singular source of nutrition: 'the surest way to find out the real nourishment of organized bodies seems to be, to inquire what is the substance without which they inevitably perish and which alone is sufficient to continue their life'. Browne, *Source book*, p. 147; Gaukroger, *Collapse of mechanism*, pp. 399–400.

manure.'[88] By now it had been established that animal dung and vegetable matter were essentially one and the same in their chemical composition.[89] Davy could look back with some detachment to the fact that 'The
vague ancient opinion of the use of nitre, and of nitrous salts in vegetation, seems to have been one of the principal speculative reasons for the
defence of summer fallows.' Now the fixing of 'nitrous salts' (nitrates)
could be explained by the combination of oxygen and azote (nitrogen).[90]

Vegetable life was considered by Davy to be no more than the
combination of elements:

> Vegetables may be truly said to be living systems, in this sense,
> that they possess the means of converting the elements of
> common matter into organized structures... but we must not
> suffer ourselves to be deluded by the very extensive application
> of the word *life*, to conceive in the life of plants, any power
> similar to that producing the life of animals... The imagination
> may easily give Dryads to our trees, and Sylphs to our flowers;
> but neither Dryads nor Sylphs can be admitted in vegetable
> physiology; and for reasons nearly as strong, irritability and
> animation ought to be excluded.[91]

In making this strong distinction between plant and animal life, Davy
was moving away from vitalist views widely held in the second half of
the eighteenth century, as discussed in Chapter 6. He belonged to a new
generation of thinkers who would reassert a language of function and
mechanism against the eighteenth-century preference for sensibility
and affinity.[92] As chemistry increasingly found itself able to accurately

---

[88] Davy, *Elements*, pp. 4–5. Davy would remain the primary influence on agricultural chemistry until Justus von Liebig's publications in the 1840s. In 1830, Loudon
appropriated nearly all his comments on the subject directly from Davy. However, a
little earlier the Earl of Dundonald, owner of a Tyneside alkali works, had absorbed
many of the recent developments in chemistry and introduced them into his work of
1795, *A treatise, shewing the intimate connection that subsists between agriculture
and chemistry addressed to the cultivators of the soil, to the proprietors of fens and
mosses, in Great Britain and Ireland, and to the proprietors of West India estates*
(London: E. Edwards, 1795).

[89] Davy, *Elements*, pp. 263, 267. Einhof conducted important research in Germany on
this issue.

[90] Davy, *Elements*, p. 316.

[91] Davy, *Elements*, pp. 221–2.

[92] Rossiter, *The emergence of agricultural science*, p. 17.

describe, explain and demonstrate by experiment the basic transformations by which plants lived, the need for some occult animating force
began to decline. But to draw a similar conclusion for animal life, to
which humans had been assimilated by some natural historians, was a
step too far. Hence the ring-fencing of plant life as a form that barely
deserved the name. Gone was the continuum of Buffon, in which plants
could be imagined as animals in permanent repose.[93] Nevertheless,
Davy still believed that the 'true nourishment of plants' consisted of
organic matter, and the service rendered by inorganic 'fossil manures'
was to improve soil texture.[94] In the eyes of Liebig, this still placed
Davy, and indeed all of Liebig's own forerunners, among the mistaken
cohorts of the vitalists, in a less metaphysical guise as purveyors of
'humus theory'.

Justus Liebig was born the son of a hardware merchant and
his wife in the small central German town of Darmstadt in spring
1803, where an early induction to chemistry came from mixing paints
and varnishes for sale. Part autodidact, part inspired by his father's
enthusiastic experimentation when economic hardship made an academic career unlikely, he became sufficiently adept in his late teens to
persuade a serendipitous family acquaintance, the professor of chemistry at the University of Bonn, to take him on as an assistant and
thus launched a famous career. By 1822 he was in Paris, consorting
with scientific luminaries such as George Cuvier and Alexander von
Humboldt, and it was at the recommendation of the latter that he
attained a chair at the University of Giessen and was able to develop
what in many ways was the first modern, systematic approach to
laboratory training for the next generation of chemists.[95] Already
a scientific star, it was an address to the British Association for the
Advancement of Science meeting in Liverpool in 1837 that was the
foundation for his published work on plant nutrition and – as we
might say – sustainability.[96]

[93] Buffon, NH, I, p. 296.
[94] See David Knight, 'Agriculture and chemistry in Britain around 1800', Annals of
Science 33 (1976), pp. 187–96.
[95] William H. Brock, Justus Liebig. The chemical gatekeeper (Cambridge: Cambridge
University Press, 1997), ch. 1.
[96] Justus von Liebig, Die Chemie in ihrer Anwendung auf Agricultur und Physiologie,
7th edition (Braunschweig: Friedrich Vieweg, 1862), pp. vii–viii; Brock, Justus Liebig,
pp. 96–7, 150–2.

Liebig was certainly not shy about his own capabilities. In submitting the manuscript to the publisher, he suggested it 'might produce a revolution'.[97] Later, he would divide the history of agriculture at 1840: that is, by the appearance of the first edition of his own book *Chemistry in its Application to Agriculture and Physiology*.[98] He noted that around the turn of the nineteenth century, when he was born, in practice farmers knew little of the causes of soil fertility (*Bodenfrucht*) but were confident that through the application of manure 'the field behaved like a machine that produced by itself again the power [*Kraft*] required for work'. Thus it seemed to be in the gift of the farmer to raise yields by managing manure, as we have seen among the cameralist writers, a notion given theoretical traction through the idea of humus and organic recycling argued by Thaer. Indeed the leading cameralist of the 1770s and 1780s, Johann Friedrich von Pfeiffer, although inclined to stress the benefits of recycling organic matter, commented that it was perfectly possible to teach a farmer good manuring practice without any reference to 'Mathesin und Physik'.[99] The soil was considered to be inexhaustible if managed properly. Liebig mocked these ideas, and also the idea that the ratios found on the experimental farms and estates of agrarian writers could be generalised into universally applicable models, although without doubt it was precisely these approaches that led him to ask the questions that would contribute to revolutionising agricultural practice.[100]

There were three key aspects to Liebig's revolution. First, contrary to what was widely thought by the early nineteenth century, plant nutrition did not lie in some kind 'organic particle' or vital force but

[97] Albeit only in the understanding of plant chemistry. Pat Munday, 'Liebig's Metamorphosis. From organic chemistry to the chemistry of agriculture', *Ambix* 38 (1991), p. 135.

[98] The work was rapidly translated into French, English, Italian, Dutch, Russian, Polish, Danish and Swedish. Brock, *Justus von Liebig*, p. 145.

[99] Pfeiffer, *Vermischte Verbeßerungsvorschläge*, pp. 5, 8.

[100] Liebig, *Die Chemie*, pp. 1–4; see also Rossiter, *Emergence of agricultural chemistry*, pp. 19–25; of course, the representativeness of experiments was a long-established theme of debate. 'Soils are so unbounded in their variety – seasons, in this climate, are also so variable in their effects on vegetation, that I much fear, whether if during a series of threescore years, the result of experiments was to be sent to this publication from every corner of the kingdom, any general and infallible axioms could be collected from the mass of information, although much real and valuable experience would certainly be gained from it.' Thomas Ruggles, 'Picturesque farming', *Annals of Agriculture* IX (1788), p. 12.

rather in the capacity of organic life to process *inorganic* minerals. The discovery of photosynthesis and understanding of the respiratory activity of plants, exchanging carbon dioxide and oxygen, with some role of nitrogen (or azote) had already pointed in this direction, and resulted in continuing controversy as to whether nitrogen was primarily supplied from the air, as the nitrogen-fixing properties of some plants such as trefoil had been noticed, or came from the soil. Liebig argued that nitrogen was fixed in the form of ammonia from the air contained in water, and one of the main uses of manure and urine as a fertiliser was that they absorbed the ammonia after putrefaction, a position he would later be forced to moderate.[101] He certainly overstated his own originality in this regard and chemistry already had advanced sufficiently by 1800 to set out the functioning of manures in non-vitalist terms, such as in the work of Charles's grandfather Erasmus Darwin as well as Davy, using the elements familiar to us today. Liebig's systematic approach and trenchant style of argument clearly set out however the management of the circulation of elements as a major problem for the agricultural system.[102]

Second, the diversity of minerals required meant that plant health was determined not by some general foodstuff but by the balance of specific minerals that acted in concert, meaning that there was a *minimum* of each required for functioning. Liebig's famous 'law of the minimum' was actually a development of an idea of Carl Sprengel, a chemist who had worked with Thaer and Einhof at their experimental farm in Möglin and to whom Liebig presented himself as rival and successor in disputes across the 1840s and 1850s.[103] Third,

---

[101] Liebig altered his positions over his career and came under sustained attack as to the details of some of his claims by various authors, especially John Lawes, the pioneer of superphosphates and director of the Rothamstead experimental farm in England from 1843. Brock, *Justus von Liebig*, pp. 166–76; J.B. Lawes, 'On some points connected with agricultural chemistry', *Journal of the Royal Agricultural Society of England* 8 (1847), pp. 227–8.

[102] Boussingault provided a clear account of these developments. J.B. Boussingault, *Rural economy in its relations to chemistry, physics and meteorology or, an application of the principles of chemistry and physiology to the details of practical farming*, trans. George Law (London: H. Baillière, 1845), pp. 29–43; Erasmus Darwin, *Phytologia; or the philosophy of agriculture and gardening* (London: J. Johnson, 1800), pp. 184–256. Brock, *Justus von Liebig*, p. 159.

[103] Liebig, *Die Chemie*, p. 38. Sprengel had also already rejected the humus theory which, it should be noted, had drawn sceptical comment from a variety of sources

Liebig noted that recycling could never be perfect because of the inevitable loss of minerals in the process of circulation and especially the consumption of the crop by the off-farm population, a kind of agrarian entropy.[104] The 'practical agriculturalist' (i.e. simple farmer) could never understand this, because he [sic] failed to perceive that problems were generated by 'himself and his system; the idea that the fault might possibly lie with him or his system can find no place in his mind'.[105] This insight was based on Liebig's model of chemical circulation within the farm, yet with its logic expanded to the polity: 'the satisfaction of needs of an ever rising population can only be secured if one returns to the fields what they lack, either from other sources or collected animal dung [Stallmiste]... it is clear, that all causes which in any way act to disturb or further these natural laws, must exert a corresponding influence on all of human life [Lebensverhältnisse der Menschen]'.[106]

Chemists were now drilling down more precisely into the elements and compounds which plants assimilated and manures could deliver, as well as the mineral content of the soil created by the longer-term weathering of rocks. Some concentrated almost entirely on the role of elements and the means by which they were absorbed through photosynthesis and the roots, only viewing organic matter as an effective, rather than essential means of delivery.[107] Others retained something of the vitalist notion of circulation in stressing the importance of humus. This was asserted by Liebig's great French contemporary Boussingault, whose work was also rapidly translated into English, and who maintained strong personal links across the Channel. Boussingault's interest in chemical cycles had been stimulated when

including those who stressed the role of photosynthesis. Brock, *Justus von Liebig*, pp. 147–8, 165.

[104] Liebig, *Die Chemie*, pp. 12–15; a more optimistic view based on the fixing of nitrogen from the air was propagated by Boussingault in the 1830s and supported by the head of the English experimental farm at Rothamstead, John Lawes. Boussingault, *Rural economy*, pp. 42–3.

[105] Justus von Liebig, *Letters on modern agriculture* (London: Walton and Maberly, 1859), p. 172.

[106] Liebig, *Die Chemie*, pp. 27, 91.

[107] See the work of Chaptal, who nevertheless bluntly stated that 'all plants exhaust the soil' and thus required appropriate fertilisers, grain crops most of all. M. le Comte de Chaptal, *Chimie appliquée a l'Agriculture. Tome 1*. (Paris: Madame Huzard, 1825), esp. pp. 272–80.

travelling and managing a mine in South America during the 1820s, expressed in a study of guano, an interest transferred into the running of an experimental farm, and a strong focus on applied agricultural chemistry in his return to France in the 1830s (he also later served as a left-leaning deputy in the French parliament).[108] He surveyed the literature available and used his own experiments to provide a table of the quality of manures ranked according to their nitrogen ('azote') and moisture content, much in the same way that Thaer, Wulffen and Thünen had contemplated 'degrees' of richness.[109] But the conclusions drawn by chemists of the 1830s and 1840s were potentially even more alarming than the calls for a balanced circulation that had prevailed before. If the essential foods of plants lay not in the general vital properties of organic matter, but the acquisition of minimum amounts of particular elements, even a well-governed system of farm recycling could not necessarily obviate the threat of degradation. But Liebig, more than any other, also pointed the way to the future solution to these dilemmas – the use of artificial fertiliser.[110]

If the political economists occasionally read natural history and agricultural chemistry, it was the agricultural chemists that attempted a more serious integration of their work into practical and economic suggestions (although the treatises of Liebig and Boussingault were in

---

[108] Boussingault displayed interest in a variety of matters relating to the relationship between inputs, biophysical processes and outputs, encompassing human and animal nutrition as well as plants. M.J. Dumas and M.J.B. Boussingault, *The chemical and physiological balance of organic nature. An essay* (London: Baillière, 1844); Dana Simmons, *Vital minimum. Need, science and politics in modern France* (Chicago, IL: University of Chicago Press, 2015), pp. 14–27; Jones, *Agricultural Enlightenment*, pp. 181–3. From their shared South American experiences he became a regular correspondent with Alexander van Humboldt, who enthused about Boussingault's works on agricultural chemistry, but was primarily interested in the relationship with atmospheric chemistry and the role of oxygen. Ulrich Päßler and Thomas Schmuck, *Alexander von Humboldt, Jean-Baptiste Boussingault, Briefwechsel* (Berlin: De Gruyter, 2015), pp. 399–402, 404–5, 416–23.

[109] He also noted that Thaer's enthusiasm for a theory based on humus may have partly derived from a mistake in Einhof's calculations as to the amount of humus present in soils, as he erroneously included the weight of water bound up in the organic matter and evaporated during the combustion used to extract the humus and estimate its mass as part of the whole. Boussingault opposed Thaer's notion that all of the food of plants resided in the soil and thus required recycling with no losses. Boussingault, *Rural economy*, pp. 266, 269–70, 391–3.

[110] On these debates, see Mårald, *Jordens kretslopp*, pp. 47–65.

truth largely reportage on experimental results and rather far from a manual that any farmer could easily employ). Liebig noted that political economy remained largely uninterested in the details of tillage, and indeed that Adam Smith's engagement had been rather incidental (illustrating this argument by quoting much the same passages as historians have subsequently done to claim that Smith was much engaged with agricultural questions).[111] Liebig noted that an understanding of soil chemistry provided an explanation of diminishing returns to labour in agriculture. Meanwhile Boussingault explained how 'where manure cannot be had from without, things must be reduced to a system; and the amount of produce which it is possible to export each year is fixed within bounds, which cannot be exceeded with impunity'.[112] There were, then, definitive limits to production. This system was, to all intents and purposes, closed. The soil, or the manure by whose application herbaceous life was animated, was made explicitly analogous to a capital stock (and industrial machinery), albeit one that could only be extended to certain limits, and at the same time easily depreciated: 'capital placed in the ground, the interest of which is represented by the commercial value of the produce of all the other agricultural operations'.[113] Hence the 'law' of diminishing returns, and the effects of soil degradation, could be explained as effectively reducing the amount of capital available per unit of labour, a point raised to argue against the export of fertiliser:

> In my opinion, any exportation, the consequence of which is
> the impoverishment of the soil, ought to be prohibited. I should,

---

[111] Schabas argues that 'Enlightenment philosophers saw the world as one integrated but complex web that linked the earth's crust, the atmosphere, plants, animals, and humans.' If they did, I have found little internal evidence in their texts that they thought this very important for their subsequent research and arguments, even if they frequently drew on analogies from nature or the sciences, as did neoclassical economists; nor thus does there seem to be a trend towards a later 'denaturalisation' as Schabas claims. In fact, one can find more references to the soil, and discussion of its qualities, in Marshall than in Smith. Schabas asserts that 'Linneaus was one of the major economists of the Enlightenment'; yet it does not appear that he was mentioned in any of the major published works of any of the political economists. Schabas, *Natural origins*, pp. 2, 5, 11, 35, 40; Liebig, *Die Chemie*, p. 135; Alfred Marshall, *The principles of economics* (London: Macmillan, 1890), passim.

[112] Liebig, *Die Chemie*, p. 147; Boussingault, *Rural economy*, p. 454.

[113] Boussingault, *Rural economy*, pp. 265, 454; see also Liebig, *Letters*, p. 178.

for instance, oppose the exportation of arable soil; and, in the same way, to allow an active manure to pass into the hands of strangers, is in my eyes tantamount to exporting the vegetable soil of our fields, to lessening their productiveness, to raising the price of the food of the poor; for as much labour is required, as much care and capital must be expended upon an ungrateful soil to obtain a little, as upon a fertile soil to procure an ample return.[114]

This was precisely the argument being raised soon after by the American economist Henry C. Carey in support of protectionist policies and against advocates of free trade such as John Stuart Mill (more of which in Chapter 8). Mill, as is well known, repeatedly emphasised the problem of diminishing marginal returns to labour on the land, and devoted far more attention to soil and cultivation than either Smith or Ricardo. Yet he remained optimistic that the availability of land on the frontier and the existence of continued existence of spare cultivable soil in every nation meant limits remained distant. This view could accommodate the reality of localised exhaustion, and even allow for the 'physical truth on which [Carey's argument] is founded; a truth which has only *lately* [italics added] come to be understood'.[115] Liebig in contrast understood the problems being faced as more profound. They were not solely a matter of trade but of the entire metabolism of an industrialising and urbanising society, in which foodstuffs were transported to cities and the excreted 'waste' and its precious load of mineral nutrients flushed away into the sea. 'The maintenance of the wealth and welfare of states and the advancement of culture and civilization is dependent on the resolution of the sewer-question [*Kloakenfrage*] of the cities', he thundered.[116] Thus did destiny become

[114] Boussingault, *Rural economy*, pp. 394-5.
[115] Henry Carey, *The harmony of interests. Agricultural, manufacturing and commercial* (Philadelphia, PA: J.S. Skinner, 1851); John Stuart Mill, *Principles of political economy with some of their applications to social philosophy* (London: Longmans & Green, 1909 [1848]), V.10.13; IV.4; II.5.8. See also quoted in Wrigley, *Energy*, p. 246; Mill was in fact an enthusiastic reader of Liebig. Pat Munday, 'Politics by other means. Justus von Liebig and the German translation of John Stuart Mill's Logic', *British Journal of the History of Science* 31 (1998), pp. 403-18.
[116] Liebig, *Die Chemie*, p. 153.

not a question of how one had been blessed or responded to one's endowment of fertility across the varied surface of the globe, but whether experts could successfully engineer the flow of nutrients in a society whose practices systematically endangered its existence. The modern problem of sustainability had arrived.

8 History and Destiny, c. 1700–1870

History

'What is this worlde but a lively image... in which God sheweth and declare himself: For albeit he be invisible in his essence, yet sheweth he himselfe by his works, to the end we should worship him.' So declared Jean Calvin, the great French-born reformer of Geneva.[1] Calvinists were particularly keen on articulating the idea that God manifested his glories in his exterior and visible works, but the notion of a providential nature suffused mainstream Christian thought.[2] Scriptural justification that the world around was a source of revelation could be found in Romans 1:20: 'For the invisible things of him from the creation of the world are clearly seen, being understood by the things that are made, *even* his eternal power and Godhead; so that they are without excuse.' As we have seen in Chapter 3, this dovetailed neatly into the idea that scientific enquiry was itself an act of praise and a recovery of God's purposes after the Fall. These arguments about God's presence in his material works could be made quite generally with no particular reflection on the particular revelation to be found in, for example, worms or eyeballs (or worms in eyeballs), but they came to be taken up by scholars of the natural world too. In the 1680s the pious taxonomist and botanist John Ray wrote of how:

[1] Cited in Walsham, *Reformation of the landscape*, p. 332.
[2] Manichean doctrines, stressing the sins of the flesh, thought otherwise, but had largely been quashed before the early modern period.

The vast multitude of Creatures... The sun, and Moon, and all the Heavenly Host are the Effects and Proofs of his Almighty Power... Their mutual Subserviency to each other, and unanimous conspiring to promote and carry on the Publick Good, are evident Demonstrations of his Sovereign Wisdom.[3]

Ray went on to explain particular instances: that 'The Armour of a Hedgehog... [was] a great instance of Design for their Defence and Security.'[4] There was an implicit notion of order and hierarchy in such ideas, although not articulated in a precise language of balance. Could the hedgehog's armour be slightly better? What message was conveyed by the vulnerability of a species like the dodo? In fact, although the latter bird was described by Clusius as early as 1605 after the Dutch began to use Mauritius as a stop for fleets of their East India Company, and was well documented by a range of seventeenth-century authors, by the age of the French Revolution there was some doubt whether the bird had ever existed at all. The issue of extinction seemed not to register in such a determinedly providential world.[5]

Yet as we move forward into the first decades of the nine-teenth century, still very much a Christian milieu, new thinking about the possibility of unsustainability presented an uncomfortable notion. Bluntly, bad things could happen to good people engaged in perfectly virtuous activities. Indeed, the rise of political economy had already confronted people with awkward ethical issues about the relationship between individual and collective morality (private vice leading to public virtue). The 'naturalisation' of investigation into anthropology and comparative religion had 'de-moralised' explanation of the differ-ential traits of human societies, including some of their most cherished practices.[6] The possibility of unsustainability raised questions about the trajectory that the whole of society might be on: a collective des-tiny. It equally raised new questions regarding what had occurred in the past. The question of sustainability became woven into the sense of historical destiny that had emerged over the previous centuries. In retrospect we might gloss the changes that occurred as the slow shift

---

[3] Ray, *The wisdom of God*, f.6v-7r.
[4] Ray, *The wisdom of God*, pp. 333-5.
[5] Mark V. Barrow, *Nature's ghosts. Confronting extinction from the age of Jefferson to the age of ecology* (Chicago, IL: University of Chicago Press, 2009), pp. 50-7.
[6] Gaukroger, *The natural and the human.*

from a sacred history to a natural History, where History is understood as the prevailing narrative of a social development. This should not be confused, however, with a general secularisation or 'disenchantment of the world'. Nor was it a straightforward, one-way process.

A naturalised historical sensibility that allowed a clear role for nature was a consequence of shifts away from a more universally providential understanding of the world. Early modern science, natural history, or natural philosophy (all these terms were current by the end of the sixteenth century and of course had their own particular forms in different languages) raised many questions as to the precise quality of God's engagement with his Creation. From the 1630s mechanistic thinkers, most strongly associated with Parisian intellectual circles (although the most famous of all, René Descartes, evaded censorship to base himself in the Netherlands) argued that the act of Creation was singular and the universe subsequently followed a course set at that original moment. The far more widespread view was that the deity maintained an active role in governing and motivating nature. This was a dynamic nature, whose characteristics might alter over time in accordance with divine will. Such opinions were related to other contemporary disputes, as we have already seen in questions of epigenesis in Chapter 6; whether matter was composed of atoms; and whether all 'natural' phenomena had to be evaluated as subject to mechanistic predetermined processes or could be interpreted as particular, prodigious and providential signs of God's intervention at that moment in time. The reception of Greek and Roman thought, that in many instances had proposed a universe subject to unbending rules, posed particular problems. The established tenets of Aristotelian thinking, with its notions of ends inherent in the nature of objects could relatively seamlessly be united with providentialism; but there was also the troublingly deity-free materialism of Epicurus and Lucretius. Hence John Ray felt it necessary to dispose of the dread triumvirate of Aristotle, Epicurus and Descartes early on in his argument for *The wisdom of God manifested in the works of Creation.*[7]

The most famous literary argument over how one might read divine intent in the state of nature was prompted by the publication of Thomas Burnett's *The sacred theory of the earth* (originally in a

---

[7] Ray, *The wisdom of God*, pp. 32–48. See also Walsham, *Reformation of the landscape*, pp. 335, 340–57.

1681 Latin edition) of 1684. Burnett, headmaster of the Charterhouse School that then lay at the northern edge of the City of London, argued that the world had originally been a perfect egg whose contemporary irregular topography was a sign of God's displeasure, primarily as a direct consequence of the Deluge. Indeed Burnett, who was assuredly not much engaged with the natural philosophy of his time, had come up with the idea of an egg-like world in an effort to explain how the amount of water in the oceans could have once covered the entire surface of the Earth when it manifestly did not now. His solution was to imagine away its post-diluvian topography. Thus the state of nature, and in particular the mountains that heaved themselves up far above the surface of the sea, were argued to be monumental markers of human sinfulness.[8] They combined divine splendour, a standing warning and admonishment. Burnett's attempt to integrate geological observations and sacred history received both criticism and mockery, as well as initially the imprimatur of both Newton and the monarch, but engaged with a fundamental question about the historicity of the natural world.[9] The polymathic scholar and non-conformist minister Nehemiah Grew, most famous for his anatomical work on plants, responded by anchoring natural history firmly to a salving rather than a wrathful providence, claiming 'Nature it self is a Standing Miracle.'[10] Yet as this literature on sacred history developed and became allied to specific scientific observations and debates, writers were confronted with the question as to whether particular phenomena might be understood as signs of beneficence or wrath.

Burnett was by no means the first to ponder how the world fared over time. Already in classical texts, as raised in Chapter 1, we find the question as to whether the world 'aged' as did plants and animals, and a related question of whether the population of living things declined with this senescence. Lucretius (99–55 BCE) answered

---

[8] Majorie Hope Nicolson, *Mountain gloom and mountain glory. The development of the aesthetics of the infinite* (Seattle, WA: University of Washington Press, 1997 [1961]), pp. 184–270.

[9] Thomas Burnet, *The sacred history of the earth* (London: John Hooke, 1719 [1684]); see also Walsham, *Reformation of the landscape*, pp. 381–7; the view that mountains were shaped by the Flood was widespread, if debated, in the seventeenth century and shared by luminaries such as Robert Hooke. Davies, *The Earth in decay*, pp. 39–40, 68–73.

[10] Cited in Walsham, *Reformation of the landscape*, p. 387.

in the affirmative, while Columella (4–70 CE) denied it. The notion of senescence proved appealing to some strands of Protestant millenarianism and was argued for by Luther.[11] It was vehemently opposed by another Calvinist clergyman (and one-time mentor to Charles I who fell out of favour), George Hakewill, who published his *Apologie of the Power and Providence of God* in 1627. Influenced by Columella as well as the idea of continual providential interventions, Hakewill applied the interesting test that the world was not obviously different to that described by Lucretius, a fact that must prove Lucretius wrong. On the other hand, by 1677 Matthew Hale could argue that the rate of deposition of soil from the mountains was so great, the Earth cannot be very ancient, and also noted that the rate of population growth was such it required a 'Corrective' delivered providentially from the deity.[12] A debate in this mode would rumble on throughout the eighteenth century, comparing the state of the present with the classical world to ascertain signs of relative decline or progress, rather than the ageing of matter itself. Much of the literature on the relationship of God and nature is now labelled as 'Physico-Theology' after William Derham's book of that name published in 1713.[13] Both providentialists and mechanists generally preferred to highlight the universality or continuity of natural processes, but attempts to more closely align scriptural precedents with observed phenomena also created space for a new kind of natural historical explanation. Derham argued, for example, that God had created a balance of species on the Earth by the careful fixing of rates of reproduction and lifespans. The fact that the Earth was manifestly more populated than when the postdiluvian survivors emerged from Noah's Ark was the reason that lives were now so much shorter than those attributed to the Old Testament patriarchs, a change effected by providence. This prevented a surfeit of people.[14] Latterly authors like

[11] Glacken, *Traces on the Rhodian shore*, pp. 69–72, 134–6; Nicolson, *Mountain gloom*, pp. 101–2; Davies, *The Earth in decay*, pp. 5–8, 47–8.

[12] George Hakewill, *An apologie of the power and providence of god in the government of the world* (Oxford: John Lichfield and William Turner, 1627); Glacken, *Traces on the Rhodian shore*, pp. 382–9; Sieferle, *Bevölkerungswachstum*, pp. 59–64; Matthew Hale, *Primitive origination*, pp. 131, 204, 226.

[13] William Derham, *Physico-Theology; or a demonstration of the being and attributes of God, from his works of creation* (London: W. Innys, 1713); Davies, *The Earth in decay*, pp. 118–22.

[14] Glacken, *Traces on the Rhodian shore*, p. 422; Sieferle, *Bevölkerungswachstum*, pp. 66–70.

the German theologian Hermann Samuel Reimarus (1694–1768) and Englishman William Paley (1743–1805) wrote in this tradition, as did indeed Thomas Malthus, who attributed the iron truths of his dismal world of 'checks' to a providential design to reward restraint.[15] Natural disasters, such as the earthquakes that shattered Lima in 1746 or most famously Lisbon in 1755, tended to revive and enliven debates over the semiotics of nature, reading them as divine punishment, acts of special providence, or seeking purely mechanical explanations.[16]

Such accounts placed human action and responsibility centre stage, but also situated human history amid an unfolding story of cosmic and worldly process. Keith Thomas has argued that as knowledge of the sheer number of species in the world grew, alongside an astronomy that opened up great vistas beyond the Earth, it became less easy to explain it all as being solely created for human purposes and subject to their dominion. Rather, humans might better be seen as the apogee of a Creation entirely suffused with the deity's purpose, humanity being that part which most resembled the deity. Given this, it seemed a less satisfactory argument that human conduct in regard to animals, for example, could be justified simply by human wants given a proclaimed dominion over nature. The self-interested satisfaction of human wants may not have been what providence intended.[17]

As well as the grand histories in the physico-theological tradition, people pondered change over time on the scale of landscapes, for which there was plenty of literary evidence. The ebb and flow of cultivated land and forest were also dramatised in larger narratives about the progress of civilisation and the state of the world. Broadly, cultivation came out well in these. The cut of the plough in the earth was a very mark of civilisational possibility; one could not cultivate the self unless someone, somewhere, was cultivating the ground, even if that was itself a boorish activity. Yet again, the classical world

---

[15] See the discussion in Sieferle. On Reimarus and Paley, see Foster, *Marx's ecology*, pp. 52, 86–7.
[16] Walsham, *Reformation of the landscape*, pp. 341–3; Charles F. Walker, *Shaky colonialism. The 1746 earthquake-tsunami in Lima, Peru, and its long aftermath* (Durham, NC: Duke University Press, 2008), pp. 22–3; John Wesley, *Some serious thoughts occasioned by the late earthquake at Lisbon* (Dublin, 1756); Maxine Van De Wetering, 'Moralizing in Puritan natural science. Mysteriousness in earthquake sermons', *Journal of the History of Ideas* 43 (1982), pp. 417–38.
[17] Thomas, *Man and the natural world*, pp. 165–72.

bequeathed a treasury of comment that was adapted, tested and employed ironically by renaissance scholars. Tacitus' *Germania* (c. 98 CE) provided a vivid contrast between the ordered and cultivated lands of the Roman Empire with the dangerous and murky forests beyond the frontier where the imperial army had repeatedly failed to enforce its writ. The conflation of the social and environmental order was equally long-established according to the medical traditions attributed to Hippocrates of Kos, where *Airs, waters, places* exercised direct effects on health and character. History could be narrated as the course of repeating or transcending such destinies inscribed in land and body.[18]

The stereotype of a civilised, light-bathed Mediterranean of field, city, vineyard and orchard in contrast to the glowering mass of northern trees could be and was inverted by reforming Germans such as Conrad Celtis and Ulrich von Hutten to acclaim the raw power of reformed ideals and comment ironically on their own election as the carriers of a divine knowledge.[19] By the later eighteenth century forest and field were not necessarily in opposition; Goethe, son of a forester, could embrace both the Grand Tour and the mighty teutonic oak. The glorification of the German forest received its visual apogee in Caspar David Friedrich's nationalist stand against French (and Latin) invasion in 1813, *Chasseur in the Forest*, and as is well-known, 'the forest' figured prominently in subsequent ethnographical interpretations of German identity.[20] Nevertheless, this was no simple story, as Friedrich could illustrate in his *Spruce Forest in Snow* of 1828, where the path into the dark woods is an ambiguous inheritance.[21] And as we have seen in Chapter 5, all woods were not alike. Increasingly after 1750, states sought to create the administered and even engineered forest, most of all in Central Europe. The interior state of the woods was itself a marker of progress towards the avowed goals of good *police* or the general happiness. Peasant grazing, old-fashioned selection felling of timber, failure to replant, all were signs of an ancient chaos still reigning in the woods. The traditional forest was now considered

---

[18] Schama, *Landscape and memory*, pp. 83–7; Arnold, *The problem of nature*, pp. 14–18.

[19] Schama, *Landscape and memory*, pp. 92–8.

[20] Schama, *Landscape and memory*, p. 106.

[21] Joseph Leo Koerner, *Caspar David Friedrich and the subject of landscape*, 2nd edition (London: Reaktion, 2009), pp. 181–2, 189–92.

'out of time', an 'anachronistic contemporaneity'.[22] Foresters schooled in the more liberal tenets of political economy, such as Hazzi who oversaw Bavaria's woods in the revolutionary era, saw common rights as vestiges of a backward feudal order. Such attitudes, where the term 'waste' acquired a pejorative meaning, had been articulated by opponents of the commons since the seventeenth century, and became the governing orthodoxy.[23] At best, common property was viewed as a 'stage' in historical development by which the land of the community had emerged from the forest, and which would be superseded by fully private, or state property. This understanding of European history would in turn find wide application in the interpretation of colonised societies and legitimation of colonial rule.[24] The landscape was a palimpsest of the logic of historical development, and its current state provided a key as to what should be done next.

Backwardness was the flip side to narratives of improvement, applied to recalcitrant groups who objected to enclosure and the schemes of foresters (see Chapter 3). During the Enlightenment the idea of backwardness came to be applied to entire nations, as stadial theories of history became prevalent, each stage strongly linked to the management of the land. Nowhere were these more forcefully articulated than among the circle of thinkers that developed in Naples. In the Italian south advocates of change were confronted with the evidence of past glories of Greek and Roman culture. Not only was the region manifestly poorer than regions to the north and more especially the maritime powers of north-west Europe, the landscape seemed diminished in productivity and population since the classical age. These thinkers lived among evidence that progressive stage theories of history, most famously associated with the Italian political thinker Giambattista Vico (1668–1744),[25] could be reversed; a land could *decline*, and this was marked by a decline in the land. Enlightened thinking could,

---

[22] Hölzl, *Umkämpfte Wälder*, pp. 47, 60.
[23] Hölzl, *Umkämpfte Wälder*, pp. 62–3; Marie-Danielle Demélas and Nadine Vivier, *Les propriétés collectives face aux attaques liberals (1750–1914). Europe occidentale et Amérique latine* (Rennes, 2003).
[24] For example, see Ravi Rajan, *Modernizing nature. Forestry and imperial eco-development 1800–1950* (Oxford: Oxford University Press, 2006).
[25] For a recent discussion of Vico's theory of history in the light of climate change, see Dipesh Chakrabarty, 'The climate of history. Four theses', *Critical Inquiry* 35 (2009), pp. 197–222.

however, set a territory back on a progressive course. To this end, the Neapolitan thinker and author of Italy's first substantial work on political economy in the 1750s, Antonio Genovesi, advocated a kind of internal colonisation of his own kingdom.[26] The notion of an internal frontier, an 'Indies' within, could be found all over Europe, and could include debates as to whether the qualities of the backward regions might actually be well-adapted to a particular climate and should thus be steered in a bespoke way towards improving projects, and not simply eradicated. Such was the case with proposals for spade-husbandry in the western Highlands that emanated from the manses and grand houses of the Scottish Lowlands, and well-proportioned edifices of Georgian Edinburgh and Glasgow, deftly analysed by Fredrik Albritton Jonsson.[27] We remember too that William Petty, who must have hearkened to debates about atomism and mechanism in a youthful sojourn in Paris, would cut his administrative teeth surveying and allotting Ireland among its improving colonial masters.

Among the most influential historians of Enlightenment Scotland was army chaplain and later professor Adam Ferguson, whose 1767 *Essay on the History of Civil Society* followed classical and renaissance models of essaying the possibility of progress through historical reflection.[28] His judgement on the qualities of the cosmopolitan metropolis and marked sympathy for the more communally orientated character he identified in the wild Gael of the Highlands made for a less starry-eyed view of progress than had been the case for many improvers and projectors. It also fitted the mien of the moment that Britain became enthralled with the gaelic romanticism of James MacPherson's Ossian poems. This 'northern time travel' represented a rather familiar, for the age, concatenation of the desire to modernise with a certain seduction exerted by the noble ways of old.[29] Progress was needed, but the new had to be built upon the greatest virtues of the old. Stages of development unfolded according to the *character* of a people that emerged in particular contexts, and to which future development must be adapted in order to transcend. These ideas were

---

[26] Barca, *Enclosing water*, pp. 16, 19.
[27] Jonsson, *Enlightenment's frontier*.
[28] For example, Niccolò Machaivelli, *Discourses on Livy* (Oxford: Oxford University Press, 2008 [1513]). See also Quentin Skinner, *Foundations of modern political thought, volume 1: The Renaissance* (Cambridge: Cambridge University Press, 1978).
[29] The phrase is from Jonsson, *Enlightenment's frontier*, p. 50.

absorbed readily in the faraway *palazzi* of Naples, where many works of the Scottish Enlightenment were translated by the 1780s, the publisher Giuseppe Galanti playing a major role.[30] Galanti would then undertake a major attempt to survey the condition and resources of the Kingdom of Naples from 1786 to 1794, and drew on historical justification for his arguments for reform, both asserting a major decline since Roman times, and that the cause for this decline had been the property relations introduced by barbarian invaders which now, in their ossified feudal form, must be swept away. Adam Smith provided a similar account of the economic consequences of the decline of Rome.[31] Yet we must be clear about the direction of causation. The dismal state of southern Italy was argued to be the *consequence* of a failed civilisation. Civilisation had not failed because of mismanagement of the land. This was entirely in line with most classical thinking, and how that was received in early modern times. Both Columella and Pliny explicitly rejected the idea that the barrenness of regions in the contemporary world could be explained by overtaxing the land in the past, although clearly they wrote with regard to some contemporaries, unknown to us, who held such a view.[32]

All these ideas however connected the condition of the land to particular steps on the ladder of progress, and civilisational fate was accordingly related to governance of nature. Ideas first given currency through the necessity to obtain particular resources, such as firewood or timber for shipping, were re-wrought to encompass a much broader view of the semiotics of nature: 'Natural history became... a means to investigate the past, and to predict the future, development of mankind.'[33] In writing influenced by physico-theology, one could draw on a putative planetary history. As in so much historical writing, on a more regional scale the exemplary case was Rome. The failure of imperial dominion, or indeed to maintain an initial 'conquest' of the 'Empire of

[30] Ferguson also published *The history of progress and termination of the Roman Republic* in 1783. John Robertson, *The case for the Enlightenment. Scotland and Naples 1680–1760* (Cambridge: Cambridge University Press, 2007), p. 398.

[31] Barca, *Enclosing water*, pp. 23–4; Robertson, *Case for the Enlightenment*, pp. 383–4; Smith, *Lectures on jurisprudence*, pp. 19–20.

[32] Columella, *On husbandry*, pp. 1, 47; this is erroneously reported, as far as I can see, in Teresa Kwiatkowska and Alan Holland, 'Dark is the world to thee. A historical perspective on environmental forewarnings', *Environment and History* 16 (2010), p. 469.

[33] Spary, *Utopia's garden*, p. 106.

Nature' that 'only exists through cares perpetually renovated', would result that 'every thing is restored to the absolute dominion of Nature', in the words of Buffon. 'Man, who can do nothing but by numbers, whose strength solely flows from union, whose only happiness consists in peace, is yet mad enough, by taking up arms, to create to himself misery, to effect his own ruin.'[34] Cupidity and strife had led to nature reasserting her empire over the glories that were once Rome.

Equally, as the notion became established that the fortunes of state could be related to resource availability, but such availability might be extended by ingenuity, trade and colonisation, thus an account of historical development could be provided that linked 'stages' of civilisation to particular challenges in the environment. One version was to divide the world into those peoples who were in some sense the victims of their climate (ripe for colonisation); and the few who were pressed by their climes to develop virtues which allowed them to escape such a destiny (colonisers).[35] Adam Smith, typically, imagined the process both as universal and a work of trial-and-error, a kind of truck and barter with nature that eventually led to the division of labour. Thus society passed through an assumed set of stages from hunter-gathering to pastoralism to agriculture and international commerce.

> But when a society becomes numerous they would find a difficulty in supporting themselves by herds and flocks. Then they would naturally turn themselves to the cultivation of land and the raising of such plants and trees as produced nourishment fit for them. They would observe that those seeds which fell on the dry bare *soil* or on the rocks seldom came to any thing, but that those[s] which entered the *soil* generally produced a plant and bore seed similar to that which was sown... And by this means they would gradually advance in to the age of agriculture. As society was farther improved, the severall arts, which at first would be exercised by each individual as far as was necessary for his welfare, would be seperated; some persons would cultivate

---

[34] Buffon, *NH*, II, p. 459.

[35] In his early work, Montesquieu argued that thinly peopled regions were not so because of their climate, but because 'savages' had an aversion to labour. Charles Louis de Secondat, Baron de Montesquieu, *Complete works, vol. 3 (Grandeur and Declension of the Roman Empire; A Dialogue between Sylla and Eucrates; Persian Letters)* (London: T. Evans & W. Davis, 1777 [1721]), Letter CCX.

one and others others, as they severally inclined. They would exchange with one an other what they produced more than was necessary for their support, and get in exchange for them the commodities they stood in need of and did not produce themselves... at last the age of commerce arises.[36]

This bore its own unquestioned assumptions. Why could pastoral peoples not develop a division of labour? Indeed, could sedentary agriculture and pastoralism not be seen as a division of labour in its own right (this appears to be true for many historical examples)? Here we also find the fate of Rome explained again, in that being placed next to the temptations of civilisation, population pressure on pasture led not to a 'natural' turn to cultivation but invasion, conquest and downfall.[37] Later, in Marx we find a similar account where the variety of natural products available will lead to a division of labour and commerce. However, where resources are not scarce, and the fertility of the land is high, people would remain indolent – a classic story to explain the 'backwardness' of the tropics.[38]

How different were all these providential and Enlightenment histories to that provided by Humphry Davy in his *Elements of Agricultural Chemistry*, as a lesson to be drawn for current and future generations:

the exportation of grain from a country, unless some articles capable of becoming manure are introduced in compensation, must ultimately tend to exhaust the soil. Some of the spots now desert sands in northern Africa, and Asia Minor, were anciently fertile. Sicily was the granary of Italy: and the quantity of corn carried off from it by the Romans, is probably a chief cause of its present sterility.[39]

Sterility and waste was not the consequence of civilisational collapse, but its cause. We have now assembled the means to explain how history could have taken this dismal turn.

---

[36] Smith, *Lectures on jurisprudence*, Friday 24 Dec. 1762.
[37] Smith, *Lectures on jurisprudence*, pp. 19–20.
[38] Karl Marx, *Capital. A critique of political economy*, vol. 1 (London: Penguin, 1976 [1867]), pp. 648–51.
[39] Davy, *Elements*, p. 321.

Collapse

In the middle of the 1780s, Thomas Jefferson, revolutionary polymath but not yet President of the United States, contemplated the course of tobacco farming, a staple activity of his native Virginia. Things were not looking good, and he identified two causes: climate change and soil exhaustion:

> its culture was fast declining at the commencement of this war...
> I suspect that the change in the temperature of our climate has
> become sensible to that plant... [I]t requires... indispensably an
> uncommon fertility of soil: and the price which it commands at
> market will not enable the planter to produce this by *manure*.
> Was the supply still to depend on Virginia and Maryland alone,
> as its culture becomes more difficult, the price would rise, so as
> to enable the planter to surmount those difficulties and to live.
> But the western country on the Missisipi, and the midlands of
> Georgia, having fresh and fertile lands in abundance, and a hotter
> sun, will be able to undersell these two states... It is a culture
> productive of infinite wretchedness. Those employed in it are
> in a continual state of exertion beyond the power of nature to
> support. Little food of any kind is raised by them; so that the
> men and animals on these farms are illy fed, and the earth is
> rapidly impoverished.[40]

Climate, soil, manure, character: through circulation, affinity and humours Jefferson connects them all. In our ecological age these interactions are, as we might say, 'perfectly natural' and self-evident. In the late eighteenth and early nineteenth century, this idea struck with a force of transformatory revelation. We cannot rehearse the emergence of this philosophy of nature, and its links with the 'romantic' sensibility in detail here. Yet it is another important piece in the puzzle; a context by which the possibility of failure in a part might lead to the collapse of the whole, and in every regard.

A *theoretical* connection of all things was no novelty in Western thought. Astrological theory or ideas of natural magic in medieval times and the Renaissance presupposed such possibilities, drawing in turn on

---

[40] Jefferson, *Works*, vol. 4, pp. 306–7.

classical Platonic thought.[41] The vastness of Creation, ranked against the deliberate placement of the most infinitesimal creature as its part, was testimony to divine power as argued by the naturalist Henry Baker in his modest little poem of 1717 about *The Universe, a Poem intended to restrain the Pride of Man*: 'Each hated toad, each crawling worm we see/ Is needful to the whole as well as he.'[42] During the Enlightenment such generalities began to acquire a more regimented form, and significantly so. The great Swedish botanist Linnaeus both famously compared the consort of plants to a marriage, and what we now call the food chain to the proper order of the cameralist state in the *Polity of Nature* of 1760: 'Thus we see Nature resemble a well regulated state in which every individual has his proper employment and subsistence, and a proper gradation of offices and officers is appointed to correct and restrain every detrimental excess.'[43] Just as the cameralist agenda for education created an exhaustive list of fields which the effective administrator should master, as we have seen in Chapters 4 and 5, so the expanding horizons of natural history drew in fields that we would now designate as chemistry, zoology, climate science, botany, geology – without having any generalised method for linking physiology and environment, a step that would only come a century later with the emergence of modern ecology. Many of the leading thinkers about nature of the late eighteenth century lined up alongside Linnaeus and the encyclopaedic volumes of natural history from Buffon, to proclaim the systematic interconnection of all things. The Genevan naturalist Charles Bonnet, for example, proclaimed in the mid-1760s how 'Everything in the world's edifice is systematic. Everything is in connection, in relation, in combination, and precise conjunction.'[44] For Bonnet, this was the expression of a continuous unfolding of the divine plan since the Creation, in which the germ of all subsequent life was given substance and imbued with powers of development. The most famous expression of such ideas came from the brothers Humboldt, who were able to combine this sensibility with the sublime experience of mountains, dashing (but purposeful) travel and the idea that communication with nature was an 'inner feeling'; in the words of Wilhelm

---

[41] See the summary in Charles G. Nauert, *Humanism and the culture of Renaissance Europe* (Cambridge: Cambridge University Press, 1995), esp. pp. 59–66.

[42] Cited in Thomas, *Man and the natural world*, p. 169.

[43] Cited in Schabas, *Natural origins*, p. 31.

[44] Reill, *Vitalizing nature*, p. 136.

describing one revelatory moment at St Jean de Luz on the Basque Coast in 1799, as 'though he were witness to the first acts of creation'. His more glamorous and garrulous brother did more than anyone to publicise such notions, especially through the *Ansichten der Natur* ('Views of nature'), and *Essai sur la géographie des plantes*, a milestone in ecological thought linking climate and botany in systemic fashion, drawing on his epic travels in the Americas and especially his ascent of the Equadorian volcano Chimborazo in 1802.[45]

Indeed, this proliferation of circulation and system was reiterated to the point of tedium. The Dutch Lutheran minister John Bruckner, a follower of Linnaeus, wrote in *Théorie du Système Animal* of 1767 (translated into English the very next year, he having already settled in Norwich), that nature was 'one continued web of life'.[46] For the botanist Georg Forster, who had travelled with Captain Cook and provided a model for Humboldt, his essay 'A look at the Whole of Nature' (1781) was also a critique of over-specialisation in the sciences. A little later in that decade, the cultural theorist Herder, more directly influenced by Buffon, breathed 'Nature is every where a living whole.'[47] Such mantras echoed through the nineteenth century. As we have seen, the statement of pieties did not necessarily mean such notions were made operational in any practical sense, even less that all elements of a system would act as *drivers* of change in all of the others. What this philosophical mood did help create was a receptivity to the possibility of mutual influence when evidence for unsustainable practice was presented. It made more plausible too the notion of a collective fate that was the product of systemic processes rather than providence. 'The whole of nature = an organization, therefore nothing in nature can arise that does not belong to this universal organism, or is subject to it; in short, nothing individual can exist in nature.' These were the words of Friedrich Wilhelm Schelling, born in the small German town

---

[45] Alexander von Humboldt and Aimé Bonpland, *Essay on the geography of plants* (1807) (translated by S. Romanowski; edited by S.T. Jackson with accompanying essays and supplementary material by S.T. Jackson and S. Romanowski) (Chicago, IL: University of Chicago Press, 2013); Alexander von Humboldt, *Ansichten der Nature mit wissenschaftlichen Erläuterungen* (Tubingen: Cotta, 1808); see Reill, *Vitalizing nature*, pp. 19–22.

[46] Cited in Donald Worster, *Nature's economy. A history of ecological ideas* (Cambridge: Cambridge University Press, 1977), p. 47.

[47] Reill, *Vitalizing nature*, p. 246; Glacken, *Traces on the Rhodian shore*, p. 542.

of Leonberg in 1775 and who went on to room with Hegel and the poet Hölderlin in Tübingen, developing his philosophy of nature in a series of books from 1797.[48] This was not just an argument that sought to bring humanity and nature into a single vision; it was a claim that natural history too was a work of the mind, thus suffusing its study with aesthetic and ethical considerations; the poet Novalis arguing that one should 'treat the history of [nature] as the history of humankind'.[49] The romantic philosophy of nature would be criticised as metaphysical hocus pocus (Liebig was certainly no fan) but contributed to a widespread sensibility that the inner soul and outer nature had an intertwined destiny, and made organic metaphors commonplace in literary and philosophical circles, just as vitalist theories of living matter peaked in popularity. This web of interconnection is itself yet to be subject to really detailed scrutiny, although it likely contributed to what would be a new century of mounting environmental anxiety. Nature was energising and elevating; but a nature mistreated was not just less resource-full for one's needs, but threatening to one's being.

One of the most important ways in which connection in the natural world had been imagined was through climate, both as determining force in human character, and a habitat for species, contrasting not just regions of the globe but local environments of upland and lowland, fen and drained land, and so on (see Chapter 3). Montesquieu was only the most famous of authors who wondered how climate might imbue human virtue or degeneracy, and it was this way of thinking that was the context for the fears of the Abbé Dubos, writing in Paris in 1714, that pollution from sewage or alum mines could cause degeneration through bad airs.[50] But if, as authors increasingly opined in that century, the climate might change, could it be altered to become more favourable for humans? The possibilities for the

---

[48] Reill, *Vitalizing nature*, p. 214.

[49] Novalis, or Georg Philipp Friedrich Freiherr von Hardenberg (1772–1810), was a mining official in Saxony as well as broadly trained in the natural sciences, a range of expertise not unlike that of the young Alexander von Humboldt. Joan Steigerwald, 'The cultural enframing of nature. Environmental histories during the early German romantic period', *Environment and History* 6 (2000), p. 459.

[50] Jean-Baptiste Fressoz, 'Losing the Earth knowingly. Six environmental grammars around 1800', in Clive Hamilton, Christoph Bonneuil and Francois Gemenne (eds), *The Anthropocene and the global environmental crisis* (Abingdon: Routledge, 2015), p. 72. Dubos also provided a theory of art derived from the effects of climate on physiology. Gaukroger, *The natural and the human*, p. 252.

transfer and acclimatisation of plants had already been a major theme among botanists since the sixteenth century, and were equally applied to animals and people.[51] Buffon had antagonised colonists, most famously Jefferson, by arguing that conditions in the New World had led to the degeneracy and shrinking of species. Throughout the nineteenth century American settlers believed that they had to become 'acclimated' as they moved west and south.[52] There would be a continuity with this line of thought into racialised theories of the later nineteenth and twentieth centuries, incorporating possibilities of climate change too, notably articulated by the Yale geographer Ellsworth Huntington.[53]

Climate change was at this time mainly associated with deforestation, giving a benign twist to a process that in some circumstances threatened scarcity. In his 1778 publication *Epoques de la nature*, Buffon had declared that, 'the entire face of the Earth now bears the imprint of man's power'. This had primarily been achieved through the extension of cultivation, a process perceived as a world-historical force as noted above. Indeed, it was suggested that it was precisely deforestation that had brought France to share the virtuous climate of Rome, making it ideal for civilisation. Previously achieved unconsciously, such civilising airs could now be achieved intentionally, humankind being able to 'alter the influence of its own climate, thus setting the temperature that suits it best'.[54] This added an extra gloss to the process of forest clearance and colonisation in

[51] Spary, *Utopia's garden*, pp. 103–4; Cooper, *Inventing the indigenous*. On Alexander von Humboldt's interest in this question of how 'plants are enmeshed in the moral and political history of humankind', see Steigerwald, 'Cultural enframing', pp. 472–81.

[52] Conevery Bolton Valencius, *Health of the country: How American settlers understood themselves and their land* (New York: Basic Books, 2002), pp. 22–34.

[53] Ellsworth Huntington, *The pulse of Asia. A journey through Asia illustrating the geographic basis of history* (Boston, MA: Archibald Constable & Co., 1907); Ellsworth Huntington, *Civilization and climate* (New Haven, CT: Yale University Press, 1915); see also James Beattie, *Empire and imperial anxiety. Health, science, art and conservation in South Asia and Australasia, 1800–1920* (Basingstoke: Palgrave Macmillan, 2011), pp. 59–60.

[54] Georges Louis Leclerc, Comte du Buffon, *Les époques de la nature* (Paris: Éditions du Muséum, 1962 [1778]); Moheau's *Recherches et considerations sur la population de la France* advanced a similar argument in regard to local climate's effects on health in the same year, as had Edward Gibbon in his history of Rome in 1776; Spary, *Utopia's garden*, pp. 120, 133; Fabien Locher and Jean-Baptiste Fressoz, 'Modernity's frail climate. A climate history of environmental reflexivity', *Critical Inquiry* 38 (2012), pp. 579–98; Foucault, *Security, territory, population*, pp. 22–3; Edward Gibbon, *The history of the decline and fall of the Roman empire*, vol. 1 (New York: Fred de Fau &

especially North America, where cultivation was argued to reduce the risks of disease, and induce rainfall in arid regions.[55] But anthropogenic environmental change was not entirely viewed in a favourable light. As we have seen in Jefferson's comments on tobacco, some colonial plantation crops were recognised to make high demands of the soil, including the commercially most important, sugar cane.[56] Caribbean islands such as Barbados and Guadeloupe became microcosms of the European wood shortage, with forests rapidly disappearing and ships bringing coal across the Atlantic, making for a convenient ballast. By the end of the seventeenth century planters had to tackle problems with soil erosion, a relative decline in yields that made manure a highly marketable commodity (introducing a peculiar kind of mixed farming by which different properties produced and consumed manure, rather than integrating them), and lack of fuel.[57]

None of these problems were new to Europe, of course, and they do not seem to have been seen as anything more than a localised problem of land management, especially when substitutes for disappearing local resources could be shipped in from elsewhere in these highly commercialised societies.[58] This may seem surprising with hindsight but may indicate both the lack of 'connected' thinking about the environment *avant le mot*, and also the greater propensity for ideas about Europe to be projected elsewhere, rather than vice versa. The role of the widespread belief in Western Europe that deforestation could affect climate, as well as cause shortages of vital resources, contributed to legislation on woodland reserves in Mauritius in 1769, and in Britain's newly acquired bounty of Caribbean islands after the Seven Years' War ended in 1763, as has been described meticulously by Richard Grove.[59] A further critique of the wastefulness of

---

[55] Valenicus, *Health of the country*, pp. 214–28.

Co., 1906 [1776]), pp. 165–6; an argument advanced by Sir John Sinclair in Britain, see Stoll, *Larding the lean earth*, p. 60.

[56] Laura Hollsten, 'Controlling nature and transforming landscapes in the early modern Caribbean', *Global Environment* 1 (2008), p. 88.

[57] Fredrik Albritton Jonsson, 'The natural history of improvement', in Philip J. Stern and Carl Wennerlind (eds), *Mercantilism reimagined. Political economy in early modern Britain and its empire* (Oxford, 2014), pp. 117–33; David Watts, *The West Indies. Patterns of development, culture and environmental change since 1492* (Cambridge: Cambridge University Press, 1987).

[58] Hollsten, 'Controlling nature', pp. 101–12.

[59] Grove also notes how for particular individuals, especially Pierre Poivre in Mauritius, encounters in Asia and with Asian thought compounded this belief. The argument

resources, and especially the soil, akin to that of Jefferson cited above, was developed in Brazil. Here the shifting frontier of cultivation was perceived to be a kind of resource-mining and wastefulness in regard to the future, a perception strongly influenced by the teaching of Italian naturalist Domenico Vandelli at the University of Portugal in Coimbra, attended at that time by many of Brazil's elite. That removing trees could lead to lands being 'sterile and without people' was being argued by the leader of Brazilian independence, José Bonifácio de Andrarda e Silva, as early as 1815 from the vantage point of Portugal.[60] On a much more localised scale the proximity of trees and hedgerows had been argued since the sixteenth century to affect field microclimates and in 1806 John Williams would make a case that the enclosure movement was also affecting the climate of England.[61]

From the 1790s the long-established narrative of wood shortage became combined in Alpine and Southern Europe with observations regarding flooding caused by the denudation of slopes (hardly a new phenomenon and one already commented on in medieval times) as well as climate anxieties.[62] This was, in part, because of a much more intensive focus by agrarian reformers on the landscape of forests and wastes over which common rights were enjoyed, and arguments for legislation to privatise such grounds.[63] Vandelli brought his experience of erosion from Italy to Portugal in the late 1780s. In France, the Chief Engineer responsible for bridges and highways in the mountainous *département* of Var in Provence, Antoine Fabre, was convinced that forest clearance in the Alps was leading to more severe flooding and published an influential work on the question in

was however being made in regard to the Holy Land as early as 1748. Grove, *Green imperialism*, pp. 124, 145–52, 156–7, 160–1, 184–6, 202, 220, 271, 304, 346, 357–8, 367; Carl Fraas, *Klima und Planzenwelt inder Zeit, ein Beitrag zur Geschichte beider* (Landshut: J.G. Wölfle, 1847), p. 28.

[60] Padua, '"Annihilating Natural Productions"'; José Augusto Padua, 'The theoretical foundations of environmental history', *Estudos Avançados* 68 (2010), p. 85; Alexander von Humboldt, *Personal narrative of travels to the equinoctial regions of the New Continent, 1797–1804* (London: Longman, Hurst, Rees, Orme & Brown, 1819), IV, p. 134.

[61] Fressoz, 'Losing the Earth', p. 584.

[62] Gabriella Corona, *Demani ed individualism agrario nel regno di Napoli 1780–1806* (Naples: Edizioni Scientifiche Italiane, 1995), p. 121; on the debated role of forests and climate in Germany, see Hölzl, *Umkämpfte Wälder*, p. 65.

[63] Demélas and Vivier, *Les propriétés collectives*.

1797. His namesake and compatriot Antoine Rauch was even more forthright in 1802, blaming flood, climate change and diminution of game on deforestation, and in traditional fashion (as we have seen in Chapter 2) castigating the excesses of the previous political regime as the prime cause. As so often, it was Alexander von Humboldt who pithily and memorably articulated – but did not invent – the danger in clearing the mountain slopes: 'men in every climate prepare at once two calamities for future generations – the want of fuel and the scarcity of water'.[64]

It was in France, where the theory of climatic influences was most developed, that such concerns also found most prominent political expression. The Interior minister penned a memorandum in 1821 on the possibility of climate change causing problems in the south of France, partly to be blamed on deforestation.[65] During the 'July Monarchy' of the 1830s, when France shifted back from a more absolutist to a more 'constitutional' regime there were continual debates over whether to keep the regulation that administrative authorisation was required for land clearance, introduced in 1803 to protect the forests. For some this turned on whether unhindered clearance caused environmental damage. On 27 February 1836, when a deputy submitted draft legislation proposing to scrap the government authorisation, the astronomer (and for many years a companion and correspondent of Alexander von Humboldt), François Arago replied listing the catastrophic consequences of land clearance, including cooling of the atmosphere, hailstones, flooding and so on; although a subsequent commission found that such claims could not be fully substantiated.[66] Boussingault, who we met in Chapter 7, considered whether agriculture and forestry could contribute to climate change and averred, drawing on Saussure 's observations of Lake Geneva having shrunk over 1,200 years and his own and Humboldt's travels in Latin America, that deforestation reduced the water cycling through the hydrological system, lessening the flows of streams and level of lakes. He cautiously

[64] Padua, '"Annihilating Natural Productions"'; Rajan, *Modernizing nature*, pp. 24–5, 27; Matteson, *Forests in revolutionary France*, pp. 163–5; on Surrell, a successor to this tradition writing in the 1840s, see Whited, *Forests and peasant politics*, pp. 56–7.
[65] Locher and Fressoz, 'Modernity's frail climate', pp. 579–80, 584–5; Foster, *Marx's ecology*, p. 126.
[66] Fressoz, 'Losing the Earth', p. 75; see also M. Becquerel, *des Climats et de l'influence qu'exercent les sols boisés et non boises* (Paris: Firmin Didot Frères, 1853), p. v.

refrained from attributing a precise cause to these effects, but as a leading scientific authority of the 1830s and 1840s helped to confirm the orthodoxy of such views and expectations.[67]

Yet all these views were also quite conventional in that their attribution of blame rested on a traditional moralising core: from the Brazilian frontier to the mountains of Southern Europe, to the forests of Germany, the problem was the covetous, the idle and the ignorant. These were not bad things happening to good people. Environmental destruction was a 'price of backwardness', as José Padua has noted, not a rebound on civilisation. Thus whether writers berated the arrogant squandering of resources, or from the mid-eighteenth century influenced by Rousseau and arcadian and edenic visions, expressed regret at the loss of a supposedly pristine (or indeed virgin) nature, solutions were still largely technical and rational. More development! Scientific forestry! Privatising the commons! Only slowly did the notion emerge that there could be a destructive logic built into the progress of civilisation itself. Such an idea came more easily to critics of the idea of 'civilisation', such as the rather idiosyncratic French socialist pioneer Charles Fourier (1772–1837) who castigated modern individualism as the source of deforestation and climate change in an essay penned in 1821 on 'The material deterioration of the planet', although not published until 1847.[68]

Dessicationist theory, arguing that stripping a land of vegetation led to a decline in rainfall, had moved into German forestry by the 1830s. It was in the 1836 edition of his classic textbook that Heinrich Cotta (see Chapter 5) introduced a list of areas that had been rendered arid by deforestation: the Volga and Don steppes, Sicily and Sardinia, Easter Island, Castile, Extramadura, Aragon and Granada, much of Persia, and parts of Chile (the latter drawn from a recent travelogue he had read). The list is instructive as a litany of vanished empires, and also in its prominence being placed at the opening of the book: warnings from history of a world without professional forestry.[69] Through the channels both of physicians primed in hydrological theory and German-trained foresters, such ideas became a staple of colonial forestry and environmental anxieties in the British Empire,

---

[67] Boussingault, *Rural economy*, pp. 673–90.
[68] Locher and Fressoz, 'Modernity's frail climate', pp. 586–7.
[69] Cotta, *Grundriß der Forstwissenschaft*, p. 2.

and by a more indigenous route, in the French Empire by the 1840s.[70] It was deforestation too that loomed as the major theme in the extraordinary work of Carl Fraas, agronomist and botanist, who took up a position in Athens whilst in his twenties and devoted himself to botanical study and a careful reading of ancient texts. Through comparison of these and contemporary findings he drew the conclusion that across the classical world, from Central Asia to Palestine, Egypt and North Africa, the retreat of forest and advance of 'steppe vegetation' led to gradual, imperceptible climate change which could be traced through the botanical record. Eventually in its wake came the demise of civilisation through 'exhausted lands, dessicated soils, disturbed climates, destroyed nature or leached-out races'.[71] A basic world-historical process was, for Fraas, a constant branching away from the old heartlands, migrants bearing with them a portmanteau of the species required for at least temporary success, leaving dessication behind. Fraas argued that writers such as Humboldt had underestimated the capacity of humans to cause climate change (a phenomenon still perceived as occurring on a local or regional, not global scale). Although writing this work up in 1846 after his return to Bavaria, Fraas was particularly preoccupied by the capacity of newly independent Greece to develop given the degraded state of its landscape.[72]

Yet the most profound critique of civilisation came from the study of the soil, because in that case there was no remedy; at least, not yet. Between the publication of his *Agricultural Chemistry* of 1840 and the appearance of the seventh edition of that book in 1862, Justus von Liebig was the most prominent advocate of this view. The totalising extent of the risk was related to his belief that:

> Nothing is for itself alone, but is always chained with one
> or more others, these again with others and so on, all bound
> together without beginning or end, so that succession of

---

[70] Grove, *Green imperialism*; Beattie, *Empire and imperial anxiety*; Rajan, *Modernizing nature*; Gregory A. Barton, *Empire forestry and the origins of environmentalism* (Cambridge: Cambridge University Press, 2002); Diana K. Davis, *Resurrecting the granary of Rome. Environmental history and French colonial expansion in North Africa* (Athens, OH: University of Ohio Press, 2007), pp. 74–9.

[71] 'ausgebrauchten Ländern, ausgesaugten Boden, gestörten Klima, zerstörter Natur oder zersetzter Race'. Fraas, *Klima und Pflanzenwelt*, pp. XIX, 5, 9–13, 22–3, 27–9, 40–3.

[72] Fraas, *Klima und Pflanzenwelt*, pp. 9, 59, 60–6.

phenomena, their arising and passing, is as a wave moving
in circulation. We consider Nature as one Whole, and all
phenomena cohering like the knots in a net of rope.[73]

In the light of *Naturphilosophie* (the details of which Liebig heartily
disliked, seeing them an inimical to good scientific practice) and the
concepts of the 'web of nature' highlighted above, we can see that
these views were in fact quite conventional. Liebig's work partly won
renown because it was so in tune with the times – despite the hearty
critique and ill-tempered debate that still raged around most topics.

Liebig thus did not limit his concerns to the leaching of previous soil nutrients and the wastefulness of the water closet. Just as
soil science revealed present dangers, it unfolded an entire interpretation of history, a sorry tale driven by the state of the sod (*Erdscholle*).
The Greek diaspora around the Mediterranean had been driven by
soil exhaustion at home. They had come to Italy and Latium, where
wise rulers had placed the woodlands under public oversight because
of their influence on the climate. But where once rose gardens and
splendid fields of cereals had once stood, now the ruins of the great
temple at Paestum were surrounded by a wasteland of meagre grass
and thistles. Loss of soil fertility in Rome had led to the downfall of the
free farmer, dependence on imports, and a once fine work ethic lost to
decadence and the dominance of an exploitative soldiery. 'What holds
together or splits asunder human society, and leads to the greatness
or disappearance of nations and states has been and always will be
the soil... a people arises and develops in relation to the fertility of
the land, and with its exhaustion, so it disappears.'[74] The same dismal
processes could be observed in the decline of Muslim Spain and now in
the contemporary United States.

[73] Liebig, *Die Chemie*, p. 87. These sentiments were in themselves quite typical of
the time. For an expression of them that stressed divine providence in ordering
the balance of circulation in the world, see James F.W. Johnston, 'The circulation
of matter', *Blackwood's Magazine* 73 (1853), pp. 550–60. The agricultural chemist
Johnston expressed these beliefs in a more prosaic context, as 'the entire economy of
vegetable and animal life, and all the changes experienced by dead matter, are parts
of one system – express, as it were, but one idea, the offspring of ONE MIND'. James
F.W. Johnston, *Catechism of agricultural chemistry and geology* (New York: William
Blackwood & Sons, 1845), p. 74.
[74] Liebig, *Die Chemie*, pp. 95–7, 102–3, 110.

Europe might seek to stave off its fate with the importation of guano from Peru, but with populations risen to an 'unnatural level', stores of guano would need to be discovered akin 'to the extent of the English coalfields'. Even the benefit of these inputs was being literally flushed away thanks to the invention of the water closet, all in all a process of 'self-annihilation'![75] In the mid-1840s Boussingault too was reflecting on this theme, and quoting Humphry Davy: 'The export-ation of grain from a country which receives nothing in exchange that can be turned into manure, must exhaust the soil in the long run', explaining the present sterility of the once breadbaskets of northern Africa, Asia Minor and Sicily.[76] Davy may have been influenced by the arguments of James Anderson, who in 1801 in his *Recreations in Agriculture* commented on the Mediterranean lands, running from Italy to Palestine through Egypt and across North Africa, 'which once swarmed with people and plenty... [are] now afflicted with irreme-diable sterility'.[77] Anderson was in fact staking a claim in the debate about populations ancient and modern, arguing that in the more agri-cultural societies of classical times labour inputs had been able to maintain the fertility of the land and intensify production (including recycling of manure), and thus supported far greater populations than modern times. Current ills were argued, in a rather Physiocratic vein, to be the result of favouring manufacturing industries. He argued a case against the assumptions of Malthus that returns to labour would diminish, and for the virtues of an agrarian society (see also Chapter 7).[78]

Davy and his successors focused explanations of imperial collapse upon chemistry. Rome had bled its colonies dry, and, as Boussingault observed, the reason for its greatness and downfall could be read in its very bones: 'Rome unquestionably contains in its catacombs quantities of phosphorus from all the countries of the earth.'[79] Liebig turned this striking image on its head with the contemporary imperial leader, industrial Britain, now to his mind

---

[75] Liebig, *Die Chemie*, pp. 120–5, 128–9.

[76] Boussingault, *Rural economy*, p. 490.

[77] James Anderson, *Recreations in agriculture, natural-history, arts and miscellaneous literature* (London: J. Wallis & R.H. Evans, 1799–1801), pp. 379–80.

[78] Anderson, *Recreations in agriculture*, pp. 368–78.

[79] Boussingault, *Rural economy*, pp. 223, 306, 490.

hanging like a vampire on Europe, plundering battlefields and ossuaries for bones to fertilise its fields. In a characteristically excoriating attack on the land he nevertheless loved and that lauded him, he raged:

> It is impossible to think that such a sinful intervention in the divine ordering of the world will remain without punishment, and the time will come perhaps earlier for England than for other countries, when for all its riches in gold, iron and coal it will not be able buy back a one-thousandth part of the conditions of life that for centuries its has so sinfully squandered.[80]

As Boussingault also noted, a soil was created in deep time, but could be carelessly and swiftly destroyed.[81] Liebig drew on arguments about the diminishing returns to labour from John Stuart Mill for later editions of the *Agricultural Chemistry*, suggesting that all the improvements of agriculture would, in the long run, be of no avail if one did not obey 'the law of replacement' (*Gesetz des Ersatzes*). It was as if society was living off its capital, he declared. Not industriousness but thrift was the cause of the increase of capital, and now losses were compounded by the flood of faecal waste borne away by sewers to the ocean.[82] In the 1850s, when Liebig moved to Bavaria, Fraas, who had been head of the Bavarian Agricultural Association since 1847, would overcome previous scepticism about the chemist's work to labour alongside him in developing research into agriculture, agricultural chemistry and the production of artificial fertilisers. Fraas wrote prolifically across these years, including *Bavaria rediviva! A contribution to the to the understanding of the downfall of peoples through soil exhaustion* in 1865.[83] Liebig, deeply embroiled and eventually disappointed in debates over the design of London's sewage system at the end of the 1850s, where he argued for the reclamation of night soil for the fields of England, would imperiously insert into the seventh edition of his opus magnus a quotation worth repeating: 'It is on the decision of the

---

[80] Liebig, *Die Chemie*, p. 133; see Brock, *Justus Liebig*, pp. vii, 94-101.

[81] Boussingault, *Rural economy*, p. 223.

[82] Liebig, *Die Chemie*, pp. 146-8, 150.

[83] Carl Fraas, *Bavaria rediviva! Ein Beitrag zur Lehre vom Völkeruntergang durch Bodenerschöpfung* (Munich: J.G. Cotta, 1865).

sewer question of the cities that the maintenance of the wealth and welfare of states and the progress of culture and civilization depends.'[84]

Repetition

By the 1840s the threat to society from self-generated environmental change had been clearly formulated across a number of fronts: climate change, resource exhaustion and perhaps most profoundly loss of soil fertility. There was a whole repertoire of anxiety available which one could more or less exhaustively mine for the dramaturgy of civilisational hubris. The soil represented the most fundamental conundrum because theorists suggested that even with best intentions, even armed with thrift and civilisation and industry, society faced an unyielding law of entropy. Even if the population ceased to grow. Even if farmers tended their land according to the very best practices. In the end, everything that had been achieved could leach away. These fears have been constant companions to debates about development, sometimes more insistent, sometimes less, ever since.

No one genius invented the dilemma of sustainability; nor do we even find the perennial head-scratcher of simultaneous invention, when a good idea's time really does seem to have come (as with the telescope, or rotary gearing for steam engines). There was no eureka moment, which is a partial explanation of why people came to find themselves debating in this domain without giving it a name, 'sustainability' in English being coined much, much later. But the lack of the force of revelation or singular invention may also explain why these discussions were not labelled with contemporary terms that do seem to have had a broad applicability in hindsight, like *Nachhaltigkeit*. They did not have that intuitive elasticity to contemporaries.

Like nearly all inventions, thinking about sustainability was a long time in coming, and many factors had to be in place before people were struck forcibly by the possibility of society undermining its environmental foundations (or at least being able to make public debate out of it, which is what we can see). This book has traced how some

---

[84] Liebig, *Die Chemie*, p. 153. On the background to the seventh edition, see Mark R. Finlay, 'The rehabilitation of an agricultural chemist. Justus von Liebig and the seventh edition', *Ambix* 38 (1991), pp. 155–66.

of these emerged: the conceptualisation of the polity (and the state that steered it) as a bounded unit that required an input of resources, whether acquired domestically or by trade; an understanding of soil fertility and the circulation of the wellsprings of organic life that was itself driven by a desire for improvement and higher yields; a range of preoccupations about limits, the idea itself being ancient but increasingly plausibly attached to essential resources; and also a critique of providential optimism, that virtuous intention would lead to virtuous outcomes. Sustainability was invented, not discovered. Like a steam engine or a painting by Titian, a new discursive field in science and politics was shaped by many micro-innovations and technologies, and often the bringing together of what were established and banal things in older domains. Yet unlike objects and machines, because it is a creation of many human minds, it is always a process of negotiation to find out to what we collectively might think it should refer.[85]

Arguably – and here we are stretching even this long history – the wider potential of the problem of 'sustainability' was realised only when a wider public began to subsume all of the natural world into one category, one that could be comprehended as being in advance or decline: 'the environment'. Then, and only in the three decades following the Second World War, could the threat be presented as of an all-encompassing magnitude and universally operative.[86] As so often, a neologism like 'the environment' could also make people think they had discovered something new, while assuming everything that had come before that seemed to fit into the new conception was just a half-glimpsed aspect of their new great truth, like the old parable of the blind men and the elephant. But the full meaning and resonance of a proposition remains of its time. People of the past were not thinking of sustainability and the environment like you or I, if even indeed we concur, which is why we can learn much by being put in conversation.

Yet I have proposed, and propose again, that as I have defined it sustainability appears in the first half of the nineteenth century. For some, it could be placed into an equation of soil 'richness' or the like, but for the historian, dealing with many perceptions, it can be seen as a

---

[85] In contrast to the argument in Grober, *Die Entdeckung der Nachhaltigkeit*.

[86] Paul Warde and Sverker Sörlin, 'Expertise for the future: the emergence of environmental prediction, c.1920–1970', in Jenny Andersson and Egle Rindzeviciute (eds), *The struggle for the long-term in transbnational science and politics. Forging the future* (New York: Routledge, 2015), pp. 36–62.

kind of problem field, an attractor of stories. It 'emerged from existing patterns of thought and practice... but was also open-ended, accepted the irremediable status of its central concerns, and resisted teleological patterns that sought to contain and resolve these concerns'.[87] In other words, even if one could find an end point by which one dilemma could be resolved (sustained-yield forestry, perhaps, or a closed system of nutrient-recycling, or more modest consumer demand, or population restraint), one could equally imagine another challenge, or even the likelihood of challenges unknown. One could of course take a different definition of sustainability – there are plenty to choose from, and nobody owns the word, even if some would like to – and tell a different story. It would, however, not obviate the stories told here; at least, not necessarily. There is place enough for many stories.[88]

From the 1840s people would, of course, find many new ways of imagining self-annihilation, not least bound up with recurrent anxieties about the effects of particular technologies. The scale and form of the scientific evidence that could be brought to bear would change enormously. Yet this is an appropriate point to bring this book towards its conclusion, for two reasons. First, we have reached the period where I argue that we find the basic parameters of sustainability thinking: the possibility of people, even inadvertently or 'virtuously', undermining the environmental conditions of their society, being quite widely articulated as a political and social problem. Thus while the substantive environmental risks would alter and indeed proliferate in the future, these were repetitions of the basic concept. Second, we have also reached the point where much modern environmental history begins, especially in the context of British imperial land management, the plantation monocultures of the Global South, and American and European conservation and preservation movements.

It is, nevertheless, instructive to connect the end point of this history to these 'future histories' more explicitly. I will do so in three regards. First, by tracing the reception of ideas about the soil in the United States in the period between the publication of the first edition of Liebig's *Agricultural Chemistry* in 1840 and that canonical text of

---

[87] I have found it helpful here to adapt points made about the discourse of dearth by Ayesha Mukherjee. Mukherjee, *Penury into plenty*, p. 21.

[88] William Cronon, 'A place for stories. Nature, history, and narrative', *Journal of American History* 78 (1992), pp. 1347–76.

American conservation, George Perkins Marsh's *Man and Nature*, published in 1864. Second, I will briefly survey the repetition of such ideas and fears of collapse in the context of the British Empire. Finally – although this is something of an excursus from our main theme – a consideration of the place of nature, and the possibility of environmental deterioration, in Marx's thought. This last theme will be taken first. It represents an excursus because it will be argued that 'environmental' considerations were not, in fact, very significant for him, and insofar as Marx was an enthusiast for Liebig, his views were entirely conventional. This seeks to be a corrective to scholars who have argued, using 'points… taken in isolation and at face value', that Marx showed particular prescience in this regard and his theories of exploitation applied also to nature. It also stands as a corrective to the idea that 'sustainability' as a concept belongs to any particular political ideology.[89]

Marx's debt to the classical economists hardly needs introduction, and he followed David Ricardo and, as we have seen, earlier thinkers in arguing both that the forces of nature were significant inputs into production, but were 'gifts'.[90] Indeed, he cited William Petty in stating 'labour is the father of material wealth, the earth is its mother', and endowed with Marx's own style, 'use values… are combinations of two elements, the material provided by nature, and labour'.[91] Yet these natural forces played no actual part in his theories of value, exploitation or economic development which rested on how value was incorporated in commodities and transmitted by exchange. 'Not an atom of matter enters into the objectivity of commodities as [exchange] values', he declared, swotting away 'the dull and tedious dispute played by nature in the formation of exchange-value'.[92] For Marx, means of production can only transmit value into the system of exchange if by doing so their own use-value is destroyed. 'If an instrument of production has

[89] The quote is from John Foster Bellamy's critique of Carolyn Merchant's characterisation of Marx, but could as well be applied to his own work, despite its many merits. Foster, *Marx's ecology*, p. 136.

[90] Schabas, *Natural origins*, p. 114; Marx, *Capital*, I, pp. 508–10, 751, 757.

[91] Marx, *Capital*, I, pp. 133–4, 138.

[92] Marx, *Capital*, I, p. 176; also III, p. 954. Marx also discussed this in comparing Adam Smith and the Physiocrats in *Grundrisse*, arguing that that latter had confused surplus value with the gift of the soil. Karl Marx, *Grundrisse. Foundations of a theory of political economy*, trans. Martin Nicolaus (London: Penguin, 1993), p. 329.

no value to lose, i.e. if it is not the product of human labour, it transfers no value to the product... This is true of all those means of production supplied by nature without human assistance, such as land, wind, water, metals in the form of ore, and timber in virgin forests.' It is quite clear then that nature played no part in Marx's core economic theories about value and exploitation, although he conceded that different natural conditions, such as the exhaustion of forests or mines, would require more labour inputs per unit of output.[93] He did, in a letter, but in none of his published works, express what we have seen to be a quite orthodox view about agriculture causing desertification leading to the decline of the Persian and Greek empires.[94]

Of course, Marx was a materialist, both philosophically from his early interest in Lucretius and Epicurus, and in building up his analysis of society from the satisfaction of its basic material needs.[95] He was also an avid reader of Liebig, and it was from Liebig that he drew the term 'metabolism' (*Stoffwechsel* – in German the term has less immediate biological resonance than in English) that has seen something of a renaissance as a socio-ecological metaphor in twenty-first-century analyses of a distinctly Marxist bent, especially as 'social metabolism'.[96] Marx's use of the term did not however necessarily relate to the flows of the natural world. He first used it within *Capital* as a way of describing the movement of goods between use- and exchange-values, and between exchange and final consumption.[97] Thus it was a comment on the different social relations with a commodity, not the material conditions which allowed the commodity to be produced. The significant lesson that Marx drew from Liebig was indeed that capitalist agriculture could destroy the soil, but we must pay very careful attention to the reasons he provides for this:

> Capitalist production collects the population together in great centres... it disturbs the metabolic interaction between man and the earth, i.e. it prevents the return to the soil of its constituent elements in the form of food and clothing; hence it hinders the

[93] Marx, *Capital*, I, pp. 287, 312; III, 369.
[94] Cited in Foster, *Marx's ecology*, p. 169.
[95] Foster, *Marx's ecology*, pp. 106, 116, passim.
[96] For example, Manuel González de Molina and Víctor M. Toledo, *The social metabolism. A socio-ecological theory of historical change* (Cham: Springer, 2014).
[97] Marx, *Capital*, I, p. 198.

operation of the eternal natural condition for the lasting fertility
of the soil.[98]

The reason for this 'metabolic rift' is the process of *urbanisation* which
prevents the nutrients contained in foods from being recycled back into
the soil, and is a lesson drawn from the sewage crisis that, as we can see,
Liebig wrote about in *Agricultural Chemistry* but that particularly preoccupied him at the end of the 1850s, being drawn into a debate about
the future development of London's sewers.[99] The risk is not the result of
property relations per se or a necessarily wanton regard for resources on
the part of capitalism; one could, certainly, suggest such disregard might
be more likely in age of footloose capital, but it is not an argument that
Marx makes.[100] One might equally enquire why one could not develop
a market in 'night soil' as James Anderson suggested (which had indeed
existed in early modern and medieval times), or why Marx did not
consider this. The truth is that far from exhibiting 'a deep concern for
issues of ecological limits and sustainability', Marx was not much preoccupied with these problems and thought that Liebig had adequately
explained what the issues were.[101] Negative evidence is, in a sense, the
fact that these brief paragraphs have already covered almost everything

[98] Marx, *Capital*, I, p. 637; he also states something very similar in III, p. 949, where
the use of 'social metabolism' is much closer to the attribution given it by scholars
today. Foster cites the same passage but fails to note clearly that *concentration of
population* is the crucial issue in this passage. Foster, *Marx's ecology*, pp. 155–6.

[99] Brock, *Justus von Liebig*, pp. 256–68.

[100] He did note a 'pulling-away of the natural ground from the foundations of every
industry, and this transfer of its conditions of production outside itself, into a general context – hence the transformation of what was previously superfluous into
what is necessary, as a historically created necessity – is the tendency of capital'. In
agriculture this requirement for external inputs and investments was exemplified by
guano, but he draws no ecological conclusions from this fact. Marx, *Grundrisse*,
pp. 527, 734.

[101] Marx, *Capital*, III, p. 878. Indeed, Marx actually wrote relatively little about Liebig.
The most sustained direct engagement with Liebig, who Marx much admired,
actually came in a twist typical of Marx in a long footnote contrasting Liebig's
'immortal merits' some of his 'gross errors' in drawing too much on John Stuart Mill
in discussing diminishing returns in the seventh edition of the *Agricultural chemistry*.
Marx, *Capital*, I, pp. 638–9. Both Marx and especially Engels were prone to express
both the desire and likelihood for a unification of the natural and human sciences (as
we would call them) – one of those things that is always easier to say than achieve.
See Friedrich Engels, *Dialectics of nature* (London: Lawrence & Wishart, 1940);
Raymond Williams, *Problems in materialism and culture* (London: Verso, 1980),
esp. p. 100.

that Marx had to say on the matter in the compendious three volumes of *Capital*, a work in which he was never inclined to spend less time on an issue than it warranted. In the extended discussion of rent in Part 6 of Volume III, Marx was not at all concerned about the *direct* impact of capitalist agriculture on the land. On the contrary, as the prospect of artificial chemical fertilisers became ever more realistic (an area of business Liebig had got into early, without success and causing some damage to his reputation), Marx was rather inclined to argue that in distinction to the rapid redundancy of machinery and the spatial limitations on its application: 'The earth, on the contrary, continuously improves, as long as it is treated correctly.' It was peasant agriculture that was most likely to cause exhaustion because of lack of investment.[102]

Our diversion into Marx demonstrates how Liebig's ideas could be absorbed into the stock of knowledge without necessarily significantly reconfiguring it. The invention of sustainability did not change everything, and not all evocations of ideas we now connect with sustainability were, in fact, about sustainability. Between the 1840s and the 1860s the immediate threat of wood shortage remained more prominent than the soil in European discourses of environmental anxiety, and indeed this fear was exported through networks of imperial management out from its European heartlands. Richard Grove, Ravi Rajan and Gregory Barton have, among others, followed this trail to the Caribbean and South Asia, not least following in the footsteps of German foresters employed by the British Crown.[103] In Germany, the height of the 'forest wars' in the early 1840s, entangled with debates about the threat of 'pauperism', were the subject of some of Marx's own earliest political journalism.[104] In the colonies argument for the regulation of forests and retention of reserves took on new justifications, sometimes linked with the climatological and hydrological theories we have seen above, but also to anxieties about the salubriousness of tropical environments for European colonisers.[105]

---

[102] Marx drew the implication that there may be a long-run higher rate of return in capital invested in agriculture because earlier investments were never lost, a rather peculiar argument which seems out of line with what he argues elsewhere and is not developed. Volume III was, of course, assembled posthumously. Marx, *Capital*, III, pp. 916, 943.

[103] See note 68.

[104] Warde, 'Fear of wood shortage'.

[105] Beattie, *Empire and imperial anxiety*, pp. 4, 32, 51, 135, passim.

The eucalyptus trees promoted by the German-born Ferdinand von Mueller ('Baron Blue Gum') in Victoria, Australia, who assisted the diffusion of the species to southern Africa, India and California with huge environmental impacts, was argued as much as a remedy against malaria (mosquitoes not yet being identified as the vector, although it was associated with swampy ground) as for supplies of timber.[106]

Importantly, however, these particular anxieties, to which technical expertise and the need to restrain profligate locals was often presented as a remedy, also became incorporated into a wider lament about the tendencies of *civilisation*. 'Let us hope that the times are past for ever when the progress of civilization was equal to the wasting and desolating the surrounding nature', stated the forester Richard Schomburgk, who worked in Adelaide and also observed deforestation and soil erosion in New Zealand. There was still hope for the future: but history, as we have seen, had become for some a path punctuated by environmental destruction and collapse. Indeed, it made what seemed the repeated evidence of civilisational failure comprehensible: 'let us hope that future generations will be wiser than the past ones'. Much of this line of thinking was shaped by the extraordinary success of the writings of Alexander von Humboldt, who indeed Schomburgk had met.[107]

Such self-critical views were nevertheless very far from universal, and, as ever, colonialists were often adept at hearing the message that suited them best, rather than perusing the literature for the most convincing argument that they then applied to their own circumstances. In Algeria, invaded by France in 1830 and subject to systematic efforts to dispossess the native population and install colonists from the mid-1840s, the example of Rome was not presented as overshoot and hubris, but as an exemplar of what could be: a return to an imperial Eden, and hence justification for expropriation. The largely evidence-free allegation that the Maghreb had been ruined by deforestation and desertification was, in this context, blamed on Arab pastoralists that a new Latin Empire might redeem, and as with British colonies, boosters for the eucalyptus in Algeria were especially enthusiastic promoters of this environmental fable, framing their own efforts as its *denouement*. The possibility of unsustainable practice could thus become a

---

[106] Beattie, *Empire and imperial anxiety*, pp. 52, 117, 119.
[107] Beattie, *Empire and imperial anxiety*, pp. 142-3.

foundational myth for 'crisis disciplines' in forestry and agronomy that rode to the rescue in a variety of different contexts.[108] Nevertheless, the widely read francophone work on deforestation and climate change by Bequerel published in 1853 set forth a similar list to Carl Fraas (see above) of the dessicated and abandoned cradles of civilisation, from the Ganges to the Euphrates, from Nineveh and Babylon to Baalbek and Palmyra. In the land of milk and honey, Canaan, was heard only 'the silence of death'. 'The progress of civilization and wars are the principal causes of deforestation', Bequerel averred, and 'In Greece, as in Persia, the most flourishing cities disappear when the environing lands become deforested.'[109]

On another frontier (from the perspective of Europeans) the question of soil became an important part of 'critical reflection on the non-human world and the impact of human society on that world'.[110] This place was the Russian steppes, where shifting cultivation for new settlers and the export market expanded rapidly from the 1840s. The supposedly inferior condition of these lands had already been blamed on Tartar rule by Catherine the Great, following the typical narrative of waste and backwardness, and the argument that the steppes had once been forested was not put to bed until the 1860s.[111] Certainly the woodlands that had been present were diminished, and as in Western Europe, and drawing on Western literature, this was linked to climate and collapse: the governor of Orenburg reported in 1835 how 'the very climate has noticeably changed, the fertility of the soil is gradually declining', a complaint frequently found alongside that of soil erosion in forestry journals of the time.[112] Liebig's *Agricultural Chemistry* was translated under the aegis of the Russian state in 1842 and rapidly disseminated in the 1860s and 1870s, where it helped shape discussions of soil exhaustion.[113] During the 1880s this problem would be associated with the possibility of civilisational collapse due

---

[108] Davis, *Resurrecting the granary*, p. 61 passim; and her recent Diana K. Davis, *The arid lands. History, power, knowledge* (Cambridge, MA: MIT Press, 2016); on the response in Swedish agronomy, see Mårald, *Jordens kretslop*, esp. p. 6.

[109] Bequerel, *Des climats*, pp. ii–iii.

[110] David Moon, *The plough that broke the steppes. Agriculture and environment on Russia's grasslands, 1700–1914* (Oxford: Oxford University Press, 2013), p. 1.

[111] Moon, *The plough that broke the steppes*, pp. 45, 61, 76, 80, 99–102, 106.

[112] Moon, *The plough that broke the steppes*, pp. 109, 119, 122–3.

[113] Moon, *The plough that broke the steppes*, p. 161.

to desertification, where Turkestan presented the historical exemplar, as north Roman and post-Roman Africa did in the west and Latin America, 'once a flourishing, well populated country' and centre of culture, gone to rack and ruin. Sand drift and dust storms made these associations particularly vivid.[114]

Davy, Liebig and the French chemist Chaptal received extensive attention on the other side of the Atlantic, where since the late eighteenth century there had been a ready market for European and especially British books on husbandry.[115] Liebig's work was rapidly pirated and sold cheaply, and contributed to what Margaret Rossiter called a 'craze' for soil analysis between 1844 and the early 1850s.[116] Travellers to Europe such as Jefferson were also careful observers, and comparisons between the Old and New World constituted a minor genre in its own right. Conditions for the colonists were, however, rather different, both because of the constant expansion of cultivation (although expansion of the tilled area was still going on in Western Europe), and because for a long time cultivation in some areas concentrated on highly fertile lands.[117] Jefferson had noted in 1793 that '*Manure* does not enter into [a good farm], because we can buy an acre of new land cheaper than we can *manure* an old one… I can affirm, that the James river low-grounds, with the cultivation of small grain, will never be exhausted.'[118] Where land was cheap and labour expensive, the incentives pointed towards frontier expansion rather than intensification and melioration of tired land, a process already described in the 1690s.[119] Nevertheless, as we have seen above, the process also generated unease, especially in the case of particularly demanding cash

---

[114] The philosopher Vladimir Solov'ev, cited in Moon, *The plough that broke the steppes*, p. 91. However, by this time leading soil scientists and developments in climate science had shifted opinion away from dessication theories of climate change due to deforestation, especially in Russia. Moon, *The plough that broke the steppes*, pp. 132–3, 139–148; Padua, 'Theoretical foundations', pp. 85–6.

[115] Benjamin Cohen has noted how this work was anything but passively received, and had precursors to these classics. Cohen, *Notes from the ground*, pp. 3, 6, 32–5, 115.

[116] Cohen, *Notes from the ground*, p. 86; Rossiter, *Emergence*, pp. 9–10, 29, 88, 102–3, 109–24.

[117] For a micro-level study of this process, see Brian Donahue, *The great meadow. Farmers and the land in colonial Concord* (New Haven, CT: Yale University Press, 2004).

[118] Jefferson, *Works*, vol. 7, 28 Jun. 1793.

[119] John Clayton, 'Mr. John Clayton, Rector of Crofton at Wake-Field, his letter to the Royal Society, giving a farther account of the soil, and other observables of Virginia', *Philosophical Transactions* 17 (1693), pp. 970–88.

crops like tobacco (a mantle taken up in the nineteenth century by cotton). The diminution of the crop by the loss of humus was already a theme articulated from the 1810s, by reformers such as the New York editor Jesse Buel or the Senator John Taylor.[120] Buel had thoroughly absorbed the European theories that 'The natural elements and agents of fertility in the soil, are organic matters, which constitute the food of farmcrops.' He dedicated the opening chapters of his main work to care of soil and provision of crop nutrients, as a critique of an attitude where 'we have regarded the soil as a kind of mother, expecting her always to give, give, without regarding her ability to give'.[121] As early as 1814 Taylor spoke of a 'rapid impoverishment of the soil of the United States'. Taylor blamed in part protectionist policies that favoured industry, a Physiocratic theme that would be a repeated source of tension between northern and southern states, and in debates about the soil, as we will see.[122] By the middle decades of the nineteenth century, the critique of poor soil management was frequently bound together with attacks on slavery that was argued to breed an inattention to good husbandry, an exploitative stance towards nature as much as to the fettered workforce. The New York legislature contrasted the relative growth of their own state to that of Jefferson's Virginia, once the most populous heart of the Union, between 1790 (the date for the first US census) and 1840, arguing that slavery 'degrades labour, paralyses industry, represses enterprise, exhausts the soil, perpetuates ignorance, and impoverishes the people'.[123] Proponents of slavery like

---

[120] Stoll, *Larding the lean earth*, pp. 17, 20, 32–4, 45, 68, 89–90, 131, 137, 144. The founding fathers continued, as with Jefferson, to express an interest in such issues, such as James Madison's speech to the agricultural society of Abermale in Virginia in 1818, linking the circulation of gases through animals, plants and the atmosphere, their mutual dependence, and problems of declining soil fertility; pp. 38–9. See also Cohen, *Notes from the ground*, pp. 37, 42, 127–8, 137–9.

[121] Jesse Buel, *The farmer's Companion, or essays on the principles and practice of American Husbandry* (Boston, MA: Marsh, Capen, Lyon & Webb, 1839). On plant nutrition, p. 54 passim. On the necessity of balance between animals and crops, see pp. 60–1. On soil as mother, p. 20.

[122] John Taylor, *Arator. Being a series of agricultural essays practical and political* (Georgetown, MD: J.M. Carter, 1814), pp. 12, 16–56.

[123] James F.W. Johnson, *Notes on North America. Agricultural, economical and social*, vol. II (Boston, MA: W. Blackwood, 1851), pp. 352–3. It should be noted that while Johnson had a lot to say about soil, it is only once and in this regard he considers soil exhaustion, generally arguing that soil fertility was a limiting factor in local development and thereby played a role in shaping the character of the people.

the enthusiastic agrarian writer Edward Ruffin (who is supposed to have personally fired the first shot of the Civil War in 1861) argued in turn that good soil husbandry was essential to preserve the slave economy of the South.[124]

Thus in the United States the question of soil fertility was bound up with movements of population westwards, a sense of declining yields after the first settlement, and increasingly arguments over free trade and tariffs as protectionist policies appeared to have consequences for the relative experience of the agricultural and industrial sector, strongly influencing demand for crops such as wheat and cotton.[125] The rapid reception of Liebig's work in the 1840s related his theories of circulation to arguments about the wisdom of an export industry that might exhaust the soil, and lead to emigration to the 'Great West'. A series of lectures and publications relating to the agriculture of New York State around 1849, for example, made precisely this point from a foundation in agricultural chemistry; in the same year so too did a report from the Agricultural Section of the Patent Office, which thundered 'nothing is more certain than the fact, that a District and State which exports largely the things which Nature demands to form breadstuffs and provisions, must sooner or later export also some of its consumers of bread and meat'.[126]

These arguments were adopted by, among others, Erasmus Peshine Smith, a Rochester-based lawyer and lecturer in mathematics who took up various public offices from 1849 and later went on to play a leading role in the Japanese government during the 1870s. In his *Manual of political economy* of 1853 he sought to develop a theory which rested first and foremost on the underlying dynamics of the forces of nature, most especially 'the law of endless circulation of nature and force' (a precursor, along with anxieties about entropy, to the second law of thermodynamics which would later become

---

[124] Cohen, *Notes from the ground*, pp. 85–94, 110–14; Edward Ruffin, 'An address on the opposite results of exhausting and fertilizing systems of agriculture' (1852), in Edwin C. Hagenstein, Sara M. Gregg and Brian Donahue, *American Georgics. Writings on farming, culture and the land* (New Haven, CT: Yale University Press), pp. 98–103; Stoll, *Larding the lean earth*, pp. 150–5.

[125] See Henry C. Carey, *The prospect agricultural, manufacturing, commercial and financial at the opening of the year 1851* (Philadelphia, PA: J.S. Skinner, 1851); Stoll, *Larding the lean earth*, pp. 23, 35, 76–7, 118–20, 147–9, 200.

[126] E. Peshine Smith, *A manual of political economy* (New York: G.P. Putnam & Son, 1853), pp. 86–7.

formalised in energetic terms). Smith presented a somewhat garbled account of plant nutrition, which was considered the basis of all life as only vegetation could assimilate inorganic elements (an observation derived from Liebig) while extraordinarily also suggesting that the main source of such elements was fixing from the atmosphere, citing the ancient and long-contradicted experiment of Van Helmont on the matter.[127] He quoted extensively from the 1849 lectures of John Pitkin Norton, the young holder of the chair of agricultural chemistry at Yale who would publish them in book form a year later as *Elements of Scientific Agriculture*, soon dying at the young age of 30 in 1852:

> We may follow any particular substance in its course from the inanimate soil to the living plant, from the plant to the living and conscious animal, and finally see it return to the soil once more. In all its changes it remains the same in its nature, but is constantly presented to us in new forms. There is an endless chain of circulation from the earth up through the plant to the animal, and then again back to the parent earth... The animals or plant dies, and also after a time disappears, but in the decay every particle furnishes food for a new series of living things.[128]

Smith combined these views not into an affirmation but a *critique* of Malthusian limits, arguing that while the exportation of organic matter was leading to 'the impoverishment of their territory, and the diminution of its power to sustain human life' by adhering to recycling by which the quantity of vital matter in circulation was maintained in each cycle, output could even be increased 'with that large interest, derived by the elements furnished from the atmosphere'. This model of natural capital was placed in direct opposition to Malthus, Ricardo, Mill and others of the 'Manchester School' who insisted on the diminishing marginal productivity of the land and labour, especially as cultivation was

[127] Smith, *Manual of political economy*, pp. 22–30.
[128] The lectures were developed by Norton at Yale where he began teaching in 1847. Norton had written the introduction to the American edition of Johnston's *Catechism of agricultural chemistry* in 1845. He was highly critical of Liebig on many points of detail. Smith, *Manual of political economy*, p. 33; John Pitkin Norton, *Elements of scientific agriculture* (Albany, NY: E.H. Pease & Co., 1850); Rossiter, *Emergence*, pp. 113, 116–17, 124.

supposed by them to move from the richest soils to more marginal ones as population grew.[129]

These arguments were taken up in turn by Smith's friend Henry C. Carey, vocal advocate for protectionism for America who duelled with John Stuart Mill over the question from the late 1840s. In his early work Carey had largely seen trade through its effects on incomes and the labour market, also arguing against the export of bulky raw materials because the higher costs of transport incurred seemed to him absurd. Carey, contra Ricardo, argued that cultivation tended to begin on poorer soils and move towards the richer.[130] His argument was especially directed against particular property arrangements and the British imperial system which helped drive the 'exhaustion' of soils by the separation of consumer and producer. The farmers of Ohio and lands to the west were denuding their land of manure through export: 'They borrow from the earth, and they do not repay: and therefore it is that they find an empty exchequer'; not so much through the loss of vital matter abroad, as the direct and indirect losses incurred through the costs of his great bugbear, transport: 'wasting on the road the manure yielded by the oxen and horses employed in the work of transportation'.[131] The ability of the British to undersell American producers of manufactured goods, argued Carey, diminished the spending power of American workers and deprived eastern farmers of their markets. It was this problem that tempted them to sell up, and drove them to the cheap lands of the west. In turn, this resulted in farming across the nation producing lower yields than if agriculture and manufacturing could be concentrated in one place, stimulating investment in the land, as he already saw happening on the coalfields of Pennsylvania.

It was only later, under the influence of Erasmus Peshine Smith, whom he quoted verbatim at length in his more famous *Principles of Social Science*, that Carey would provide a more scientifically grounded theory of soil exhaustion derived from Liebig, arguing that the iniquities of export were also that America was squandering its

---

[129] Smith, *Manual of political economy*, pp. 34–7.

[130] Carey, *The prospect*, pp. 73–4 passim; Henry C. Carey, *The past, the present and the future* (Philadelphia, PA: Carey & Hart, 1848), p. 430.

[131] Carey, *The past*, pp. 430–1, 433, 438, 462–3; On Carey's anti-Britishness, built on the experiences of his Irish patriot father, see the otherwise highly anachronistic reading of Carey in Michael Perelman, 'Henry Carey's ecological economics', *Organization & Environment* 12 (1999), pp. 281–4.

reserves of soil fertility.[132] He also drew upon the German biologist Matthias Schleiden, who used Liebig and Boussingault's views of circulatory processes in his own physiological studies, and the 1855 lecture of the young George Waring, an agricultural chemist who succinctly formulated the problem of loss of fertility to the cities. At the end of his short quantitative survey of American agriculture, Waring attempted an estimate of the loss of soil minerals through export to urban populations, thundering against the unaccounted 'earth butchery' by which the country would grow 'feeble from this loss of its life-blood; but the hour is fixed when, if our present system shall continue, the last throb of the nation's heart shall have ceased, and when America, Greece and Rome shall stand together among the ruins of the past'. Following a trajectory suggested in Liebig's own work, Waring would later become a major sanitarian and played a major role in the development of effective sewage and drainage systems for New York City and Memphis.[133]

Waring would later be cited, via Carey, by no less an authority than Liebig himself. Thus was knowledge circulated and recycled. And no less important, as it emerged in new political contexts, the shape and significance of the arguments changed, even when delivered by the same authors. The manure-based nutrient-recycling theory emerging from eighteenth-century European though had provided the 'scientific' basis for arguments from Carey and others, although by the mid-nineteenth century this was only one strand in the repertoire of environmental anxiety. It was largely theorists of the soil who had anchored these ideas in a form of political economy, while political economy was increasingly engaging with stadial theories of history. This in turn provided the possibility (with variants focusing to a greater or lesser degree on deforestation) of a soil-based

---

[132] Henry C. Carey, *The principles of social science* (Philadelphia, PA: J.J. Lippincott & Co., 1858), pp. 67–8.

[133] Schleiden co-developed cell theory in the 1830s. On Matthias Jacob Schleiden's interest in questions of circulation and the 'law of the minimum', see *Die Pflanze und ihr Leben. Populäre Vorträge* (Leipzig: Vieweg, 1850), pp. 210, 221–31; John Bellamy Foster, '"Robbing the Earth of its capital stock". An introduction to George Waring's *Agricultural Features of the Census of the United States for 1850*', *Organization & Environment* 12 (1999), pp. 293–7; George Waring, 'Agricultural features of the Census of the United States for 1850', *Organization & Environment* 12 (1999), pp. 305–7.

theory of the rise and decline of civilisation, concerns that seemed especially pertinent on the colonial frontier whether proximate to Europe in the Mediterranean, in the Americas, or elsewhere. Such accounts of decline and fall, and the apparent immediacy a crisis of American farmers leaching west, gave saliency to the theoretical positions on sustainability adopted by those studying the soil, although the theories have moved on from their eighteenth-century origins. In turn, of course, theories of soil exhaustion gave a patina of solid scientific authority to the political positions presented in American debates, and not least, to the politicians themselves.

No works exemplify this history better than those of Liebig himself, who (whether happily or not for those who have to read them) produced numerous, regularly updated editions of his thoughts on these matters. We have previously seen that Liebig adapted and refined his arguments as critical commentary was unleashed, and new information became available. Already in 1842 the new edition of *Agricultural Chemistry* was less trenchantly focused on nitrogen. Liebig's increasing caution about the centrality of nitrogen to plant growth actually led to him removing the problem of its dissipation to the city and hence into the sewers altogether in another substantially revised edition of 1843, although he continued to argue that English fields were subject to exhaustion in a letter to the prime minister Robert Peel.[134] But engagement with American debates would see the argument come roaring back, with a Malthusian fear of overpopulation sharpened by seeing the wretched conditions of post-famine Ireland in a visit of 1851.[135] The rapidly rising importation of guano was taken as confirmation of his ideas across the years 1856–8, as he corresponded with Carey and continued to read voraciously. By the time he published his *Letters of modern agriculture* of 1859, a more readable digest of his ideas in this field, Liebig was sketching more clearly the theory of history finally delivered in the seventh edition of *Agricultural Chemistry* of 1862. He imperiously defined the agriculture that did not adhere to his system of recycling as 'a system of spoliation' that he identified above all on the east coast of America, where parts of the east coast were allegedly

[134] Justus Liebig, *Chemistry in its application to agricultural and physiology* (Cambridge: John Owen, 1842); also Rossiter, *Emergence*, pp. 40–3; Brock, *Justus Liebig*, pp. 121–2.

[135] Brock, *Justus Liebig*, pp. 108–9.

'turned into deserts', in Brazil, and in a less manifest form, even as the destiny of English high farming, and delivered a full-blooded and excoriating chapter on how Rome was fatally weakened by mismanagement of the land. The remedy, he declared, would require an intervention akin to the forest ordinances of Germany that had developed over previous centuries: the rational response to 'The dangers threatening the state and society from the wanton spoliation.'[136] Because, in the end, sustainability was an issue that always had been attached to state and society, and visions of what that should be.

[136] Liebig, *Letters*, pp. 179–82, 188, 196.

CONCLUSION: ENDS AND BEGINNINGS

In June 1955, 72 men and one woman gathered at the Princeton Inn, amid the genteel lots and smart lawns of Princeton, New Jersey, to discuss 'Man's role in changing the face of the Earth'. It was a landmark interdisciplinary conference on assessing environmental change. This was held in the wake of a flurry of doomsaying books that emerged after the war, their critique of man's [*sic*] destructiveness sharpened by that conflagration: William Vogt's *The road to survival*, Fairfield Osborn's *Our plundered planet*, Harrison Brown's *The shadow of man's future*, and posthumously, Aldo Leopold's classic *Sand County almanac*. One could also pick up the reissue of Paul Sears's *Deserts on the march*, first written amid the dust bowls of the 1930s that had inspired works such as Whyte and Clark's *The rape of the earth* and Lowdermilk's *Conquest of the land through seven thousand years*, who surveyed 'the graveyard of empires' in much the same way as had Fraas and Bequerel a century previously, and warned of 'danger signs in America'.[1] In many ways, these post-war years saw the emergence of a new environmentalism, one that self-consciously employed

---

[1] William L. Thomas (ed.), *Man's role in changing the face of the Earth* (Chicago, IL: University of Chicago Press, 1956); Paul B. Sears, *Deserts on the march* (Norman, OK: University of Oklahoma Press, 1947 [1935]); Osborn, *Our plundered planet*; William Vogt, *Road to survival* (London: Gollancz, 1948); W.C. Lowdermilk, *Conquest of the land through seven thousand years*, USDA report, Aug. 1953; G.V. Whyte and R.O. Jacks, *The rape of the earth. A world survey of soil erosion* (London: Faber & Faber, 1939); Aldo Leopold, *A Sand County almanac. Sketches here and there* (Oxford: Oxford University Press, 1949).

the term 'the environment' and sought to save it from destruction. It marked a beginning, but was equally the culmination of developments in ecological understanding and new techniques for measuring and imagining the world over the previous decades. This was recognised by the conference organisers. The opening address evoked honoured precursors to the endeavours at the conference, including the Russian soil scientist Voeikov (see Chapter 8). But the presiding saint was George Perkins Marsh, one-time senator for Vermont, ambassador to the Ottoman court and Italy, and author of *Man and nature, or physical geography as modified by human action* of 1864, undoubtedly the canonical text of American conservationism up until the publication of Rachel Carson's *Silent spring* a century later.[2]

Marsh was an eclectic polymath, largely an autodidact although he made significant political contributions to the setting up of the Smithsonian Institution, and was also widely respected as a linguist.[3] As old as the century, he had presented criticisms of the effects of logging in his home state in the 1840s, and later made use of his foreign diplomatic missions for very extensive journeys around Southern Europe, Egypt and Palestine, fervidly observing and taking botanical notes. Everywhere he was struck, as he had been since his youth, by the capacity of humans to transform the land. Thus when he finally put pen to paper on the subject in the early 1860s, he was highly critical of geographical writing that inclined towards deterministic explanations of human societies, of the notion that climate and geographical factors shaped the character and political institutions of 'man'.[4] He charted the assault on the forests, the repeated and large-scale movement of species around the world whether consciously or in the wake of human activity, hydrological changes and sand drift and desertification. He gave very little attention to soil, apparently did not read Liebig directly, and discussed Boussingault only in relation to the latter's work on lake levels and climate. Above all, he drew on German and French writing regarding forestry and climate,[5] including those discussed above who

---

[2] George Perkins Marsh, *Man and nature. Or, physical geography as modified by human action* (New York: Charles Scribner, 1864).

[3] David Lowenthal, *George Perkins Marsh. Versatile Vermonter* (New York: Columbia University Press, 1958).

[4] 'it's a little volume showing that whereas Ritter and Guyot think that earth made man, man in fact made the earth'. Cited in Lowenthal, *George Perkins Marsh*, p. 248; see also Foster, *Marx's ecology*, p. 122.

[5] Davis, *Resurrecting the granary*, pp. 63–4.

were engaged with the contemporary colonisation of Algeria and the alleged despoliations of nomads: Bequerel, Boussingault, Evelyn, Fraas, Humboldt, Palissy, Schleiden, Ritter all feature among his references, but not Liebig, Pershine Smith, Carey or Waring.[6] But whilst Marsh dealt surprisingly little with the American writing on soil husbandry and the great migrations west, he echoed a sentiment already established in works such as John Lorain's 1824 book on the health of the land in Pennsylvania, *Nature and reason harmonized in the practice of husbandry*: 'Man is the most destructive animal in the universe, when he considers that his resources cannot fail.'[7]

Man and nature was, as Marsh's biographer David Lowenthal notes, above all a work of 'synthesis'.[8] The work triggered widespread interest, and in that sense, was a new beginning and remembered as such – at least, until the next new beginning. Yet it relied like most writing on much work that had gone before. It was suffused with many of the observations and anxieties around environmental and climatic interpretations of history that were accumulated over the decades before Marsh lifted his pen. He had travelled across what were the dead heartlands of dessicationist theory, the Mediterranean and Middle East, 'now completely exhausted of its fertility' for the most part 'entirely withdrawn from human use... [as] the result of man's ignorant disregard of the laws of nature, or an incidental consequence of war, and of civil and ecclesiastical tyranny and misrule', the latter being 'the brutal and exhausting despotism which Rome itself exercised... [then the] host of temporal and spiritual tyrannies which she left as her dying curse'.[9] Note that Marsh did not take the line that the Romans had inadvertently undermined soil fertility, but rather the despotism of the regime had led to abandonment, a pattern continued under feudal and Catholic rule that Marsh, a fervent anti-papist, saw as the Imperium's direct successor. The oppression of Rome found a distant echo in the contemporary world as archaic institutions and moribund economies forced thousands on to the boat to America to find 'new hives for the emigrant swarms', another example of how emigration and environment were linked at this time.[10] He provided an extraordinary and

---

[6] Marsh, *Man and nature*, p. vii.
[7] Stoll, *Larding the lean earth*, p. 104.
[8] Lowenthal, *George Perkins Marsh*, p. 276.
[9] Marsh, *Man and nature*, p. 5.
[10] Marsh, *Man and nature*, pp. 27, 48.

varied catalogue of change (mostly negative) attendant upon human action, alive both to depredations long past and the potential hazards of new industrial technologies.[11] He was a master of the repertoire, albeit not applying it comprehensively by any means. And *Man and nature* was not just history or reportage, but a jeremiad that held out the hint of redemption:

> The earth is fast becoming an unfit home for its noblest
> inhabitants, and another era of equal human crime and human
> improvidence, and of like duration with that through which
> traces of that crime and that improvidence extend, would
> reduce it to such a condition of impoverished productiveness,
> of shattered surface, of climatic excess, as to threaten the
> depravation, barbarism, and perhaps even extinction of the
> species.[12]

Like every other individual mentioned in this book, George Perkins Marsh was also a person of his time. His views had been shaped by observations of deforestation on the logging frontier when a young man in Vermont, by his travels (and expectations acquired from literature) in Europe, Africa and the Levant, and also his readings on contemporary colonial expansion which he set against historical experience. He was not as a consequence a doomsayer when it came to modernity, because he saw within it a capacity for learning and rescue. There was even a certain enthusiasm for engineering, praising drainage schemes, irrigation, reclamations from the sea and re-afforestation. There was hope. 'The destructive agency of man becomes more and more energetic and unsparing as he advances in civilization, until the impoverishment, with which his exhaustion of the natural resources of the soil is threatening him, at last awakens him to the necessity of preserving what is left, if not of restoring what has been wantonly wasted.'[13] Despite the increased scale of humanity's transformative powers:

> In the successive stages of social progress, the most destructive
> periods of human action upon nature are the pastoral condition,
> and that of incipient stationary civilization, or, in the newly

[11] For example, Marsh, *Man and nature*, pp. 122–3.
[12] Marsh, *Man and nature*, p. 43.
[13] Marsh, *Man and nature*, pp. 39–41, 45.

discovered countries of modern geography, the colonial, which corresponds to the era of early civilization in older lands. In more advances states of culture, conservative influences make themselves felt; and if highly civilized communities do not always restore the works of nature, they at least use a less wasteful expenditure than their predecessors in consuming them.[14]

This was a new gloss on the old stage theory, in which colonial frontiers are a species of 'archaic contemporaneity' (in reality of course often driven by demand from 'highly civilized communities'), and civilisation itself is defined by its restorative inclinations. Marsh, a figure renowned and familiar in the corridors of power even with his long sojourn as ambassador in Italy, found a ready reception in America for what would be by far his best-remembered work.

As we draw this book to a close, *Man and nature* can be situated in the story of sustainability in two (at least) significant ways. First, his lifetime traversed an era of transformation in what Rolf-Peter Sieferle called a 'field of plausibility'.[15] Writing in the early 1860s, the litany of environmental damage he provided possessed a resonance for the future of 'civilisation', and indeed American Empire, that had not hitherto been the case. There had been, as we have seen, plenty of thought about forests, water, sands and climates before, but only over time had they acquired a more existential dimension for human society, becoming bound into questions of human action and responsibility in novel ways. These changes cannot be traced to a eureka moment, the approach of any one author, but legion (if not quite innumerable) influences that shaped the discursive field of sustainability.

This brings us to the second point of significance: by the time Marsh was writing, any writer on the theme of sustainability had available a whole repertoire of gloomy prognostications and failed states on which to draw. Refuting any one case represented as evidence would not undermine the basic problematic. Marsh did not have to write anything about the soil to inhabit a tradition profoundly shaped by authors such as Liebig or Thaer. Equally, the widespread questioning of Liebig's theories in the 1850s and 1860s, often on the basis of field experiments, did not eradicate the fundamental anxieties around

---

[14] Marsh, *Man and nature*, p. 49.
[15] Sieferle, *Bevölkerungswachstum*, p. 82.

nutrient recycling.[16] William L. Thomas, who wrote the introduction to the proceedings of the 1955 conference, hailed Marsh as an 'intellectual font', who had produced 'the first great work of synthesis in the modern period to examine in detail man's alteration of the face of the globe'.[17] Perhaps the really intriguing historical question is not why it was George Perkins Marsh that wrote *Man and nature*, but how he was able to produce a synthesis. In some ways this book has become an answer to that question, although it was conceived looking in the other direction, from the agrarian societies of Renaissance Europe. Marsh represents both an end and a beginning, and *represents* is perhaps the word to stress, as he helped crystallised for American readers a whole genre of thought.

Across all of these discussions it would seem wrong, or at least not demonstrable, to argue that people became 'more' or 'less' preoccupied with nature at particular times, or indeed that nature evoked a common set of properties or ideas in their minds.[18] Equally, whilst one can certainly trace the enduring significance of certain propositions, motifs or techniques, this does not mean that this significance was invested with the same *meaning* by different people. Patterns of thought matter, and can endure. Passed down to and held in the minds of people at any one time, those patterns in turn shape their thoughts, and in this sense genealogy is an essential part of historical explanation.

But context and mood matter too. We are neither hidebound nor trapped by ancient intent, and often we cannot be sure what that intent was. Debates over the alleged vainglory and hubristic prcolamations of Francis Bacon will doubtless continue, especially as to the tenor and intent of his injunction that 'nature is only to be commanded in obeying her'. This was part of an argument about the need to understand causation, in that an effect cannot be reproduced unless you know what causes it. For some, this has been seen as a step towards claims to dominion. But others interpreted the idea much more modestly, as an argument *against* vainglorious expectations, which should also act as a reminder to examine the wider context in which Bacon wrote. 'Nature does not follow [the *Haus-Vater*'s] economy [*Haushaltung*], rather this

---

[16] Rossiter, *Emergence*, pp. 142–8.
[17] Thomas, *Man's role*, pp. xxviii–xxix.
[18] It is, as Raymond Williams famously pointed out, a most complex, elusive and elastic concept.

must follow hers', advised Florinus to the estate manager around 1700. This was in fact an adaptation of a point already made by Colerus in the 1590s.[19] When an Agricultural Institute was opened at Hohenheim outside Stuttgart in 1818, its new director, Johann Nepomuk Schwerz, drew on the exemplary lesson to be found in the *Novum Organum* of 'Bacon of Verulam', but went on to draw the conclusion that one should 'Give Nature a helping hand, but not master her; follow her lead, but not dictate to her.'[20] Words are an ambiguous inheritance and cannot by themselves dictate behaviour. Nor can any particular view-point own them.

These thoughts lead me to two final, seemingly paradox-ical observations. The first is that the idea of sustainability is not 'discovered', as if its principles are obvious and one simply requires wise and well-informed people to come upon them (or in declensionist mode, to cause us trouble by forgetting them).[21] I have in fact defined sustainability in a particular way, as the idea that it was a problem that society may inadvertently undermine the ecological conditions for its own survival. But even this leaves many questions. The very necessity of definition might suggest 'sustainability' is not some artefact lying about simply to be dug up, polished and displayed. Presenting sustainability as something to be 'discovered' naturalises the idea as something self-evident (to the insightful) and largely serves to create whiggish stories of wisdom gained or declensionist narratives of wisdom lost. Such stories can certainly serve worthy political objectives (unworthy ones too). But they turn history into a chronicle of blindness slowly healed (at best), or of a wilful aversion of the gaze to a manifest truth (at worst). Such arguments tend to imply that truths exist for all time and their uptake at particular times is explained by *interests*, in the sense of the search for advantage, a category altogether less flattering and honour-able than truth. Such views seem to do a disservice to the effort people put in to making sense of their circumstances, and rendering their lives liveable. The 'truth' of an idea like sustainability can take on many forms. This is not to deny that interest (or put another way, power) and truth have a great role in intellectual history. And I am conscious that

[19] 'weil die Natur sich nicht nach seiner Hasuhaltung/ sondern diese nach jener sich richten muß'. Colerus referred to 'the earth' rather than nature. Cited in Sieglerschmidt, 'Virtuelle Landwirtschaft', pp. 243–4.
[20] Sieglerschmidt, 'Virtuelle Landwirtschaft', p. 246.
[21] Contra Grober, *Entdeckung*.

this book has not really been able to do justice to the complex history of either of these things, especially in the interaction between socio-economic life and argument. I hope that it will be a stimulus to produce better and more rounded works on the themes I have raised.

However, the second observation is that neither is it a fruitful exercise to seek for the 'origins' of sustainability thinking, or environmentalism – or if it is, only in the sense that one can speak of one's familial 'origins' as a useful way into a story which within a very few generations becomes a trail marked out by obfuscation and forgetting. The interest in such an approach is obvious: we like histories of when we became 'us'. Thus a story about origins tells us more about... us, which does not mean it is uninteresting (if I may speak for myself). But it is an approach prone to hagiography and partiality, and consequently to histories of diffusion from some critical point, usually one that the author happens to have spent a long time researching (how many investigations of origins conclude that they are to be found 'not here'?).[22] The search for origins is, in reality, an endlessly recursive exercise, always chasing shadows. Hence I have instead employed the term *invention*, hardly perfect, but emphasising the *work* that is always being done. As has been written in a rather different context, 'There are... important limitations associated with making use of the concept of causation in historical explanation... [but] in relation to many of the topics discussed in this book the concept of positive and negative feedback is particularly helpful.'[23] Thus to use a metaphor from electronics, I have sought to show how such feedback generated a field of plausibility for the idea of sustainability.

And the work goes on. Society may seek to repeat itself but like the proverbial river we do not step into it twice. The similarity of utterances by John Norden, Georg von Hartig or Gro Harlem Brundtland do not mean that they could have written or fully understood each other's works. Even less is it true that a single figure like Carlowitz either 'invents the word' or that he 'sketches out the entire structure of the modern sustainability

[22] For a critique of diffusionist as opposed to 'circulatory' histories, see Prasenjit Duara, *The crisis of global modernity. Asian traditions and a sustainable future* (Cambridge: Cambridge University Press, 2015), esp. p. 82.

[23] E.A. Wrigley, *The path to sustained growth. England's transition from an organic economy to an Industrial Revolution* (Cambridge: Cambridge University Press, 2016), p. 203.

discourse'.[24] As Clarence Glacken observed in the greatest work of intellectual history on environmental thinking, *Traces on the Rhodian shore*, 'There is nothing disembodied about [ideas]... one literally tears and wrenches them out... and the cut is not clean. They are living small parts of complex wholes; they are given prominence by the attention of the student.'[25]

Arguably, what is striking in the continual debates about sustainability in which we are still deeply engaged is the lack of consensus over what 'it' is, and a tendency to treat opposing opinions as an abdication from sustainability thinking, rather than a different response to a similarly shaped problem. In his magnificent and path-breaking study *Green imperialism*, Richard Grove argued that 'Without the Romantic cult of islands (itself the outgrowth of much older Utopian and paradisal traditions), a fully fledged environmentalism, rather than a rather utilitarian shadow of it, could not have emerged.'[26] It is obvious that this presents a notion of what a 'fully fledged' environmentalism looks like, that was elsewhere defined by Grove as 'the safeguarding and nurturing of the natural order [that] therefore became a vital condition for sustaining a physical and social Utopia'.[27] Grove's interests have strong affinities with my arguments, but I am nervous about the anachronistic 'environmentalism', precisely because it is treated as a juvenile to be measured against a 'fully fledged' form. For Grove, who certainly went far beyond a simple diffusionist model of knowledge and who has been a lodestar in developing early modern environmental history especially in its global dimensions, the crucial point of egress for environmentalism was the tropical island (that he happened to study). In my account of sustainability, there can be no fully fledged form, because it defines not a prescription but a *problem*.

J.H. Bernadin de St Pierre was a French official on Mauritius and companion of Rousseau who returned home to publish what

---

[24] Of course, pioneering histories of a field have the great virtue of opening it as a worthwhile object of study, and it would be very surprising indeed if they produced definitive works. Grober, *Entdeckung*. A lecture by Grober is also cited in Jeremy L. Caradonna, *Sustainability. A history* (Oxford: Oxford University Press, 2014), p. 36. The first chapter of Caradonna's book covers some of the ground of this volume, but, derived from a course at the University of Alberta, is a brief introductory survey of some secondary literature to which this book tends to take a different view.

[25] Glacken, *Traces on the Rhodian shore*, p. viii.

[26] Grove, *Green imperialism*, p. 223.

[27] Grove, *Green imperialism*, p. 229.

Grove rightly calls 'remarkable' texts in the early 1780s. In one of these he angrily questioned 'To what degree have our speculations and our prejudices degraded her [nature]? Our treatises on agriculture show us, on the plains of Ceres, nothing but grain; in the meadows, the beloved haunt of nymphs, only bundles of hay and in the majestic forests only cords of wood and faggots.'[28] For St Pierre, the accounting and techno-cratic gaze, this system of making nature legible for utilitarian ends, was precisely what degraded 'her', debasing the true natural order. On the other hand, we have the techno-optimism of George Perkins Marsh, of a restorative and wise civilisation. And then there are the arguments of Justus Liebig, who thought his chemistry was the key to a natural order and sustainable future that only the theorist could truly grasp, and by utilising it:

> The farmer will be able to keep an exact record of the produce of his fields in harvest, like the account book of a well-regulated manufactory; and then by a simple calculation he can determine precisely the substances he must supply to each field, and the quantity of these, in order to restore their fertility.[29]

What belonged to nature's order and is worthy of articulation was varied and could well take on rather different forms in the mind of the same person. Thus the appeal to that order opened a field of debate, rather than providing a solution. Appealing to the natural order is a useful idea, to paraphrase Bruno Latour, aside from the problem with the two words 'natural' and 'order'. As a problem ever-emergent, sus-tainability seems to demand again and again a response that we might call inventive. And as we invent, we differ.

---

[28] Cited in Grove, *Green imperialism*, p. 250.
[29] Justus Liebig, *Familiar letters on chemistry* (London: Taylor & Walton, 1843), p. 171. Also cited in Brock, *Justus Liebig*, p. 180.

BIBLIOGRAPHY

Manuscript Sources

British Library

BL Additional MS 10038
BL Additional MS 38444

Glasgow University Library

MS Cullen 435/1–8

The National Archive

CSPD 1591–4
CUST 3
E190 Customs

Printed Primary Sources

Gottfried Achenwall, *Die Staatsklugheit nach ihren ersten Grundsätzen*, 2nd edition (Göttingen: Witwe Vandenhoeck, 1763)

James Anderson, *Recreations in agriculture, natural-history, arts and miscellaneous literature* (London: J. Wallis & R.H. Evans, 1799–1801)

James Anderson, *A calm investigation of the circumstances which have led to the present scarcity of grain in Britain, suggesting the means of alleviating that evil, and of preventing the recurrence of such a calamity in future* (London: John Cumming, 1801)

Anon., 'Enquiries concerning Agriculture', *Philosophical Transactions* 1 (1665–6), pp. 91–4

John Asgill, *Several assertions proved, in order to create another species of money, than gold and silver* (London: E. Curll, T. Jauncy & W. Boreham 1720 [1696]), p. C2

Francis Bacon, *Novum Organum in works of Francis Bacon*, ed. Basil Montagu (London: William Pickering, 1825)

Francis Bacon, *The advancement of learning*, ed. William Aldis Wright (Oxford: Clarendon, 1868 [1605])

Francis Bacon, *Historia Vitae et Mortis* (London: Matthai Lownes, 1623)

Francis Bacon, *Sylva sylvarum; or A naturall historie In ten centuries* (London: William Rawling, 1627)

Johann Joachim Becher, *Politischer Discurs von den eigentlichen Ursachen deß Auf- und Abnehmens der Städt, Länder und Republicken* (Frankfurt: Johann David Zunner, 1668)

J.G. Beckmann, *Gegründete Versuche und Erfahrungen der zu unsern Zeiten höchst nöthigan Holzsaat, zum allgemeinen Besten* (4th Auflage, Chemnitz: Johann Christoph Stößel, 1777 [1755, 1759])

M. Becquerel, *Des Climats et de l'influence qu'exercent les sols boisés et non boisés* (Paris: Firmin Didot Frères, 1853)

J.B. de Beunie, 'Annalysis of soils', *Annals of Agriculture* II (1784)

Walter Blith, *The English improver, or, A new survey of husbandry discovering to the kingdome, that some land, both arable and pasture, may be advanced double or treble other land to a five or tenfold, and some to a twenty fold improvement, yea, some now not worth above one, or two shillings, per acree, be made worth thirty, or forty, if not more: clearly demonstrated from principles of sound reason, ingenuity, and late but most certaine reall experiences, held forth under six peeces of improvement* (London: J. Wright, 1649)

Walter Blith, *The English improver improved or the survey of husbandry surveyed discovering the improueableness of all lands*, 3rd edition (London: John Wright, 1652)

Gerald Boate, *Irelands naturall history being a true and ample description of its situation, greatness, shape, and nature, of its hills, woods, heaths, bogs, of its fruitfull parts, and profitable grounds* (London: John Wright, 1657)

Jean Bodin, *The six books of common-weale* (London: G. Bishop, 1606)

Ioannis Botero, *Von der Stätten / Auffgang / Grösse und Herzligkeit / kurtzer / doch gruntlicher Bericht* (Strassburg, 1596)

Giovanni Botero, *Gründlicher Bericht von Anordnung der Policeyen Regiments auch Fürsten und Herren Stands sampt Gründliche... ung der Ursachen wodurch Stätt zu Auffnemmen und hochheiten komen mögen* (Strassburg: Zetzner, 1596)

Giovanni Botero, *On the causes of the greatness and magnificence of cities*, trans. Geoffrey W. Symcox (Toronto: University of Toronto Press, 2012)

J.B. Boussingault, *Rural economy in its relations to chemistry, physics and meteorology or, an application of the principles of chemistry and physiology to the details of practical farming*, trans. George Law (London: H. Baillière, 1845)

Robert Boyle, *General heads for the natural history of a country great or small drawn out for the use of travellers and navigators* (London: J. Taylor & S. Hedford, 1692)

Richard Bradley, *A general treatise of agriculture, both philosophical and practical* (London: W. Johnston etc., 1757 [1727])

Jesse Buel, *The farmer's Companion, or essays on the principles and practice of American Husbandry* (Boston, MA: Marsh, Capen, Lyon & Webb, 1839)

Georges Louis Leclerc, M. de Buffon, 'Memoire sur la conservation et le retablissement des forests', *Memoires de l'Academie Royale* (8 Apr. 1739), pp. 140–156

Georges Louis Leclerc, Comte de Buffon, 'Of nutrition and growth', 'Recapitulation', and 'Experiments on the method of generation', in trans. J.S. Barr in J. Lyon and Phillip R. Sloan, *From natural history to the history of nature. Readings from Buffon and his critics* (Notre Dame, IN: University of Notre Dame Press, 1981)

Georges Louis Leclerc, Comte de Buffon, *The Natural History of Animals, Vegetables and Minerals with the Theory of the Earth in general. 7 vols.*, trans. W. Kendrick and J. Murdoch (London: T. Bell, 1775)

Georges Louis Leclerc, Comte de Buffon, *Les époques de la nature* (Paris: Éditions du Muséum, 1962 [1778])

Thomas Burnet, *The sacred history of the earth* (London: John Hooke, 1719 [1684])

Richard Cantillon, *Essay on the nature of trade in general*, ed. and trans. Henry Higgs (London: Frank Cass & Co., 1959)

Henry C. Carey, *The past, the present and the future* (Philadelphia, PA: Carey & Hart, 1848)

Henry Carey, *The harmony of interests. Agricultural, manufacturing and commercial* (Philadelphia, PA: J.S. Skinner, 1851)

Henry C. Carey, *The prospect agricultural, manufacturing, commercial and financial at the opening of the year 1851* (Philadelphia, PA: J.S. Skinner, 1851)

Henry C. Carey, *Principles of social science* (Philadelphia, PA: J.J. Lippincott & Co., 1858)

Hanns Carl von Carlowitz, *Sylvicultura oeconomica oder haußwirtschaftliche Nachricht und naturmäßige Anweisung zue Wilden Baum-Zucht nebst gründlicher Darstellung wie zu förderst durch göttliches Benedeyen dem attenthalben und unsgemein einreissenden grossen Holz-Mangel...* (1st edition, Leipzig: Johann Friedrich Braun, 1713; 2nd edition, Leipzig: Johann Friedrich Braun Erben, 1732)

Marcus Porcius Cato, *On Agriculture*, trans. William Davis Hooper (Cambridge, MA: Harvard University Press, 1934)

M. le Comte de Chaptal (Jean Antoine Chaptal, Comte de Chanteloup), *Chimie appliquée a l'Agriculture. Tome 1.* (Paris: Madame Huzard, 1825)

Rock Church, *An old thrift newly revived* (London: Richard Moore, 1612)

John Clayton, 'Mr. John Clayton, Rector of Crofton at Wake-Field, his letter to the Royal Society, giving a farther account of the soil, and other observables of Virginia', *Philosophical Transactions* 17 (1693), pp. 970–88

Rev. H. Close, 'Experiments on potatoes', *Annals of Agriculture* I (1784)

Iohannis Colerus, *Oeconimicae oder Hausbuch* (Wittenberg: Paul Hefrig, 1598 [1595])

Lucius Junius Moderatus Columella, *Of husbandry*, trans. (London: A. Millar, 1745)

The Complete Farmer; Or a General Dictionary of Husbandry in All Its Branches, Containing the Various Methods of Cultivating and Improving Every Species of Land, 4th edition (London: Longman, Law, Robinson, Robinson, Cadell, Baldwin, Otridge and Lowndes, 1793)

Moses Cook, *The manner of raising, ordering, and improving forrest-trees. Also, how to plant, make and keep woods, walks, avenues, lawns, hedges etc. With several figures proper for avenues and walks to end in, and convenient figures for lawns* (London: Peter Parker, 1676)

Heinrich Cotta, *Grundriß der Forstwissenschaft. 2 Auflage* (Dresden: Arnold, 1836–8)

Pieter de la Court, *The true interest and political maxims of the Republic of Holland*, trans. John Campbell (London: J. Nourse, 1746)

'Encouragement of agriculture by the Empress of Russia, extracted from Mr Coxe's travels', *Annals of Agriculture* II (1784), pp. 233–7

Hector St. John de Crèvecouer, *Letters from an American farmer* (London: Thomas Davies, 1782)

Erasmus Darwin, *Phytologia; or the philosophy of agriculture and gardening* (London: J. Johnson, 1800)

Humphry Davy, *Elements of Agricultural Chemistry* (London: Longman, Hurst, Rees, Orme & Brown, 1813)

G.U. Däzel, *Ueber Forsttaxierung und Ausmittelung des jährlichen nachhaltigen Ertrages* (Munich: Joseph Lindauer, 1793)

William Derham, *Physico-Theology; or a demonstration of the being and attributes of God, from his works of creation* (London: W. Innys, 1713)

Leonard Digges, *A boke named Tectonicon briefelye shewynge the exacte measurynge, and speady reckenynge all maner lande, squared tymber, stone, steaples, pyllers, globes* (London: Felix Kyngston, 1556)

H.W. Döbel, *Neueröffnete Jägerpraktika* (Leipzig: Johann Samuel Heinsii Erben, 1746)

William Dugdale, *The history of imbanking and drayning of divers fenns and marshes, both in forein parts and in this kingdom, and of the improvements thereby extracted from records, manuscripts, and other authentick testimonies* (London: Alice Warren, 1662)

Henri-Louis Duhamel du Monceau, *De l'exploitation des bois. 2 vols* (Paris: H.L. Guerin, L.F. Delatour, 1764)

Henri-Louis Duhamel du Monceau, *The Elements of Agriculture*, trans. P. Miller (London: Vallaint & Durham; and Baldwin, 1764)

M.J. Dumas and M.J.B. Boussingault, *The chemical and physiological balance of Organic Nature. An essay* (London: Baillière, 1844)

Earl of Dundonald, *A treatise, shewing the intimate connection that subsists between agriculture and chemistry addressed to the cultivators of the soil, to the proprietors of fens and mosses, in Great Britain and Ireland, and to the proprietors of West India estates* (London: E. Edwards, 1795)

William Ellis, *Chiltern and vale farming explained, according to the latest improvements* (London: Weaver Bickerton, 1733)

Friedrich Engels, *Dialectics of nature* (London: Lawrence & Wishart, 1940)

Charles Estienne, *Maison rustique, or The countrey farme*, trans. Richard Surflet, and further edited by Gervase Markham (London: John Bill, 1616)

John Evelyn, *Fumifugium, or, The inconveniencie of the aer and smoak of London dissipated together with some remedies humbly proposed* (London: G. Bedel & T. Collins, 1661)

John Evelyn, *Sylva. Or, a discourse of forest trees* (London: Jo. Martyn & Ja. Allestry, 1664)

John Evelyn, *A philosophical discourse on Earth relating to the Culture and Improvement of Vegetation, and the Propagation of Plants, etc.* (London: John Martyn, 1676)

Simon d'Ewes (ed.), *Journal of the House of Commons* (Shannon: Irish University Press, 1682)

William Falconer, *Remarks on the influence of climate on the Disposition and Temper of Mankind* (London: C. Dilly, 1781)

Farmer, *An essay on the theory of agriculture, intended as an introduction to a rational system of that art. By a farmer* (London: T. Becket, 1760)

Roger Fisher, *Heart of Oak. The British Bulwark* (London: J. Johnson, 1763)

John Fitzherbert, *Boke of surveyinge and improumentes* (London: Rycharde Pynson, 1523)

John Fitzherbert, *The boke of husbandrie* (London: Thomas Berthelet, 1533)

John Fitzherbert, *Boke of Husbandry* (London: Thomas Berthelet, 1540)

Francis Philipp Florinus, *Oeconomus Prudens et Legalis oder allgemeiner kluger und Rechts-verständinger Haus-Vatter* (Nürnberg: Christoph Riegels Wittib, 1750 [1701])

George Fordyce, *Elements of agriculture and vegetation* (London: J. Johnson, 1771)

Carl Fraas, *Klima und Planzenwelt inder Zeit, ein Beitrag zur Geschichte beider* (Landshut: J.G. Wölfle, 1847)

Carl Fraas, *Bavaria rediviva! Ein Beitrag zur Lehre vom Völkeruntergang durch Bodenerschöpfung* (Munich: J.G. Cotta, 1865)

C.F. Germershausen, *Der Hausvater in systematischer Ordnung* (Leipzig: Junius, 1783)

Carl August Geutebrück, *Kurze Anweisung wie mit dem Anbau des Holzes, zu gedeylich anzuhoffenden Anwuchs desselben zu Werck zu gehen?* (Erfurt: Johann Friedrich Weber, 1757)

Edward Gibbon, *The History of the decline and fall of the Roman empire*, vol. 1, ed. J.B. Bury (New York: Fred de Fau & Co., 1906 [1776])

John Graunt, *Natural and political observations made upon the bills of mortality* [1662] in Peter Laslett (ed.), *The earliest classics* (Farnborough: Gregg International, 1973)

Nehemiah Grew, *The anatomy of plants with an idea of a philosophical history of plants, and several other lectures, read before the royal society* (London: W. Rawlins, 1682)

Nehemiah Grew, 'A demonstration of the number of acres contained in England, or South-Britain; and the use which may be made of it', *Philosophical Transactions* 27 (1710), p. 269.

Martin Grosser, *Kurze und gar einfeltige Anleitung zu der Landwirtschaft, beides im Ackerbau und in der Viehzucht nach Art und Gelegenheit dieser Land und Ort Schlesien*, ed. Gertrud Schröder-Lembke (Stuttgart: Fischer, 1965 [1589])

George Hakewill, *An apologie of the power and providence of god in the government of the world* (Oxford: John Lichfield and William Turner, 1627)

Matthew Hale, *The Primitive Origination of Mankind* (London: William Shrowsbery, 1677)

Thomas Hale Esq., *A compleat body of husbandry. Containing rules for performing, in the most profitable manner, the whole business of the farmer and country gentleman, ... Compiled from the original papers of the late Thomas Hale, ... Illustrated with a great number of cuts, ...* Vol. 1, 2nd edition (London: Tho. Osborne, Tho. Trye & G. Crowder, 1758–9)

Edward Harries, 'A Hint to the Minister of the Crown Lands', *Annals of Agriculture* V (1786)

Edward Harries, 'General observation on the state of oak timber, &c.', *Annals of Agriculture* XV (1791)

William Harrison, *An historical description of the Island of Britain* (London: John Harrison, 1577)

Georg Ludwig Hartig, *Anweisung zur Taxation der Forste oder zur Bestimmung des Holzertrags der Wälder* (Giessen: Heyer, 1795)

Samuel Hartlib, *An essay for advancement of husbandry-learning* (London: Henry Hills, 1651)

Samuel Hartlib, *The reformed husbandman* (London: J.C., 1651)

Samuel Hartlib, *A discoverie for division or setting out of land, as to the best form published by Samuel Hartlib esquire, for direction and more advantage and profit of the adventurers and planters in the fens and other waste and undisposed places in England and Ireland; whereunto are added some other choice secrets of experiments of husbandry; with a philosophical quere concerning the cause of fruitfulness, and an essay to shew how all lands may be improved in a new way to become the ground of the increase of trading and revenue to this common-wealth* (London: Richard Wodenothe, 1653)

Samuel Hartlib, *The compleat husband-man; or, A discourse of the whole art of husbandry; both forraign and domestick* (London: Edward Brewster, 1659)

S. Hayes, *A practical guide to planting and the management of woods and coppices* (London: Allen & West, 1794)

J. Headrick, 'Effects of Manures in the Production of Plants', *Annals of Agriculture* XXXIII (1799)

Conrad Heresbach, *Rei rusticae libri quatuor* (Köln: Johann Birckmann, 1570)

Conrad Heresbach, *Foure books of husbandry*, trans. Barnaby Googe (London: John Wight, 1577)

Conrad Heresbach, *The whole art of husbandrie contained in foure books*, trans. Richard Surflet and enlarged by Gervase Markham (London: Richard More, 1631)

Thomas Hobbes, *Leviathan*, ed. R. Tuck (Cambridge: Cambridge University Press 1996 [1651])

Herr von Hohberg, *Georgica Curiosa Aucta, das ist. Umständlicher Bericht und klarer Unterricht adelichen Land- und Feldleben* (Nürnberg: Martin Endte, 1701 [1682])

Rev. Edward Holmes, 'On the food of plants', *Annals of Agriculture* VI (1786)

Francis Home, *The principles of agriculture and vegetation* (Edinburgh: G. Hamilton & J. Balfour, 1757)

Francis Home, *Les principes de l'agriculture et de la vegetation* (Paris: Prault, 1761)

Henry Home, Lord Kames, *Sketches of the History of Man Considerably enlarged by the last additions and corrections of the author*, vol. II (London: W. Strahan & T. Cadell, 1778)

John Houghton, *A collection for the improvement of husbandry and trade* (London: Woodman & Lyon, 1727–8)

Alexander von Humboldt and Aimé Bonpland, *Essay on the geography of plants* (1807) (trans. S. Romanowski; ed. S.T. Jackson with accompanying essays and supplementary material by S.T. Jackson and S. Romanowski) (Chicago, IL: University of Chicago Press, 2013)

Alexander von Humboldt, *Ansichten der Nature mit wissenschaftlichen Erläuterungen* (Tubingen: Cotta, 1808)

Alexander von Humboldt, *Personal narrative of travels to the equinoctial regions of the New Continent, 1797–1804* (London: Longman, Hurst, Rees, Orme & Brown, 1819)

David Hume, *A treatise of human nature. Being an attempt to introduce the experimental method of reasoning in moral subjects* (London: James Noon, 1739)

J. Ch. Hundeshagen, *Encyclopädie der Forstwissenschaft* (Tübingen: Heinrich Laupp, 1821)

Ellsworth Huntington, *The pulse of Asia. A journey through Asia illustrating the geographic basis of history* (London: Archibald Constable & Co, 1907)

Ellsworth Huntington, *Civilization and climate* (New Haven, CT: Yale University Press, 1915)

Francis Hutcheson, *System of Moral Philosophy*, vol. I (London: A. Millar & T. Longman, 1755)

John Ingenhousz, *Experiments upon vegetables discovering the great power of purifying the common air in the sun-shine it and of injuring it in the shade and at night* (London: P. Elmsly & H. Payne, 1779)

Thomas Jefferson, *The works of Thomas Jefferson*, federal edition (New York and London: G.P. Putnam's Sons, 1904–5)

William Stanley Jevons, *The coal question. An enquiry concerning the progress of the nation, and the probable exhaustion of our coal mines* (London: Macmillan, 1865)

James F.W. Johnston, *Catechism of agricultural chemistry and geology* (London: William Blackwood & Sons, 1845)

James F.W. Johnson, *Notes on North America. Agricultural, economical and social*, vol. II (London: W. Blackwood, 1851)

James F.W. Johnston, 'The circulation of matter', *Blackwood's Magazine* 73 (1853), pp. 550–60

Journal of the House of Commons: volume 1: 1547–1629 (1802)

Journal of the House of Lords
Journals of all the Parliaments during the reign of Queen Elizabeth (1682)
Johann Gottlieb von Justi, *Staatswirtschaft oder systematische Abhandlung aller Oekonomischen und Cameralwissenschaftn, die zur Regierung eines Landes efodert [sic] werden* (Leipzig: Bernhard Christoph Breitkopf, 1758)
Johann Gottlieb von Justi, *Die Nature und das Wesen der Staaten als die Grundwissenschaft der Staatskunst, der Policey und aller Regierungswissenschaften* (Berlin: Johann Heinrich Rüdiger, 1760)
Johann Gottlieb von Justi, *Die Grundfeste zu der Macht und Glückseligkeit der Staaten; oder ausführliche Vorstellung der gesamten Policey-Wissenschaft. 1er Band.* (Königsberg: Johann Heinrich Hartungs Erben, 1760)
Johnan Gottlieb von Justi, *Politische und Finanzschriften über wichtige Gegenstände der Stattskunst, der Kriegswissenschaften und des Cameral- und Finanzwesens* (Kopenhagen und Leipzig: Rothenschen Buchhandlung, 1761)
Rev. Mr Kedington, 'On the proper husbandry for a gentleman', *Annals of Agriculture* VI (1786), pp. 11–17
Gregory King, *Natural and political observations and conclusions upon the state of England* (London, 1696), in Peter Laslett (ed.), *The earliest classics* (Farnborough: Greggs International, 1973)
Gregory King, 'The LCC Burns journal', in Peter Laslett (ed.), *The earliest classics* (Farnborough: Greggs International, 1973)
Richard Kirwan, 'What are the manures most advantageously applicable to the various sorts of soils? And what are the causes of their beneficial effect in each particular instance?', *Annals of Agriculture* XXIII (1795)
Sheila Lambert, ed., *House of Commons sessional papers of the eighteenth century. Vol. 76. George III. Reports of the Commissioners of Land Revenue 1–7. 1878–1790* (Wilmington, DE: Scholarly Resources, 1975)
Batty Langley, *A sure method of improving estates* (London: Francis Clay & Daniel Browne, 1728)
James F. Larkin and Paul L. Hughes (eds), *Stuart Royal Proclamations. Vol. 1. Royal proclamations of King James I 1603–1625* (Oxford: Clarendon, 1973)
J.B. Lawes, 'On some points connected with agricultural chemistry', *Journal of the Royal Agricultural Society of England* 8 (1847), pp. 227–8
Joseph Lee, *Eutazia tou agrou: or a vindication of regulated Inclosure* (London: Thomas Williams, 1656)
Justus Liebig, *Chemistry in its application to agricultural and physiology* (Cambridge: John Owen, 1842)
Justus Liebig, *Familiar letters on chemistry* (London: Taylor & Walton, 1843)

Justus von Liebig, *Letters on modern Agriculture* (London: Walton and Maberly, 1859)

Justus von Liebig, *Die Chemie in ihrer Anwendung auf Agricultur und Physiologie*, 7th edition (Braunschweig: Friedrich Vieweg, 1862)

Louis Liger, *Oeconomie générale de la champagne ou nouvelle maison rustique* (Paris: Claude Prudhomme, 1701)

Louis Liger, *Le nouvelle maison rustqiue* (Paris: Claude Prudhomme, 1721)

Carl Linneaus and Issac J. Biberg, *Oeconomica Naturae* (Uppsala: na, 1749)

Carl Linneaus, *Oeconomy of Nature* in Bernard Stillingfleet (ed.), *Miscellaneous tracts relating to natural history, husbandry and physic* (London: J. Dodsley, S. Baker & T. Payne, 1762)

John Locke, *Two treatises of government* (London: Awnsham & John Churchill, 1694)

Niccolò Machiavelli, *Discourses on Livy* (Oxford: Oxford University Press, 2008 [1513])

Thomas R. Malthus, *Essay on the principle of population* (London: J. Johnson, 1798)

Thomas Malthus, *An Essay on the Principle of Population, Or a View of Its Past and Present Effects on Human Happiness; with an Inquiry Into Our Prospects Respecting the Future Removal or Mitigation of the Evils which It Occasions*, 2nd edition (London: J. Johnson, 1803)

Thomas R. Malthus, *Principles of political economy, with a view to their practical application*, 2nd edition (London: William Pickering, 1836; first edition 1820)

Gerald Malynes, *Englands view, in the unmasking of two paradoxes with a replication unto the answer of Maister Iohn Bodine* (London: Richard Field, 1603)

Bernard de Mandeville, *The fable of the bees. Or, private vices, public benefits* (London: J. Tonson, 1724)

John Manwood, *A treatise and discourse of the laws of the Forrest* (London: Thomas Wight & Bonham Norton, 1598)

Gervase Markham, *Markhams farwell to husbandry or, The inriching of all sorts of barren and sterill grounds in our kingdome, to be as fruitfull in all manner of graine, pulse, and grasse as the best grounds whatsoeuer together with the anoyances, and preseruation of all graine and seede, from one yeare to many yeares. As also a husbandly computation of men and cattels dayly labours, their expences, charges, and vttermost profits. Attained by trauell and experience, being a worke neuer before handled by any author: and published for the good of the whole kingdome.* (London: Roger Jackson, 1620)

Gervase Markham, *The English husbandman* (London: William Sheares, 1635)

George Perkins Marsh, *Man and Nature. Or, Physical geography as modified by human action* (New York: Charles Scribner, 1864)

Alfred Marshall, *The principles of economics* (London: Macmillan, 1890)

William Marshall, *Experiments and observations concerning agriculture and the weather* (London: J. Dodsley, 1779)

Karl Marx, *Capital. A critique of political economy*, Vols I–III (London: Penguin, 1976–81 [1867])

Karl Marx, *Grundrisse. Foundations of a theory of political economy*, trans. Martin Nicolaus (London: Penguin, 1993)

Noé Meurer, *Vom forstlicher Oberherrligkeit und Gerechtigkeit* (Pforzheim: Georg Rab, 1560)

Noé Meurer, *Jag und Forstrecht* (Frankfurt: Paul Keffeler, 1576)

John Stuart Mill, *Principles of political economy with some of their applications to social philosophy* (London: Longmans & Green, 1909 [1848])

John Mills, *A new system of practical husbandry*, Volume 1 (London: J. Johnson & B. Davenport, 1767)

Marquis du Mirabeau, *The oeconomical table, an attempt towards ascertaining and exhibiting the source, progress, and employment of riches, with explanations* (London: W.Owen, 1766)

Charles-Louis de Secondat, Baron de La Brède et de Montesquieu, *De l'Esprit des Lois* (Paris: Barillot et fils, 1748)

Charles Louis de Secondat, Baron de Montesquieu, *Complete Works*, vol. 3 (*Grandeur and Declension of the Roman Empire; A Dialogue between Sylla and Eucrates; Persian Letters*) (London: T. Evans & W. Davis, 1777 [1721])

Adam Moore, *Bread for the poor, and advancement of the English nation promised by enclosure of the wastes and common grounds of England* (London: Nicholas Bourn, 1653)

J. Moore, *A target for tillage briefly containing the most necessary, pretious, and profitable vse thereof both for king and state* (London: William Jones, 1612)

Thomas More, *Utopia, or, the Happy Republic*, trans. G. Burnet (Glasgow: Hamilton and Balfour, 1743)

John Mortimer, *The whole art of husbandry. Or, the way of managing and improving of land*, 2nd edition (London: H. Mortlock & J. Robinson, 1708 [1707])

John Norden, *The surveyors dialogue* (London: Hugh Astley, 1607)

W.G. Moser, *Grundsätze der Forst-Oeconomie* (Frankfurt and Leipzig: Heinrich Ludwig Brönner, 1757)

Monsieur Mouron, 'Observations on Agriculture', *Annals of Agriculture* III (1785)

Otto von Münchhausen, *Der Hausvater* (Hannover: Nic. Försters und Sohns 1765)

John Pitkin Norton, *Elements of scientific agriculture* (Albany, NY: E.H. Pease & Co., 1850)

Timothy Nourse, *Campania Fœlix. Or, a discourse of the benefits and improvements of husbandry; containing directions for all manner of tillage, pasturage, and plantation*, 2nd edition (London: Tho. Bennet, 1700)

Timothy Nourse, *Of the fuel of London*, in *Campania Foelix*

Christoph Oettelt, *Praktischer Beweis, dass die Mathesis bei dem Forstwesen unentbehrliche Dienste tue* (Eisenach: Georg Ernst Witterkindt, 1765)

Palladius, *The work of farming (Opus Agriculturae)*, trans. John G. Fitch (Totnes: Prospect, 2013)

John Parkinson, *Paradisi in sole paradisus terrestris or A garden of all sorts of pleasant flowers which are English ayre will permit to be noursed up* (London: Humfrey Lownes & Robert Young, 1629)

Ulrich Päßler and Thomas Schmuck, *Alexander von Humboldt, Jean-Baptiste Boussingault, Briefwechsel* (Berlin: De Gruyter, 2015)

Johann Friedrich Penther, *Praxis geometriae worinnen nicht nur alle bey dem Feld-Messen vorkommende Fälle, mit Stäben, dem Astrolabio, der Boussole, und der Mensul, in Ausmessung eintzeler Linien, Flächen und gantzer Revier, welche, wenn deren etliche angräntzende zusammen genommen, eine Land-Carte ausmachen, auf ebenen Boden und Gebürgen, wie auch die Abnehmung derer Höhen und Wasser-Fälle, nebst beygefügten practischen Hand-Griffen, deutlich erörtert, sondern auch eine gute Ausarbeitung der kleinesten Risse bis zum grösten, mit ihren Neben-Zierathen, treulich communiciret werden* (Augsburg: Jeremias Wolffs Erben, 1761)

William Petty, *The advice of W.P. to Mr. Samuel Hartlib for the advancement of some particular parts of learning* (London: na, 1647)

William Petty, *Treatise of Taxes and Contributions* (London: Edward Poole, 1662)

William Petty, *Another essay in political arithmetic, concerning the growth of the city of London; with the measures, periods, causes and consequences thereof* (London: Mark Pardoe, 1683)

William Petty, *Political Arithmetick* (London: Robert Clavel & Henry Mortlock, 1691)

Johann Ludwig von Pfeiffer, *Vermischte Verbeßerungsvorschläge und freie Gedanken über verschiedene, den Narungszustand, die Bevölkerung und Staatswirtschaft der Deutschen, betreffende Gegenstände* (Frankfurt: Eßlinger, 1778)

Johann Ludwig von Pfeiffer, *Grundsätze der Universal-Cameral-Wissenschaft* (Frankfurt: Eßlinger, 1783)

Mr. Pitt 'Miscellaneous Observations', *Annals of Agriculture* VIII (1787)

Sir Hugh Plat, *The iewell house of art and nature* (London: Peter Short, 1594)

Sir Hugh Plat, *Floraes paradise* (London: William Leake, 1608)

Gabriel Plattes, *A discovery of infinite treasure, hidden since the worlds beginning* (London: George Hutton, 1639)

Robert Plot, *The natural history of Oxfordshire, being an essay toward the natural history of England* (London: Moses Pits & Millers, 1677)

Robert Plot, *The natural history of Staffordshire* (Oxford: Theater, 1686)

Robert Powell, *Depopulation arraigned, convicted and condemned, by the lawes of God and man a treatise necessary in these times* (London: Richard Badger, 1636)

Governor Pownall, 'On the necessity of regulating the making and selling of flour, and on the bread assize', *Annals of Agriculture* IX (1788), pp. 557–627

François Quesnay, 'Fermiers', in August Oncken (ed.), *Oeuvres économiques et philosophes de F. Quesnay, fondateur du systéme physiocratique* (New York: B. Franklin, 1969 [1888]), pp. 159–92

François Quesnay, 'Grains', in August Oncken (ed.), *Oeuvres économiques et philosophes de F. Quesnay, fondateur du systéme physiocratique* (New York: B. Franklin, 1969 [1888]), pp. 193–249

John Ray, *The wisdom of God manifested in the works of Creation*, 3rd edition (London: Sam Smith & Benj. Walford, 1701)

A.L. Reyscher, *Vollständige, historisch and kritisch bearbeitete Sammlung der württembergischen Gesetze*, vol. XII (Tübingen: na, 1841)

David Ricardo, *On the principles of political economy and taxation* (London: John Murray, 1817)

Edward Ruffin, 'An address on the opposite results of exhausting and fertilizing systems of agriculture' (1852), in Edwin C. Hagenstein, Sara M. Gregg and Brian Donahue (eds), *American Georgics, Writings on farming, culture and the land* (New Haven, CT: Yale University Press, 2011), pp. 98–103

Thomas Ruggles, 'Picturesque Farming', *Annals of Agriculture* IX (1788)

Jean-Baptiste Say, *A treatise on political economy*, trans. C.R. Prinsep (Philadelphia, PA: Lippincott, Grambo & Co., 1855 [1803])

Veit Ludwig von Seckendorff, *Teutscher Fürsten-Staat* (Jena: Johann Meyer, 1737 [1655])

Antonio Serra, *[Breve tratatto] A short treatise on the wealth and poverty of nations*, trans. Sophus A. Reinert (London: Anthem Press, 2011 [1613])

Olivier de Serres, *Théâtre d'Agriculture* (Paris: Saugrain, 1600)

Matthias Jacob Schleiden, *Die Pflanze und ihr Leben. Populäre Vorträge* (Leipzig: Vieweg, 1850)

John Shaw, *Certaine easie and profitable points in husbandrie* (London: Barnard Alsop, 1637)

John Shaw, *Certaine helpes and remedies vnder God to prevent dearth and scarcitie* (London: B. Alsop, 1638)

John Sinclair, 'Plan for establishing a Board of Agriculture and Internal Improvement', *Annals of Agriculture* XX (1793)

Adam Smith, *Lectures on Jurisprudence*, ed. R.L. Meek, D.D. Raphael and P.G. Stein (Indianapolis, IN: Liberty Classics, 2005 [1762])

Adam Smith, *An Inquiry into the Nature and Causes of the Wealth of Nations* (London: W. Strahan & T. Cadell, 1776)

John Smith, *England's improvement reviv'd digested into six books* (London: Tho. Newcomb, 1670)

E. Peshine Smith, *A manual of political economy* (New York: G.P. Putnam & Son, 1853)

Sir Thomas Smith, [published as Gentleman, W.S.], *A compendious or briefe examination of certayne ordinary complaints* (London: Thomas Marshe, 1581)

Adolphus Speed, *Adam out of Eden or Asbtract of divers excellent experiments touching the advancement of Husbandry* (London: Henry Brome, 1658)

George Ernest Stahl, *Philosophical principles of universal chemistry; Or, the foundation of a scientifical manner of inquiring into and preparing the natural and artificial bodies and the uses of life*, trans. Peter Shaw (London: Osborn and Longman, 1730)

Arthur Standish, *The commons complaint* (London: William Stansby, 1611)

Arthur Standish, *New directions of experience authorized by the kings most excellent Maiesty, as may appeare, for the planting of Timber and Fire-Wood* (London: Nicholas Okes, 1614)

Arthur Standish, *New directions of experience authorized by the kings most excellent Maiesty, as may appeare, for the increasing of Timber and Fire-Wood* (London: N. Okes, 1616)

Statutes of the Realm

Benjamin Stillingfleet, *Miscellaneous tracts relating to natural history, husbandry, and physic. To which is added the calendar of flora*, 2nd edition (London: R. & J. Dodsley, S. Baker, & T.Payne, 1762)

Friederich Ulrich Stisser, *Forst- und Jagd Historie der deutschen* (Jena: Johann Friedrich Ritter, 1737)

Johann Peter Süßmilch, *Die göttliche Ordnung in denen Veränderungen des menschlichen Geschlechts* (Berlin: Buchhandlung der Realschule, 1741)

Rev. Swayne, 'Reply to Mr. Holmes' queries on lime', *Annals of Agriculture* 4 (1785), pp. 37–47

Publius Cornelius Tacitus, *On Germany*, trans. Thomas Gordon (New York: P.F. Collier & Son, 2012)

John Taylor, *Arator. Being a series of agricultural essays pratical and political* (Georgetown, MD: J.M. Carter, 1814)

Silvanus Taylor, *Common-good; or, the improvement of commons, forests and chases, by inclosure, wherein the advantage of the poor, the common plenty of all, and the increase and preservation of timber, with other other things of common concernment* (London: Francis Tyton, 1652)

Albrecht D. Thaer, *The principles of Agriculture*, trans. William Shaw and Cuthbert W. Johnsson (London: Ridgway, 1844)

Johann Heinrich von Thünen, *Der isolirte Staat in Beziehung auf Landwirtschaft und Nationalökonomie* (Rostock: G.P. Leopold, 1842 [1826])

Jethro Tull, *Horse-hoeing husbandry; or, an essay on the principles of vegetation and tillage*, 4th edition (London: A. Miller, 1762)

A.R.J. Turgot, *Reflections on the Formation and the Distribution of Riches*, trans. William J. Ashley (New York: Macmillan, 1898 [1770])

Thomas Tusser, *Fiue hundred pointes of good husbandrie* (London: Henrie Denham, 1580)

Marcus Terentius Varro, *On Agriculture*, trans. William Davis Hooper (Cambridge, MA: Harvard University Press, 1934)

Johann Ehrenfried Vierenklee, *Mathematische Anfangsgründe der Arithmetik und Geometrie für Forstleute* (Leipzig: na, 1767)

Virgil, *The Georgics* (London: Penguin, 1982)

Robert Wallace, *A dissertation on the numbers of mankind in antient and modern times; in which the superior populousness of Antiquity is maintained* (Edinburgh: G. Hamilton & J. Balfour, 1753)

Robert Wallace, *Various prospects of Mankind, Nature and Providence* (London: A. Millar, 1761)

George Waring, 'Agricultural Features of the Census of the United States for 1850', *Organization & Environment* 12 (1999), pp. 305–7

Sir Richard Weston, *A discours of husbandrie used in Brabant and Flanders* (London: Samuel Hartlib, 1650)

John Winthorp, 'The description, culture, and use of maiz. Communicated by Mr. Winthorp', *Philosophical Transactions* 12 (1677)

Christian Wolff, *Anfangs-Gründe aller mathematischen Wissenschaften* (Halle: Renger, 1710)

Christian Wolff, *Vernünfftige Gedancken von den Kräfften des menschlichen Verstandes und ihrem richtigen Gebrauche in Erkäntnis der Wahrheit* (Halle: Renger, 1713)

John Worlidge, *Systema agriculturae* (London: Samuel Speed, 1669)

Carl von Wulffen, *Die Vorschule der Statik des Landbaues* (Magdeburg: Wilhelm Heinrichshofen, 1830)

Carl von Wulffen, *Entwurf einer Methodik zur Berechnung der Feldsysteme* (Berlin: Veit und Comp., 1847)

Xenophon (trans. G. Hervet) *Treatise of housholde* (London: Thomas Berthelet, 1532)

Andrew Yarranton, *England's improvement by land and sea*, vol. 1 (London: T. Parkhurst & N. Simmons, 1677)

Arthur Young, *A course of experimental agriculture* (London: J. Dodsley, 1770)

Arthur Young, *Rural oeconomy; or, essays on the practical parts of husbandry...* *To which is added, The rural Socrates: being memoirs of a country philosopher* (London: T. Becket, 1770)

Arthur Young, *Rural Oeconomy or, Essay on the practical parts of Husbandry* (London: T. Becket, 1773)

Arthur Young, 'Hints to the correspondents', *Annals of Agriculture* I (1784)

Arthur Young, 'Experiments on manures', *Annals of Agriculture* II (1784), pp. 17–32

Arthur Young, 'Experiments to ascertain how far, and in what form, Phlogiston is the food of plants', *Annals of Agriculture* I (1784), pp. 139–89

Arthur Young, 'Conclusion', *Annals of Agriculture* I (1784)

Arthur Young, 'On the Conduct of Experiments in Agriculture', *Annals of Agriculture* V (1786)

Arthur Young, 'On the Air Expelled from Earths, &c.', *Annals of Agriculture* VI (1786), pp. 265–324

Arthur Young, 'Experiments on the Food of Plants', *Annals of Agriculture* VI (1786), pp. 442–52

Arthur Young, 'Experiments on expelling air from soils', *Annals of Agriculture* XII (1789)

Arthur Young, 'An essay on manures', *Annals of Agriculture* XXXIII (1799), pp. 577–620

H.D. von Zanthier, *Abhandlungen über das theoretische und praktische Forstwesen. 2e Sammlung* (Berlin: C.W. Hennert, 1799)

Georg Heinrich Zinck, *Anfangsgründe der Cameralwissenschaft worinne dessen Grundriß weiter ausgeführet und verbessert wird. Part II* (Leipzig: Carl Ludwig Jacobi, 1755)

Secondary Sources

Wilhelm Abel, *Geschichte der deutschen Landwirtschaft*, 2nd edition (Stuttgart: E. Ulmer, 1967)

Wilhelm Abel, *Massenarmut und Hungerkrisen in vorindustriellen Europea. Versuch einer Synopsis* (Berlin: Parey, 1974)

Londa Achiebinger and Claudia Swan (eds), *Colonizing botany. Science, commerce, and politic in the early modern world* (Philadelphia, PA: University of Pennsylvania Press, 2005)

Walter Achilles, *Landwirtschaft in der frühen Neuzeit* (Munich: R. Oldenbourg, 1991)

Jorma Ahvenainen, 'Man and the forest in northern Europe from the Middle Ages to the 19th century', *Vierteljahrschrift für Sozials- und Wirtschaftsgeschichte* 83 (1996)

V.V. Alexejev. Y.V. Alexejeva and V.A. Shkerin, 'Russian forest. Its dimensions and use', in Simonetta Cavaciocchi (ed.), *L'uomo e la foresta secc. XIII–XVIII* (Florence: Le Monnier, 1996)

Robert C. Allen, *Enclosure and the yeoman* (Oxford: Oxford University Press, 1992)

Robert C. Allen, *The British Industrial Revolution in global perspective* (Cambridge: Cambridge University Press, 2009)

Joachim Allmann, *Der Wald in der frühen Neuzeit* (Berlin: Duncker & Humbolt, 1989)

Mauro Ambrosoli, *The wild and the sown. Botany and agriculture in Europe 1350–1850* (Cambridge: Cambridge University Press, 1997)

Andrew B. Appleby, *Famine in Tudor and Stuart England* (Liverpool: Liverpool University Press, 1978)

J.O. Appleby, *Economic thought and ideology in seventeenth-century England* (Princeton, NJ: Princeton University Press, 1978)

Karl Appuhn, *A forest on the sea. Environmental expertise in Renaissance Venice* (Baltimore, MD: Johns Hopkins University Press, 2009)

Tom Arkell, 'Illuminations and distortions. Gregory King's Scheme calculated for the year 1688 and the social structure of later Stuart England', *EcHR* 59 (2006), pp. 39–59

David Arnold, *The problem of nature. Environment, culture and European expansion* (Oxford: Oxford University Press, 1996)

Eric H. Ash, 'Expertise and the early modern state', in Eric H. Ash, 'Expertise. Practical knowledge and the early modern state', *Osiris* 25 (2010), pp. 1–24

Elizabeth Baigent, 'Boate, Gerard (1604–1650)', in *Oxford Dictionary of National Biography* (Oxford: Oxford University Press, 2004)

Anne Pimlott Baker, 'Ellis, William (c.1700–1758)', in *Oxford Dictionary of National Biography* (Oxford: Oxford University Press, 2004)

Stefania Barca, *Enclosing water. Nature and political economy in a Mediterranean valley, 1796–1916* (Cambridge: White Horse Press, 2010)

Toby Barnard, 'Petty, Sir William (1623–1687)', in *Oxford Dictionary of National Biography* (Oxford: Oxford University Press, 2004)

Mark V. Barrow, *Nature's ghosts. Confronting extinction from the age of Jefferson to the age of ecology* (Chicago, IL: University of Chicago Press, 2009)

Gregory A. Barton, *Empire forestry and the origins of environmentalism* (Cambridge: Cambridge University Press, 2002)

Bas van Bavel and Auke Rijpma, 'How important were formalized charity and social spending before the rise of the welfare state? A long-run analysis of selected Western European cases, 1400–1850', *EcHR* 69 (2016), pp. 159–87

James Beattie, *Empire and imperial anxiety. Health, science, art and conservation in South Asia and Australasia, 1800–1920* (Basingstoke: Palgrave Macmillan, 2011)

E.S. de Beer, 'John Evelyn F.R.S (1620–1706)', *Notes and Records of the Royal Society of London*, vol. 15 (Jul. 1960)

Wolfgang Behringer, *Witchcraft persecutions in Bavaria. Popular magic, religious zealotry and reason of state in early modern Europe* (Cambridge: Cambridge University Press, 1997)

Wolfgang Behringer, *Kulturgeschichte des Klimas. Von der Eiszeit biz zur globalen Erwärmung* (Munich: Beck, 2007)

Wolfgang Behringer, Hartmut Lehmann and Christian Pfister (eds), *Kulturelle Konsequenzen der "Kleinen Eiszeit"/Cultural consequences of the "Little Ice Age"* (Göttingen: Vandenhoeck & Ruprecht, 2005)

William Beik, *A social and cultural history of early modern France* (Cambridge: Cambridge University Press, 2009)

Bernd Bendix, 'Zur Biographie eines Vordenkers der Nachhaltigkiet, Hans Carl von Carlowitz (1645–1714)', in Sächsische Carlowitz-Gesellschaft (eds), *Die Erfindung der Nachhaltigkeit. Leben, Werk and Wirkung des Hans Carl von Carlowitz* (Munich: Oekom verlag, 2013), pp. 175–216

August Bernhardt, *Geschichte des Waldeigenthums, der Waldwirtschaft und Forstwissenschaft in Deutschland* (Berlin: J. Springer, 1872–5)

T.C.W. Blanning, *The culture of power and the power of culture. Old regime Europe 1660–1789* (Oxford: Oxford University Press, 2002)

Peter Blickle (ed.), *Deutsche ländliche Rechtsquellen* (Stuttgart: Klett-Cotta, 1977)

Peter Blickle (ed.), *Landgemeinde und Stadtgemeinde in Mitteleuropa. Ein struktereller Vergleich* (Munich: R. Oldenbourg, 1991)

Carol Blum, *Strength in numbers. Population, reproduction and power in eighteenth-century France* (Baltimore, MD: Johns Hopkins University Press, 2002)

Christian van Bochove, *The economic consequences of the Dutch. Economic integration around the North Sea, 1500–1800* (Amsterdam: Askant, 2008)

André J. Bourde, *The influence of England on the French agronomes 1750–1789* (Cambridge: Cambridge University Press, 1953)

Julie Bowring, 'Between the corporation and Captain Flood. The fens and drainage after 1663', in R. Hoyle (ed.), *Custom, improvement and the landscape in early modern Britain* (Farnham: Ashgate, 2011), pp. 235–61

Michael Braddick, *God's fury, England 's fire. A new history of the English civil wars* (London: Penguin, 2008)

Stefan Brakensiek, *Agrarreform und ländliche Gesellschaft. Die Privatisierung der Marken in Nordwestdeutschland 1750–1850* (Paderborn: Schöningh, 1991)

Helmut Brandl, *Der Stadtwald von Freiburg* (Freiburg: Wagnersche Univ.- Buchhandlung K. Zimmer, Kommissionsverlag, 1970)

Annabel S. Brett, *Changes of state. Nature and the limits of the city in early modern natural law* (Princeton, NJ: Princeton University Press, 2011)

Peter Brimblecombe, *The big smoke. A history of air pollution in London since medieval times* (London: Methuen, 1987)

William H. Brock, *Justus Liebig. The chemical gatekeeper* (Cambridge: Cambridge University Press, 1997)

Charles A. Browne, *A source book of agricultural chemistry* (Waltham, MA: Chronica Botanica Co., 1944)

Charles A. Browne, *Thomas Jefferson and the scientific trends of his time* (Waltham, MA: Chronica Botanica Co., 1944)

Peter Buck, 'People who counted. Political arithmetic in the eighteenth century', *Isis* 73 (1982), pp. 28–45

Jaap Buis, *Historia forestis. Nederlandse bosgeschiedenis* (Utrecht: HES, 1985)

Graham Burchell, Colin Gordon and Peter Miller (eds), *The Foucault effect. Studies in governmentality* (Chicago, IL: University of Chicago Press, 1991)

Peter Burke, 'The language of orders in early modern Europe', in M.L. Bush (ed.), *Social orders and social classes in Europe since 1500* (London: Routledge, 1992), pp. 1–12

Matthias Bürgi, 'How terms shape forests. "Niederwald", "Mittelwald" and "Hochwald" and their interaction with forest development in the canton of Zürich, Switzerland', *Environment and History* 5 (1999), pp. 325–244

Bob Bushaway, *By rite. Custom, ceremony and community in England 1700– 1880* (London: Junction Books, 1982)

Piero Camporesi, *Bread of dreams. Food and fantasy in early modern Europe* (Cambridge: Polity, 2005)

Jeremy L. Caradonna, *Sustainability. A history* (Oxford: Oxford University Press, 2014)

Charles F. Carroll, *The timber economy of New England* (Providence, RI: Brown, 1973)

William Cavert, 'The environmental policy of Charles I. Coal smoke and the English monarchy 1624–40', *Journal of British Studies* 53 (2014), pp. 310–33

William Cavert, *The smoke of London. Energy and environment in the early modern city* (Cambridge: Cambridge University Press, 2016)

Dipesh Chakrabarty, 'The climate of history. Four theses', *Critical Inquiry* 35 (2009), pp. 197–222

Loïc Charles, 'The visual history of the Tableau Économique', *The European Journal of the History of Economic Thought* 10 (2003), pp. 527–50

Benjamin R. Cohen, *Notes from the ground. Science, soil and society in the American countryside* (New Haven, CT: Yale University Press, 2009)

C.W. Cole, *Colbert and a century of French mercantilism* (Hamden, NY: Columbia University Press, 1939)

Harold J. Cook, *Matters of exchange. Commerce, medicine and science in the Dutch golden age* (New Haven, CT: Yale University Press, 2007)

Hadrian F. Cook and Tom Williamson (eds), *Water meadows. History, ecology and conservation* (Oxford: Windgather, 2007)

Alix Cooper, *Inventing the indigenous. Local knowledge and natural history in early modern Europe* (Cambridge: Cambridge University Press, 2007)

Gabriella Corona, *Demani ed individualism agrario nel regno di Napoli 1780–1806* (Naples: Edizioni Scientifiche Italiane, 1995)

Andrée Corvol, *L'homme et l'arbre sous l'Ancien Regime* (Paris: Economica, 1984)

Andrée Corvol, 'La decadence des forêts. Leimotiv', in Andrée Corvol (ed.), *La Forêt malade. Débats anciens et phénomènes nouveaux XVIIᵉ–XXᵉ siècles* (Paris: L'Harmattan, 1994)

Andrée Corvol, 'La belles futaies d'antan', in Andrée Corvol (ed.), *La Forêt malade. Débats anciens et phénomènes nouveaux XVIIe–XXe siècles* (Paris: L'Harmattan, 1994)

Andrée Corvol, 'Les communautés d'habitants et l'approvisionement énergetique. Les combustibles ligneux', in *Economia e energia secc. XIII–XVIII* (Florence: Le Monnier, 2003), pp. 737–64

William Cronon, *Changes in the land. Indians, colonists and the ecology of New England* (New York: Hill & Wang, 1983)

William Cronon, 'A place for stories. Nature, history, and narrative', *Journal of American History* 78 (1992), pp. 1347–76

Gordon L. Davies, *The Earth in decay. A history of British geomorphology 1578–1878* (London: Macdonald & Co, 1969)

Diana K. Davis, *Resurrecting the granary of Rome. Environmental history and French colonial expansion in North Africa* (Athens, OH: University of Ohio Press, 2007)

Diana K. Davis, *The arid lands. History, power, knowledge* (Cambridge, MA: MIT Press, 2016)

Peter Dear, *Discipline and experience. The mathematical way in the scientific revolution* (Chicago, IL: University of Chicago Press, 1995)

Peter Dear, 'Mysteries of state, mysteries of nature. Authority, knowledge and expertise in the seventeenth century', in Sheila Jasanoff (ed.), *States of knowledge. The co-production of science and social order* (Abingdon: Routledge, 2004), pp. 205–9

Peter Dear, 'The meanings of experience', in Katherine Park and Lorraine Daston (eds), *The Cambridge history of science. Vol. 3. Early modern science* (Cambridge: Cambridge University Press, 2006), pp. 106–31

Allen G. Debus, 'Palissy, Plat and English agricultural chemistry in the 16th and 17th centuries', *Archives internationals d'histoire* 21 (1968), pp. 67–88

Allen G. Debus, *The chemical philosophy. Paracelsian science and medicine in the sixteenth and seventeenth centuries* (Mineola, NY: Science History Publications, 1977)

Allen G. Debus, *Chemistry, alchemy and the new philosophy 1550–1700* (London: Variorum Collected Studies, 1987)

Allen G. Debus, 'The Paracelsian Aerial Niter', in Allen G. Debus (eds), *Chemistry, alchemy and the new philosophy* (London: Variorum Collected Studies, 1987), IX

Allen G. Debus, 'Chemistry and the quest for a material spirit of life in the seventeenth century', in Allen G. Debus, *Chemistry, alchemy and the new philosophy* (London: Variorum Collected Studies, 1987), X

Burkhard Dietz, 'Wirtschaftliches Wachstum und Holzmangel in bergisch-märkischen Gewerberaum vor der Industrialisierung', www.lrz-muenchen. de/~MW?Hardenstein/Dietz/htm

Brian Donahue, *The Great Meadow. Farmers and the land in colonial Concord* (New Haven, CT: Yale University Press, 2004)

Richard Drayton, *Nature's government. Science, imperial Britain, and the 'improvement' of the world* (New Haven, CT: Yale University Press, 2000)

Prasenjit Duara, *The crisis of global modernity. Asian traditions and a sustainable future* (Cambridge: Cambridge University Press, 2015)

J.H. Eddy Jr, 'Buffon, organic alterations, and man', in *Studies in the History of Biology* 7, eds William Coleman and Camille Limoges (Baltimore, MD: Johns Hopkins University Press, 1984), pp. 22–39

Frank N. Egerton, 'Bradley, Richard (1688?–1732)', in *Oxford Dictionary of National Biography* (Oxford: Oxford University Press, 2004)

Per Eliasson and Sven G. Nilsson, 'Rättat efter skogarnes aftagende – en miljöhistorisk undersökning av den svenska eken under 1700- och 1800-talen', *Bybeyggelsehistorisk Tidskrift* 37 (1999), pp. 33–64

Siegfried Epperlein, *Waldnutzung, Waldstreitigkeiten und Waldschutz in Deutschland im hohen Mittelalter. 2. Hälfte 11. Jahrhundert bis ausgehendes 14. Jahhundert* (Stuttgart: Steiner, 1993)

Christoph Ernst, *Den Wald entwickeln. Ein Politik- und Konfliktfled in Hunsrück und Eifel im 18. Jahrhundert* (Munich: De Gruyter Oldenbourg, 2000)

Heather Falvey, 'Marking the boundaries. William Jordan's 1633 pre-enclosure survey of Duffield Frith (Derbyshire)', *Agricultural History Review* 61(I) (2013), pp. 1–18

James R. Farr, *Artisans in Europe 1300–1914* (Cambridge: Cambridge University Press, 2000)

Mark R. Finlay, 'The rehabilitation of an agricultural chemist. Justus von Liebig and the seventh edition', *Ambix* 38 (1991), pp. 155–66

John Bellamy Foster, '"Robbing the Earth of its capital stock". An introduction to George Waring's *Agricultural Features of the Census of the United States for 1850*', *Organization & Environment* 12 (1999), pp. 293–7

John Bellamy Foster, *Marx's ecology. Materialism and nature* (New York: Monthly Review Press, 2000)

Sally Foster and Thomas Christopher Smout, *The history of soils and field systems* (Aberdeen: Scottish Cultural Press, 1994)

Paula Findlen, 'Francis Bacon and the reform of natural history in the seventeenth century', in Donald R. Kelley (ed.), *History and the disciplines. The reclassification of knowledge in early modern Europe* (Rochester, NY: University of Rochester Press, 1997), pp. 239–60

Andrea Finkelstein, *Harmony and balance. An intellectual history of seventeenth-century English economic thought* (Ann Arbor, MI: University of Michigan Press, 2000)

Michel Foucault, *Security, territory, population lectures at the Collège de France, 1977–78*, ed. Michel Sellenart (London: Palgrave Macmillan, 2009)

Adam Fox, 'Printed questionnaires, research networks, and the discovery of the British Isles, 1650–1800', *The Historical Journal* 53 (2010), pp. 593–625

Jean-Baptiste Fressoz, *L'apocalypse joyeuse. Une histoire du risqué technologique* (Paris: Seuil, 2012)

Jean-Baptiste Fressoz, 'Losing the Earth knowingly. Six environmental grammars around 1800', in Clive Hamilton, Christoph Bonneuil and Francois Gemenne (eds), *The Anthropocene and the global environmental crisis* (Abingdon: Routledge, 2015), pp. 70–83

Robert von Friedeburg, 'The making of patriots. Love of fatherland and negotiating monarchy in seventeenth-century Germany', *Journal of Modern History* 77 (2005), pp. 881–916

Bo Fritzbøger, *A windfall for the magnates. The development of woodland ownership in Denmark, c.1150–1850* (Odense: Syddansk Universitetsforlag, 2004)

George E. Fussell, *The old English farming books from Fitzherbert to Tull 1523–1730* (London: C. Lockwood, 1947)

George E. Fussell, *Farming technique from prehistoric to modern times* (Oxford: Pergamon, 1965)

George E. Fussell, *Crop nutrition. Science and practice before Liebig* (Lavenham: Tortoise Shell Press, 1971)

George E. Fussell, *Jethro Tull. His influence on mechanized agriculture* (Reading: Osprey Publishing, 1973)

Malcolm Gaskill, *Between two worlds. How the English became Americans* (Oxford: Oxford University Press, 2013)

Stephen Gaukroger, *Francis Bacon and the transformation of early-modern philosophy* (Cambridge: Cambridge University Press, 2001)

Stephen Gaukroger, *The collapse of mechanism and the rise of sensibility. Science and the shaping of modernity 1680–1760* (Oxford: Oxford University Press, 2010)

Stephen Gaukroger, *The natural and the human. Science and the shaping of modernity 1739–1841* (Oxford: Oxford University Press, 2016)

E.F. Gay, 'The authorship of the Book of Husbandry and the Book of Surveying', *The Quarterly Journal of Economics* 18(4) (Aug. 1904), pp. 588–93

John G. Gazley, *The life of Arthur Young 1741–1820* (Philadephia, PA: American Philosophical Society, 1973)

Charles Coulsen Gillispie, *Science and polity in France. The end of the Old Regime* (Princeton, NJ: Princeton University Press, 2009)

Clarence Glacken, *Traces on the Rhodian Shore. Nature and culture in Western thought from ancient times to the end of the eighteenth century* (Berkeley, CA: University of California Press, 1967)

Jan Golinski, *British weather and the climate of Enlightenment* (Chicago, IL: University of Chicago Press, 2007)

Margaret Grabas, 'Krisenbewältigung oder Modernisierungsblockade? Die Rolle des Staates bei der Überwindung des "Holzenergiemangels" zu Beginn der Industriellen Revolution in Deutschland', *Jahrbuch für europäische Verwaltungsgeschichte* 7 (1995), pp. 43–75

Christa Graefe, *Forstleute. Von den Anfängen einer Behörde und ihren Beamten Braunschweig-Wolfenbüttel 1530–1607* (Wiesbaden: Kommission bei Harrassowitz, 1989)

Hamish Graham, 'Fleurs-de-lis in the forest. 'Absolute' monarchy and attempts at resource management in eighteenth-century France', *French History* 23 (2009), pp. 311–35

Marion W. Gray, 'From the household economy to "rational agriculture". The establishment of liberal ideals in German agricultural thought', in Konrad H. Jarausch and Larry Eugene Jones (eds), *In search of liberal Germany. Studies in the history of German liberalism from 1789 to the present* (New York: Berg, 1990), pp. 25–54

Mark Greengrass, 'Hartlib, Samuel (*c.*1600–1662)', in *Oxford Dictionary of National Biography* (Oxford: Oxford University Press, 2004)

Bernd-Stefan Grewe, *Der versperrte Wald. Ressourcenmangel in der bayerischen Pfalz (1814–1870)* (Köln: Böhlau, 2004)

Bernd-Stefan Grewe, '"Man sollte sehen und weinen!" Holznotalarm und Waldzerstörung vor der Industrialisierung', in Frank Uekötter and Jens Hohensee (eds), *Wird Kassandra heiser? Die Geschichte falscher Ökoalarme* (Stuttgart: Steiner, 2004), pp. 24–41

Ulbrich Grober, *Die Entdeckung der Nachhaltigkeit. Kulturgeschichte eines Begriffs*, 3rd edition (Frankfurt: Kunstmann, 2010)

Richard H. Grove, *Green imperialism. Colonial expansion, tropical island Edens and the origins of environmentalism 1600–1860* (Cambridge: Cambridge University Press, 1995)

Ian Hacking, *The emergence of probability*, 2nd edition (Cambridge: Cambridge University Press, 2006)

Marie Boas Hall, *Henry Oldenburg. Shaping the Royal Society* (Oxford: Oxford University Press, 2002)

Marie Boas Hall, 'Oldenburg, Henry (*c.*1619–1677), in *Oxford Dictionary of National Biography* (Oxford: Oxford University Press, 2004)

Garrett Hardin, 'The tragedy of the commons', *Science* 162 (13 Dec. 1968), pp. 1243–8

Deborah Harkness, *The Jewel House. Elizabethan London and the scientific revolution* (New Haven, CT: Yale University Press, 2007)

Esmond Harris, Jeanette Harris and N.D.G. James, *Oak. A British history* (Macclesfield: Windgather, 2003)

Peter Harrison, *The Bible, Protestantism, and the rise of natural science* (Cambridge: Cambridge University Press, 1998)

K. Härter (ed.), *Policey und frühneuzeitliche Gesellschaft* (Frankfurt: Klostermann, 2000)

K. Härter, *Polizey und Strafjustiz in Kurmainz. Gesetzgebung, Normdurchsetzung und Sozialkontolle im frühneitzeitlichen Territorialstaat* (Frankfurt: Klostermann, 2005)

Beryl Hartley, 'Exploring and communicating knowledge of trees in the early Royal Society', *Notes and Records of the Royal Society of London* 64(3) (20 Sep. 2010), pp. 229–50

Karl Hasel and Ekkehard Schwartz, *Forstgeschichte. Ein Grundriss für Studium und Praxis*, 3rd edition (Remagen-Oberwinter: Kessel, 2006)

Albert Hauser, *Wald und Feld in der alten Schweiz* (Zurich: Artemis Verlag, 1972)

John Hatcher, *The history of the British coal industry. Vol I. Before 1700. Towards the age of coal* (Oxford: Clarendon, 1993)

Dorothea Hauff, *Zur Geschichte der Forstgesetzgebung und Forstorganisation des Herzogtums Württemberg im 16. Jahrhundert* (Stuttgart: Landesforst verwaltung Baden-Württemberg, 1977)

Eli F. Heckscher, *Mercantilism*, revised edition, ed. E.F. Söderlund (London: Allen & Unwin, 1955)

Blanche Henrey, *British botanical and horticultural literature before 1800. Vol. I. The sixteenth and seventeenth centuries* (Oxford: Oxford University Press, 1975)

Steve Hindle, 'Dearth, fasting and alms. The campaign for general hospitality in late Elizabethan England', *Past & Present* 172 (2001), pp. 44–86

Steve Hindle, *On the parish? The micro-politics of poor relief in rural England, c.1550–1750* (Oxford: Oxford University Press, 2004)

Steve Hindle, 'Dearth and the English revolution. The harvest crisis of 1647–50', *EcHR* 61(S1) (2008), pp. 64–98

Stephen Hipkin, 'The structure, development and politics of the Kent grain trade, 1552–1647', *EcHR* 61(S1) (2008), pp. 99–139

Wolfgang von Hippel, 'Bevölkerung und Wirtschaft im Zeitalter des 30 jährigen Krieges', *Zeitschrift für historische Forschung* (1978), pp. 412–48

Richard C. Hoffmann, *An environmental history of medieval Europe* (Cambridge: Cambridge University Press, 2013)

André Holenstein, *'Gute Policey' und lokale Gesellschaft im Staat des Ancien Régime. Das Fallbeispiel der Markgrafschaft Baden(-Durlach)* (Epfendorf/Neckar: Bibliotecha Academica, 2003)

Laura Hollsten, 'Controlling nature and transforming landscapes in the early modern Caribbean', *Global Environment* 1 (2008), pp. 80–113

Richard Hölzl, *Umkämpfte Wälder. Die Gscichte einer ökologischen Reform in Deutschland 1760–1860* (Frankfurt: Klostermann, 2010)

Julian Hoppitt, 'Political arithmetic in eighteenth-century England', *EcHR* 49 (1996), pp. 519–33

Richard Hoyle, 'Famine as agricultural catastrophe. The crisis of 1622–4 in east Lancashire', *EcHR* 63 (2010), pp. 974–1002

Michael Hunter, 'Grew, Nehemiah (*bap.* 1641, *d.* 1712)', in *Oxford Dictionary of National Biography* (Oxford: Oxford University Press, May 2009)

Terence Hutchison, *Before Adam Smith. The emergence of political economy, 1662–1776* (Oxford: Oxford University Press, 1988)

Vladimir Jankovic, *Reading the skies. A cultural history of English weather, 1650–1820* (Chicago, IL: University of Chicago Press, 2000)

Lisa Jardine and Alan Stewart, *Hostage to fortune. The troubled life of Francis Bacon* (London: Gollancz, 1998)

Mark Jenner, 'The politics of London Air. John Evelyn's Fumifugium and the Restoration', *The Historical Journal* 38 (1995), pp. 535–51

Elisabeth Johann, *Geschichte der Waldnutzung in Kärnten unter dem Einfluß der Berg-, Hütten- und Hammerwerke* (Klagenfurt: Verlag des Geschichtsvereines für Kärnten, 1968)

Peter Jones, *Agricultural Enlightenment. Knowledge, technology, and nature, 1750–1840* (Oxford: Oxford University Press, 2016)

Peter Jones, 'Making chemistry the "science" of agriculture, c. 1760–1840', *History of Science* 54 (2016), pp. 169–94

Richard Jones, 'Why manure matters', in Richard Jones (ed.), *Manure matters. Historical, archaeological and ethnographic perspectives* (Farnham: Ashgate, 2012), pp. 5–8

Fredrik Albritton Jonsson, *Enlightenment's frontier. The Scottish highlands and the origins of environmentalism* (New Haven, CT: Yale University Press, 2013)

Fredrik Albritton Jonsson, 'The natural history of improvement', in Philip J. Stern and Carl Wennerlind (eds), *Mercantilism reimagined. Political economy in early modern Britain and its empire* (Oxford: Oxford University Press, 2014), pp. 117–33

Robert Jütte, *Obrigkeitliche Armenfürsorge in deutschen Reichsstädten der frühen neuzeit. Städtischen Armenwesen in Frankfurt am Main und Köln* (Köln: Böhlau, 1984)

Robert Jütte, 'Klimabedingte Teuerungen und Hungersnöte. Bettelverbote und Armenfürsorge als Krisenmanagement', in Behringer et al., *Kulturelle Konsequenzen*, pp. 225–37

Astrid Kander, Paolo Malanima and Paul Warde, *Power to the people. Energy in Europe over the last five centuries* (Princeton, NJ: Princeton University Press, 2013)

Stephen L. Kaplan, *Bread, politics and political economy in the reign of Louis XV* (The Hague: Martinus Nijhoff, 1976)

H.S.K. Kent, *War and trade in northern seas. Anglo-Scandinavian economic relations in the mid-eighteenth century* (Cambridge: Cambridge University Press, 1973)

Eric Kerridge, *The agricultural revolution* (London: George Allen & Unwin, 1967)

R.W. Ketton-Cremer, *Felbrigg. The story of a house* (London: Rupert Hart-Davis, 1962)

Richard Keyser, 'The transformation of traditional woodland management. Commercial sylviculture in medieval Champagne', *French Historical Studies* 32 (2009), pp. 353–84

Andreas Kieser, *Alt-Württemberg in Ortsansichten und Landkarten, 1680–1687* (Stuttgart: Theiss, 1985)

Peter King, 'The production and consumption of bar iron in early modern England and Wales', *EcHR* 58(1) (2005), pp. 1–33

Judy L. Klein, *Statistical visions in time. A history of time series analysis 1662–1938* (Cambridge: Cambridge University Press, 1997)

Isabelle Knap, 'Die Anfänge "wissenschaftlicher" Frstleuten am Beispiel des *Allgemeinen oeconomischen Forst-Magazins* (1763–1769)', in Marcus Popplow (ed.), *Landschaften agrarisch-ökonomischen Wissens. Strategien innovativer Ressourcennutzung in Zeitschfiften und Sozietäten des 18. Jahrhunderts* (Münster: Waxmann, 2010), pp. 61–78

David Knight, 'Agriculture and chemistry in Britain around 1800', *Annals of Science 33* (1976), pp. 187–96

Mark Knights, 'Commonwealth. The social, cultural, and conceptual contexts of an early modern keyword', *The Historical Journal 54* (2011), pp. 663–7

Martin Knoll, *Umwelt – Herrschaft – Gesellschaft. Die landesherrliche Jagd Kurbayerns im 18. Jahrhundert* (St. Katharinen: Scripta Mercaturae, 2004)

Joseph Leo Koerner, *Caspar David Friedrich and the subject of landscape*, 2nd edition (London: Reaktion, 2009)

Lisbet Koerner, *Linnaeus. Nature and nation* (Cambridge, MA: Harvard University Press, 1999)

J.T. Kolitaine, *Russia's foreign trade and economic expansion in the seventeenth century. Windows on the world* (Leiden: Brill, 2005)

Detlef Krannhals, *Danzig in der Weichselhandel in seiner Blütezeit vom 16. bis zum 17. Jahrhundert* (Leipzig: Hirzel Verlag, 1942)

K. Krüger, *Finanzstaat Hessen 1500–1567. Staatsbildung im Übergang vom Domänstaat zum Steuerstaat* (Marburg: Elwert, 1980)

Teresa Kwiatkowska and Alan Holland, 'Dark is the world to thee. A historical perspective on environmental forewarnings', *Environment and History 16* (2010), pp. 455–82

Erich Landsteiner, 'The crisis of wine production in late sixteenth-century central Europe. Climatic causes and economic consequences', *Climatic Change 43* (1999), pp. 323–34

Achim Landwehr, *Policey im Alltag. Die Implementation frühneuzeitlicher Policeyordnungen in Leonberg* (Frankfurt am Main: Klostermann, 2000)

Achim Landwehr, 'Die Rhetorik der "Guten Policey"', *Zeitschrift für historische Forschung 30* (2003), pp. 251–87

James L. Larson, *Interpreting nature. The science of living form from Linneaus to Kant* (Baltimore, MD: Johns Hopkins University Press, 1994)

Sidney Lee, 'Plat, Sir Hugh (*bap.* 1552, *d.*1608)', rev. Anita McConnell, in *Oxford Dictionary of National Biography* (Oxford: Oxford University Press, 2004)

Reginald Lennard, 'English agriculture under Charles II. The evidence of the Royal Society's "Enquiries"', *EcHR 4* (1932), pp. 23–45

Aldo Leopold, *A Sand County almanac. Sketches here and there* (Oxford: Oxford University Press, 1949)

Keith Lindley, *Fenland riots and the English revolution* (London: Heinemann Educational, 1982)

Alexis D. Litvine, 'The industrious revolution, the industriousness discourse, and the development of modern economies', *Historical Journal* 72(2) (2014), pp. 531–70

Fabien Locher and Jean-Baptiste Fressoz, 'Modernity's frail climate. A climate history of environmental reflexivity', *Critical Inquiry* 38 (2012), pp. 579–98

A. Low, *The Georgic revolution* (Princeton, NJ: Princeton University Press, 1985)

W.C. Lowdermilk, *Conquest of the land through seven thousand years*. USDA report, Aug. 1953

David Lowenthal, *George Perkins Marsh. Versatile Vermonter* (New York: Columbia University Press, 1958)

H.E. Lowood, 'The calculating forester. Quantification, cameral science and the emergence of scientific forestry management in Germany', in T. Frängsmyr, T.L. Heilbronn and R.E. Rider (eds), *The quantifying spirit in the 18th century* (Oxford: Oxford University Press, 1990), pp. 315–42

S. Todd Lowry, 'The agricultural foundation of the seventeenth-century English oeconomy', *History of Political Economy* 35(Suppl. 1) (2003), pp. 74–100

Katherine Lynch, *Individuals, families, and communities in Europe, 1200–1800. The urban foundations of Western society* (Cambridge: Cambridge University Press, 2003)

Friedrich Mager, *Der Wald in Altpreussen als Wirtschaftsraum* (Köln: Böhlau, 1960)

Lars Magnusson, 'Comparing cameralisms. The cases of Sweden and Prussia', in Marten Seppel and Keith Tribe (eds), *Cameralism in practice. State administration and economy in early modern Europe* (Woodbridge: Boydell & Brewer, 2017)

Erich Bauer Manderscheid, *Los montes de España en la historia* (Madrid: Ministerio de Agricultura, Pesca y Alimentación, 1991)

Kurt Mantel, *Forstgeschichte des 16. Jahrhunderts unter dem Einfluß der Forstordinungen und Noe Meurers* (Hamburg: Parey, 1980)

Erland Mårald, *Jordens kretslop. Landbruket, staden och den kemiska vetenskapen 1840–1910* (Umea: Umea Universitet, 2000)

Kieko Matteson, *Forests in revolutionary France. Conservation, community, and conflict, 1669–1848* (Cambridge: Cambridge University Press, 2015)

Donald R. McCloskey, 'The Prudent peasant. New findings on open fields', *Journal of Economic History* 51 (1991), pp. 343–55

Ted McCormick, *William Petty and the ambitions of political arithmetic* (Oxford: Oxford University Press, 2009)

Ted McCormick, 'Population. Modes of seventeenth-century demographic thought', in Philip J. Stern and Carl Wennerlind (eds), *Mercantilism reimagined. Political economy in early modern Britain and its empire* (New York: Oxford University Press, 2014), pp. 25–45

Andrew McCrae, 'To know one's own. Estate surveying and the representation of the land in early modern England', *Huntington Library Quarterly* 56 (1993), pp. 332–57

Andrew McCrae, *God speed the plough. The representation of agrarian England, 1500–1660* (Cambridge: Cambridge University Press, 1996)

Andrew McRae, 'Tusser, Thomas (c.1524–1580)', in *Oxford Dictionary of National Biography* (Oxford: Oxford University Press, 2004)

Carolyn Merchant, *The death of nature. Women, ecology, and the scientific revolution* (San Fransisco, CA: Harper & Row, 1980)

Carolyn Merchant, *Reinventing Eden. The fate of nature in Western culture* (New York: Routledge, 2003)

Carolyn Merchant, 'Secrets of nature. The Bacon debates revisited', *Journal of the History of Ideas* 69(1) (2008), pp. 147–62

Gregg Mitman, *The state of nature. Ecology, community, and American social thought, 1900–1950* (Chicago, IL: University of Chicago Press, 1992)

Michael Mittrauer and Reinhard Siedler, *The European family. Patriarchy to partnership from the Middle Ages to the present* (Oxford: Blackwell, 1982)

Manuel González de Molina and Víctor M. Toledo, *The social metabolism. A socio-ecological theory of historical change* (Cham: Springer, 2014)

David Moon, *The plough that broke the steppes. Agriculture and environment on Russia's grasslands, 1700–1914* (Oxford: Oxford University Press, 2013)

Martina de Moor, Leigh Shaw-Taylor and Paul Warde (eds), *The management of common land in north west Europe 1500–1850* (Turnhout: Brepols, 2002)

John E. Morgan, 'Flooding in early modern England. Cultures of coping in Gloucestershire and Lincolnshire', PhD thesis, University of Warwick, 2016

Sara Morrison, 'The Stuart forests. From venison pie to wooden walls', PhD thesis, University of Western Ontario, 2004

Chandra Mukerji, 'The great forest survey of 1669–1671. The use of archives for political reform', *Social Studies of Science* 37(2) (2007), pp. 593–625

Chandra Mukerji, *Impossible engineering. Technology and territoriality on the Canal du Midi* (Princeton, NJ: Princeton University Press, 2009)

Ayesha Mukherjee, *Penury into plenty. Dearth and the making of knowledge in early modern England* (London: Routledge, 2015)

Craig Muldrew, *Food, energy and the creation of industriousness. Work and material culture in agrarian England, 1550–1780* (Cambridge: Cambridge University Press, 2011)

Craig Muldrew, 'From commonwealth to public opulence. The redefinition of wealth and government in early modern Britain', in Steve Hindle, Alexandra Shepard and John Walter (eds), *Remaking English society. Social relations and social change in early modern England* (Woodbridge: Boydell & Brewer, 2013), pp. 317–39

Thomas Munck, *Seventeenth century Europe 1598–1700* (Basingstoke: Palgrave Macmillan, 1990)

Pat Munday, 'Liebig's Metamorphosis. From organic chemistry to the chemistry of agriculture', *Ambix* 38 (1991), pp. 135–54

Pat Munday, 'Politics by other means. Justus von Liebig and the German translation of John Stuart Mill's *Logic*', *British Journal of the History of Science* 31 (1998), pp. 403–18

Charles G. Nauert, *Humanism and the culture of Renaissance Europe* (Cambridge: Cambridge University Press, 1995)

Majorie Hope Nicolson, *Mountain gloom and mountain glory. The development of the aesthetics of the infinite* (Seattle, WA: University of Washington Press, 1997 [1961])

Katia Occhi, *Boschi e mercanti. Traffici di legname tra la contea di Tirolo e la Repubblica di Venezia (secoli XVI–SVII)* (Bologna: Il Mulino, 2006)

Brian Ogilvie, *The science of describing. Natural history in Renaissance Europe* (Chicago, IL: University of Chicago Press, 2005)

Fairfield Osborn, *Our plundered planet* (Boston, MA: Little, Brown, 1948)

R.B. Outhwaite, *Dearth, public policy and social disturbance in England, 1550–1800* (Basingstoke: Macmillan, 1991)

José Augusto Pádua, '"Annihilating Natural Productions". Nature's economy, colonial crisis and the orgiins of Brazilian political environmentalism (1786–1810)', *Environment and History* 6 (2000), pp. 255–87

José Augusto Pádua, 'The theoretical foundations of environmental history', *Estudos Avançados* 68 (2010), pp. 81–101

Walter Pagel, *Joan Baptista van Helmont. Reformer of science and medicine* (Cambridge: Cambridge University Press, 1982)

Silvana Patriaca, *Numbers and nationhood. Writing statistics in nineteenth-century Italy* (Cambridge: Cambridge University Press, 1996)

Michael Perelman, 'Henry Carey's ecological economics', *Organization & Environment* 12 (1999), pp. 281–4

Philip A.J. Pettit. *The royal forests of Northamptonshire. A study in their economy 1558–1714* (Gateshead: Northumberland Press/ Northamptonshire Record Society, 1968)

Christian Pfister, 'Climatic extremes, recurrent crises and witch hunts. Strategies of European societies in coping with exogenous shocks in the late sixteenth and early seventeenth centuries', *The Medieval History Journal* 10 (2007), pp. 1–41

Christian Pfister and Rudolf Brázdil, 'Climatic variability in sixteenth century Europe and its social dimension. A synthesis', *Climatic Change* 43 (1999), pp. 5–53

Marcus Popplow, 'Die ökonomische Aufklärung als Innovationskultur des 18. Jahrhunderts zur optmierten Nutzung natürlicher Ressourcen', in Marcus Popplow (ed.), *Landschaften agrarisch-ökonomischen Wissens. Strategien innovativer Ressourcennutzung in Zeitschfiften und Sozietäten des 18. Jahrhunderts* (Münster: Waxmann, 2010), pp. 2–48

Marcus Popplow, 'Von Bienen, Ochsenklauen und Beamten. Die ökonomischen Aufklärung in der Kurpfalz', in Marcus Popplow (ed.), *Landschaften agrarisch-ökonomischen Wissens. Strategien innovativer Ressourcennutzung in Zeitschfiften und Sozietäten des 18. Jahrhunderts* (Münster: Waxmann, 2010), pp. 175–235

Theodore M. Porter, *The rise of statistical thinking 1820–1900* (Princeton, NJ: Princeton University Press, 1986)

Theodore Porter, *Trust in numbers. The pursuit of objectivity in science and public life* (Princeton, NJ: Princeton University Press, 1995)

John Prest, *The garden of Eden. The botanic garden and the re-creation of paradise* (New Haven, CT: Yale University Press, 1981)

Oliver Rackham, *Ancient woodland. Its history, vegetation and uses in England* (London: Edward Arnold, 1980)

Joachim Radkau, 'Holzverknappung und Krisenbewußtsein im 18. Jahrhundert', *Geschichte und Gesellschaft* 4 (1983), pp. 513–43

Joachim Radkau, 'Zur angeblichen Energiekrise des 18. Jahrhunderts. Revisionistische Betrachtungen über die "Holznot"', *Vierteljahrschrift für Sozials- und Wirtschaftsgeschichte* 73 (1986), pp. 1–37

Joachim Radkau, 'Warum wurde die Gefährdung der Natur durch den Menschen nicht rechtzeitig erkannt? Naturkult und Angst vor Holznot um 1800', in Hermann Lübbe and Elisabeth Ströker (eds), *Ökologische Probleme im kulturellen Wandel* (Paderborn: Wilhelm Fink Verlag, 1986), pp. 47–78

Joachim Radkau, *Holz – wie ein Naturstoff geschichte schreibt* (Munich: Oekom verlag, 2007)

Joachim Radkau, 'Das Rätsel der städtischen Brennholzversorgung im "Hölzernen Zeitalter"', in Dieter Schott (ed.), *Energie und Stadt in Europa. Von der vorindustriellen 'Holznot' bis zur Ölkrise der 1970er Jahre.* Beihefte der Vierteljahrschrift für Sozials- und Wirtschaftsgeschichte 155 (Stuttgart, 2007), pp. 43–75

Mark Raeff, *The well-ordered police state. Social and institutional change through law in the Germanies and Russia, 1600–1800* (New Haven, CT: Yale University Press, 1983)

Ravi Rajan, *Modernizing nature. Forestry and imperial eco-development 1800–1950* (Oxford: Oxford University Press, 2006)

Graham Rees, 'Francis Bacon and *Spiritus Vitalis*', in Marta Fattori and Massimo Bianchi (eds), *Spiritus. IV° Colloquio internazionale del lessico intellettuale Europeo* (Rome, 1984), pp. 265–81

Peter Hanns Reill, *Vitalizing nature in the Enlightenment* (Berkeley, CA: University of California Press, 2005)

Sophus Reinert, 'Introduction', in Antonio Serra, *A short treatise on wealth and poverty of nations (1613)*, ed. Sophus Reinert (London: Anthem Press, 2011), pp. 1–85

Harriet Ritvo, *The dawn of green. Manchester, Thirlmere and modern environmentalism* (Chicago, IL: University of Chicago Press, 2009)

John Robertson, *The case for the Enlightenment. Scotland and Naples 1680–1760* (Cambridge: Cambridge University Press, 2007)

Elly Robson, 'Improvement and epistemologies of landscape in seventeenth-century English forest enclosure', *Historical Journal* (Oct. 2016), pp. 1–36

Alessandro Ronacglia, *The wealth of ideas. A history of economic thought* (Cambridge: Cambridge University Press, 2005)

Lyndal Roper, '"The common man", "the common good", "common women". Gender and meaning in the German Reformation commune', *Social History* 12 (1987), pp. 1–22

Margaret W. Rossiter, *The emergence of agricultural science. Justus Liebig and the Americans, 1840–1880* (New Haven, CT: Yale University Press, 1975)

Emma Rothschild, *The inner life of empires. An eighteenth century history* (Princeton, NJ: Princeton University Press, 2011)

Heinrich Rubner, *Forstgeschichte im Zeitalter der industriellen Revolution* (Berlin: Duncker & Humbolt, 1967)

Andrea A. Rusnock, *Vital accounts. Quantifying health and population in eighteenth-century England and France* (Cambridge: Cambridge University Press, 2002)

Margaret Schabas, *The natural origins of economics* (Chicago, IL: University of Chicago Press, 2005)

Ingrid Schäfer, '*Ein Gespenst geht um*'. *Politik mit der Holznot in Lippe 1750–1850. Eine Regionalstudie zur Wald und Technikgeschichte* (Detmold: Naturwissenschaftlicher u. Historischer Verein f. d. Land Lippe, 1992)

Simon Schama, *Landscape and memory* (London: Fontana, 1996)

Winifried Schenk, *Waldnutzung, Waldzustand und regionale Entwicklung in vorindustrieller Zeit im mittleren Deutschland* (Stuttgart: Steiner, 1996)

Jürgen Schlumbohm, 'Gesetze, die nicht durchgesetzt warden – ein Strukturmerkmal des frühneuzetlichen Staates', *Geschichte und Gesellschaft* 23 (1997), pp. 647–63

Uwe E. Schmidt, *Der Wald in Deutschland im 18. und 19. Jahrhundert. Das Problem der Ressourcenknappheit dargestellt am Beispiel der Waldressourcenknappheit in Deutschland im 18. und 19. Jahrhundert – eine historisch-politische Analyse* (Saarbrücken: Conte, 2002)

Ivo Schneider, 'Mathematisierung des Wahrscheinlichen und Anwendung auf Massenphänomene im 17. und 18. Jahrhundert', in Mohammed Rassem and Justin Stagl (eds), *Statistik und Staatsbeschreibung in der Neuzeit vornehmich im 16.–18. Jahrhundert* (Paderborn: Schöningh, 1980), pp. 53–66

Ernst Schubert, 'Der Wald. Wirtschaftliche Grundlage derspätmittelalterlichen Stadt', in Bernd Herrmann (ed.), *Mensch und Umwelt im Mittelalter* (Stuttgart: Deutsche Verlags-Anstalt, 1987), pp. 257–69

Winifried Schulze, 'Vom Gemeinnutz zum Eigennutz', *Historische Zeitschrift* 243 (1986), pp. 591–625

A.F. Schwappach, *Handbuch der Forst-und Jagdgeschichte Deutschlands* (Berlin: J. Springer, 1886)

Elizabeth Scott, 'The secret nature of seeds. Science and seed improvement, c. 1520–1700', PhD thesis, University of East Anglia, 2016

James C. Scott, *Seeing like a state. How certain schemes to improve the human condition have failed* (New Haven, CT: Yale University Press, 1998)

Paul B. Sears, *Deserts on the march* (Norman, OK: University of Oklahoma Press, 1947 [1935])

Bill Shannon, 'Approvement and Improvement in the lowland wastes of early modern Lancashire', in R. Hoyle (ed.), *Custom, improvement and the landscape in early modern Britain* (Farnham: Ashgate, 2011), pp. 175–202

Barbara Shapiro, *A culture of fact. England, 1550–1720* (Ithaca, NY: Cornell University Press, 2000)

Lindsay Sharp, 'Timber, science, and economic reform in the seventeenth century', *Forestry* 48 (1975), pp. 60–1

Leigh Shaw-Taylor, 'The management of common land in the lowlands of southern England, c. 1500–c. 1850', in de Moor et al., *The management of common land*, pp. 59–85

James Sheehan, *German history 1770–1866* (Oxford: Oxford University Press, 1989)

Rolf Peter Sieferle, *Bevölkerungswachstum und Naturhaushalt. Studien zur Naturtheorie der klassischen Ökonomie* (Frankfurt: Suhrkamp Verlag, 1990)

Rolf-Peter Sieferle, *The subterranean forest. Energy systems and the Industrial Revolution* (Knapwell: White Horse Press, 2001)

Jörn Sieglerschmidt, 'Die virtuelle Landwirtschaft der Hausväterliteratur', in Rolf Peter Sieferle and H. Brueninger (eds), *Natur-Bilder. Wahrnehmungen von Natur und Umwelt in der Geschichte* (Frankfurt: Campus, 1999), pp. 223–54

Dana Simmons, *Vital minimum. Need, science and politics in modern France* (Chicago, IL: University of Chicago Press, 2015)

T. Simon, *'Gute Polizey'. Ordnungsleitbilder und Zielvorstellungen politischen Handelns in der frühen Neuzeit* (Frankfurt: Klostermann, 2004)

Quentin Skinner, *Foundations of modern political thought, volume 1: The Renaissance* (Cambridge: Cambridge University Press, 1978)

Paul Slack, *Poverty and policy in Tudor and Stuart England* (London: Longman, 1988)

Paul Slack, *From Reformation to improvement. Public welfare in early modern England* (Oxford: Oxford University Press, 1999)

Paul Slack, *The invention of improvement. Information and material progress in seventeenth-century England* (Oxford: Oxford University Press, 2014)

A.W. Small, *The cameralists. The pioneers of German social policy* (New York: Burt Franklin, 1909)

T.C. Smout, Alan R. MacDonald and Fiona Watson, *A history of the native woodlands of Scotland, 1500–1920* (Edinburgh: Edinburgh University Press, 2005)

Jacob Soll, 'Accounting for government. Holland and the rise of political economy in seventeenth-century Europe', *Journal of Interdisciplinary History* XL (2009), pp. 215–38

Emma Spary, *Utopia's garden. French natural history from Old Regime to Revolution* (Chicago, IL: University of Chicago Press, 2000)

Emma Spary, '"Peaches which the patriarchs lacked". Natural history, natural resources, and the natural economy in France', *History of Political Economy* 35(Suppl. 1) (2003), pp. 14–41

David Souden, 'Nourse, Timothy (c. 1636–1699)', in *Oxford Dictionary of National Biography* (Oxford: Oxford University Press, 2004)

L. Sporhan and W. Von Stromer, 'Die Nadelholzsaat in Nünrberger Reichswäldern zwischen 1469 und 1600', *Zeitschrift für Agrargeschichte und Agrarsoziologie* 17 (1969), pp. 79–106

Matthew Steggle, 'Markham, Gervase (1568?–1637)', in *Oxford Dictionary of National Biography* (Oxford: Oxford University Press, 2004)

Joan Steigerwald, 'The cultural enframing of nature. Environmental histories during the early German romantic period', *Environment and History* 6 (2000), pp. 451–96

P.-M. Steinsiek, *Nachhaltigkeit auf Zeit. Waldschutz im Westharz vor 1800* (Münster: Waxmann, 1999)

Philip J. Stern and Carl Wennerlind (eds), *Mercantilism reimagined. Political economy in early modern Britain and its empire* (New York: Oxford University Press, 2014)

Stephen M. Stigler, *Statistics on the table. The history of statistical concepts and methods* (Cambridge, MA: Harvard University Press, 1999)

M. Stolleis, 'Was Bedeutet 'Normdurchsetzung' bei Poiceyordnungen der frühen Neuzeit?', in R.H. Helmholz (ed.), *Grundlagen des Rechts* (Paderborn: F. Schöningh, 2000), pp. 740–57

Steven Stoll, *Larding the lean earth. Soil and society in nineteenth-century America* (New York: Hill and Wang, 2002)

Martin Stuber, '"dass gemeinnüzige wahrheiten gemein gemacht werden" – Zur Publikationstätigkeit der *Oekonomischen Gesellschaft Bern 1759–1798*', in Marcus Popplow (ed.), *landschaften agrarisch-ökonomischen Wissens. Strategien innovativer Ressourcennutzung in Zeitschriften und Sozietäten des 18. Jahrhunderts* (Münster: Waxmann, 2010), pp. 121–53

M. Teich, 'Circulation, transformation, conservation of matter and balancing of the biological world in the eighteenth century', *Ambix* 29 (1982), pp. 17–28

Malcolm Thick, 'Garden seeds in England before the late eighteenth century', *Agricultural History Review* 38 (1990), pp. 58–71

Malcolm Thick, *The neat house gardens. Early market gardening around London* (Totnes: Prospect, 1998)

Malcolm Thick, *Sir Hugh Plat. The search for useful knowledge in early modern London* (Totnes: Prospect, 2010)

Joan Thirsk, *Economic policy and projects. The development of a consumer society in early modern England* (Oxford: Clarendon, 1978)

Joan Thirsk, 'Plough and pen. Agricultural writers in the seventeenth century', in T.H. Aston, P.R. Coss, C. Dyer and J. Thirsk (eds), *Social relations and ideas. Essays in honour of R.H. Hilton* (Cambridge: Cambridge University Press, 1983), pp. 297–9

Joan Thirsk, 'Agricultural innovations and their diffusion', *AHEW* V (Cambridge: Cambridge University Press, 1985), pp. 533–89

Joan Thirsk, 'The Crown as projector on its own estates, from Elizabeth I to Charles I', in Richard Hoyle (ed.), *The estates of the English crown, 1558–1640* (Cambridge: Cambridge University Press, 1992), pp. 298–352

Joan Thirsk, 'Blith, Walter (*bap.* 1605, *d.* 1654)', in *Oxford Dictionary of National Biography* (Oxford: Oxford University Press, 2004)

Joan Thirsk, 'Standish, Arthur (*fl.* 1552–1615)', in *Oxford Dictionary of National Biography* (Oxford: Oxford University Press, 2004)

Keith Thomas, *Man and the natural world* (London: Penguin, 1984)

William L. Thomas (ed.), *Man's role in changing the face of the Earth* (Chicago, IL: University of Chicago Press, 1956)

Sara Trevisan, '"The murmuring woods euen shuddred as with feare". Deforestation in Michael Drayton's Poly-Olbion', *The Seventeenth Century* 26(2) (2011), pp. 240–63

Keith Tribe, *Land, labour and economic discourse* (London: Routledge & Kegan Paul, 1978)

Keith Tribe, *Governing economy. The reformation of German economic discourse 1750–1840* (Cambridge: Cambridge University Press, 1988)

Keith Tribe, *Strategies of economic order. German economic discourse 1750–1950* (Cambridge: Cambridge University Press, 1995)

Anthony Turner, 'Natural philosophers, mathematical practitioners and timber in later 17th century England', *Nuncius* 9 (1994), pp. 619–31

Conevery Bolton Valencius, *Health of the country. How American settlers understood themselves and their land* (New York: Basic Books, 2002)

Liana Vardi, *The Physiocrats and the world of the Enlightenment* (Cambridge: Cambridge University Press, 2012)

William Vogt, *Road to survival* (London: Gollancz, 1948)

Andre Wakefield, *The disordered police state. German cameralism as science and practice* (Chicago, IL: University of Chicago Press, 2009)

Charles F. Walker, *Shaky colonialism. The 1746 earthquake-tsunami in Lima, Peru, and its long aftermath* (Durham, NC: Duke University Press, 2008)

D.P. Walker, 'Francis Bacon and *Spiritus*', in Penelope Gouk (ed.), *Music, spirit and language in the Renaissance* (London: Variorum Reprints, 1985)

Alexandra Walsham, *The Reformation of the landscape. Religion, identity and landscape in early modern Britain and Ireland* (Oxford: Oxford University Press, 2011)

John Walter and Roger Schofield (eds), *Famine, disease and the social order in early modern England* (Cambridge: Cambridge University Press, 1989)

Paul Warde, *Ecology, economy and state formation in early modern Germany* (Cambridge: Cambridge University Press, 2006)

Paul Warde, 'Subsistence and sales. The peasant economy of Württemberg in the early seventeenth century', *EcHR* 59 (2006), pp. 289–319

Paul Warde, 'The fear of wood shortage and the reality of the woodland in Europe, c. 1450–1850', *History Workshop Journal* 62 (2006), pp. 28–57

Paul Warde, 'The origins and development of institutional welfare support in early modern Württemberg, c.1500–1700', *Continuity and Change* 22 (2007), pp. 459–87

Paul Warde, *Energy consumption in England and Wales 1560–2000* (Naples: CNR, 2007)

Paul Warde, 'The invention of sustainability', *Modern Intellectual History* 8 (2011), pp. 153–70

Paul Warde, 'The idea of improvement, c. 1520–1700', in Richard Hoyle (ed.), *Custom, improvement and the landscape in early modern Britain* (Farnham: Ashgate, 2011), pp. 127–48

Paul Warde, 'Imposition, emulation and adaptation. Regulatory regimes in the commons of early modern Germany', *Environment and History* 19 (2013), pp. 313–37

Paul Warde, 'Early modern "resource crisis". The wood shortage debates in Europe', in A.T. Brown, A. Burn and R. Doherty (eds), *Crisis in economic and social history* (Woodbridge: Boydell Press, 2015)

Paul Warde, 'Sustainability, resources and the destiny of states in German cameralist thought', in K. Forrester and S. Smith (eds), *Nature, action, and the future. Political thought and the environment* (Cambridge: Cambridge University Press, 2018), pp. 43–69

Paul Warde, 'Trees, trade and textiles. Potash imports and ecological dependency in British industry, c. 1550–1770', *Past & Present* (2018)

Paul Warde and Sverker Sörlin, 'Expertise for the future. The emergence of environmental prediction, c.1920–1970', in Jenny Andersson and Egle Rindzeviciute (eds), *The struggle for the long-term in transnational science and politics. Forging the future* (New York: Routledge, 2015), pp. 36–62

Charles Watkins, *Trees, woods and forests. A social and cultural history* (London: Reaktion, 2014)

Tessa Watt, *Cheap print and popular piety 1550–1640* (Cambridge: Cambridge University Press, 1991)

David Watts, *The West Indies. Patterns of development, culture and environmental change since 1492* (Cambridge: Cambridge University Press, 1987)

John C. Weaver, *The Great Land Rush and the making of the modern world* (Montreal: McGill-Queen's University Press, 2003)

Charles Webster, 'Introduction', in C. Webster (ed.), *Samuel Hartlib and the advancement of learning* (Cambridge: Cambridge University Press, 1970), pp. 1–72

Charles Webster, *The great instauration. Science, medicine and reform 1626–1660* (London: Duckworth, 1975)

Maxine Van De Wetering 'Moralizing in puritan natural science. Mysteriousness in earthquake sermons', *Journal of the History of Ideas* 43 (1982), pp. 417–38

Lynn Townsend White, 'The historical roots of our ecological crisis', *Science*, New Series, 155 (10 Mar. 1967), p. 1205

Tamara L. Whited, *Forests and peasant politics in modern France* (New Haven, CT: Yale University Press, 2000)

G.V. Whyte and R.O. Jacks, *The rape of the earth. A world survey of soil erosion* (London: Faber & Faber, 1939)

Nicola Whyte, 'Landscape, memory and custom. Parish identities, *c.* 1550–1750', *Social History* 32 (2007), pp. 166–86

Nicola Whyte, *Inhabiting the landscape. Place, custom and memory, 1500–1800* (Oxford: Windgather, 2009)

Nicola Whyte, 'An archaeology of natural places. Trees in the early modern landscape', *Huntington Library Quarterly: Studies in English and American History and Literature* (2013), pp. 508–16

Merry E. Wiesner, *Women and gender in early modern Europe*, 2nd edition (Cambridge: Cambridge University Press, 2000)

L.P. Wilkinson, 'General introduction', in Virgil (ed.), *The Georgics* (London: Penguin, 1982)

Raymond Williams, *Problems in materialism and culture* (London: Verso, 1980)

Steffi Windelen, 'Die vollkommene Landwirtschaft, der vernünftige Landwirt und die Erdflöhe. *Die Berliner Beyträge zur Landwirtschaftswissenschaft* (1774–1791)', in Marcus Popplow (ed.), *Landschaften agrarisch-ökonomischen Wissens. Strategien innovativer Ressourcennutzung in Zeitschfiften und Sozietäten des 18. Jahrhunderts* (Münster: Waxmann, 2010), pp. 79–96

John T. Wing, 'Keeping Spain afloat. State forestry and imperial defense in the sixteenth century', *Environmental History* 17 (Jan. 2012), pp. 116–145

Verena Winiwarter, 'Böden in Agrargesellschaften. Wahrnehmung, Behandlung und Theorie von Cato bis Palladius', in Rolf-Peter Sieferle and H. Breuninger (eds), *Natur-Bilder. Wahrnehmungen von Natur und Umwelt in der Geschichte* (Frankfurt: Campus, 1999), pp. 181–221

Verena Winiwarter, 'Soils in ancient Roman agriculture. Analytical aporoaches to invisible properties', in H. Novotny and M. Weiss (eds), *Shifting boundaries of the real. Making the invisible visible* (Zurich: vdf Hochschulverlag AG an der ETH, 2000)

Charles W.J. Withers, 'William Cullen's agricultural lectures and writings and the development of agricultural science in eighteenth-century Scotland', *Agricultural History Review* 37 (1989), pp. 144–56

Nathaniel Wolloch, *Nature in the history of economic thought. How natural resources became an economic concept* (Basingstoke: Palgrave Macmillan, 2017)

Andy Wood, *The 1549 rebellions and the making of early modern England* (Cambridge: Cambridge University Press, 2007)

Andy Wood, *The memory of the people. Custom and popular senses of the past in early modern England* (Cambridge: Cambridge University Press, 2013)

J.R. Wordie, 'The chronology of English enclosure, 1500–1914', *EcHR* 36 (1983), pp. 483–505

Donald Worster, *Nature's economy. A history of ecological ideas* (Cambridge: Cambridge University Press, 1977)

William John Wright, *Capitalism, the state, and the Lutheran Reformation. Sixteenth-century Hesse* (Athens, OH: Ohio University Press, 1988)

E.A. Wrigley, *Continuity, chance and change. The character of the industrial revolution in England* (Cambridge: Cambridge University Press, 1988)

E.A. Wrigley, *Energy and the English Industrial Revolution* (Cambridge: Cambridge University Press, 2010)

E.A. Wrigley, *The path to sustained growth. England's transition from an organic economy to an Industrial Revolution* (Cambridge: Cambridge University Press, 2016)

Clemens Zimmermann, *Reformen in der bäuerlichen Gesellschaft. Studien zum aufgeklärten Absolutismus in der Markgrafschaft Baden 1750–1790* (Ostfildern: Scripta Mercaturae, 1983)

H. Zins, *England and the Baltic in the Elizabethan era* (Manchester: Manchester University Press, 1972)

INDEX